BY MICHAEL LOYND

All Things Irish: A Novel

The Watermen

THE WATERMEN

THE
WATERMEN

THE BIRTH OF
AMERICAN SWIMMING
AND ONE YOUNG MAN'S
FIGHT TO CAPTURE
OLYMPIC GOLD

MICHAEL LOYND

BALLANTINE BOOKS
NEW YORK

LIBRARY OF CONGRESS CATALOGING-IN-PUBLICATION DATA
NAMES: Loynd, Michael, author.
TITLE: The watermen: a young swimmer's fight for America's first gold
and the birth of the modern Olympics Michael Loynd.
DESCRIPTION: First edition. | New York: Ballantine Books, [2022] |
Includes bibliographical references.
IDENTIFIERS: LCCN 2021052317 (print) | LCCN 2021052318 (ebook) |
ISBN 9780593357040 (hardcover) | ISBN 9780593357057 (ebook)
SUBJECTS: LCSH: Daniels, Charles M., 1885-1973. |
Swimmers—United States—Biography. | Olympic athletes—
United States—Biography. | Swimming—History—20th century. |
Olympics—History—20th century.
CLASSIFICATION: LCC GV838.D35 L69 2022 (print) |
LCC GV838.D35 (ebook) | DDC 797.2/1092 [B]—dc23/eng/20211207
LC record available at https://lccn.loc.gov/2021052317
LC ebook record available at https://lccn.loc.gov/2021052318

Printed in the United States of America on acid-free paper

randomhousebooks.com

1st Printing

First Edition

Title-page photo courtesy of the Daniels family archive
Book design by Barbara M. Bachman

To my family.

They make everything worthwhile.

What stands in the way
becomes the way.

—MARCUS AURELIUS

CONTENTS

PART FOUR
SPEED SWIMMING

PART FIVE
SWAMBLING

THE WATERMEN

PROLOGUE

FIFTEEN THOUSAND BRITISH SPECTATORS GATHERED INSIDE LONdon's Olympic stadium to see if the human fish could actually crawl on top of the water. Despite the morning rains, the crowds came on a cloudy July afternoon in 1908 to bear witness to what newspapers on both sides of the Atlantic had been writing about over the past two years. But when the young American walked onto the damp lawn, he didn't look anything like a fish. He wore a dark blue swim cap over his short blond hair, a heavy, navy-colored wool bathing suit that stretched from shoulders to knees, and a long white robe that moments later would be at the center of an international scandal.

At a time when only top royalty and powerful heads of state were known beyond their country's borders, the name of the so-called American fish, Charles Daniels, was on people's lips throughout North America, Europe, and Australia. No one quite knew where he came from. The origins of his swimming prowess remained equally mysterious. And whatever fueled his unlikely rise was made all the more inexplicable by the fact that almost no one in America swam. The country's measly six hundred competitive swimmers had been discarded as laughingstocks compared with the superior Europeans. Yet somehow this twenty-three-year-old, who admittedly could not muster a decent stroke four years earlier, held every American swimming record from fifty yards to the mile. He had willed into being the first U.S. Olympic swim team. Invented the modern-day freestyle stroke. Popularized an obscure sport whose minimal attire and openness to all genders challenged the day's narrow-minded Victorian attitudes that oppressed so many. And now he claimed world records in the sport England had invented and dominated for the past seventy years.

The sport's supreme authority, England's Amateur Swimming Association, denounced him as a fraud, refusing to validate his achievements. And what had begun four years earlier as a personal struggle to overcome crippling anxiety and improve his and his mother's bleak existence now placed him at these fourth Olympic Games with the chance to accomplish what no one believed possible: becoming the first non-British swimmer to seize the world's No. 1 ranking. America loved a winner. What Charles didn't realize was that London's Olympic organizers were conspiring to ensure that never happened.

The European champion was already rumored to be posting world-record times after copying Daniels's unique crawling technique. With a body forged from steel, an incredible wingspan, and a shaved head that signaled he was all business, the European champ had beaten him during their first encounter at the 1904 Olympics. Then won again last year at the 1907 English Championships, this time with the underhanded help of the same British swim judges who now officiated these London Games.

The fact that the Olympic officials were all British presented a major conflict of interest that the International Olympic Committee would never allow to happen again. The Brits operated all the stopwatches. They made the call on close finishes. Any complaint filed by the American team over the British referees' hometown bias or blatant cheating was ruled upon by the same British officials. Unless he won by a clear margin, the opportunity for the judges to rule in another competitor's favor remained very real. And Charles needed to do more than just win. To leave no room for the British Empire's swimming authorities to again dismiss him, he had to break their world record. Which they had made more difficult by designing an outdoor pool four times longer than any concrete tank in the world (twice as long as what would become standard for a modern Olympic-sized pool). Its hundred-meter length eliminated Charles's superior off-the-wall turning advantage that the British press insisted was the only reason he could ever defeat one of their champions. On top of that, England's Olympic officials "randomly" assigned him to the farthest lane, the hardest position to hear the starting call or see one's opponents, and the most likely spot to face more resistance from the displaced waves rebounding off the side wall and back onto the swimmer. Yet, despite all these disadvantages, they sneaked in one final measure to guarantee his defeat and extinguish his growing legacy.

A sense of anticipation buzzed inside the stadium as Charles walked across the grass in front of the king's royal box and onto the wooden starting deck of the infield's pool to begin the hundred-meter race. All of his teammates had met defeat at the hands of Britain's superior watermen, and other than a tiny section of flag-waving countrymen relegated to the stadium's far corner, the entire crowd hoped to see the American fish defeated.

The official starter, a mustachioed Brit named Mr. Hudson, called out, "Take your marks," to signal the swimmers to remove their robes. Charles had his robe half drawn off, listening intently for Mr. Hudson's next call, "Are you ready?"—but the next word from Mr. Hudson was "Go!"

Every opponent vanished. Charles's head whipped around in panic as he realized the trick. Loud splashes and the fast-departing churn of water exploded beneath him. His competitors had all been forewarned. They now had an insurmountable head start while Charles was still yanking his arms out of his sleeves.

Mr. Hudson and his fellow officials grinned.

The American fish was defeated before he got wet. The officials knew it. Everyone in the stadium knew it. But as Charles ripped off his robe and dove into the water, he knew only that he was in for the fight of his life.

PART ONE

DROWNING

THOMAS P. DANIELS, 1897
(FATHER OF CHARLES DANIELS)

1.

THE DROWNING BOY

—

1896-1899

THE PATH THAT LED CHARLES DANIELS TO THE WATER THAT DAY was a long, hard, thorny bushwhack that he should never have survived.

Some said it started with a handful of misfits at the New York Athletic Club fantasizing about defeating the unbeatable British Empire. Others claimed it began with a mother and son fighting to keep each other from financial and social ruin.

Charles never forgot the first time he saw the word that would become his destiny. It was a cool April morning in 1896. He was eleven, inhaling the sweet smell of newsprint and fresh ink. Under the yellow hue of his apartment's gaslights and chandeliers, he sat in a spot where he often lost himself in reports of athletic triumphs. Out of New York's fifteen daily English-language newspapers, sports aficionados like Charley preferred William Randolph Hearst's *Journal* because, unlike other papers that lumped news together like goulash, it introduced the then revolutionary concept of a section dedicated entirely to sports.

Charley flipped through those pages, combing through every article about athletic contests. There was one on Harvard's track men fighting through back-to-back defeats against Princeton and Columbia. Another about Yale's oarsmen training for the Grand Challenge Cup of the prestigious fifty-seventh Henley Royal Regatta in London, which no American team had ever won. The Brooklyn Bridegrooms were preparing to kick off the professional baseball season in front of thousands of anticipated fans in the wooden bleachers at Eastern Park. And then, near an ad claiming any person was behind the times if they did not join New York City's fifteen thousand other telephone subscribers, appeared an utterly foreign headline: "The Olympic Games."

Like most people at the time, Charley had never heard of an Olympian. The sound of trolley cars, horse carriages, and pedestrians below the apartment window faded as he read on. The short article described a seemingly mythical stadium in Athens with a mind-boggling fifty thousand gleaming white marble seats that stretched beautifully to the sky, with fifty thousand more spectators sitting on a hillside overlooking the venue's basin. The image seemed lifted straight from Greek myth.

The concept of a stadium had been lost to history. Not since the last ancient stadiums of the Greek and Roman empires crumbled to ruin had the world known such a breathtaking athletic arena. Accounts of Rome's unmatched 200,000-seat Circus Maximus or Greece's 50,000-seat stadium at Olympia had been reduced to legend. Only the bones of Rome's Colosseum still bore proof that such colossi once existed on Earth, compared with the day's uninspiring wooden grandstands that held several thousand bodies. Yet, halfway across the world, these new Olympic Games had inspired the Greeks to restore the ruins of Athens's ancient venue to its former glory.

The fourteen brave young warriors from Princeton University and Boston who had stepped into this gladiatorial arena were not the top college stars whom Charley regularly read about in the paper. He discovered that, strangely, the world's best athletes had not participated. There were several reasons for this. As a practical matter, most of the top amateur athletes could afford neither the time nor the expense to travel abroad. There was no precedent for raising money for such a venture. There were no uniform international rules to govern such competitions. And other than the Americans, Germans, and subjects of the British Empire, most of the world showed little enthusiasm for sports and no enthusiasm for international competition.

The powerful amateur athletic unions of the British Empire and America thought the very concept of international play suspicious and refused to support such a boondoggle. Of the 74 foreign athletes who traveled to compete that year with the 167 Greeks in the first modern Olympic Games, most were self-selected. In America's case, the biggest criterion for participating was the financial means to make the twelve-day journey by ship and, of course, knowing the Games existed in the first place. The wealthy college boys who went on a lark, seeing it as an amusing jaunt on their European spring vacation, won a surprising nine of the twelve track-and-field events. In the Games' opening contest, a triple jumper from Harvard became the first Olympic champion in more than fifteen hundred years. The Americans' eleven total first-place medals surpassed even the host nation's ten victories, stunning the Greeks. Only the lone American swimmer was badly outclassed during a three-quarter-mile race back to shore in the freezing Greek sea that turned into a harrowing, hypothermic ordeal, with waves six feet high. The winning Hungarian swimmer later said, "My will to live completely overcame my desire to win."

Each victor's prize was much greater than simply the thrill of meeting a real-life king. While the Greek monarch awarded each first-place champion a wreath of wild olive branches made from the trees of Olympia, a diploma, and a silver medal, with second place receiving copper (there was no prize for third), these prizes too were nothing compared with looking up at more than 100,000 Greeks seated within the stadium and on the overlooking hillside, while thunderous applause reverberated deep within the victor's soul. That was the true reward. In more than a thousand years, only kings had experienced such adulation. The medals were mere tokens of that fleeting instant when each man felt like a god.

These first modern Olympic Games made little impact on the sporting world beyond those 100,000 Greek spectators, but Charley never forgot about them. Like all boys who daydream about scoring the game-winning point, the undersized Charley marveled at the notion of standing triumphantly before throngs of cheering fans. He wondered if he had what it took to become an Olympic champion.

NEW YORK SOCIETY WOULD later wonder how the Daniels family became such a cautionary tale of disgrace and ruin. They came from "good stock." Charley's illustrious paternal grandfather served an exemplary twenty-eight years on the New York Supreme Court and two terms as a U.S. congressman and established the University at Buffalo Law School, becoming its first dean. Charley's maternal grandfather founded the most successful department store in Buffalo. His maternal grandmother was the grandniece of the legendary Massachusetts senator Daniel Webster, who would have been president, the family long held, if he could have laid off the booze.

The Danielses hailed from one of the wealthiest per capita societies in the country. While New York City claimed 352 millionaires, their much smaller hometown of Buffalo claimed as many as 60. Nestled on Lake Erie's easternmost shore, the cozy town had flourished as a major shipping port ever since the 1825 opening of the Erie Canal. Buffalo's Delaware Avenue was one of the most illustrious addresses in America. Nowhere was the Gilded Age on fuller display than in the massive mansions along this wide tree-lined thoroughfare, dubbed Millionaires' Row. Two of the avenue's most famous residents were Millard Fillmore, thirteenth president of the United States, and America's legendary humorist Mark Twain, who lived for a brief stint at 472 Delaware while working as the editor and co-owner of *The Buffalo Express*. Twain's wealthy father-in-law had acquired the home as a surprise wedding present in 1870, and it was said that Twain hung a plaque on the front door that read, "Mark Twain lives here, and his father-in-law pays the rent." Even the world's first superstar athlete, the English swimmer Matthew Webb, the only man at the time to have swum the English Channel, paid a visit to the great city of Buffalo in July 1883 to attempt another impossible aquatic feat—crossing the deadly Whirlpool Rapids below Niagara Falls. This time luck was not on Webb's side, and he perished beneath the roiling waves.

Glamour and prominence abounded in this special nook that one resident described as exuding "a wild, sweet, enthralling zestfulness" and where everybody knew everybody else, as well as all there was to know about everyone else. The wealthy residents employed plenty of live-in help, usually Irish or German girls, along with a coachman and his family, who lived in the carriage house in back. The well-off shopped at the same fashionable stores, attended the same private clubs, worshipped at one of the many corner churches whose towering spires marked the Delaware Avenue skyline. Their children played together and attended the city's private prep schools and finishing schools, and all ages intermingled at polo matches, boating on Lake Erie, winter sleigh rides, and the extravagant seasonal balls and abundant dinner parties. Their sons attended Ivy League colleges or went straight to work in a thriving family business, while their daughters prepared for their coming-out parties at age nineteen, and most of these promising young adults aspired to one day live, work, and raise their own children in this comfortable world.

Yet as one resident noted about living on Delaware Avenue during this time, "Life flowed on in an apparently commonplace way until, once in a while, something happened." Like the rest of America's wealthy who were insecure about their country's identity and felt a cultural inferiority to Europe, Buffalo society borrowed heavily from the Victorian aristocratic notions of separate classes. But unlike Europeans who were born into their social class, Americans achieved high status through hard work, with the almighty dollar constituting the country's only aristocracy. Victorian England's ultraconservative values and customs that placed men far atop the pecking order were especially influential, granting few rights to women and children other than to serve and obey the head of the household.

Charley's mother, Alice, knew, and Charley soon learned, that they existed to provide a good reflection of their patriarch, Tom Daniels. Learning to love and value themselves was not part of that equation.

ALICE MELDRUM WANTED MORE out of life than attending a finishing school that prioritized teaching social and domestic skills over academics. As the eldest daughter of six children, the dark-haired, blue-eyed, five-foot-three beauty attended Buffalo's only public high school, where she learned to hold her own against the opposite sex. In 1882, she graduated as a star scholar in a class of twenty-three girls and sixteen boys, two being the sons of her father's two business partners who failed to achieve similar high honors. Her peers might well have called Alice a "goody-goody" because of her genuine love for learning and study. She was even among the select few Central High students commended with a special rosette ribbon for integrity.

Unfortunately, for women like Alice, few educational opportunities existed beyond high school. In an upper-class society that groomed men to work hard and women to be charming—but ultimately let men do the serious thinking—Alice was encouraged to downplay her intellectual prowess so as not to frighten away suitors. Whatever her true ambitions, Victorian society insisted that her sense of self-worth be found strictly in a good marriage and motherhood. Now that Alice had completed her schooling and traveled Europe with her parents, her next expectation was to marry well and raise good children, particularly good men.

A favorite in the society pages, Alice enjoyed hosting parties at her family's North Street mansion, which lay a block off Delaware Avenue. During Buffalo's long snowy winters, she liked sleigh rides with friends, and in warmer weather, showing off her athletic abilities as an equestrian at a time when seeing a woman on horseback was as rare as spotting an electric trolley. She helped put on pageants for the local orphanage, led her Christian youth group, played the piano, which, in an era before records and radio, was one of the few ways to enjoy music, and loved to dance. She and her close friend Ida Reid hosted dance parties at their homes. Among the numerous young eligible bachelors who attended was Tom Daniels.

Two years older than Alice, Tom was tall, handsome, popular, and abundantly charming, loved being the center of attention, and had a keen eye for opportunity. He grew up a few blocks from Alice in a mansion that did not buzz with warm family energy as did the Meldrums' loving home. Tom understood the advantages of fitting in, being well liked, and projecting an image of success. Always impeccably dressed, he showed an early attraction for the finer things— something his earnest father eschewed. While his older brother, Charles junior, followed their highly respected father into the profession of law, Tom intended to make a grander splash in business. An important ingredient in that pursuit was social status.

As Tom knew well, strong social standing was a passkey to posher relationships, more exclusive parties, elite clubs, and key connections that could generate lucrative business opportunities and greater wealth. The quality of one's housing, clothing, servants, club affiliations, net worth, family reputation, and marriage were all visible marks of membership and rank. In major cities like Buffalo, the Social Register published the names and addresses of society's elite members. It was a list Tom aspired to, and Alice fit nicely into that equation.

THE SAME SUMMER OF 1883 that Britain's international swimming star Matthew Webb drowned in Niagara's waters, twenty miles away, Tom and Alice stood at the altar of Central Presbyterian church as one of four groomsmen and bridesmaids at a mutual friend's wedding. Like the other bridesmaids, Alice wore a white dress that adhered to the modest Victorian standards of the day, covering her from neck to feet with layers of fabric, undergarments, and long white gloves that ensured she exposed as little skin as possible. A painful tight-laced corset squeezed her waist into the fashionable hourglass figure meant to showcase a woman's desirable childbearing hips. These gently reared bridesmaids would remember to pinch their cheeks and bite their lips to bring out a bit of color, since Victorians connected makeup with prostitutes and actresses. There wasn't much distinction between the two. If a woman did wear makeup, she applied its subtle colors with care, along with powder or lotions to give her skin that translucent, oh-so-close-to-death look. Pale complexions were all the rage, reflecting a woman's nobility by showing she could afford not to work outdoors like some field hand. Her goal was to appear the delicate flower that gentlemen wanted to dominate and protect.

The wedding reception provided a safe social opportunity for single young women like Alice who were otherwise never allowed alone in mixed company. Since decorum forbade Alice to address a gentleman on her own initiative unless they were very close, a proper introduction needed to be made by a mutual friend, with the gentleman introduced first, then the lady, accompanied by the man's slight bow. They would address each other as "Miss Alice" and "Mr. Daniels," until acquainted enough to permit the other to drop such formalities. The two young adults socialized that evening at the bride's family residence among several hundred guests, eating, enjoying refreshments, and sharing a dance or two together. Any more was inappropriate. When Mr. Daniels asked Miss Alice's permission to "call" on her, she agreed.

Under the Meldrums' approving but ever watchful eye, a series of formal chaperoned visits ensued between these two scions of well-regarded families, which involved sitting gracefully in the Meldrums' front parlor or drawing room as the two engaged in polite conversation for about fifteen minutes, with no physical contact, of course, and Alice's mother close enough to hear every word. As their courtship progressed, Alice could take walks with Tom, maintaining an appropriate social distance, and always with a chaperone, usually her mother. Touching was out of the question, unless Tom extended a hand to help Alice into a carriage or over a rough spot on the street. The only acceptable means of expressing their emotional intimacy was to write love letters, which was an art in itself. Such a customary prelude to marriage demanded parental approval, with many topics of discussion taboo. Alice needed to write guardedly to maintain her dignity. One misstep on any of these crucial rules could ruin her reputation beyond repair. But they also limited Alice's ability to truly know her soon-to-be fiancé.

Their 1884 June wedding was Buffalo society's most anticipated social event, hosting a Who's Who of guests including Judge Charles Folger, secretary of the U.S. Treasury; Mr. and Mrs. William "Willy" Waldorf Astor, the former being one of the richest men in America; and the current New York governor and ex-mayor of Buffalo, Grover Cleveland, who five months later would be elected president. When the ceremony ended, *The Evening Telegraph* reported that 115 carriages filed up to the Lafayette Street Presbyterian Church and conveyed the guests a mile east down Delaware Avenue, where an elaborate reception awaited them at the Meldrums' flower-festooned mansion. The newlyweds spent their honeymoon at New York's playground to the wealthy, Saratoga Springs, with its adult Disneyland of grand hotels, high-stakes casinos, racetracks, and fashionable health spas. It was there Alice gave herself to Tom completely and fulfilled her highest wifely duty by getting pregnant.

Whatever aspirations Alice had for herself, she was now Mrs.

Thomas Porter Daniels—for better or for worse—entrusting her life, future, and unborn child's well-being to a man she hoped would be a loving husband and father, a dependable provider, and a model of integrity. When they returned from their honeymoon, she had no say when Tom promptly moved her four hundred miles away from her family, friends, and beloved Buffalo.

TOM'S WANDERING EYE FOR opportunity had seen just that in Dayton, Ohio. The working-class town on the banks of the Miami River's canal to Lake Erie was about a fourth the size of Buffalo. The homes were modest, mostly built on narrow lots, far different from the prominent Gilded Age neighborhood of their upbringing.

Having worked a brief stint at his father-in-law's dry goods store in Buffalo, Tom decided to become master of his own universe. In what was fast becoming one of Ohio's wealthiest cities thanks to the booming National Cash Register Company and other manufacturers of everything from railroad cars to cigars, Tom, with an investment from his father-in-law, partnered with two friends to start a dry goods store. Leasing prime space in a prominent new building off Main Street, Tom spared no expense in decorating the store with exquisite handcrafted wood shelving, opulent chandeliers, and the finest luxury items for sale. For the grand opening, Tom took out big ads. Alice's whole family made the daylong journey by train to take part, including her Scottish-born father, always so full of positive energy. Despite the weekend's storms, the crowds at Whitmarsh, Daniels & Robbins surpassed all expectations. Tom was on track to provide an admirable level of success for his new family—the ultimate measure of a Victorian man—until shortly before Alice was to give birth, when he announced the dissolution of his partnership. Mr. Whitmarsh and Mr. Robbins no longer cared to be in business with Tom.

Alice had spent the last eight months coping with any homesickness and loneliness by trying to ingratiate them with Dayton society, make friends, and settle into her role as supportive wife. They lived in the desirable Dayton View neighborhood, with its broad, tree-lined streets, and Alice worked hard to turn their impressive house into a happy home for Tom and their future children. Popular guidebooks like *Hill's Manual of Social and Business Forms,* first published in 1874, helped new housewives like herself understand their duties. "Whatever may have been the cares of the day, greet your husband with a smile when he returns. Make your personal appearance just as beautiful as possible. Let him enter rooms so attractive and sunny that all the recollections of his home, when away from the same, shall attract him back."

Even in 1885, childbirth was still the leading cause of death for women. For Alice to give birth for the first time in an unfamiliar city, with a new doctor, far away from the support of family and friends, was frightening enough, let alone having to worry about Tom's business difficulties. Tom made arrangements to buy out his partners' interest, most likely with the help of his father-in-law. He changed the store's name to Daniels and, unfortunately, now needed to spend a lot more time away from a very pregnant Alice.

In the early morning hours of March 24, the doctor was at the Daniels home helping Alice give birth. After nine months of feeling the baby grow inside her, Alice finally laid her loving eyes upon her son, who, for the first time, felt his mother's embrace.

Born on the same day as Tom's father, the baby was named after the esteemed judge. Meanwhile, Tom himself was a mile away at Daniels Dry Goods. The Dayton *Herald* would later note that "Mr. T. P. Daniels greeted his numerous customers this morning with an unusually pleasant smile, but with a look that plainly showed his thoughts were at home with a new ten-pound boy, who will soon call him 'Papa.'"

That evening, Alice's mother arrived by train to help with her first grandchild and care for her daughter, while Tom remained a slave to his store. In late June, Tom and Alice took baby Charley to visit Buffalo. While Tom needed to return after the Fourth of July holiday to tend to his business, Alice spent the entire summer with baby Charley in her parents' North Street home, showing him off to friends and enjoying her family and beloved hometown. When she arrived back in Dayton that September, she brought back someone who could both help alleviate homesickness and fill the much-needed partner role for Tom.

Alice's nineteen-year-old brother, Fred, had been working at their father's Buffalo department store the past two years and, most impor-

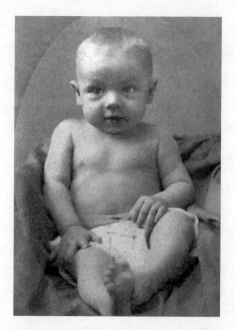

CHARLES MELDRUM DANIELS,
FOUR MONTHS OLD

tant, was the type who got along with everyone. Handsome and outgoing, Fred was the closest in age to Alice of all her five siblings. They shared childhood friends, enjoyed Europe together with their parents and older brother Arthur, and graduated as star scholars from Central High. With Alice in her first trimester with a second baby, Fred was a godsend, quickly becoming a favorite in Dayton society.

Tom renamed the store Daniels & Meldrum. The brothers-in-law worked hard to make it a success, and for fun they helped found Dayton's Ruckawa Canoe Club, since canoeing had grown quite fashionable after adventure authors like Robert Louis Stevenson romanticized its rugged manliness in exploration.

In 1885, sport was just being deemed an appropriate activity. From America's earliest colonial period, New England Puritanism viewed sport as a sinful waste of time better spent on prayer. But after the Civil War, Mark Twain observed that sports were "the very symbol, the outward and visible expression of the drive and push and rush and struggle of the raging, tearing, booming nineteenth century." As the newly industrialized nation surged like a phoenix from the ashes of war, this golden age of invention saw the appearance not only of the telephone, electric lightbulb, camera, and phonograph but of the first intercollegiate football match between Rutgers and Princeton, the creation of a professional baseball league, and the birth of amateur athletic clubs. Americans began channeling their fighting spirit into pounding one another on the playing field or, in Tom's case, outracing opponents in his canoe.

Life in the young Daniels family was on track. On March 29, 1886, Alice gave birth to a second son, whom they named after Fred. A month later, Charley took his first steps, beginning his journey to becoming the proverbial "chip off the old block." Tom was enjoying shuttling around town in a fancy new open carriage and expensive new horse. He hired a servant to help with Alice's household duties and give them status. He had a small boathouse built for his canoe on the Miami River. Now, with a partner to tend to the store, Tom made plans for his growing family to summer at the fashionable Put-in-Bay island resort on Lake Erie, cheek by jowl with Ohio's high society. Tom was even becoming a bit of a local celebrity thanks to Daniels & Meldrum's central location and its prominent daily advertisements in the Dayton *Herald*.

On June 19, as Tom and Alice celebrated their second wedding anniversary with two beautiful little boys and Tom's winning partnership with Fred, an attorney friend arrived with a telegram from Balcony Falls, Virginia. A week earlier, Fred had departed for a brief holiday with a fellow Ruckawa member, Frank Fowler, to celebrate his twentieth birthday with a canoe trip down the James River. What they expected to be a telegram from Fred wishing them a happy anniversary turned out to be one from Frank Fowler, notifying them that Fred's canoe had overturned in the rapids. Fred had struck a rock and was believed to have drowned.

At a time when most people could not swim, Fred was a good swimmer. Alice was optimistic, insisting she join the search for her brother. The family wired Frank Fowler to spare no expense in finding Fred. Tom closed up the store, and he and Alice boarded a train Sunday morning, leaving Charley and baby Fred with household care. On Wednesday, June 23, the fifteen-man search party found Fred's drowned body a mile downriver. Alice and Tom were devastated.

Following a sad train ride back to Buffalo, where they held a funeral that Saturday at the Meldrum family's North Street mansion, Alice and Tom returned to Dayton, only to discover that three-month-old Fred had contracted cholera. Then Charley too fell ill.

The infection appeared frighteningly similar to the one five-year-old Tom had watched take his mother's life. Its onset was fast, leading to severe diarrhea and dehydration, followed by terrible seizures. The bacteria spread through contaminated water from the city's poor sanitation system, which baby Fred had likely consumed during Alice's absence via a water-diluted breast-milk substitute. On Sunday evening, July 4, baby Fred died.

With Tom once again left alone to run every aspect of the store, business began a slow, steady downward slide. A week before Charley's third birthday in March 1888, the store's shortfall forced the Danielses to dismiss their domestic help and sell off most of the furnishings that Alice had acquired to make Dayton feel more like home. Tom explained to friends that they were just simplifying their life, and kept up appearances by taking the family for another summer hobnobbing at Put-in-Bay, where he won prizes at the annual canoe regatta. By the spring of 1890, with Daniels & Meldrum unable to stop the bleeding, Tom held a "Great Retirement Sale," sold the store and their house, and pulled up stakes in the only home five-year-old Charley had known.

Had Alice wanted to move back to her beloved Buffalo to be close to family and friends, her wish would have been vetoed. As head of the household, Tom's say was all that mattered. It was Alice's job to conform to whatever Tom decided and find a way to make it work for their family.

During Tom's previous buying trips to New York City, he had become enamored of a particular breed of businessman. They wore expensive suits, dined at the best restaurants, traveled in fancy carriages, belonged to all the top clubs, attracted pretty young girls, and seemed to make ridiculous money with far less work than running a dry goods store. Tom saw himself becoming one of these new masters of the universe. Tom relocated the family to this big, overcrowded, bustling metropolis with 3.8 million residents, opened an office, and proclaimed himself a banker. He moved the family into the majestic Hotel Gerard, the luxurious thirteen-story residential building in Manhattan's trendy Theater District that dominated West Forty-fourth Street's skyline. One of his first moves was to join the prestigious New York Canoe Club on the waters of Brooklyn's Gravesend Bay, which provided a good social network and, he believed, a potential stepping-stone into the more exclusive athletic clubs like the Knickerbocker or the New York. The family attended Sunday services at the fashionable St. Michael's Episcopal Church on Manhattan's Upper West Side, which *The New York Times* proclaimed one of the finest houses of worship in the country and a popular Sunday destination for New York's affluent. St. Michael's was *the* church in which to be seen, helping Tom further expand his network of wealthy friends and potential business investors.

Tom's appetite for the good life only grew a year after their arrival when Alice's beloved fifty-eight-year-old father, whose heartbreak over Fred's death had sent his health into a tailspin, passed away, leaving each Meldrum child a $50,000 inheritance (about $1.4 million today), which Tom certainly saw as his own personal piggy bank. Alice grieved that the next time she returned to her dear Buffalo, her family's North Street home would feel much emptier. And now being four hundred miles east, after Tom refused to move back home following Dayton, she was unable to provide her widowed mother with regular company.

New York City seemed so uncomfortably foreign in comparison to Buffalo and Dayton. There were no yards or open streets for Charley to run around in. The tall buildings blocked out the sun and breeze. The constant smell of manure and urine choked the air and filled the streets. More than 100,000 horses lived in the city, each day generating 2.5 million pounds of manure and 25,000 gallons of urine that threatened to bury the city. People weren't as friendly and seemed to be constantly rushing to catch a train. Alice once again needed to start over, trying to make friends, create a home in an apartment they did not own, and ingratiate the family with the ultra-wealthy and more elitist New York society. She was now a very small fish in an enormous ocean, too unknown and financially insignificant to earn any mention in Manhattan's society pages that were dominated by names like Vanderbilt,

Rockefeller, and Astor, as well as visiting European royalty. But Tom aspired to one day make the country's most affluent Social Register. The first step was to outwardly look like the epitome of success. And he expected his family to reflect the same, especially his son.

AS WIFE AND MOTHER, Alice bore the full responsibility of caring for and educating Charley. Already baby Fred had died under her watch. The guilt of leaving him to search for her brother certainly haunted her. Now her only child seemed to be suffering with what today we would call a sort of post-traumatic stress that kept him a constant ball of nerves. Charley seemed so anxious about making the slightest mistake that he had trouble engaging in sports and other social activities with boys his age. Despite his anxiety, he kept trying to please his father, even though his failed attempts never sat well with Tom.

While Alice continually agonized over how to help Charley, fathers were not expected to communicate with their children more than once a day, with that encounter often revolving around a berating or even a beating if the child needed to be set straight. Affection was not part of Victorian parenting. The prevailing belief was that it softened a child. Kissing or hugging was not encouraged, with only perhaps a bedtime peck on the forehead if a mother really couldn't resist.

There was no known treatment for Charley's anxiety and depression. The condition had been defined in medical books only twenty-five years earlier, and society avoided the stigma of mental illness by calling it "nerves." Everyone was said to possess a certain amount of "nervous energy," and when life grew too hectic, it caused "nervousness." For women it was attributed to too much stimulus outside the home. For businessmen who were confined to their offices, it was blamed on too little outdoor activity. Doctors believed the condition was a by-product of a highly evolved brain and nervous system, most commonly inherent in members of the upper class, especially the most sensitive among them.

With psychiatry still in its infancy, the medically recommended "cure" differed for each sex. For women's so-called delicate nerves, doctors prescribed the "rest cure," which entailed six to eight weeks of

isolated bed rest in the home or, for the wealthy, in a fashionable sana-
torium. Sometimes it included the administration of unregulated
tonics that used dubious ingredients such as strychnine, morphine,
laudanum, or cocaine. In contrast, a man was encouraged to rechannel
his nervous energy by engaging in rigorous physical activity, preferably
in the outdoors and optimally out west, roping cattle, riding horses,
and mixing it up with cowboys, until the sheer manliness of it all revived him. Walt Whitman documented his "West Cure" journey in
parts of his memoir, *Specimen Days*. The novelist Owen Wister's West
Cure inspired his 1902 bestselling novel, *The Virginian,* giving birth to
the wildly popular Western genre. Tom had a different cure in store for
his son.

One afternoon, when Charley was around eleven, Tom marched
him several blocks east to Fifth Avenue and Forty-fifth Street, where
they entered a tall brownstone. Tom paid a fee to an attendant and led
Charley past a small room where ropes and harnesses dangled from the
ceiling. His father referred to this place as Gebhard's Natatorium, a
private swimming facility that catered to some of New York's wealthiest families. Walking through another door, Charley felt his clothes
dampen as he hit a wall of sticky humidity. More ropes, harnesses, and
a trapeze dangled off the ceiling before them. They stood on an elevated gallery, about twelve feet above the floor below, where Charley
saw glistening green water. A huge rectangular swimming tank
stretched sixty-five feet in length and forty-five feet wide. There was a
slight echo as his father firmly directed him down the stairs to a poolside changing booth. Perhaps Tom provided Charley with a bathing
suit, but perhaps not, because nudity was common during the swimming hours reserved exclusively for men.

Like 99.99 percent of American boys, Charley had never taken a
swimming lesson. He had never received instruction on what to do
when water entered his ears and nose and mouth and overtook his
entire body. When he emerged from the changing booth, Tom, a good
breaststroker, tied a rope around Charley's skinny waist. The rope attached to the end of a long wooden pole that Tom held like a fishing
rod. The last thing Charley probably heard before he plunged into the
pool was Tom pushing him in with the mandate "Swim!"

Charley hit the water and sank. His arms thrashed, churning the surface and drowning out whatever instructions Tom was yelling from the other end of the pole.

Charley gulped for air, only to suck water. As his terror of drowning intensified, he kept fighting and splashing to avoid failing his father yet again. By the time Tom pulled the traumatized boy from the pool, Charley recalled that he had "swallowed enough water to sink a warship."

Charley didn't want to go near water ever again. Although he never fully described the aftermath of that dreadful afternoon, we can imagine how severely Tom stonewalled him. Charley changed back into his street clothes, and if he had tried to address his father, Tom would have stiffened. They likely departed Gebhard's Natatorium with Tom walking briskly ahead while Charley lagged behind, head down, wet hair dangling in his face.

THE FOLLOWING SUMMER OF 1897, Charley faced another test from his father. This time Tom seemed intent on shaming the anxiety out of him.

In July, Tom took the family away from the city's stifling heat, about fifty minutes south by train to Brooklyn's popular seaside resort town of Bath Beach. The exclusive summer playground of Victorian upper-class homes overlooked the sandy beach along the yacht-dotted Gravesend Bay, where Tom's New York Canoe Club made its home. For the next two months, while Tom commuted back and forth to his job in the city, the family stayed at Kathleen Villa, an upscale hotel on three acres of beachfront property, where they hobnobbed with affluent Brooklynites and Manhattanites. For Charley, this socializing came with the added stress of trying not to let his many anxieties embarrass his father, which now included his fear of the water.

The vast majority of beachgoers, like Charley and his mother, dressed head to toe in their Sunday best. The men wore suits, white shirts with starched collars, ties, and panama hats or bowlers, while the ladies wore white dresses, stockings, and large floppy hats and carried colorful parasols to protect their fashionable pale skin. Most harbored no aquatic ambitions beyond dipping their feet in the cool surf. Even those sun-tanned fellows in fancy striped bathing costumes rarely ventured be-yond the waist-high waves. Nine times out of ten, like the overwhelming majority of Americans, those "beach posers" could hardly swim a stroke. Tom Daniels, however, was one of the few Americans who could, hav-ing acquired the self-taught skill as a boy growing up on Lake Erie, and Charley felt the pressure to live up to his standards.

Standing in his bathing suit, Tom looked the ideal male specimen, tall, strong, and confident. He was one of the New York Canoe Club's champion swimmers, and he liked to show off his skills by breaststrok-ing half a mile out to sea. As Tom rounded the far buoy and made his way back to shore, the skinny, undersized twelve-year-old Charley was left sitting on the beach to watch.

For Charley, his father's display was a painful reminder of his own failure at Gebhard's Baths. There was one report that Tom even refused to take him canoeing until he learned to swim. Whatever attempts Charley made that summer to push past his fears and enter the water in an attempt to learn a workable breaststroke, they failed to produce anything other than near drownings and greater anxiety, and Victorian society made it almost impossible for Alice to help.

The decency standards that required women to wear weighty wool or flannel bathing gowns, made of up to nine yards of fabric, cloaking every square inch of their figures so as not to arouse male passions, made actual swimming downright dangerous. Unexpected waves were known to have lassoed the excess fabric around women's legs, dragging them down, drowning them in the shallows. Such restrictive garb made it impossible for women to learn a decent stroke, so most demurred. And Tom seemed to have too much going on at work to waste hours trying in vain to teach his anxiety-ridden son how to swim. Not when he was about to finally strike it rich.

THAT JULY, CRIES OF "Gold! Gold! In the Klondike!" electrified Amer-ica. After two Alaskan ships made port in San Francisco with more than a million dollars' worth, tens of thousands of wide-eyed fortune seekers flooded into the makeshift tent towns of Skagway and Dyea, hoping to get lucky.

Tom aimed to get a jump on them by partnering with a group that advertised themselves as "prominent New York businessmen" and incorporating what he named the United States Alaska Gold Company. By late July, the new company took out national ads to attract prospective investors, boasting about plans to send to the Klondike a delegation of experienced mining engineers, accompanied by representatives of the stockholders, whose purpose it would be, after careful investigation, to buy from the holders the best claims in the district, taking "no chances of failure." The company touted a capitalization of one million dollars at ten dollars per share. In the ads, Tom listed himself as "Thomas P. Daniels of Porter & Daniels." Porter, his partner, however, did not exist; that was Tom's middle name. It was a minor fabrication for a man who anticipated becoming as rich as Rockefeller and who now had no time when Charley finally mustered the courage to ask to return to Gebhard's Natatorium.

One fall day, while Tom was at work—he seemed always "at work" these days—Charley returned with Alice to Gebhard's during the hours reserved exclusively for women and children. This time, they employed a proper instructor to allow Charley all the time he needed to ease into the water, using the ropes and harnesses, and eventually learn to breaststroke like his father. Charley was determined to keep at it no matter how long that meant. What normally took five lessons took Charley twelve.

"An even dozen was my lucky number," he later quipped, but he never stopped believing he could do it. By his own account, he had a long way to go before he could keep up with his father, but he was committed to putting in the work. That Christmas, however, everything began to unravel.

It all started five days before the holiday, when Charley's grandfather collapsed at his Buffalo law office. By the time Tom, Alice, and Charley arrived by train the following evening, Judge Daniels was dead. Newspapers across the country eulogized the judge's legendary integrity, work ethic, and extraordinary career.

A few days after the funeral, Judge Daniels's handwritten will revealed what he truly thought of his younger son. After the judge bequeathed to twelve-year-old Charley his gold pocket watch and chain, he named three executors to his estate: his elder son, Charles H. Daniels; his only daughter, Jeanie; and his daughter-in-law Alice, completely excluding Tom. Adding greater insult, since the judge's wife, Mary Enos, was already wealthy on her own account, he had divided his $40,000 estate (about $1.2 million today) equally into thirds: one outright to Charles, one outright to Jeanie, and the remaining third held in trust for Tom under the exclusive control of Charles, Jeanie, and Alice.

Like a child, Tom could not even cash an inheritance check for groceries without his siblings' and wife's consent. The judge had never approved of Tom's showiness and infatuation with wealth, nor his flighty financial schemes. And indeed Tom's latest "can't-miss" gold venture was looking to be a total bust. All of the legitimate claims had been snapped up, and the only people making money were the entrepreneurs who outfitted all the starry-eyed prospectors who eventually returned from the goldfields more broke than when they started. The judge had made it crystal clear that he trusted Alice's integrity and judgment over his spendthrift son's.

It was the ultimate insult. Only two decades earlier had the United States even made it legal for a wife to have any say in or ownership of her own inheritance, let alone her husband's, and England still forbade it. What made it even worse was that Buffalo newspapers published the judge's will for all to see, including Charley.

That summer of 1898, Tom took the family to the trendy Long Island beach community of Rockaway, at Arverne by the Sea, over the Fourth of July holiday, but this time rented a cottage for Charley and Alice to remain until the beginning of the fall school year. While he commuted back and forth to the city either by train or by the twenty-five-hundred-passenger *General Slocum* steamboat that departed twice a day out of Brooklyn, he began spending longer stints away from them.

Using some of his father's inheritance—with Alice's and his siblings' consent, of course—Tom had bought into an established partnership with the Henry V. Brandenburg brokerage company on Wall Street and was more determined than ever to make a tremendous success of himself. When he did make it down for a weekend at Rockaway, his impressive routine of breaststroking half a mile out to sea and back earned him a mention in *The Brooklyn Daily Eagle*, which mistakenly reported Tom as a "former champion swimmer of the New York Athletic Club." It is unclear if the reporter misheard him or if Tom felt the need to embellish his associations with one of the country's most prestigious athletic clubs and swim teams. While Charley still struggled to produce a breaststroke worthy of his father's respect, Alice began to suspect Tom was having an affair.

The very possibility was crushing.

The prevailing view among upper-class wives of such behavior was to look the other way, so long as their husbands were being discreet. It was pure survival: for their family, for their social standing, for their financial well-being. It was unthinkable for a woman of Alice's class to work for pay. Without Tom, she had no prospects. No ability to earn a living. No means to participate in society. Her only self-support was whatever Tom didn't squander of her father's inheritance. Once that ran out, the streets of New York offered a daily reminder of what could become of Alice without a husband. Charley would be her only hope of financial survival after that. Except that he was someone whom Tom and the rest of their circle already deemed an anxiety-ridden weakling, hardly capable of fending for himself, let alone his mother.

When Alice confronted Tom that October, he insisted her suspicions were all in her mind. But she knew otherwise and did not back down. No matter what was said, the confrontation ended with Tom storming out of the apartment and not returning. He did not get back in touch, nor try to work things out. He did not provide them with one penny of support. In fact, Tom no longer acknowledged that he had a wife and son. Before he walked out the door, one wonders if he even said goodbye to Charley.

2.

CASTAWAYS

—

1900-1902

As THE WEEKS ROLLED BY WITHOUT HEARING FROM HIS FATHER, a boy Charley's age could only wind and rewind the movie reel of his life, scrutinizing everything he'd done wrong to make his dad want nothing more to do with him. Thanksgiving came and went with an empty chair and a turkey in need of a new carver. Charley and Alice faced putting up a Christmas tree on their own, as people all around crowded into dry goods stores like the one Tom had once owned, buying presents and making plans for merry family gatherings. As fathers led their gussied-up families into Christmas Mass, Alice and Charley found themselves in the awkward position of needing to make an excuse for Tom's absence on one of the holiest days of the year. They avoided going home to Buffalo for seemingly the same reason. A week later, they bade adieu to 1899, and without Tom to raise a glass, they could only wonder what the twentieth century would bring. In March, Charley's fifteenth birthday passed without so much as a belated card or note from Tom.

Alice heard from Tom's siblings that he now owned a home in Staten Island with his mistress—a blond twenty-year-old whom Tom was introducing to neighbors as his wife, making no mention of having a family back in Manhattan, and definitely no mention of Charley.

Divorce still seemed an unthinkable measure. It went against Alice's vows before God, the church, and Charley's and her very survival.

Even back in Buffalo, where members of society had an unspoken understanding to pretend to ignore each other's closeted skeletons so long as one kept up appearances, divorce was unacceptable. Alice needed only to consider the fate of Alva Vanderbilt, the former queen of the exclusive "Four Hundred"—the crème de la crème of New York society—to understand its consequences.

At her peak, Alva threw legendary balls, owned a 264-foot yacht, resided in palatial manors along New York's Fifth Avenue and in her famed Marble House at Newport, Rhode Island, but in 1895, when she divorced her philandering husband, Willie, she brought a hailstorm of unsavory press down upon the family that made her an instant outcast. As the wife, she was blamed for not creating a home environment that would dissuade Willie from straying. Friends who for years bent over backward to curry favor suddenly shunned her. Invitations no longer came. People no longer called on her. When her ex-sister-in-law threw the biggest wedding of the season that year, Willie was welcomed with open arms, while Alva remained persona non grata. The queen bee had been banished from her own hive. Not even a divorce settlement that would equate to $350 million today could save her socially.

Even if Alice could stay afloat with the remaining inheritance from her father, as a divorced woman she'd have been an outcast. Divorce was so distasteful and rare, of the fifty cases filed in Manhattan annually, male-run newspapers recorded them in special sections reserved for public shaming. Because a divorce on any grounds placed a black mark on the entire family, most unhappy couples remained married in name only. Some separated, pretending to be single or widowed, and some even remarried in another state without ever filing for a divorce, which risked public humiliation.

For their own survival, Alice and Charley had to maintain the public façade of an intact family. In the 1900 U.S. census, Alice listed Tom Daniels as still living with them. She knew too well that if friends and neighbors ever caught wind of the truth, not only would their glaring eyes condemn Alice for driving away Tom, but worse, they'd look down on Charley for not having a father. Respectable families did not want their children associating with those from broken homes. For his part, Charley had to be careful not to say too much. One slip and he would become an even bigger target of ridicule than his anxiety already made him.

Charley knew he needed to be the man of the house, but after Tom left, his anxieties only increased. Whatever words of comfort Alice offered weren't much help in the school's gymnasium. Engaging in physical activities with boys his age seemed to always result in embarrassing himself or letting down his teammates. Aggressive sports rattled his nerves. The ball came at him too quickly. Bodies flew too fast around the field. Boys were tackling or being tackled, and he was one of the scrawniest boys out there. Such a physical disadvantage made it nearly impossible to stand his ground in contact sports. He wanted to be a better athlete just as his father always pushed him to be, but neither his physicality nor his anxiety was improving. And now many of his classmates had hit growth spurts. Some shot up as much as a foot and gained twenty pounds of muscle. Boys his age suddenly looked and talked like young men. Charley had always been one of the small guys, struggling to compete with stronger, faster, taller schoolmates. But now he was in serious jeopardy of being *the* small guy, with no father to support or champion him.

He was the classic case of trying to become the son his father would be proud of, and Tom's abandonment only exacerbated it. Charley had failed at every sport on land, but his father's sport of swimming still intrigued him. He became even more interested after reading a small newspaper blurb about a contest between speed swimmers from New York's elite athletic clubs. But the art of competitive swimming remained a mystery for a majority of the country, with its secrets known by only an elite few.

THROUGHOUT MOST OF WHAT the British dubbed the "civilized world," swimming had been lost for the last millennium. As society grew more conservative with the rise of Christianity, the medieval church opposed the state of undress required for immersion in the water. Christian doctrine's hostility toward self-indulgence added further taboo to the "luxury" of bathing, which prompted the historian Jules Michelet to describe the Middle Ages as "one thousand years without a bath." By the fifteenth century, barely anyone in Europe swam. Bodies of water became dark mysterious realms filled with sea monsters, serpents, and mermaids, depicted on medieval maps as scientific truths. As Europeans began sailing around the world, they observed many of the scantily clad native peoples in Africa and the Americas swimming and linked the behavior to "savagery."

A rise in drownings in the sixteenth century further provoked bans on swimming in Germany and England. In 1571, Cambridge passed a law that any student caught entering the Cam River would receive a severe public flogging, a fine of ten shillings, and a day in the stocks. Sixteen years later, the Cambridge scholar Everard Digby had the radical idea that a better way to prevent drownings was to teach people to swim. Drawing from ancient military and medical treatises that described swimming, along with his own experimentation, Digby wrote his 1587 opus, *The Art of Swimming*. The book became the go-to text in England for teaching the breaststroke and backstroke, as well as giving practical tips on how to cut one's nails while floating and advising readers not to swim when rain is washing dung into the water. However, Digby's fledgling movement suffered a bit of a public relations setback after he was caught in Guy Fawkes's failed Gunpowder Plot attempting to blow up the House of Lords, and hanged. About eighty years after Digby's premature end, Europe's oldest known operational outdoor swimming pool was built at Cambridge University.

The eighteenth century's age of Enlightenment began justifying swimming on the grounds of health and lifesaving. Soon, English schools like Eton, with its honored tradition of rowing, began to encourage their students to learn to swim. Eton designated several bathing spots as early as 1727 to keep the nakedness contained. By the 1770s, swimming in England gained further notoriety when King George III, the English king who lost America—and his mind—liked to lose his britches for a plunge.

A few decades later, after suffering crushing defeats by Napoleon's French army, the trio of Germany, Austria, and Hungary opened floating pools, making them essential parts of male citizens' physical development and military training. In support, the German educator Johann

Guts Muths published a book on the art of the breast- and backstroke based on the teachings of Benjamin Franklin.

By the nineteenth century, swimming's popularity had exploded across the British Empire. Glorious indoor facilities sprang up in almost every village and town across England. Boys became excellent watermen by the time they reached manhood. While on the other side of the pond, America spurned swimming as an activity of degenerates—first and foremost among them being Benjamin Franklin.

Franklin thought nothing of dropping his drawers and parading into the water with all his manhood on display—especially awkward in an era when Puritan sensibilities still prevailed. Learning to swim before age ten from the 1696 French instructional book by M. Thevenot, a successor of Digby's, Franklin regularly swam naked in the Thames as a young typesetter in London, in the Schuylkill River back home in Philadelphia, and in the Seine as an elder statesman in Paris. Franklin even invented his own wooden swimming fins and, as a young man, considered opening a swimming school in London. Yet, despite all of Franklin's sway on American culture, his fondness for swimming—as well as his daily routine of naked air baths—never took hold.

In the early nineteenth century, a fresh new generation of young rabble-rousers embraced Franklin's aquatic exhibitionism. Working-class men without tenement bathing facilities went down to the river in the evenings to disrobe and bathe, drawing the ire of offended passersby. As a result, New York and other U.S. cities banned swimming in urban waterways. By the summer of 1870, temporary public baths had sprung up along the river for the great unwashed masses. These large floating pontoon baths became quite popular with naked boys on hot summer days, though far less so with men, and even less so with women and girls. Americans' Puritanism made most too prudish to bathe with strangers. Unable to justify using public funds for mere recreational facilities for youths, support for more expensive, year-round public baths waned. And so swimming in America remained synonymous with indecency, the uncouth, and the poorest and dirtiest of society.

The few indoor pools like Gebhard's Natatorium in Midtown were not conducive to practicing speed swimming, nor did they have the instructors to teach such advanced techniques. Manhattan's only two year-round competition pools where Charley could learn the secrets of British speed swimming remained locked away in the restricted basements of the Knickerbocker and New York Athletic Clubs. Access to this exclusive world was strictly reserved for first-rate gentlemen handpicked by its members. A boy without a father was not candidate material.

CHARLEY DID NOT HAVE many men in his life to guide him on his way. His grandfathers were both dead. His uncles lived in Buffalo, and he and his mother had not gone back since his father left. Even if his mother had longed to relocate back home closer to family, it could not happen without her broken marriage being discovered. She couldn't risk it.

With still no contact from Tom, Alice was left desperately trying to hold together the shattered pieces of their lives. While other parents boasted about their children's accomplishments—academic honors, sports achievements, popularity, social triumphs—Alice could only hope to see her son freed from the anxiety and sense of worthlessness that overwhelmed his life. She no longer could be the delicate porcelain doll she was raised to be. As Charley's only parent, she needed to be a quiet warrior for her son and somehow fill Tom's role to guide him into manhood. Together, she and Charley had to find a way to make it through this dark time. Charley needed to be morally and physically fit to brave a world that promised to be tough on him. So, in their first summer without Tom, Alice dipped into what remained of her inheritance to follow the example of America's newest hero, Teddy Roosevelt, whose accolades in the recent American war to liberate Cuba from Spain had made him New York's current governor. Like Charley, Roosevelt suffered from severe nervousness most of his childhood. At age three, he described the feeling as a "toothache in my stomach." His sensitivity kept him from engaging in physical activities with other boys until a doctor prescribed strenuous activity in the great outdoors.

The concept that an excursion into the wilderness could actually be pleasurable had begun to take hold only three decades earlier, after a young Yale-educated preacher, William H. H. Murray, published a bestselling Adirondack guidebook. Murray contended that hiking, canoeing, and fishing in nature offered the ultimate spirit-enhancing tonic for anxiety-ridden city dwellers. Within five years, the popularity of Murray's book led to the building of some two hundred hotels and camps in the Adirondacks, with new stagecoach services clattering up from the freshly erected rural train stations and steamboats traveling up and down the lakes. The Adirondacks' summer population grew from three thousand in 1869 to twenty-five thousand in 1900. The Vanderbilts, Rockefellers, Carnegies, Morgans, and other wealthy industrialists built spectacular mansions on its lakes' most coveted shorelines, which they quaintly dubbed camps. As a result of these New York socialites' "vacating" their homes for their summer retreats, the term "vacation" was born into the American lexicon, replacing the British term "holiday."

When Charley's college preparatory, Dwight School, let out in June, he and Alice boarded a train for the Adirondacks, hoping to find some reprieve from his nervousness. After ten hours in the stale, swaying belly of the train cars, they stepped out into a mountainous Garden of Eden that welcomed them with birdsong, fresh air, and the crisp scent of balsam and evergreens. A stagecoach took them the remaining twelve miles over a rough dirt road, and soon they passed the gateway into a wilderness where the days of the week no longer mattered. The three-hour bumpy ride ended deep in the woods, along the crystal waters of Stony Creek Ponds, where the rustic Hiawatha Lodge rested cozily in the shadow of Seward Mountain. The large white main building overlooked the lake, together with a little commune of white cottages with private baths. The settlement included a general store, daily mail service, a resident physician, and a telegraph and telephone office—quite the luxury at a time when less than 1 percent of Americans had phones.

Charley and Alice needed to be careful what they said about their absent patriarch to the lodge's other hundred or so guests, which consisted mostly of wives and children until their hardworking husbands abandoned their sweaty city offices in July for cooler surroundings. During organized outdoor activities and daily communal meals in the rustic dining room, it would not have been uncommon for Charley to

HIAWATHA LODGE ON
STONY CREEK PONDS, ADIRONDACKS

be asked if he was related to the late New York Supreme Court justice and congressman bearing his name. Families who knew Buffalo would certainly inquire if Alice was from the same Meldrum family as the department store Meldrums. And questions naturally arose about the line of work of everyone's husbands back in the city and when they were expected to arrive. If pressed, Alice and Charley probably divulged that Mr. Thomas Daniels was a Wall Street banker with his own firm. Beyond that, they would not have been chatty about their personal affairs. When husbands began to arrive to reunite with their wives and children, Alice persuaded her youngest sister, twenty-one-year-old Flossie, to join them. It appears Alice had confided in her as to the painful truth behind why they had not visited Buffalo in nearly a year.

All summer, Charley sought to escape his reality by exploring the trails, woods, and three connecting ponds that made up Stony Creek. The lodge rested on the shore of half-mile-long First Pond, where one could canoe to the connecting mile-long Middle Pond, then into the much smaller Third Pond. There was a popular trail used to shuttle canoes between Stony Creek Ponds and the bigger Saranac Lake, in which Charley met and befriended some of the local guides who shared tips on tracking, hunting, and handling a rifle. He particularly liked to use the lodge's birch canoes to practice the "manly" art of canoeing, just like his father.

During the hot summer days, nothing beat a cool mountain lake. Charley would dive into this other world, float weightless, perform underwater flips and handstands. In the water, he was strong and capable and happy. He practiced his father's breaststroke, which he had so admired and fifty years later would still recall watching with pride. Perhaps, in some strange way, the water was the one thing that still let him feel connected to his father.

One of the most magical times in the water was at dusk when the lake became glass and the conical spires of trees reflected off the surface with the last few glimmers of sunlight. The haunting, howl-like wail of a loon reverberated off the lake, the bird seeming to be calling out in a desperate search for others. Moments later, a different part of the lake resounded with another long, mournful wail, as if to say, "You're not alone. I'm over here," and back and forth the pair would call out, aching to connect with each other and no longer feel so alone. Then the sky illuminated with more stars than Charley could ever wish upon.

In August, Charley looked forward to the daily stagecoach delivery of newspapers that brought reports about the 1900 Olympic Games in Paris, though the papers said virtually nothing about the Games' swimming contests. What little Charley found about the second modern Olympiad as he flipped through the pages centered on brief reports of the twenty-one track-and-field events the Americans competed in. As he read, he daydreamed about standing in the cleats of America's Olympic champions—heroes like Penn's Alvin Kraenzlein, whose innovative straight-leg hurdling won four events with record times. Or the New York Athletic Club's Ray Ewry, who won all three standing jumps with such superiority the French called him "the human frog." In total, the American team took eighteen victories, thirteen second places, and eleven thirds, being dominated only by the long-distance men of England—the only English runners participating at these Games. The one small blurb about swimming said that the contests took place in the river Seine and the self-selected American in the two-hundred-meter qualifier was "outclassed and did not finish." Nothing else. No winning times. Not even a list of the other events or who won. Charley wouldn't have known this yet, but if there had been more information, it would have shown complete domination by the watermen of the British Empire.

As the days grew shorter and summer drew to an end, Charley heard the last call of the loons. He took one final swim and, after the bumpy twelve-mile wagon ride through the woods, took his last big inhalation of fresh pine air. Then he and Alice boarded a train for home. With the scream of the train whistle, a loud hiss of steam, the smell of coal fire singeing the air, he rolled out of the station to the sound of the clanging bell and watched the marvelous paradise of woods and lakes slowly fade into memory. Somewhere in the surrounding wilderness and distant mountains, come dusk, the loons would be calling him back to the lake.

CHARLES DANIELS,
STONY CREEK PONDS, ADIRONDACKS

IN LATE SEPTEMBER, the arrival of the 1900 fall semester brought Charley all the anxieties that came with a new school year, as well as fresh challenges that included feeling like an awkward foreigner in his new gangly, growing body. Dwight School had hired a new athletic director who looked like Hercules and was unlike anyone Charley had ever met.

Dr. Philip M. Seixas, or "Doc" as the boys called him, embodied Teddy Roosevelt's new persona of rugged manliness. Broad-chested, steely-muscled, with intense dark eyes, Doc was an all-around athlete and outdoorsman who made even gangly kids like Charley believe they could turn themselves into top-notch athletes. At age twenty-six, Doc had already made a name for himself as one of New York's premier physical educators. He had graduated from Columbia University with a medical degree, reportedly lettered in five sports—football, baseball, track, water polo, and swimming—and counted Teddy Roosevelt as an admirer and friend. But his most impressive accomplishment was his work with the National Sportsmen's Association—a prominent organization for wildlife preservation—to establish one of the nation's first youth scouting troops.

Like Roosevelt, Seixas believed in a vigorous outdoor lifestyle to rid boys of any nervousness and mold them into strong, active men. At Dwight that fall, Doc exposed the boys to just about every kind of sport. Once they discovered one they enjoyed, Doc offered further instruction. Only when a boy found athletics fun did Doc believe he attained all the necessary exercise and body development that put him on the path to becoming a first-rate competitor.

As Doc liked to point out, many great athletes of the day started out as physically weak. Among them was the Olympic jumping champion Ray Ewry, confined to a wheelchair by polio until he turned to rigorous exercise to walk again. Another was E. Carroll Schaeffer, who took up swimming at the University of Pennsylvania to strengthen his polio-stricken legs and now held just about every swimming record in America. Even Teddy Roosevelt overcame asthma and frailty to become not only a model of rugged athleticism but, that November, President McKinley's new vice president.

All year, Doc and Charley worked on finding a sport the undersized teen could excel in. They tried running and high-jumping, baseball, the new sport of basketball, and various other sports in Dwight's gymnasium, but all to no avail. In February, Doc introduced Charley and the boys to scouting at the National Sportsmen's Show, which turned Madison Square Garden into an outdoorsman's paradise with painted mountain canvas backdrops, a man-made lake, and a wooded island where the junior branch scouts re-created Camp Rainbow, their previous summer's Adirondack tent encampment. Charley became enamored with scouting.

That July, Doc again opened up Camp Rainbow for two months of scouting adventures in the Adirondacks. Reports seem to indicate that the troop ranged from a dozen to forty boys. For most of them like Charley, it would be their first time managing their own affairs, figuring out things with little adult help, and taking care of themselves and each other. All summer long, they lived in four-man tents on Bluff Island on Lower Saranac Lake. Doc empowered the boys to take responsibility for themselves and their fellow scouts, setting their own agendas, trying new things, and making mistakes without the worry of an authority figure coming down on them. Doc emphasized the importance of developing good swimming and outdoor skills that could help the troop. Here, if Charley shot a rabbit, his unit enjoyed a rabbit dinner that evening. If he learned to navigate the woods, it helped his team find their way. And his determination to master swimming helped others who might be struggling in the water. Doc Seixas made it mandatory to swim each morning before breakfast, and every time the water put a smile on Charley's face. Without a father in his life to offer proper guidance on how to be a man, the environment at camp under Doc provided a desperately needed road map. Most important, the daily access to the lake allowed him to swim to his heart's content.

Not until they returned to New York in September did they learn that an assassin's bullet had struck down President McKinley at Buffalo's World's Fair, making their hero, Teddy Roosevelt, the youngest president of the United States.

CHARLEY HAD NOT SEEN or heard from his father in the two years since Tom had abandoned them, when advertisements began to appear in *The New York Times* and other newspapers promoting the Wall Street banking firm of Daniels & Company. Some ads solicited stock investors for extraordinary opportunities to invest in Colorado and California gold-mining companies. Others gave Daniels & Company's seal of approval to extend credit to various produce and logging companies. Most of the advertisements simply read:

———

ADDITIONAL CAPITAL SUPPLIED.

STOCK COMPANIES ORGANIZED.

CHARTERS SECURED IN ANY STATE.

STOCKS AND BONDS UNDERWRITTEN OR

SOLD UNDER GUARANTEE AND ON COMMISSION.

GOOD INVENTIONS MARKETED.

CASH FURNISHED FOR ANY GOOD ENTERPRISE.

DANIELS & CO.,

BANKERS, 6 WALL ST., NEW YORK

ALSO LONDON, PHILADELPHIA,

BOSTON, SAN FRANCISCO

———

Alice was walking down a crowded New York street one day when, for the first time since Tom had left, she saw him. Dressed impeccably, he looked his usual buoyant and successful self, only with a little less hair. She had heard that his Staten Island home had burned down and that he now lived farther south on the island in a bigger, grander estate with a barn, a groundskeeper, and his young mistress, whom he continued to introduce to everyone as "Mrs. Daniels." He had still not sent Alice a penny of support nor acknowledged Charley's existence. Whatever Alice had imagined saying to him if such a moment ever arose, the words failed her. She was confident that he did not see her, and she did not make her presence known. What he had done to her and Charley, no words could make better.

IN EARLY MARCH 1902, a few weeks before his seventeenth birthday, Charley had a chance to prove to his father that he was more than just the anxiety-ridden boy his father walked out on. He joined his fellow scouts at the two-week National Sportsmen's Show that brought his beloved Adirondacks to Madison Square Garden. Painted pine-covered mountains rose high above the Garden floor on an enormous drop curtain. A trout stream wound around a large man-made wooded island on the arena floor, with dirt paths and wooden bridges that Charley could follow to big game enclosures of live moose and deer and the shoreline camps of wilderness guides and Ojibwe teepees. The scouts re-created daily life at their Adirondack summer camp and held their national junior rifle-shooting contest, which Charley entered along with seventy-three other boys. At stake was a silver trophy donated by the legendary sharpshooter Annie Oakley and, most important, a write-up in the newspaper, which might get his father's attention.

Although shooting required little athleticism—which was good for Charley—sharpshooting demanded mental precision and psychological calm. Breath control was essential to keep the heart from beating too fast and making the arms shaky. Squeezing the trigger of a .22-caliber rifle needed to be a smooth motion, not jerky, or it would throw off your aim. Miss by a little and you missed by a mile. This was a sport that required him to settle his nerves and remain laser focused on the mark.

At the end of two weeks, Charley found himself in a first-place shoot-out against the current scouting champion and fellow Dwight classmate. If he won, his father would see his name in the paper and might finally reach out and congratulate him. With a big crowd watching and everything on the line, Charley's nerves caused his worst performance of the week, as he hit only twenty-one of thirty targets. Lucky for Charley, his opponent hit only nineteen. The Annie Oakley trophy was the first time Charley won anything of such magnitude or received accolades from his peers. The next morning, buried on page 6 of *The New York Times* for all to see was a subhead, "Daniels Wins Rifle Trophy."

Charley never heard from his father. Not only that, but his accomplishment suddenly seemed more insignificant compared with the headlines made by a high school phenom at the National Sportsmen's Show in Boston, whom the press described as tall, muscular, handsome, popular, and an all-around athlete that any father would be proud to call his son.

Each day, newspapers touted a new American swimming record by the eighteen-year-old Harry LeMoyne. First sixty yards, then eighty yards, then LeMoyne broke the esteemed hundred-yard American century record. Newspapers across the country called LeMoyne a "star," "wonderful," "marvelous," and "the coming champion short-distance swimmer of the world." *The Boston Post* and New York's *Evening World* hyped up a match race between the teen marvel and America's East Coast champion, E. Carroll Schaeffer. *The Buffalo Enquirer* even went so far as to tout LeMoyne as showing every promise of being the one American to equal the records of the top-notch English and Australian swimmers.

The mere suggestion that an American could compete against the British Empire's unbeatable stable of watermen was unheard of. As the *Enquirer* even admitted, "American record holders have never been able to approach the figures set by their British relatives or even those of far off Australia." Yet, with the recent announcement that Chicago would host the third Olympiad in 1904, the *Enquirer* heralded LeMoyne as the country's only real hope to defend America's honor against the seemingly unbeatable British. To accomplish such an impossible feat would impress even Tom Daniels.

3.

THE UNBEATABLE
BRITISH EMPIRE

—

IN 1902, THE BRITISH EMPIRE KNEW NO EQUAL ON THE WATER. ITS
Royal Navy ruled the seas. Its commercial fleet enjoyed unrivaled
dominance over global trade. Its sovereignty extended over six conti-
nents and ruled over a fourth of the world's inhabitants, giving truth to
the expression "the sun never sets on the British Empire."

Even though Germany and America had superseded Britain as in-
dustrial powers, the empire still reigned supreme on the waves, with a
naval fleet larger than the combined armadas of its next two rivals,
France and Russia, and ten times bigger than its American counter-
part. Its iron hulls and steam-powered ships made it the most advanced
navy in the world. And Britain's aggressive culture of imperialism
found its ultimate expression in sport. One of the earliest versions of
soccer was said to have originated as a war game when Englishmen
began kicking around the severed head of a Danish prince they had
defeated in battle. And nowhere was Britain's athletic superiority more
on display than among its oarsmen and swimmers, who had dominated the previous century.

Britain had long used sports' aggressive play to groom a culture of
young, middle-class, able-bodied soldiers who projected a masculine
image to the world. These competitions were a key element in asserting
control over all who lived under its flag. As the father of modern sports,
the empire oversaw all the rule books, presided over every "official"
world record, and regarded its own athletic governing bodies—the first

and oldest—as the only ones that mattered. Colonists who sought to compete were subject to the authority of the empire, which vetted, adjudicated, recorded, and had the authority to reject any outcome or disqualify any participant. Athletes outside the empire were not taken seriously unless they competed in the British Empire's annual championships and against its best sportsmen.

The Crown used sports among its colonies to help eradicate native customs and games and instill a proper British culture. Seeking a homogeneous society throughout its vast empire, it began justifying its conquest of undeveloped countries in Asia and Africa on the moral mission of "civilizing" them, with sports playing an important role. Sports allowed British athletes to dominate the less experienced colonials and natives in competition, reinforcing the Crown's superiority over its subjects. And by dividing teams between "gentlemen" and members of the working class, and excluding certain races entirely, the British helped perpetuate their notions of a social hierarchy.

THE FIRST BRITISH SWIMMING competitions took place in the 1830s. Only a decade earlier, England had sought to combat cholera outbreaks that originated from fecal-contaminated water in areas with inadequate sewage and bathing facilities by reintroducing the ancient Roman tradition of public bathhouses. No sooner had the baths gone up than the patrons began amusing themselves by racing one another. When more cholera outbreaks necessitated additional bathing facilities, municipalities designed them with larger pools to accommodate the growing popularity of swimming races. The installation of water mains around the mid-nineteenth century allowed city planners to construct aquatic facilities in the inner city, making swimming more accessible to the public.

Unlike America, where the few public baths operated in the poorest parts of town, England built facilities near some of the city's swankiest neighborhoods. And not just baths. It erected aquatic cathedrals, with big multistory glass atriums, grand skylighted domes, pillared galleries, and enormous tanks. Some indoor complexes contained as many as four swimming pools—one first-class bath for gentlemen and another for ladies, and separate second-class baths for commoners— with different entrances to protect the highborn from mingling with the masses. To ensure class segregation, the first-class bath cost six- pence, about three times higher than the second-class bath admission fee of twopence.

The popularity of swimming races incited the search for faster strokes. For thousands of years, the breaststroke, which resembles the movement of a frog swimming in water, had been the most efficient way to navigate from point A to point B. The head remained above water, the arms made leisurely semicircular synchronous movements beneath the chest, and the legs thrusted wide underwater, requiring not a lot of effort if the right technique was applied, which was good for long distances. Then, in 1855, the Australian C. W. Wallis intro- duced a new speed technique. Lying on his side with arms and legs working beneath the surface, Wallis demonstrated what he observed aborigines doing Down Under. The empire promptly claimed the in- novation as its own and dubbed it the English sidestroke.

Eighteen years later, the twenty-one-year-old Englishman John Trudgen shocked the British swimming establishment by bringing his arms out of the water. No one had ever seen such a thing. Lying flat on his chest, with his head carried high in the air and legs using the frog kick, Trudgen lifted one arm out, followed by the other. The radical overarm technique was used by the indigenous swimmers of Buenos Aires,* where Trudgen had recently visited. He observed how the Ar- gentinian swimmers' arms encountered less resistance as they came out of the water, inducing greater speed. Trudgen promptly took full credit for the technique and named the overarm stroke after himself.

The exertion required to maintain the trudgen's flywheel arm move- ment made most long-distance swimmers stick to the leisurely breast- stroke. But over short distances, the British Empire's swimmers soon

---

* Some sources claim Trudgen learned the stroke on a trip to South Africa; however, this is unlikely, given that the South Americans had a much greater reputation for being outstanding swimmers.

ditched the sidestroke to adopt Trudgen's speedy revolution, enabling them to set new world records.

Two years later, in 1875, when Captain Matthew Webb conquered the swimming world's Mount Everest by breaststroking across the English Channel, every lad in England wanted to swim.

By 1900, hundreds of state-of-the-art indoor swimming facilities dotted the English landscape, with more than eleven hundred swimming clubs across the country. Australia did even better, thanks to a climate that permitted outdoor bathing throughout the year. Besides the splendid open-water facilities along its coast, there were numerous magnificent pools at swimmers' disposal. Sydney alone supported a dozen enormous public establishments where every accommodation, including competent instruction, could be had for a nominal fee.

England's Amateur Swimming Association—the first such governing body of its kind—recorded, vetted, and maintained all of the world's swimming records, and the British and Australians held just about every record since it began. Their fast times were a level above those of the rest of Europe and light-years ahead of the United States. Each year the English swimming championships drew a reported 100,000 enthusiastic spectators, while America's annual championship was lucky to attract 100.

It is an undeniable fact that in sport, as in all else, the achievement of excellence is proportionate to the number of participants. In 1900, England registered about nine thousand competitive amateur swimmers. The Australian city of Sydney alone boasted more than twelve hundred racing men. The United States claimed only six hundred and none of them very good.

For one thing, America completely lacked adequate public pools. New York's few indoor facilities and competitive meets were exclusive to elite athletic clubs, with very little exposure to the public. Even the New York Athletic Club's heralded twenty-five-yard basement pool, with its two levels of encircling galleries, seemed like a flooded bunker compared with the beautiful aquatic atriums of London. Given the abysmal state of public swimming facilities, or total lack thereof, America's swimming culture withered under a multipronged dearth of interest, talent, and leadership.* Swimming against such a mediocre field of competitors was not conducive to any Americans advancing to the highest level of skill.

Then, in 1901, a young Austrian Jewish immigrant had the crazy dream to make American swimmers the greatest in the world. He just needed to find a champion to help him get started.

ON A SNOWY DAY in February 1901, Otto Wahle (pronounced "Wally") stood on the deck of a transatlantic steamer, staring through a veil of flurries to catch his first glimpse of the Statue of Liberty. The distant island of Manhattan looked dreamlike. Until that moment, London's fourteen-story Queen Anne's Mansions was the tallest building Wahle had ever seen that wasn't a cathedral. Now his wide gray eyes spotted several of the so-called skyscrapers jutting up from this urban forest of tall towers, some as high as thirty stories, all striving symbols of America's ambition.

As the United States sought to take its first big steps to legitimize itself alongside the great world powers of Europe under its sports-crazed, energetic young president, Teddy Roosevelt, Wahle believed that the country was ripe for a hero who exemplified that gritty underdog spirit on a global stage. Someone whose victories could bring joy, hope, and inspiration to the toiling masses. And he asked himself, why couldn't that hero be a swimmer?

Wahle had used swimming to transcend the growing anti-Semitism in his hometown of Vienna. As a celebrated champion who brought honor to his country, he was fortunate enough to be viewed first and foremost as a fellow Austrian. But throughout his city, he couldn't ig-

---

* Ironically, in 1896, in the remote western hinterland of San Francisco, far beyond the eyes of the East, Adolph Sutro, a German Jewish immigrant who made a fortune in the Comstock Lode, built the world's largest indoor swimming pool (500 feet by 254 feet) under a glass atrium roof, with seven huge slides and springboards, rivaling anything in England or the rest of Europe, all because he wanted Americans to learn to swim for their own health and safety. Unfortunately, Sutro's vision did not catch on in the rest of the country.

nore the way Vienna's mayor, Karl Lueger, fanned the flames of anti-Semitism that would grow to later influence a struggling young resident artist named Adolf Hitler.

All his life Wahle fought to disprove the cruel stereotypes that said Jews were physically weak and unathletic. At age twenty, his achievements in swimming allowed him to compete at the Paris Olympics and ultimately, after a brief stint in London, escape the old-world prejudices of Europe for a brighter future in New York City, where a quarter of the population was Jewish. Taught perfect English in school and trained as a bookkeeper, Wahle made a good living as a clerk, but his true calling remained swimming. The sport had saved him, and he wanted to use it to save others.

His determination was only bolstered a few months before departing London for the United States when English newspapers reported that a hurricane had leveled the thriving city of Galveston, Texas, littering its beaches with thousands of bodies of people who could not swim. One account reported the death toll as high as twelve thousand. Lifeless children were found tethered to drowned mothers and fathers. Thousands could have survived had they only known how to simply keep themselves afloat.

Wahle thought swimming should be an activity for everyone, rather than being exclusive to men, like most sports. Women, children, rich and poor, gentile and Jew, should learn to swim. As he had experienced himself, swimming had the power not only to strengthen the body and save lives but to liberate those who found themselves on the outside looking in. Even if just in the world of swimming, it allowed a marginalized individual like himself to rise above his or her circumstances and enjoy a sense of dignity. No other sport had the potential to be so inclusive and save so many. Yet, for now, America's elite clubs were the only thing giving competitive swimming a pulse. If you did not belong to one of them, you had no chance of competing. Wahle needed to find an athletic club with a pool to call home. Unfortunately, the two in Manhattan that fit that bill did not allow Jews.

Modeled on the London Athletic Club in 1868, the New York City version was one of the first in the country to organize amateur sports contests and championships like swimming. What started with a handful of former college athletes renting an apartment together to store weights and workout equipment to stay in shape evolved over the next two decades into several different exclusive social societies. They tried to outdo one another by building palatial clubhouses, one grander than the next, and acquiring summer estates, like the New York Athletic Club's Travers Island, for yachting and swimming and creating superior outdoor track-and-field venues. At a time when baseball was the only professional team sport—and geared toward the working-class fan—athletic clubs provided upper-class sports enthusiasts a chance to watch sports and be associated with the winners. Wahle soon discovered that the majority of the NYAC's members were more interested in smoking cigars, sipping brandy, and raising a glass to their athletes' triumphs—in the way one would toast a prized stallion or well-bred hunting dog—than in competing themselves. As *Scribner's Magazine* noted in an 1895 article, "The athletes of the clubs became hired performers, and they were often kept like a pack of hounds," to be taken out as needed.

Of course, the club could not afford to list a Jew as an official member on its annual report, nor allow him the right to vote or hold office, but it could assign him the special designation of an "athletic member." This allowed the NYAC to take superior athletes like Wahle without the need to vet them with the same Waspishness that was required of official members. Certain "undesirable attributes" could be overlooked. As long as Wahle contributed to the club's trophy cases, it allowed him use of its basement pool. It was understood that the lounges and dining areas were off-limits unless he was invited by a proper member. But the arrangement gave Wahle a chance to compete, and perhaps change a few hearts.

Ironically, being a Jew did not make Wahle feel like a second-class citizen so much as did being a swimmer. The NYAC's twenty watermen felt the constant pressure to keep winning trophies, or their minor sport would cease to be relevant for funding. Even the powerful Amateur Athletic Union viewed swimming as an unwanted stepchild. The 1901 American championships held that June in a muddy lake at Buffalo's World's Fair drew only a small gathering of curiosity seekers, who seemed more interested in seeing if the lake's resident ducks would interfere with the swimmers than the actual outcome of the races. Wahle was even more disturbed when the *Buffalo Courier* called him "nothing short of marvelous" after he broke every American record from 660 yards to the mile with times that would not even earn a top-three finish at England's championships. His half-mile American record was a whole three minutes slower than the British champion John Jarvis had swum the previous summer in Paris, and the other competitors' times were abysmal. Only two American champions even knew how to swim the faster trudgen stroke—both of them taught by former British champions living in America.

There were no rules or standards. No official governing body like England's Amateur Swimming Association. In many events, Wahle was shocked to see there were only as many entrants as medals. Amer-

OTTO WAHLE, TRAVERS ISLAND, 1907

icans ran races so close together that it became almost impossible for the few good swimmers, still winded from their previous contest, to compete in the next event. In many instances, Wahle witnessed second-raters floating across the finish line in front of tired champions. After only six months in his new country, Wahle took it upon himself to write an American version of the official rule book on swimming, based on England's of course. But the horrible state of American swimming needed a complete cultural revolution to turn it around.

The sport demanded more year-round pools and exposure. Somehow American youth needed to be encouraged to take to the water early in life, like the Brits. Slight advantages gained at a young age resulted in huge gains later. But none of that could happen without Americans of all ages first being inspired to swim. The only way that might happen was if some underdog American born with exceptional natural ability defied all odds to beat the Brits and Aussies at their own game. Just as Matthew Webb's amazing swim across the English Channel had stirred England's youth to take to the water, Wahle needed an American swimmer who could go up against the watermen of the British Empire and inspire the country to dream. It was a chicken-and-egg enigma, or rather, fish-and-egg. How one could happen first without the other posed an impossible dilemma.

4.

THE KNICKERBOCKER
PREDICAMENT

—

1902

FACING TIGHTER FINANCES AND THE THREAT OF NEIGHBORS growing wise to their "unseemly" situation, Alice and Charley moved two miles south to a more affordable, pre-furnished two-room Greenwich Village apartment along the south side of Washington Square Park, where the influx of immigrants and bohemianism over the prior few decades had scared off the upper class. The Village's avant-garde residents, mostly artists, writers, radicals, and Italian immigrants attracted to its cheap rents, lived lifestyles outside the traditional nuclear family. There was a growing feminist movement, and the neighborhood was one of the first to allow an openly gay presence. The move opened both Alice's and Charley's eyes to the wider world, full of people unlike those they'd grown up with. It was also an area where women worked.

Each morning, hundreds of young immigrant women, many of whom did not speak English, walked east across Washington Square Park. Among them were teenagers, some even younger, who walked half a block off the park down Washington Place, and disappeared into the ten-story Asch Building. There, a freight elevator carried them nine floors to slave away for twelve hours on a sewing machine line at the Triangle Shirtwaist Factory's cramped, unventilated sweatshop, for a meager two dollars per day. It was a constant reminder of what might be in store for Alice if their situation did not improve, because what remained of her diminished inheritance provided only modest living expenses and Charley's tuition, but little else.

Alice had fallen far from the life she had known. Back home in Buffalo, all of her siblings had been enjoying the close-knit, small-scale Buffalo society that they were raised to be part of. Her two brothers Arthur and Herbert lived in stately homes, both with Victorian wives who spent their time volunteering, socializing with the right families, and raising three adored children. They summered in lakeshore cottages and wintered down south. Alice's sister Jessie, seven years younger, lived just outside Buffalo in a beautiful home in the quaint village of East Aurora, married to a prominent chemist. Even her youngest sister, Flossie, sixteen years her junior at age twenty-three, lived with their mother at Buffalo's swanky residential hotel, the Lenox, not far from the family's old North Street mansion, which became too much upkeep for Alice's mother. The two of them liked to escape Buffalo during the cold and hot seasons, wintering in California and summering by a lake or beach.

Alice's younger brother Herbert had accomplished in Buffalo exactly what Tom and Alice had set out and failed to do in Dayton, building his own successful department store, H. A. Meldrum Company. He held leadership positions at Buffalo's chamber of commerce, the Buffalo Club, the Aero Club, and the Automobile Club. Alice's older brother Arthur had worked for their late father's department store, Adam, Meldrum & Anderson, and now ran his own underwear manufacturing company.

Just about all of Alice's childhood friends remained in Buffalo. Her two closest, Ida Reid and Gertrude Fargo, both bridesmaids at her wedding, were living the life that all three used to dream about. Both had married well and resided in large homes, close to their families, raising their children in the beloved society they grew up in. All of their lives seemed so perfect compared with her own failed marriage and the state she now found herself in. But even Alice's childhood friends would not be so welcoming if they discovered the truth about her marriage situation, and the rest of Buffalo society would be downright cruel.

Alice could only fantasize about what would have happened if Tom had planted roots in their home city as Alice's other siblings had. Charley could have enjoyed an idyllic Buffalo childhood. Alice would now be scoping out young ladies who might one day make a "good match" for her son. In a year or two, Charley would have been attending Buffalo's exclusive balls and coming-out parties. He would have been meeting debutantes like the daughter of Grandma Meldrum's neighbor eighteen-year-old Miss Florence Goodyear, whom society pages proclaimed "the most stunning girl of the younger set." But Charley would experience none of that. He would never be in those social spheres that Ida's and Gertrude's children would enjoy. Not without a father. Charley would somehow have to find his own way.

EACH WEEKDAY MORNING, CHARLEY walked a block west to Sixth Avenue, where the overhead iron scaffolding of train tracks cast the sidewalks in shadow. He ascended the metal stairs to the elevated platform, paid the five-cent fare, and crowded into the El train for a loud, rickety, coal-choking three miles north at a speedy twelve miles per hour, twice the speed of a horse-drawn streetcar.

A little before 9:00 A.M., 110 secondary school boys dressed in coat and tie entered the four-story brick town house on West Forty-third Street to begin the day at Dwight School with the Pledge of Allegiance, followed by college prep work in English, mathematics, and the sciences. Some classmates by Charley's age had already been deemed "college ready" and moved on to the Ivy Leagues, while he continued struggling to find his way. His anxiety and family situation did not help. And his growing interest in such an obscure activity as swimming made him only more of an odd kid.

Normal American boys participated in popular sports like football, baseball, rowing, track and field, or newer sports like basketball, hockey, golf, or lawn tennis. Swimming wouldn't even constitute the proverbial road less traveled. It was more akin to beating a desperate path through uncharted swampland. The few competitive swimmers in America all seemed like outcasts—immigrants, mavericks, loners, or discards from somewhere else—until the great Harry LeMoyne.

Charley hadn't much of a clue how fast he really was, or if he was fast at all. He had never been timed, nor raced anyone. There was the obvious problem of having no competitive public pools to race in or public swim clubs to join. Neither of those really existed in New York, other than those maintained by the city's elite athletic clubs. He just knew that he enjoyed swimming in the cool lakes of the Adirondacks.

The New York Athletic Club had the top swimming team in the country, made up of a passionate bunch of watermen whose lofty goals would have evoked outside laughter if anyone cared to listen. They strove to become not only the best watermen in America but the best in the world. To that end, they sought only proven champions who could help elevate their status.

The NYAC's written application not only required each candidate to list his full name, residence, and place of business but had to be signed by the two club members who proposed and seconded him, with references and remarks. This helped the membership committee place an applicant in the social hierarchy and determine if he was "clubbable." Initiation fees of around a hundred dollars (three thousand dollars in today's money) and annual dues half that amount were another means of discouraging undesirables. Membership into the club's elite ranks was precisely the type of pedigree that Charley's father prized.

Charley wanted to find a way to swim. He wanted to learn the British Empire's racing secrets. But, then again, Charley never had ready access to a swimming pool, nor to a proper instructor who could teach him the latest speed swimming stroke, like the trudgen.

When *The Boston Post* asked the high school phenom Harry LeMoyne for advice on how to swim fast, LeMoyne responded, "The only way . . . is to go into the water and stay there. Go every day, and if there is speed in you it will soon show."

Charley was determined to find that opportunity.

A FEW BLOCKS EAST of Dwight School, at the southeast corner of Madison Avenue and Forty-fifth Street, rose the five-story red-stone palace of the Knickerbocker Athletic Club. On par with the New York

Athletic Club's prestige, its more than fifteen hundred members consisted of the city's wealthiest and most distinguished gentlemen, including the czar of American amateur athletics, Jim Sullivan, who
served as club president. *The New York Times* called the Knickerbocker
headquarters "the finest athletic clubhouse in the world," with the biggest indoor pool in the city and one of the country's most esteemed
aquatic instructors, Alex Meffert. It also did not allow guests younger
than nineteen years old. Not unless they were the son of a member,
which Charley clearly was not.

One spring day after school, Charley walked up the broad white
marble steps to the Knickerbocker's imposing front door. To even set
foot inside required proper attire: suit, tie, and, if a true gentleman, a
handsome derby or top hat. Charley looked like a boy trying to play
adult in an oversized off-the-rack jacket. Walking into the Knickerbocker felt like entering a palace, its rooms rich with fancy red-and-
gold wallpaper, paintings, and grand chandeliers. Numerous statues of
muscular athletes—the darting sprinter, the heaving shot-putter, the
thrusting fencer, the hoisting weight lifter—were equally imposing to
a newcomer. The smell of rich oak and fine tobacco lingered in the air.
Distinguished gentlemen in snugly fit, tailor-made suits socialized in
its elegant smoking lounges, card parlors, and enormous billiards room.
Its private upper floors boasted a fifteen-hundred-seat concert hall, an
unrivaled gymnasium that covered the entire fifth floor, and a rooftop
tennis court and ice rink. If you did not belong, you were made to
feel it.

Eyebrows certainly were raised as a seventeen-year-old Charley
checked in at the front desk beneath the glass chandelier. Despite his
prohibited age, the desk clerk humored him by looking through the
guest book. Sure enough, he found the name Charles M. Daniels.
Alongside Charley's name was the member who vouched for him,
most likely either the club's president, Jim Sullivan, or the club's athletic director, Harry Cornish, whom Doc would've contacted to arrange the special tryout.

The club's admissions committee had the discretion to elect gentlemen under the age of nineteen to a junior membership. With reduced

annual dues of ten dollars (three hundred dollars today), these young members could gain access to the athletic facilities until 6:00 P.M., when the club's regular members showed up after work. So long as the young individual was personally known and nominated by at least one full-fledged member, the proposed candidate could present an application endorsed either by both parents—a problem for Charley—or by the headmaster of a preparatory school of "recognized standing." The admissions committee could then take it under advisement and, in confidential discussion, determine if the young candidate was indeed "clubbable" and enough of an outstanding athlete to contribute to their trophy cases. And unlike the New York Athletic Club's star-studded swim team, the Knickerbocker, although tops in water polo, was in need of another short-distance speedster.

The clerk directed him to descend the grand staircase, where upon reaching the bottom step he encountered eight bowling alleys, a 125-foot-long shooting gallery, and a 60-foot pistol range. Beyond that, he passed the Turkish baths and entered the well-appointed dressing room, where members confidently exhibited their expensive bathing suits and manly physiques.

Charley undressed, exposing his lanky twig of a body, and changed into his cheap wool swimsuit. The bottom half stretched down to his knees. Stepping in one skinny leg at a time, he pulled the top half up over his bony chest and, grabbing the split shoulder strap on each side, conjoined each one at the top of his shoulders with its button.

The Knickerbocker's intimidating stable of watermen included some of the top amateurs in the country. There was the burly Leo "Budd" Goodwin, a brute water polo center and champion long-distance swimmer who was only a year older than Charley and, like Doc, looked like Hercules. Also the fast twenty-two-year-old George Van Cleaf from Brooklyn's Bath Beach; the friendly thirty-two-year-old Dave Bratton, who knew no strangers; the tough twenty-three-year-old Joe Ruddy, an Irish jokester and ruffian whose savage water polo technique made him the most feared player in the country; and the twenty-eight-year-old Louis de B. Handley, a sports journalist and team captain whose notorious "flying salmon" (jumping off the backs of teammates to shoot a goal) made him the nation's top scorer. They all played on the Knickerbocker's undefeated, six-time-champion water polo team.

At a time when strong swimmers were rare, these champions regularly made the newspapers for saving people from drowning in the waters around New York, giving each one a bit of a superhero status. And while the Amateur Athletic Union refused to sanction any swimming contests for women, the Knickerbocker's watermen appeared at local aquatic carnivals around Long Island's beaches to help draw crowds to support swimming exhibitions by their friend the twenty-year-old Ethel Golding. With female swimming teams and clubs not yet in existence, the few ocean races open to females were an oddity, organized as stunts by local newsmen to sell more papers, and Ethel, performing in a controversial low-cut swimming dress that exposed her stockings just below the knee, won them all, even though she had no access to an adequate year-round swimming facility like the all-male athletic clubs' indoor pools.

The Knickerbocker's impressive basement pool stretched thirty-three yards in length, a little over half the size of a modern Olympic pool. A brass railing enclosed it like the ropes around a boxing ring. Only the tank's far ends remained open to grant access to swimmers. A line of gaslit lamps hung lengthwise above the middle of the tank, illuminating the water with a yellow hue. There were no black lines on the pool floor, no swim lanes, nor any side gutters or troughs to alleviate churn—all these had yet to be invented. Proper filtration systems and the use of chlorine were still ten years away. Except for days when the club sanitized the pool by draining and refilling it with fresh water, it usually looked some shade of brown.

Charley met the Knickerbocker's famed swimming instructor. He was a husky fellow who wore a tight, dark tank top that had probably fit him ten years earlier. Born around 1865 in New York to German immigrants, Alex Meffert grew up, like Charley, in a fatherless home. In his youth, he had happily shocked passersby as one of the East River's notorious naked swimming urchins. At age fifteen, Meffert worked as a telegraph employee to help support the family and began making a name for himself around the waters of Manhattan for feats other than

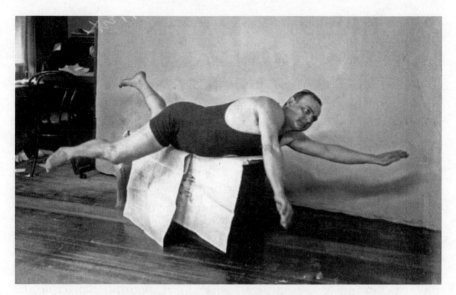

ALEX MEFFERT, FAMED SWIMMING EXPERT
AND CHAMPION, DEMONSTRATING THE
SIDESTROKE WITH SCISSOR KICK

nudity. He established some of the first swimming records ever recorded in the United States, winning the mile championship in 1887,
1889, and 1890, as well as Montreal's one-mile championship. Back
then, Meffert was described as a modest young man, with a mop of
dark hair and a chiseled physique. Newspapers published tales of his
heroic rescue of half a dozen people from drowning. One report told of
a child falling from a boat into the East River and Meffert diving in to
save him. Another story spoke of Meffert's jumping into the river in
clothes and boots to single-handedly save two young boys he saw
drowning. And still another spoke of his rescuing a woman from a
shark.

Now thirty-seven, Meffert had put on weight since his competitive
days but still possessed the quintessential swimmer's barrel chest and
muscular limbs. The sight of the lanky Charley would have made the
legendary waterman tilt his head and rub his jaw, trying to make heads
or tails of the skinny boy. The day's perception of an ideal swimmer's
body included some girth to help him float. Charley looked light
enough to hang on a clothesline and watch flap in the wind.

Meffert disliked swimmers who learned the basics without good formal instruction. They often developed faults in their stroke that became fixed habits. People like that never became fast swimmers, he was known to say. He declared that he would rather take hold of a man who couldn't even stay afloat than train a swimmer with faulty technique.

Charley's tryout was over one hundred yards, a race dubbed "the century." This was regarded as the optimum distance to maintain a stroke at full sprint before the technique's demands began to tire the swimmer. The century record was currently held by England's twenty-three-year-old John "Rob" Derbyshire, who used the trudgen to clock a speed of 60.2 seconds—one-fifth of a second from what many experts believed the limit of human speed. America's times were more modest. Beyond a few outliers like Penn's E. Carroll Schaeffer, the Harvard-bound Harry LeMoyne, and San Francisco's J. Scott Leary, who all swam the century at around 64 seconds, most American sprinting champions clocked times closer to 69, which was what Charley needed to swim if he ever hoped to compete. However, that kind of speed could not be accomplished with his father's breaststroke.

Charley had one shot. And if Meffert detected bad habits, even a satisfactory time might not save him.

Truth was, until that moment, Charley probably had never swum a hundred yards in one go. Not formally. Not timed. Certainly not in a pool.

Charley stood on the water's edge staring down at the longest swimming pool he had ever laid eyes on. The white marble tank required three laps for the hundred-yard century swim—down, back, and down again. It entailed two turns off the wall—something else Charley had no experience with.

The pressure of the moment began to mount. Blood pounded in Charley's ears, his heart hammered against his rib cage, breathing came hard, and his limbs began to tremble. It was the same anxiety that happened in target shooting, until deep breathing settled the nerves so one could focus on the bull's-eye, which in this case was the other end of the pool.

Charley bent over ninety degrees. His upper body hung over the water with his bony arms outstretched in front of him. He did not know how to swim the more advanced two-arm overhead trudgen stroke that Harry LeMoyne, E. Carroll Schaeffer, J. Scott Leary, and the British Empire's speed swimmers used. His only chance was a sidestroke that he had experimented with in the Adirondacks.

At the signal, Charley dove in and made a desperate effort to cover the distance in as close to sixty-nine seconds as possible. He later described his stroke that day as a half overarm, with legs frog-kicking underwater. Meffert would have described it as a complete mess.

Everything about his sidestroke and kick looked wrong. Charley's turns off the wall looked as graceless as a caught fish flopping against the side of a boat. He appeared to be moving slowly, almost lazily across the pool. When Charley touched the final edge, Meffert clicked his stopwatch. Seventy-five seconds.

The time was Meffert's absolute cutoff to work with someone. And Charley still needed to master basic leg techniques that most English boys learned in primary school. But there was a determination in the boy. Meffert no doubt could see that he wanted it badly, however laughable or unrealistic his prospects seemed. The veteran swim coach also probably saw Charley's inability to hold eye contact, and maybe his fidgeting.

"A powerful effective kick is indispensable to correct swimming," Meffert said. He would probably regret his decision, but for now he would make sure Charley had no more trouble at the front desk. The boy could use the basement pool after his track practice. And Meffert agreed to work with him on the fundamentals. But no further instruction would happen unless Charley mastered a proper scissor kick.

Charley was ecstatic.

Several afternoons a week, Charley showed up and Meffert taught him the importance of bringing the legs together sharply, forcing a V of water between them.

"Remember," Meffert instructed, "speed is maximized by the pressure exerted by your legs and not the violence of the kick."

Charley needed to learn to stretch his legs as wide apart as possible underwater and then bring them together with a snap resembling the closing of a pair of scissors, but no further. Often the feet tended to pass each other, forming an X that caused a double drag, stalling momentum.

Charley slowly traversed the pool again and again, diligently working on his leg movement. For the time being, he did not seem to worry about his stats or other people's superior times or records. He knew he lacked the natural strength and speed inherent in most of the club's champions. He also knew that if he failed to keep progressing, Meffert could end the relationship.

Each day, Charley strove to execute his kick better than he had the day before. He loved the sensation of the water, the gentle resistance against his body, the weightlessness, the freedom and inner peace when he swam. Such a unique feeling could not be found anywhere else. And he was committed to seeing how far he could push himself.

That summer, he and his mother again returned to the Hiawatha Lodge, only this time with both Aunt Flossie and Grandma Meldrum, who by this point was fully aware of their situation. Along the banks of First Pond, Charley measured off a hundred-yard course and had a friend in a canoe time him. Surely some of the Hiawatha's guests who saw him swimming every day in the lake shook their heads and laughed at the crazy boy who thought he was a fish. Charley even made the twelve-mile canoe trek to the Lower Saranac to join Doc and forty of his fellow scouts, where they had pitched tents to spend another summer on Bluff Island.

All summer long, he practiced his leg work. It became a joyful obsession. In early August, he entered the hundred-yard century race at the Hiawatha's annual aquatic festival against three older contestants. Because guests had seen him swimming so much that summer, the official tried to even the contest by assigning Charley's three competitors handicaps that gave them each a ten- to twenty-yard head start, yet with his sweeping overhand sidestroke Charley still won. *The Brooklyn Daily Eagle* called it "by far the best contested race of the day. Mr. Daniels' swimming was faultless." Charley no doubt wondered if his father read about his little victory. But another dark cloud loomed over the Danielses.

Earlier that summer, as they left New York for the Adirondacks, they had made an urgent detour to Buffalo. It was the first time the city's society pages reported Alice visiting in more than two years. She kept up appearances as Mrs. Thomas P. Daniels. But a rather frightful skeleton was about to escape the Meldrums' closet, and Alice felt compelled to be with her family when it did.

Arthur's underwear manufacturing company had failed, and he now faced personal bankruptcy, a trauma akin to a serious physical illness. In society, not paying one's debts was deemed an abomination and regarded as a crime, rather than as a legally sanctioned way to close down a failing business, and the social ostracism was chilling.

The late Alexander Meldrum had worked hard to build a strong reputation for their family, so much so that newspapers had talked about renaming North Street after him. Now one of the esteemed Meldrum family was facing public humiliation. A week after Alice and Charley had arrived in Buffalo that June, local papers published the court filing that labeled Arthur Meldrum a "bankrupt."

Alice and Charley stayed for several weeks to help circle the family wagons and offer support. Arthur's failed business venture had not only sucked up his inheritance but cost him his very honor. Herbert offered his eldest brother a job at his department store to help him survive, but Arthur's reputation in Buffalo was ruined. The shame of bankruptcy would hang over him and his family the rest of their lives. It would tarnish his children's future. Such disgrace even jeopardized the survival of his marriage. They all knew it.

Seeing her elder brother so utterly gutted with no real hope certainly weighed heavily on Alice, probably conjuring the same bleakness she felt at her brother Fred's funeral. For all practical purposes, the Arthur they knew was dead. The family disgrace also brought to mind the ruinous future that awaited Alice and Charley should their shameful secret ever leak beyond the Meldrums' inner circle, which the whole family likely feared was just a matter of time.

BY THE END OF summer, with a friend standing on the shore and timing him, Charley recalled swimming his makeshift hundred-yard century course on Stony Creek Pond in about the same time that had been winning races in New York. He had finally broken seventy seconds.

Charley buzzed with confidence and a clear sense of purpose, eager upon his return to slip into the Knickerbocker's cherry diamond colors for his first official AAU-sanctioned race and make a headline for his father to see. However, when he bounded up the Knickerbocker's front marble steps, excited to show his new speed to Meffert, his big glowing smile quickly melted away upon finding the Knickerbocker's doors padlocked shut.

5.

CHASING THE
GOD OF SPEED

—

1903

Historians later dubbed it America's first trial of the century. The entire country was riveted by wild accusations inside the Knickerbocker of sex, betrayal, and "moral degeneration" (that is, homosexuality) stemming from a series of shocking high-society murders that rocked New York. The accused murderer was the former Knickerbocker Roland Molineux, a pretentious Manhattan socialite and chemist whose family had made a fortune in the chemical dye business. Newspapers printed tales of his trips to opium dens in Chinatown, his frequent buying of impotence cures, his visits to a gay bordello patronized by a secret homosexual ring of club members, and his deadly love triangle over the beautiful singer Blanche Chesebrough. His first victim, Henry Barnet, was a fellow Knickerbocker who had been sleeping with Chesebrough, the girl Molineux was determined to marry. His second victim, Kate Adams, was the landlady of his intended target, Harry Cornish, the Knickerbocker's athletic director, who had forced Molineux to resign from the club after Molineux's intolerable snobbery became too extreme for even his fellow snobs. Both victims were poisoned with cyanide disguised in a bottle of a popular hangover elixir that each intended victim had received as an anonymous gift in his club mailbox. Unfortunately for Kate Adams, she sampled some of Cornish's.

Predictably, the highly sensationalized ordeal sullied the Knickerbocker's reputation. The first murder trial had lasted from November

1899 to February 1900, making it, at the time, the longest and most expensive in New York history. It ended with a sentence of death by electric chair. However, after a New York appeals court reversed the conviction on the grounds of improper admission of evidence, the retrial was set to begin that October of 1902, and once again the Knickerbocker found itself at the epicenter of the scandal when another blow hit the club.

Years of extravagances and fiscal mishandling had finally come to roost. An action was filed in the New York Supreme Court to foreclose on the Knickerbocker's $400,000 clubhouse mortgage. With the Molineux retrial damaging the club's reputation, members struggled to assemble the necessary financing to keep its palatial doors open. In early September, creditors posted a prominent notice in the main corridor announcing to members that their exclusive club was no more.

Alex Meffert lost his job, but he encouraged Charley to stick with his training. If he committed himself to swimming, Meffert told him, he might eventually show enough speed to justify entering an amateur competition. Only now, it was no longer up to Meffert. Charley needed to prove himself to the team.

The Knickerbocker's former watermen formed a new organization called the Knickerbocker Aquatic Club. It included well-known club members such as the dapper Louis de B. Handley, whom they called L. de B.; the six-foot-two, brawny Leo Goodwin, whom they called Budd; the feisty Joe Ruddy, whom they called Spike; the heroic George Van Cleaf, whose red hair made for an easy nickname; and the gregarious David H. Bratton, whom they simply called Dave because he was too great a guy to call anything else. Until you earned a nickname, you remained an outsider.

Meffert put in a good word for Charley and touted him as a potential champion.

"Any healthy, normal child can be built up into a champion of something," Joe Ruddy would say in his gruff voice. "Being a champion of something—if it's just wiggling your ears—is better than being a never-waser." Whether Charley had it in him to be a champion swimmer remained to be seen.

By mid-September, the creditors offered Meffert temporary management duties of the Knickerbocker's baths when they opened the club to anyone in the public willing to pay for the enjoyment of its facilities. Meffert arranged for the team to train at their old clubhouse, but by November the new owners forced the Knickerbockers to vacate. Charley was two weeks from his first race, and now the team had no place to swim. The contest was scheduled for mid-November against their most formidable rival, the New York Athletic Club. There was a big-time feel about swimming at the famed NYAC pool, where so many American records had been broken. For swimmers, it was their Madison Square Garden.

Later, it was the butterflies in his stomach that Charley remembered most about his first race, followed by the hundred or so spectators from the club looking down at him from the two tiers of packed galleries, the cold wet pool deck under his bare feet, and lining up alongside three college men, all novices like him, who by definition were swimmers who at the time of competing had not won in a similar class of open competition. Then there was the crack of the gun, the fight through the water against a bunch of sidestroke swimmers like himself, touching the final wall, and discovering that he was, in his own words, "soundly beaten."

After that, there was no next time. The Knickerbocker Aquatic Club disbanded, and Charley was left discouraged, frustrated, and without a pool to swim in.

OVER THE HOLIDAYS, GRANDMOTHER Meldrum and Aunt Flossie tried to liven up Thanksgiving and the Christmas season with a three-week visit to New York City before heading out west to Pasadena for the winter. Even Alice's successful younger brother Herbert and his wife came for the week of Thanksgiving to attend the National Horse Show at Madison Square Garden and offer some family cheer. Conversations surely dwelled on their brother Arthur's bankruptcy. They all worried about its effect on the whole family but particularly on his three children's societal standing and future marriage prospects. Alice and Charley's troubled situation also remained a concern. Charley would reach adulthood in a few years. He needed to start thinking about and preparing for his future, rather than wasting all this time on an unpromising activity that he clearly wasn't very good at.

BY JANUARY, CHARLEY FELT like a fish that had been out of water too long. And he was troubled as to why he could not repeat the times he'd achieved in the Adirondack lakes. Even if he had lost a few seconds with poor turns at the New York Athletic Club, that still failed to explain why his performance fell embarrassingly short of his winning times at Stony Creek Ponds. He wanted the chance to try again.

Charley managed to reconnect with one of the Knickerbocker's former watermen, Dave Bratton, who wasted no time joining the New York Athletic Club after the Knickerbocker's demise and was in the process of assembling an all-star water polo team of his former teammates. Handsome, well connected, and beloved by all, Dave was Mr. Positive, uplifting everyone and never speaking an unkind word. Married with two young daughters, he made a good living as a carpet salesman. He belonged to New York's most well-regarded lodges, like the prestigious Knights Templar, and held memberships at three of the country's most accomplished athletic clubs—Chicago, San Francisco's Olympic, and now New York. Bratton had already brought Lou Handley, Budd Goodwin, Joe Ruddy, and George Van Cleaf over to the NYAC. What Charley didn't know was that before Alex Meffert left for his new club swimming instructor job in St. Louis, he'd entrusted Dave with one parting request: "Keep an eye on Daniels."

The New York Athletic Club's top mid-distance swimmer, Otto Wahle, was the foremost expert on England's speed strokes, including the cutting-edge English trudgen. The stroke had just become known in America in 1898 after Penn's English swimming coach began teaching it to E. Carroll Schaeffer. Its unique double overarm was difficult to learn. It unnaturally required a person to swim facedown, forcing him to lift his head straight out of the water to take quick breaths and glance at where he was going. The trudgen also demanded that the swimmer's body contort in an uncomfortable position, with the torso facing forward, chest even with the surface, while the waist twisted the lower half sideways for the scissor kick. Those rare few in America who mastered it were record setters.

If Charley wanted to learn its secrets, he needed to show Wahle that he had the makings of a champion. He needed to figure out how to repeat his Adirondack times. But before Dave Bratton could arrange a trial, word broke from the British Empire that changed everything.

DAVID BRATTON

The news was shocking if it could be believed. Otto Wahle, Lou Handley, and several other watermen huddled around the New York Athletic Club's basement pool trying to make heads or tails of the report from London.

Fifty-eight-point-six seconds.

Over a second faster than what many experts thought humanly possible in the hundred-yard century race. The article reported that the unbelievable feat was achieved by the visiting Australian champion, eighteen-year-old Dick Cavill.

Some still expressed doubt as to the accuracy of the figure. After all, the fastest century recorded by England's great champion Rob Derbyshire was 60.2 seconds. And the great Australian champion Freddie Lane had recently hit 60 seconds dead on. But 58.6 seconds! Even from a great swimmer like Dick Cavill, who hailed from Australia's most famous swimming family, such a speed defied logic.

Their only hint into the secret of Cavill's accomplishment was the article's mention that he used a surprising new swimming style never before seen in England. *The Sun* of New York and the *Buffalo Courier* picked up the report from England noting that Cavill "kept his head entirely underwater" and said "his leg kick was a revelation and was a sort of a cross between the 'trudgeon' and the English racing stroke." *The Sun* called it a "crawl." The description proved too vague to adequately visualize, and unfortunately the article featured no accompanying photographs. Not that any were expected.

For a photograph to be transmitted via telegraph lines, an exact likeness had to be drawn by an artist on a sheet of tinfoil, carefully wrapped around the fax-like machine's eight-inch metal cylinder, and then transmitted to an identical machine that took about thirty minutes to make a grainy carbon duplicate. Only a few media outlets possessed such a machine, so most photographs of faraway events had to be sent via mail, train, or boat. High-speed wire photographs were still thirty years away.

Even without photographs and an adequate description, what was perfectly clear about Cavill's new stroke was that the British Empire and its commonwealth of Australia had once again flexed its supremacy over the rest of the swimming world.

MOST OF THE NEW YORK Athletic Club's top sprinters had only begun to adopt the trudgen under Wahle's tutelage. Having observed some of the British Empire's watermen at the 1900 Paris Olympics, Wahle carefully analyzed their advanced techniques. A good trudgen was difficult to perfect. Maybe one in a thousand swimmers accomplished such a feat. Only a few years earlier, Penn's E. Carroll Schaeffer was the first American to perform it successfully, thanks to the school's English champion instructor, George Kistler. And now, with Americans yet to fully master the trudgen, they needed to contend with the British Empire's new mysterious "crawl." Charley was even further behind in the process, still swimming with the old one-armed English sidestroke. And his sixty-nine seconds from the Adirondacks that he was trying to repeat no longer seemed good enough.

THE FIRST TIME TWENTY-THREE-YEAR-OLD Otto Wahle and Charley met in the frigid early months of 1903, the seventeen-year-old's shy nature brought to mind a poet rather than a determined athlete. Charley's six-foot height had five inches on Wahle, but the skinny teenager's still-developing muscles left Charley uncoordinated and not fully in command of his body.

Wahle's gray eyes viewed newcomers skeptically. The only people who ever wandered down to such a forlorn place as the NYAC's basement pool, other than the rare true watermen, were either mavericks looking for the avant-garde, the lame searching for a sport where their leg disability didn't matter, or outcasts seeking a sense of belonging. The shy boy appeared too insecure to be a maverick. He wasn't limping. Which left only two scenarios—and he didn't look like a true waterman.

About all that Wahle knew about Charley was that he attended a swanky prep school. His father was supposedly a big Wall Street banker. In a year, a prep schooler like Charley would be off to Yale or Columbia or some other fancy college like so many other privileged boys. The only thing slightly out of profile was that Charley wore a cheap swimsuit. Either way, Wahle had no time for lightweights or long-term projects. Just about every one of the club's top watermen were "athletic members" who had to deliver. Wahle needed proven champions. And unless an American emerged to challenge Europe's Goliath, the U.S. watermen were not just going to be beaten at the third Olympiad but going to be humiliated in full view of their countrymen.

Using his overarm sidestroke, Charley traversed the pool and once again failed to repeat his Adirondack performance. The notion came up—most likely from the Austrian—that perhaps Charley's lake course had been inadvertently measured short, which would account for inflated Adirondack times. Wahle had already been a national champion at Charley's age. If Charley truly was meant to be a competitive swimmer, it seems the seventeen-year-old would have distinguished himself by now.

"You can't make a peach out of a persimmon," Joe Ruddy said. "And you can't make anything else out of an athlete but an athlete."

CHARLEY NEEDED MORE TIME to prove he belonged. With neither Wahle nor Handley showing any interest, Dave Bratton put his impeccable reputation on the line to propose Charley's name as a junior member to the club's admissions committee. Dave also roped in a friend to second the nomination. Then Charley's name was posted as a proposed candidate for junior membership on the club's bulletin for ten days so that anyone opposed had reasonable time to lodge an objection. On the second Tuesday of February, the sixteen-member board of governors met to review the candidates and elect any desirable athletes. One blackball doomed a candidate's chances. Bratton made sure not only that he secured the necessary support but that neither Wahle nor Handley would lodge an objection. Junior membership status bought Charley one year to prove himself. After that, it either terminated on his nineteenth birthday or the club's board of governors had the power to award him an athletic membership if he distinguished himself as an athlete who could bring honors to the club. Failing to win was a quick way to be shown the door.

Almost every afternoon, Charley made the mile journey north from Dwight School to the large redbrick building of the New York Athletic Club. Dressed in a tie and suit that hung loosely off his skinny frame, he rushed between the horse and buggy traffic along Fifty-ninth Street and entered the club's imposing granite archway entrance. The spacious lobby carried a hint of fine cigars from the upstairs smoking lounges. Beyond the front desk that resembled a grand hotel's, Charley turned to his right and faced two huge hardwood staircases.

Atop a carved newel-post at the base of the ascending staircase stood a bronze statue of the club's mascot, Mercury, the god of speed. The deity's winged foot was emblazoned in red on all the club's navy-blue jerseys and banners, inspiring the club's nickname, the Winged Foot.

Charley took the descending steps that led into the basement, passing the washrooms, bowling alleys, rifle range, and barbershop before he reached the indoor pool facility, or what they called back then the natatorium.

The cavernous space stretched thirty feet high with the upper two of its three stories lined with pillared galleries overlooking the green water. The tank stretched twenty-five yards in length by seven yards wide, or the width of about three swimming lanes today.

Charley emerged from the locker room in his cheap swimsuit and slipped into the pool with little notice. His junior membership allowed use of the swimming tank until five o'clock in the afternoon, when the club's champion swimmers and water polo players usually arrived after work. A novice like Charley was more likely to cross paths with the champions on weekends, when they practiced during regular hours.

Each day, Charley pushed himself to reach the wall faster than the day before, but whatever conditioning his daily aquatic routine accomplished was not revealed in his swimming times. When he occasionally swam a friendly race against one of the watermen, he lost. Nothing about his performance drew attention except for the fact that he was becoming as familiar a fixture as the pillars that lined the pool.

As for the coaching he hoped to gain access to, that proved the biggest challenge. The modern role of coaching was mostly a foreign concept in the early twentieth century. To actually pay someone to train athletes violated the purity of amateurism, so the role fell upon the team captain or a volunteer graduate who helped out. English amateur sports banned coaching outright. But then again, the aristocratic English sporting establishment had long brandished the ethos of "amateurism" to maintain an advantage over the working class. The idle rich had ample leisure time to train, while the commoner, who labored twelve hours a day, six days a week, often returning home after dark exhausted, lacked the free time, daylight, and energy to train and stay competitive. Even at that, many of England's amateur sports authori-

ties enforced a prohibitive "mechanics" clause that defined manual la-
borers as "professionals," barring them from amateur competition. The
only way workingmen could make time to train was not to work, and
the only way they could afford not to work was to be paid for their
athleticism. The sporting aristocracy chastised such arrangements, associating these "professionals" with mercenaries and the seedy under-
side of gambling versus proper gentlemen who participated for the
pure joy of competition.

However, America's drive to win began to outweigh the more elitist
aspects of amateurism. In 1873, Cornell hired its first professional rowing coach, and Harvard and Yale soon followed. By 1882, Harvard employed a professional coach for its track-and-field team. In 1896, a
group of Penn alumni raised funds to hire a coach to oversee America's
first college swim team.*

The next year, Penn's new coach, George Kistler, an English champion, quickly organized the first intercollegiate swim meet between
Penn and the New York Athletic Club's swimmers who attended Columbia University (Yale and Harvard would not form swim teams
until 1900). The following spring of 1898, Kistler joined forces with Jim
Sullivan, the head of the Amateur Athletic Union, to stage the first
"national"—though it was far from it—collegiate championship between Penn and Columbia at the National Sportsmen's Show in Boston's Mechanics Hall. A temporary tank was constructed, and a
reported fourteen thousand of the show's attendees watched Penn beat
Columbia in both swimming and water polo. The following year, in
1899, the collegiate championship was held at the National Sportsmen's Show at New York's Madison Square Garden, where a large
crowd witnessed Penn's emerging star, E. Carroll Schaeffer, introduce
the double-overarm trudgen to America. Over the next two years,
Schaeffer broke just about every American short-distance speed rec-

* Although Vassar College became the first American college to build a swimming
tank for its all-female student body, in 1890, Victorian society still forbade women to
form athletic teams that engaged in intercollegiate competition because they worried
that a woman's frail constitution could suffer "nervous fatigue" if competitions became too strenuous. Therefore, Penn became America's first college to form an actual
swim team.

ord, which wasn't exactly a high bar but was still a feat never before accomplished.

Charley had little luck with the NYAC's longtime professional swimming instructor, Gus Sundstrom. The forty-three-year-old former champion offered basic lifesaving skills and swimming lessons to adult members, from 11:00 A.M. to 3:00 P.M. each day when Charley was in school. On Saturdays, Sundstrom offered a special session from 9:00 A.M. to 12:00 P.M. for high schoolers and younger boys, but only if they were the sons of members. As for more advanced competition training, the role of coach for the swimming and water polo teams was filled mostly by the team captains—Otto Wahle and Lou Handley. To obtain their instruction, Charley needed to first make the team. How he was going to do that without a good coach seemed an insurmountable problem.

WITH NONE OF THE club's athletic members interested in Charley, he tried to pick up pointers by watching them swim and eavesdropping on their conversations as they puzzled over Dick Cavill's mysterious new "crawl" stroke.

Athletic members were the closest thing in the amateur world to professional athletes. None came from means. Only two of the club's swimming champions attended college: twenty-four-year-old Fred Wenck, who had graduated from Yale Law School and worked as a journalist; and twenty-year-old Conrad "Con" Trubenbach, currently enrolled at Columbia. Charles Ruberl, twenty-one, and Otto Wahle, twenty-three, were both Austrian immigrants and former Paris Olympians who worked as clerks. Lou Handley, twenty-nine, had grown up in Rome and now made a modest living as a freelance journalist, reporting on the swimming scene. Joe Ruddy, twenty-four, who always walked with a slight limp, worked for New York City's Civil Service Commission and had ties with Tammany Hall. Edgar Adams, the oldest at thirty-five, was an author and journalist who walked with a cane when he wasn't swimming, due to the fact that his left leg was shorter than his right. And Budd Goodwin, only nineteen, toiled all morning on his father's Manhattan Island ferry. Budd showed up at the club each day around noon, swam as many laps as time allowed, then quickly dressed and grabbed a sandwich from the club's kitchen before racing out the door and back to the docks for the afternoon excursions, where he caught an earful from his father about his obsessive swimming nonsense. All these young athletes hoped to gradually earn more interest and respect for aquatics.

Charley enjoyed feeling a part of something, even if he was only on the periphery. The watermen all took their training seriously but found time to laugh and joke around the pool. Joe Ruddy, who had arms like a blacksmith's, was not only the toughest but one of the funniest. To anyone who was griping about anything, like a drill sergeant Joe would bark out his cure-all. "Your wind is bad? Go swimming! You're cross-eyed? Go swimming! Your grammar is poor? Go swimming! If you want a happy, healthy existence—Go swimming!" Sometimes Ruddy would even pontificate. "On a planet that is two thirds water, what discovery was more important for mankind's quest to control his own destiny than swimming?"

Wahle and Handley were able to provide a wealth of knowledge about the natatorial art. Dave Bratton was everyone's biggest cheer-leader. Gus Sundstrom would occasionally provide entertainment by diving into the pool with a lit cigar, swimming underwater, and emerging at the other end with the cigar still lit. And after Doc Seixas gave Charley the heartbreaking news that he was leaving Dwight School at the end of the spring semester, this small band of basement misfits would become his only source of good male role models.

Doc had accepted a position at the New York Military Academy, about a hundred miles upstate at Cornwall-on-Hudson, after being offered an annual salary of three thousand dollars, the largest of any school athletic director in the country. He had been a father figure and friend when Charley desperately needed one. Now, just like his father and Alex Meffert, Doc walked out of his life. And if Charley failed to make the Winged Footers' swim team by winter, his last lifeline would be taken away.

As Charley worked hard on perfecting his sidestroke and scissor kick in the spring of 1903, the British Empire's watermen were only growing faster with this mysterious new "crawl" that no one in America could figure out. Wahle and Handley were wringing their hands over how to give American swimmers a fighting chance the following summer of 1904 at what they were calling the third, and perhaps last, Olympiad, which raised the bar for making the team that much higher.

After school let out in June, Charley and Alice returned to the Hiawatha Lodge, where Charley was determined to discern the mystery about what happened to his previous year's speed. He carefully remeasured his century course along the banks of First Pond to see if Otto Wahle was right. Sure enough, last year's measurement had been ten yards short.

Maybe Charley didn't have speed after all. Maybe he never would. Or maybe he had just not spent enough time in the water. Either way, the bug had bitten him, and he was determined to see what would happen if he stayed the course.

Each morning, amid a surrounding forest of songbirds, Charley waded into the lake's still waters that gleamed with bits of fallen sky. He took the time and care needed to measure a proper hundred-yard course. He even brought up from New York City motivational clippings like the one describing the great Harry LeMoyne's recent century race of 61.4 seconds, which shattered J. Scott Leary's American record. All June and July, Charley worked on breaking 70 seconds. And once again he went up to visit his fellow scouts at their camp on the Lower Saranac, which this year included boys from Doc's new school. It would be his last time under the tutelage of his favorite teacher.

Now six feet tall and not quite as gangly, and growing more handsome each day, the eighteen-year-old began to show muscles and started resembling more of the man of the house he had to become. That's when Tom Daniels reappeared in his life.

6.

SKELETONS OUT
OF THE CLOSET

—

1903

Some of the Hiawatha Lodge's hundred guests had to already be talking about it on that early August morning. The ruinous headlines had arrived with the daily stagecoach's load of supplies, mail, and latest newspapers. By dinner, everyone would know. There would be pointing, whispering, and no decent person would dare sit with Charley and Alice at mealtime, let alone wish to be staying at the same resort. At home in New York and back in Buffalo, family and friends would be gossiping about them. Across the nation perfect strangers now read about their most painful secrets. They would be the butt of all society. And day after day, new headlines arrived, exposing more scandalous details.

Tom Daniels and six of his alleged partners had been arrested.

A little before noon on August 5, police had raided Tom's Wall Street offices. The papers reported how his seven women stenographers began screaming and did not calm down until police assured them that they were there to arrest only Tom and his six associates. Newspapers reported that one associate, Charles Brown, was caught attempting to destroy several letters that turned out to be protests from customers. They also incorrectly referred to him as Tom's "brother-in-law," an easy mistake given that he was the brother of the woman Tom now called his "wife."

Detectives uncovered Daniels & Company circulars advertising branch offices in Philadelphia, San Francisco, London, Boston, Atlanta, Cincinnati, Chicago, and St. Louis, even though Daniels & Company operated no offices outside No. 6 Wall Street. The company promoted itself as a "banker and broker," yet it was not legally registered as a bank nor did it conduct a banking business.

Newspapers reported how Daniels & Company offered to supply capital for all sorts of enterprises, the preliminary condition being that "no application will be considered unless a check for $250 is deposited with us at the time of sending in the application." The amount was more than half of what most people earned in a year. Daniels & Company collected a lot of fees, yet no evidence showed they had ever committed capital to a single company.

An Iowa man claimed that after he answered one of their advertisements, he paid Tom "organizing expenses" to the tune of $840 to help create a real estate company but said that the creation of his company was just as far off as it was when he answered the advertisement. One newspaper reported that a Kansas firm paid Daniels & Company more than $70,000 (over $2 million today). One upstate newspaper called it "one of the greatest Wall Street get-rich-quick concerns yet unearthed."

Tom Daniels and his associates were taken to police headquarters and booked. When the court arraigned Tom on a charge of grand larceny, the press reported that he broke down and wept bitterly. Perhaps the shame he brought to his virtuous father's name weakened his knees. Maybe the pain and humiliation he now brought down upon himself, Alice, and Charley sickened him. Or maybe he was just sorry he got caught.

When the judge ordered Tom sent to "the Tombs," the same city jail that had recently held the Knickerbocker's accused murderer, Roland Molineux, newspapers reported that Tom was in such a state that it almost became necessary for guards to carry him to his cell.

Headlines blared "Late Justice Daniels' Son Under Arrest" and "Thomas P. Daniels Held for Larceny." For weeks, newspapers around the country proclaimed Tom Daniels a fraud and a swindler. They accused him of running a confidence game. They claimed he had defrauded people from all over the United States. His victims ranged from sophisticated businessmen and high-class families to average Americans. One poor man was swindled out of his pension. A West

Virginia man who sent money to Daniels & Company to monetize his inventions had just filed a civil suit after discovering that Mr. Daniels's promises were bogus. Tom's former boss, Henry Brandenburg, told reporters that shortly before Tom started Daniels & Company, they dismissed Tom because the firm's customers objected to his questionable methods. Just about all the newspapers highlighted the sensational fact that he was the son of the late New York Supreme Court justice Charles Daniels. And many of the papers made sure to mention that Tom was married to Alice Meldrum Daniels, the daughter of the late Alexander Meldrum, a successful dry goods store owner in Buffalo.

After Tom had spent a week behind bars, papers described how a woman appeared at the Tombs to sign for his two-thousand-dollar bail bond, giving as security their Staten Island home valued at ninety-five hundred dollars, then signed her name "Mrs. Minnie Brown Daniels," claiming to be Tom's wife.

Whatever appearance Charley and Alice had managed to maintain over the past few years to protect their good name and reputation was now painfully exposed with Tom's arrest and scandalous affair. The fraud charges against him promised to sink the one life preserver—a respected family name—that had kept Alice and Charley afloat. And because Alice had refused to subject their family to the ruin of divorce, their tether to Tom Daniels promised to drown them right along with him.

For Charley, always uncomfortable in the spotlight, especially the damning one that now glared on his family, the shame and embarrassment were searing. The thought of people whispering about him, pointing and snickering, would have been devastating. Friends in school might have approached him, saying: *"I saw your father in the paper." "Did your father really do that?" "Is your father going to jail?" "Are your parents getting divorced?"* Undoubtedly, some of his meaner classmates taunted and shamed him.

Tom Daniels continued to blame others for his predicament, insisting on his innocence, while the federal authorities and district attorney identified more and more victims across the country prepared to testify against him. The *Buffalo Times* even posted a front-page list of local residents whom Tom had swindled or planned to swindle, much to the added humiliation of Alice's whole family.

Charley watched his innocent mother suffering through the disgrace. Alice was twenty when she married Tom Daniels and would turn forty that November. Even after she separated from Tom, so much of her identity hung on being "Mrs. Thomas P. Daniels." For almost twenty years, the once star student who had received a rosette for her honesty and integrity, who had worked hard to build a law-abiding, respectable family, now faced the sad reality that this is what had become of that legacy.

Mother and son could no longer show their faces in decent society. No more would anyone call on them. One suspects that Alice's family, for their own social survival, had to distance themselves. Alice and Charley would be forced to live out the rest of their days in shame and isolation. And the New York Athletic Club did not associate with disreputable families.

Charley's opportunity to become a speed swimmer appeared to be over. And his dream to become an Olympic champion dead before it started.

PART TWO

FIGHTING TO STAY AFLOAT

PIERRE DE COUBERTIN,
FOUNDER, OLYMPICS

JAMES E. SULLIVAN,
SECRETARY, AMERICAN
AMATEUR ATHLETIC
UNION

7.

A GAME FOR
BARBARIANS

—

O N A MILD OCTOBER DAY IN 1900, WHEN MARGARET ABBOTT, A young American studying in France, walked off the golf course outside Paris in her full-length dress, having just shot a forty-seven over the nine-hole tournament that she and her mother entered on a lark, she had no idea that she had just competed in the second Olympic Games. Nor would she ever realize that the porcelain bowl she was awarded for her victory would later be considered by historians the first "gold medal" ever won by an American woman. She would die in 1955 never knowing she was an Olympian.

The 1900 Olympic Games ended in Paris as unceremoniously as they had begun. There would be no closing ceremony, just as there had been no opening one. No parade of athletes. No spectators. There was not even an Olympic stadium. In fact, the Paris World's Fair Committee under whose charge the competitions were placed had never once used the word "Olympic." Their French founder, Baron Pierre de Coubertin, felt afterward that the Olympic movement was now utterly torn to shreds, confiding in friends that it would be a miracle if the Games survived.

For almost a decade, the petite five-foot-three Frenchman had been preaching his vision of the modern Olympics through his remarkable handlebar mustache, which swept out from his small head like the lowered longhorns of a bull. But what Coubertin lacked in stature and natural charisma, he compensated for with passionate energy, all of it directed toward this single pursuit upon which he had staked his entire reputation, despite his family's objections.

Coubertin's father, Baron Charles de Coubertin, like most French aristocrats, had long believed that countries distinguished themselves through contributions to the arts, sciences, law, and politics, not by running after a ball in shorts. As a nation, France saw sport as Anglo-Saxon. More British and German and simply not French. Such a frivolous pursuit threatened to tarnish the Coubertin name that had taken centuries to build.

The Coubertins, whose surname was Frédy, gained noble affiliation in 1477, when the first Pierre de Frédy, a chamberlain to the king, was granted a coat of arms, allowing the family to prosper. A century later, a grandson bought the prestigious Château de Coubertin, thus acquiring the title and an estate to pass from father to eldest son. After many generations of Frédys had made valuable noble alliances and distinguished themselves on the battlefield, King Louis XVIII bestowed the designation of "baron" upon Coubertin's grandfather in 1821. But unlike Pierre's two taller, more handsome older brothers, who, under the hereditary laws of nobility, would receive the lion's share of the family's wealth and titles, which included palatial family estates and generous trusts so that they might build upon the family name, Pierre, as third son, would receive no such birthright. He would inherit enough so as not to have to earn a living, but beyond that he was inconsequential.

Nine years junior to his next sibling, a young Pierre traveled with the seasons among the family's four homes and an artist colony along the pretty northwestern seaside town of Étretat. It is here where his father aspired to distinguish himself as a great religious painter and hoped for Pierre to one day discover a similar noble vocation. But the early trauma of war would forever set the youth on a divergent path.

From their five-story town house in Paris, a few blocks from where the Eiffel Tower would one day rise, Pierre had witnessed the conclusion of the French emperor Napoleon III's grandiose vision for a new, modern city. For seventeen years, the massive urban reconstruction made scaffolding the city's official tree and hammers its official bird. When completed, the place that was once described as "an immense workshop of putrefaction, where misery, pestilence and sickness work in concert...where plants shrivel and perish, and where, of seven small infants, four die during the course of the year," was now rightfully dubbed the most beautiful city in the world. Napoleon III's ambitious plan, carried out by Baron Haussmann, defined the modern Parisian landscape. But the glory was short-lived. In 1870, as the final stage of renovations was about to begin, the thunder of German cannon fire and smell of discharged gunpowder exploded in the streets.

With shocking swiftness, the glorious new city fell to a better-equipped, better-trained, and more physically fit German army. Young Pierre was traumatized as German troops with bayonets and spiked helmets stormed the family's castle in Normandy, stole the boy's croquet box, stuffed it with explosives, and blew up the nearby overpass to cut the train line into Paris. When the family finally returned to Napoleon III's city of dreams, the dream was over.

Eight-year-old Pierre observed the war's aftermath from his bedroom window, with the smell of burned charcoal rising up from the dirty cobblestoned streets. As Coubertin later recalled in his memoirs, he withdrew into his room for the next two years, reading and creating an imaginary kingdom where he restored stability and imagined a peaceful world. Like most of France, he was consumed by the bitterness and shame of the humiliating loss to Germany. It was during this period of self-isolation, in his twelfth year, that he read the popular English novel *Tom Brown's School Days*. The book introduced the lonely youth to the world of English prep schoolboys and the important life lessons they learned on the sporting fields at Rugby School. A century and a half later, Thomas Hughes's story would inspire J. K. Rowling's *Harry Potter*. That same year, 150 miles farther north of Pierre's father's artist colony, on the beaches of Calais, the Englishman Matthew Webb crawled out of the waves after breaststroking for twenty-two hours across the Channel to become the first international sports superstar, reaffirming the British Empire's athletic supremacy. The only thing more inspiring to Pierre would have been if Webb had been French.

Coubertin eventually came to believe that the only way for France to reinvigorate its military and regain its status as a leading world power was to strengthen its young men through sport. He took up rowing and fencing, until his parents clamped down on his freethinking and rebellious nature and sentenced Pierre to seven years of strict Jesuit boarding school. The oppressive atmosphere of those years only reaffirmed his belief that education needed to include a proper physical outlet, just as the schoolboys had enjoyed in *Tom Brown*.

Against his parents' wishes, Pierre rejected careers in the law and military, or in fact any career at all, and instead spent his time trying to incorporate school athletics into the French curriculum. With his copy of *Tom Brown* accompanying him, he crossed the English Channel to see how youth sports developed character and turned boys into good soldiers. He would be convinced that what he saw on England's athletic fields was the cornerstone of the British Empire. As was so aptly stated by the Duke of Wellington, the British commander who defeated the great Napoleon Bonaparte, "The Battle of Waterloo was won on the playing fields of Eton."

Coubertin created his own self-funded leadership role to infuse sports into French culture, which mortified his proud family. He unsettled them further by spending some of his modest inheritance to support fledgling school athletic associations and to travel here and there to organize sports meetings. In 1889, Coubertin, at age twenty-six and still no closer to his goal, placed a personal ad in English newspapers seeking further expertise on the benefits of English sports. In response, a letter arrived from Dr. William Penny Brookes, an eighty-year-old country doctor, inviting him to be an honored guest at his village's annual athletic festival, which Dr. Brookes referred to by a strange Greek name.

DR. BROOKES WAS BORN, practiced medicine, and would die in his small English village of Much Wenlock. An aficionado of ancient Greece, for nearly forty years Brookes promoted a healthy, active culture among his fellow Wenlockians by annually resurrecting an ancient Grecian festival of strength and agility. Unlike those original events that forbade the participation of "barbarians," which meant any non-Greek, these Games, he insisted, would be accessible to every grade of man, stirring up controversy among England's highborn sporting establishment. By 1868, his festival's popularity had evolved into a three-day national event, held now at London's Crystal Palace before ten thousand people. Its national prominence lasted only a few years, however, when it was squelched by England's Amateur Athletic Association's determination to preserve sport strictly for gentlemen.

In October of the following year, when Pierre de Coubertin arrived in Brookes's medieval village to observe his now reduced, so-called Olympian Festival, gray skies and rain marred the day, but not Dr. Brookes's enthusiasm. The burly, white-haired octogenarian greeted Coubertin with a volunteer marching band and a large cavalcade of athletes and men on horseback, who paraded their honored guest to the village's playing field, where Brookes had erected a beautiful archway displaying a banner: "Welcome to Baron Pierre de Coubertin, and Prosperity to France." The Olympic sports played that rainy day included tilting (a form of jousting whereby the horseman tries to insert his lance through small metal rings) and tent pegging (where the charging equestrian tries to pick up small wooden ground pegs with a spear), as well as long jumping, high-jumping, and footraces at a time when modern track and field remained in its infancy.

The festival ended with the band playing Handel's "See, the Conquering Hero Comes" and schoolgirls strewing flowers along the victors' path as they all paraded back into town. At that evening's Olympian Society dinner, Coubertin listened to Brookes talk about the three prior attempts, starting back in 1859, to revive the ancient Olympiad in Greece. None were well executed or internationally supported, attracting only athletes from the Greek-speaking world. Yet Brookes still wrote regularly to the Greek minister in London, trying to persuade him to hold a truly international Olympics in Athens. Now in the twilight of his life, Dr. Brookes saw in the young Frenchman a possible successor to carry the torch of his Olympic dreams. Coubertin was not interested.

The young noble was having an impossible enough time persuading French schools to adopt England's athletic curriculum. The Olympics would take an enormous international effort that seemed unachievable. Over the next two years, Coubertin led the formation of the Union des Sociétés Françaises de Sports Athlétiques, which combined more than sixty-two amateur sporting societies in France with seven thousand members, but the continued resistance from his countrymen to incorporating sports in schools, and their accusations calling him an Anglophile, made Coubertin reconsider Dr. Brookes's impractical idea. The romantic notion of warring Greek states more than a thousand years ago gathering every four years to compete in the spirit of peace and reconciliation posed an alternative solution to save France from the growing German threat on its border. If not strength through sport, Coubertin contemplated, then perhaps peace through international competition?

Two years after meeting Dr. Brookes, Coubertin stood before a large delegation at the Sorbonne's great lecture hall and gave an impassioned speech advocating the reestablishment of the Olympic Games. Staring back at him was a sea of indifferent faces. His big finish, "Let us export our fencers, our runners, our rowers to other lands . . . and the day we do it the cause of peace will have received a strong and vital ally," was greeted with some polite claps, then snickers and laughter that ebbed into a silence as cold as that November afternoon.

A year later, Coubertin tried again, this time in America, before a gathering at New York City's University Club hosted by William Sloane, a friend and French history professor at Princeton. The Frenchman hoped to promote his Olympics to leaders of both American college sports and the country's powerful Amateur Athletic Union. Professor Sloane was wildly enthusiastic about the project. Everyone else in the room thought it an inevitable failure. And the blunt opinion from the young, straight-talking, hard-line head of the AAU, Jim Sullivan, clashed with the Frenchman's overly genteel diplomatic style to not offend.

A few months later, in February 1894, Coubertin pitched the Olympic idea in England and found their disinterest even stronger. One by one, his intimate audience at the London Sports Club dwindled, until he had emptied the room. Britain, as the father of modern sport, was not about to let an outsider tell it how best to handle its own child. Charles Herbert, the powerful secretary of the English Amateur Athletic Association, considered the Olympic Games neither "viable nor useful." Coubertin admitted, "Nowhere did the idea for the revival of the Olympic Games meet with the enthusiasm it deserved."

Several months later, in June, Coubertin called another meeting at the Sorbonne. This time he wisely hand-selected his audience. The fifty-eight Frenchmen he invited represented twenty-four sports organizations and clubs. Another twenty men from Belgium, Great Britain, Greece, Italy, Russia, Spain, Sweden, and the United States represented thirteen sports federations as athletes or authorities. Of the seventy-eight total invitees, half were connected to the peace movement—six were future Nobel Peace Prize winners—and all were strong allies in his call for peace through the Olympic Games. Dr. Brookes, too old to travel, sent his regrets for not being there in person. Professor Sloane was the lone American to make the trip. Charles Herbert, the real power behind England's Amateur Athletic Association, did not bother to attend the vote.

Coubertin stood at the amphitheater's lectern and gave a stirring speech that touched upon the spirit of peace and harmony aroused by the ancient Olympic Games, dating from 776 BC and lasting twelve hundred years, until the Roman emperor Theodosius abolished them in AD 394 because of their pagan roots. This time when Coubertin called for the Olympics' revival, his proposal was met with overwhelming approval. However, his wish to make Paris the inaugural host city during its 1900 World's Fair was outvoted. The majority felt six years was too long to wait. With the world's sports leader, England, showing no interest in such a venture, the delegation voted in favor of awarding this enormous inaugural undertaking, set for 1896, to the country of the Olympiad's birthplace, in the city of Athens. Somehow the voters overlooked the rather obvious problem that Greece had no money to fund these Games. Furthermore, not a single railroad line connected the country to the rest of Europe and boats to Athens were scarce, making it nearly impossible to attract world-class athletes.

Ignoring these fatal flaws, the delegation went on to decide that the competitions would be open to amateurs of all nations so long as they were men. Women's participation was never considered. Prizes would be souvenirs, not monetary awards. And if there was a second Games, they could be held in Paris.

Still determined, Coubertin proposed the establishment of the International Olympic Committee, or IOC, as its official governing body.

It appointed Coubertin the IOC's secretary-general, the de facto leader, and allowed him a free hand in selecting the committee's members.

Coubertin planned to operate the IOC out of his parents' town house at 20 Rue Oudinot in Paris, where as a boy he had fantasized about ruling over a peaceful kingdom. He appointed fourteen other members, including the soft-spoken Professor Sloane as America's representative, and since he needed England's credibility, he selected its powerful amateur athletic czar, Charles Herbert, despite Herbert's complete lack of interest. Nobody at the delegation seemed concerned that Coubertin chose almost all absentee members. Coubertin later admitted that he needed elbow room at the start. He avoided anyone with a strong, engaged attitude who might oppose his decisions or want to seize the helm or modify his own autocratic direction.

That November of 1894, when Coubertin arrived in Athens to begin preparations for the 1896 Games, Greece's prime minister informed him that funding his novelty promised economic ruin, and refused to host the Games. Not surprised, the Frenchman sought the support of the Greek royal family, as well as almost a million drachmas in funding from a philanthropic Greek shipping tycoon. Despite continuous opposition from the financially strapped government, Coubertin and the Greek royal family, along with the sizable philanthropic gift, kept the dream alive.

After seventeen months of struggle and uncertainty, on April 6, 1896, as Greece celebrated the seventy-fifth anniversary of its war of independence against the Turks, the Greek royal family, Coubertin and his new bride, Marie, and about fifty thousand Athenians poured into the newly renovated Panathenaic Stadium for the first modern Olympiad. Few in the crowd had ever seen a formal athletic contest, and the nine-day festival turned into more of a patriotic celebration of Greece's past greatness rather than the start of a promising international athletic event. Dr. Brookes, their biggest enthusiast, had sadly died four months before seeing his lifelong vision realized. But hardly any people outside Greece cared or even knew that the Olympics had been revived.

Coubertin later complained that the limited international press they received treated the Games as merely a flash-in-the-pan novelty.

Only a handful of newspapers carried regular reports on the Games. France's *Le Figaro* covered it with some enthusiasm but gave Coubertin no credit. The London *Times* published a daily summary of events in its foreign affairs section that read as dry as a crop report. *The New York Times,* which had no special correspondent in Athens, gave it modest attention only because the Americans won so many victories. That curiosity alone prompted other American newspapers to publish one or two reports off the wire. Otherwise, the revival of this ancient Greek event would not have warranted any American ink.

The failure of the Games to attract the world's top athletes prompted Caspar Whitney, editor of *Outing,* a premier U.S. sports magazine, to criticize Coubertin's IOC as inefficient, mismanaged, and incapable. And given the lack of British interest, newspapers in the U.K. expressed doubt that an athletic contest not officially patronized by English sportsmen could be a success.

When the Games ended, the Greeks were so intoxicated with nationalistic pride that they credited its entire success to the Greek royal family and never once gave Coubertin his rightful due. They then tried to seize control, demanding the Games make their permanent home in Athens, and insisted that anything less was national theft. Even Coubertin's fellow IOC members believed they had no choice but to bow to the Greek king's wishes and dissolve themselves. When Coubertin left Athens to plan the 1900 Games in Paris, the Greek newspapers called him "a thief, trying to strip Greece of one of its historic jewels." One British tourist who competed in the Games cheekily noted that it was so nice of the French to allow Greece to hold their ancient games in Athens as a "special favor."

When Coubertin returned home, his father weighed in. Charles de Coubertin had painted a gathering of ancient Olympia, with the goddess Athena and god Apollo high on a throne, crowning the modern Olympic athletes, which included a fencer, rower, cyclist, equestrian, and rugby player—all sports practiced by his son—with the Eiffel Tower rising beyond the temple ruins as a symbol of the upcoming Paris Olympics. He called it *Rétablissement des Jeux Olympiques— allégorie aux sports* (Restoration of the Olympic Games—allegory of sports). Charles never verbally approved of his son's sports fixation, but the surprising work showed that he had not only been following Pierre's efforts but been moved by them. Pierre saw Paris as a chance to finally vindicate his modern Olympic Games and perhaps, more personally, prove that his father's gesture of support was not misguided.

Paris's Exposition Universelle in 1900 promised to draw nearly fifty million people, offering the perfect stage for a glorious coming-out party. When its World's Fair Committee began agonizing over what iconic new landmark to unveil that could equal the 1889 fair's Eiffel Tower or the 1893 Chicago fair's Ferris wheel, Coubertin approached them with a grand vision: to build a glorious, state-of-the-art Olympic stadium, the likes of which mankind had never seen. Around it, they would construct the world's greatest athletic mecca by re-creating the ancient site of Olympia, which would display great works of art depicting athletes, with his father's *Jeux Olympiques* taking its place of prominence. This would be the global awakening of what Coubertin called "Olympism," a movement that promised to advance world peace by uniting all of humanity through athletic competition. Unmoved, the organizers settled on painting the Eiffel Tower yellow.

Behind closed doors, the fair's committee laughed at the very term "Olympism," calling it a superfluous, made-up word. The fair's director, Alfred Picard, thought sport a useless and absurd activity and disliked the idea of including the second Olympics within the fair. When the committee published the fair's official program, they splintered Coubertin's sports contests across the fair's various exhibits. Track and field was listed under charities, gymnastics under activities of schoolchildren, and most astonishing, skating and fencing under cutlery. Even more devastating, the program excluded any use of the term "Olympic," making these events indistinguishable from other "sport" competitions like kite flying, delivery van driving, pigeon racing, cannon firing, and firefighting. So blasé about sports was the fair's committee that in golf, lawn tennis, and sailing they allowed women to unofficially compete, which Coubertin insisted in no uncertain terms was "impractical, uninteresting, unaesthetic, and . . . incorrect." He believed that the female body was "not cut out to sustain certain shocks" and, more significantly, believed it indecent to see a woman sweat. Coubertin shared the era's view that "horses sweat, men perspire, and women glow." The final blow came when the fair refused to even construct proper athletic venues.

All the track-and-field events took place on an uneven field outside Paris, where one leg of the grass running course passed through a grove of trees. Several of the discus and hammer throwers' attempts inadvertently hit the large oak tree that occupied the middle of the throwing field. And virtually no one came to watch these events except for the American delegation who showed up to support their fellow countrymen. As Coubertin stated, "Nothing could be more difficult than trying to persuade a number of French spectators to attend a sports meeting."

Not even the awards bore the name "Olympiad" as they had in Athens. Victors received an inconsistent hodgepodge of either a trophy, a rectangular one-and-a-half-by-two-and-a-half-inch silver or bronze medal, a ribbon, a bowl, or, as in the case of one victorious swimmer, a fifty-pound bronze statue of a horse.

Caspar Whitney proclaimed the Paris Games utterly insignificant compared with the Olympic Games in Athens. "The Paris games," he wrote in an *Outing* article, "were no more, no less, than an American intercollegiate meet. With the exception of the English half-miler, the English hurdler, and Stanley Rowley, the New South Wales champion sprinter, there were positively no really good men entered except from America. England, Ireland, Scotland or Germany sent no champions, and but for the Americans the games would have been the complete fiasco, in athletics and in spectators, they really deserved to be."

The only British publication to carry any real coverage of the 1900 Paris Games, *The Field*, called it a disastrous affair, stating, "The whole series of sports produced nothing but muddles, bad arrangements, bad management, bad prizes, and any amount of ill-feeling amongst the various nationalities engaged."

The Australian Stanley Rowley, running for the British Empire, summed up the feelings of many athletes: "To treat these events as world's championships would be really an insult to the important events they are supposed to be. They are treated by most of the competitors as a huge joke and when it comes to that one has come all this way from Australia to compete in them, it really seems ridiculous."

Basically, one could argue that the Games did not really take place in 1900. Even Coubertin stated, "There was nothing Olympic about them."

Coubertin regretted his part in allowing the Games to become dependent upon a world's fair. And worse, his father showed no further interest in his work.

Jim Sullivan, the czar of America's Amateur Athletic Union, was so disgusted by the mess of it all and the IOC's total spinelessness in standing up to the fair's committee and ensuring the Games' success that he sought to save the Olympic movement from the one person he viewed as its worst enemy—Pierre de Coubertin.

JAMES EDWARD SULLIVAN WAS someone who knew with absolute certainty what God put him on this earth to do and went after it as if he knew, at age thirty-seven, that he had only fourteen years left on this earth to do it. Such clarity made him see the world in black and white, good versus evil, right versus wrong, friend or enemy. Broad-shouldered and big-chested, and almost a foot taller than Coubertin, the former athlete walked with a bold stride and didn't mince words, no matter whom it offended. But he was not a cold man. He was always willing to help a friend in need, never forgot a name or face, and knew no strangers. Yet even when he was laughing and joking with pals, his obsession with making America the greatest sporting nation in the world was ever present.

Born a mere six weeks before Coubertin, Sullivan grew up in the hardscrabble Irish slums of New York, unlike the Frenchman's aristocratic upbringing. He wrestled and boxed in the alleys, swam in the East River, and eventually made a bit of a name for himself as a distinguished mile runner. The more he competed, the deeper his interest grew and the more he saw this new field as a way up and out of his life.

At sixteen, determined not to be a laborer like his father, he found work at a publishing house, learning every aspect of the business while continuing to participate in sports. When editors dedicated to respectable journalism were giving sports minimum coverage, eighteen-year-old Jim self-published one of America's first, albeit short-lived, all-sports magazines, *The Athletic News,* modeled after Britain's popular sporting publications that had existed for more than half a century. He then helped initiate a sports department at the *New York Morning Journal* and three years later became editor of another newspaper, *The New York Sporting Times.* He obsessed over amateur sports, making the acquaintance of the world's best nonprofessional athletes in person or through correspondence. He kept files on their records. Memorized their stats. Learned the rules of their games and contests. Watched their advancement. He became a walking, talking sports encyclopedia at a time when game playing was still viewed by many with disdain. In 1891, when leaders at the New York Athletic Club took another page from England and created the country's first Amateur Athletic Union to organize and oversee this growing field of nonprofessional contests, they appointed Jim Sullivan its volunteer leader.

No man could say where Jim Sullivan ended and the Amateur Athletic Union began. He wrote the rules for many of the amateur track-and-field sports, kept all of the books and records, vetted the athletes, and in all amateur matters acted as judge, jury, and enforcer, and then reported the events in the *Sporting Times.*

In 1896, when word of America's track-and-field dominance in Athens reached him, Sullivan began to rethink his opposition to the Olympics. The 13 Americans took eleven victories, one more than attained by their Greek hosts' 167 athletes. Even the discus, a contest unknown outside Greece, was won by a Princeton shot-putter who had never thrown one before. If this is what happened with Professor Sloane's handful of self-selected recruits from Princeton and Boston, imagine the results if America sent a delegation of its best. The Olympics offered the perfect world stage to challenge the British Empire's athletic supremacy, and Sullivan believed Americans should pursue the challenge with the same aggressive spirit they used in warfare. He just needed someone willing to fund it, and he had just the person in mind.

Albert G. Spalding's competitive drive and love of sports matched Sullivan's. In the 1870s, Spalding gained fame as a dominant pitcher with the newly formed National Association of Professional Base Ball Players, where he quickly rose from player-manager to owner of the Chicago White Stockings at age thirty-one, to the head of the newly formed National League, and made the simple leather glove worn over his bare catching hand a popular piece of baseball equipment. During his baseball tenure, he wrote the game's official playing rules, brought his players down to Hot Springs, Arkansas, to initiate baseball's first spring training, cleaned up the gambling and drinking that were ruining the sport, and took his White Stockings and an all-star team on an 1889 world tour to broaden the game's appeal.

Later, to ingratiate baseball as "America's pastime," he formed a commission to perpetuate the myth that the game was a distinctly homegrown sport, created on U.S. soil by Abner Doubleday, and not, as it was in fact, born from the English sport of rounders. In 1876, while still a player-manager, Spalding and his brother Walter scraped together eight hundred dollars to launch a Chicago sporting goods company that went on to manufacture the first official baseball glove and ball; develop the modern bat with the bulge at its business end; design the American football, basketball, and volleyball; introduce Americans to the Scottish game of golf; and in all sports make sure the rules read, "The ball made by A. G. Spalding & Bros. shall be the official ball."

To further enhance his reputation as the leading supplier of all things sports, he went on to found the American Sports Publishing Company, envisioning a series of "Spalding Guides" that ranged from rule books, to instructional manuals (such as *How to Play First Base*), to individual sports almanacs summarizing the previous year's history, statistics, and accomplishments—all, of course, featuring prominent sections advertising Spalding's products, which now ranged from baseball gloves to ice skates, tennis rackets to track spikes, bicycles to golf clubs, and initiating the use of top athletes to endorse the products. The man Spalding handpicked to run his publishing empire in 1893 was none other than Jim Sullivan.

Like Spalding, Sullivan believed that athletic performance reflected a nation's strength and the morality of its men. Athletics required hard work and discipline. One could not drink, smoke, or carouse and still perform at one's best. Spalding liked that Sullivan was an American first and foremost, and both were determined to build an athletic culture to one day rival the gold standard of England's. As Spalding firmly believed, "Everything is possible to him that dares."

Sullivan and Spalding assembled an exploratory group that included Professor Sloane and Caspar Whitney among several other leading sportsmen. Spalding successfully lobbied President McKinley's administration to officially create an American Olympic commission and appoint him as leader, with Jim Sullivan as his deputy. The two sports titans drew up a list of the country's best amateurs of track and field, a sport Sullivan believed was the ultimate display of athleticism and machismo. They then used their stature to persuade the selected athletes' colleges and athletic clubs to pay their expenses to Paris.

Shortly before the American Olympic delegation set sail for France with its fifty-three handpicked athletes, word arrived that no stadium had been built for the Games, nor the promised running track constructed, nor were the British sponsoring a team. Coubertin had not even bothered to establish a set of international rules, an oversight that would cause all kinds of misunderstandings and arguments arising from each country's different nuances of play. From almost the moment they arrived in Paris, Sullivan, Whitney, and European athletic leaders from Italy, Sweden, Denmark, and even France, which included a few members from Coubertin's Union des Sociétés Françaises de Sports Athlétiques, began taking steps to form the new International Athletic Union to supplant Coubertin's IOC.

The new union's goal was to establish a uniform set of rules for international play and to abandon the quadrennial Olympic cycle after countries like Italy, Denmark, Sweden, and France felt it necessary to hold an international meeting in a different country every year to build momentum. Sullivan also had little interest in "minor" sports like swimming and sought to make all future Olympic Games strictly an international track-and-field affair. Before leaving Paris, the group adjourned with orders to obtain the approval of each of their country's amateur athletic associations and reconvene in Paris by year's end to formalize the new union.

With the coup growing serious, Coubertin appealed to the secretary of the English Amateur Athletic Association, Charles Herbert, the most powerful voice in athletic competition. The rest of the amateur world revolved around the British Empire's brilliant burning sun. Coubertin desperately needed what he called the "luster" and "incomparable prestige bestowed by Old England." He wrote to Herbert requesting that England submit an application to host the 1904 Games, hoping to reaffirm the IOC's legitimacy.

However, unlike the Americans who were warming to the Olympic concept, England had made no effort to send a team to Paris. Those British athletes who participated did so on their own shilling. And the British sporting establishment was underwhelmed by the reports they heard about the rank failure in Paris.

The British attitude had always been that if any first-rate athlete wanted to test his mettle, he need only enter one of their championships in London, the world's largest city and unrivaled sports capital, where he would be treated to an actual cinder track, proper swimming pools, west London's Stamford Bridge stadium, tens of thousands of spectators, and, of course, the world-class competition of Britain's superior athletes.

Ultimately, what mattered most to the British was the empire. It had its own international sporting network among its colonies without ever having to go outside its ranks. Hailing from the premier sporting nation, the British had no incentive to play under someone else's rules and lesser standards. They held practically all the world records, with no need to prove themselves to anyone.

One of England's leading sports publications, *The Referee,* stated, "Surely the annals of athletics, harking back to the days of the Greek Olympian games even, bear no parallel to the Championship meeting at Stamford Bridge."

As Coubertin anxiously awaited Herbert's answer in the fall of 1900, even the Greeks stopped clamoring for the Olympic Games. After their newfound nationalism emboldened them to pick a war with the Turks, only to be swiftly crushed and sent home humiliated, their economy now lay in shambles and their once volcanic Olympic spirit dormant. Coubertin's most enthusiastic supporter was gone, making England's backing all the more critical. By October, Coubertin had received Herbert's answer.

"The Olympic Games held at, let me say, Stamford Bridge, London, would not draw two hundred people," Herbert explained. "An international match between England and Ireland, Scotland or America would draw 20,000 spectators, but your Olympian festival would be a frost pure and simple." Herbert had no interest in playing wet nurse to Coubertin's Olympic baby. Especially one that now seemed stillborn.

Herbert concluded, "We do not want it."

ON OCTOBER 14, 1900, overhead vultures appeared to be circling the IOC, especially after several newspapers across the United States not only reported Herbert's lethal blow but stated the next Olympics would be held the following year at Buffalo's Pan-American Exposition. The *Buffalo Courier* ran a front-page headline: "Buffalo Has Secured Olympic Games of 1901." Several other papers throughout the United States reprinted the story off the wire. Newspapers attributed Buffalo's selection as host city to the efforts of Caspar Whitney and Jim Sullivan, the latter of whom was likely behind Buffalo's hosting assertion, which Coubertin had not authorized.

From a European perspective, holding the Games in America made little sense. Coubertin's entire mission was to bring the world together through sport and create peace among neighbors in a way that ultimately benefited France and the rest of Europe. It was hard enough getting European athletes to come to a remote place like Athens, let alone trying to lure them more than four thousand miles overseas. Europe's aristocracy still saw America as an undesirable colonial backwater, with bad food served in large portions, railroad travel that did not have the decency to divide the cars by class, and American manners as rough as its roads. As Walt Whitman observed, after America's recent Cuban victory over Spain, the European powers that had for centuries enjoyed a leading hand in "civilization's and humanity's eternal game" grew wary of America's ambition to take a seat at their table. The old-world aristocracy in which Coubertin was raised viewed the American experiment as a dangerous trend that threatened their class system and way of life.

Even for Coubertin, the high cost of such travel and the long time away from home, compounded by marriage troubles, made the prospect of going to America unmanageable. He preferred to work among

Europe's leisurely, white-gloved lords and princes, bowing and intro-ducing, being properly received, dining with finger bowls, praising and being praised back, rather than dealing with America's fast-paced, blunt-speaking, bare-knuckle culture that congregated around spit-toons. An Olympics so far away would do nothing to ingratiate the movement in Europe. And an Olympics without a strong foreign showing would be another complete disaster, killing what little enthu-siasm remained for the movement.

Coubertin's and Sullivan's war for Olympic control was about to get bloody.

CHARLES M. DANIELS,
EIGHTEEN YEARS OLD

8.

UNDERWATER

—

1903

IT WAS LATE SEPTEMBER WHEN CHARLEY STEPPED ONTO THE UP-
town elevated train. The shy, lanky high schooler in his school uniform
jacket and tie tried to slip aboard unnoticed. With his father still making headlines, people holding newspapers must have made him uneasy.
Especially if their eyes looked up from their papers and settled on him.
He had undoubtedly endured enough finger-pointing, snickers, and
condemning glares during that first week back for his senior year at
Dwight.

Perhaps on the train he sought to make his six-foot frame smaller
by scooting against the window and turning away from any onlooking
passengers, praying not to be recognized. The thought of what awaited
him at his destination could not have been pleasant. If he tried to ease
any anxiety by gazing down at the passing streets, his hopelessness
would have only amplified at seeing the world outside brimming with
optimism.

A cultural revolution was afoot as America began to discover its
vast potential. As Charley clattered along the rails three stories above
Sixth Avenue, the embodiment of the new twentieth-century America
passed below him. A glimpse of the future rattled amid all the horse-
drawn buggies and wagons in the form of a fancy new motorcar—a toy
for the wealthy at the cost of twice what an average worker earned in a
year. Even the mix of people walking in the street looked different.
Half a million immigrants a year now arrived on American shores,

lured by the promise of unbridled freedom to pursue their own idea of happiness. Women were discovering a new sense of independence with the invention of the chain-driven bicycle, which had replaced the dangerous penny-farthing. They no longer were beholden to a male escort's horse-drawn carriage to go places. Some female bicyclists were rebellious enough to shed their cumbersome dresses for the very symbol of the growing suffrage movement—bloomers.

With the public disgrace of Tom Daniels and the family name in ruins, Charley's own chance at the American dream seemed over. As his train approached West Forty-fourth Street, he was reminded of his bleak future by the sight of the prominent thirteen-story Hotel Gerard, where he had once lived with his mother and father. Condemned to a life of shame, as newspapers continued to drag his family's name through the mud, Charley was unlikely to ever find a way back.

His destination that day was the New York Athletic Club. Charley approached its arched entryway with uncertain steps. Inside, the daily newspapers lay on the lounge tables. Rushing past any damning headlines, he hurried down the grand staircase, past the familiar basement barbershop, bowling alleys, and rifle range, and quickly slipped into the locker room before someone asked him to leave. He changed into his bathing suit, then bravely opened the door and stepped onto the wet tiles.

Any of the watermen who had picked up a newspaper in the last month probably never expected to see him at the club again. Not after what was being written about his father in every major newspaper from the East Coast to California.

The little confidence Charley had developed since his father abandoned him four years earlier came not from any God-given talent but from working hard each day, focusing all his energy on achieving one small goal and then another, step by small step, hoping they might begin to show him a way forward. It seemed that swimming was now his only chance to prove he was more than the son of a notorious Wall Street swindler. Even if just in this one place, in this basement among this small group of misfits, he could become a first-class swimming champion and earn their respect, that would almost be enough. Such a dream was his last lifeline to prove he had value, and the New York Athletic Club had every reason to sever it.

His junior membership was conditional on two stipulations. Number one, that he represented the club as a gentleman. And two, that he brought the club honors as a champion. He had fulfilled neither, but the former failing warranted immediate expulsion according to the club's constitution as "conduct injurious to the good order, peace, or interests of the club." Had the members previously known about even his parents' separation, they never would have allowed him in the door.

Charley walked into the basement natatorium that day like a deer stepping into an open meadow during hunting season. Yet none of the watermen seemed to have fired a shot. Not Wahle. Not Lou Handley. Perhaps the shock of his appearance froze them all.

As Charley quietly headed to the tank during what was surely the longest walk of his life, he had to be questioning how many laps he could swim before they came to their senses and asked him to leave. One lap? A dozen? He would keep swimming until they threw him out.

The cool water let him feel something that wasn't negative. For more than half an hour, he worked on his scissor kick and sidestroke, and no one came to stop him. Maybe Wahle and Handley were too flabbergasted to say anything. Maybe everybody was. But at some point, he would have to leave the water and come face-to-face with the man who first vouched for his character—Dave Bratton—with the full knowledge that he had horribly let him down. When that awkward encounter happened, Dave had a story to share.

The prior summer, Dave was swimming off Manhattan Beach, a mile and a half out to sea, leading a group of six others, when a dense fog rolled in. Unable to see a hundred feet before them, they soon lost all sense of direction, and the other swimmers began to panic. Bratton tried to calm their fears as they swam slowly along, but even he couldn't tell whether the tide was coming in or going out. If it was coming in, he knew that it would eventually carry them to within a short distance of Rockaway Inlet at Sea Gate Point. If it was going the other way, he feared that it would carry them out to sea.

After what felt like hours of treading water in the fog, one of the men suffered a leg cramp and shouted for help. Bratton wrapped an arm around the man's upper waist, towing him with a sidestroke as they searched in vain for any sign of the inlet. The man's pain worsened. All this time an eerie silence engulfed them, with not so much as a steamboat whistle. They shouted for help until they were hoarse, but the fog only grew thicker. After what felt like another two hours, their muscles aching and at nearly the point of exhaustion, they began to lose all hope. Even the ever-positive Bratton was certain that by now they must have passed Sea Gate Point and were far out to sea. They knew they couldn't stay afloat much longer and began to believe this was the end.

That's when Bratton thought he heard a bell. His hopes and ears perked up, for it sounded like the bell on a buoy. Knowing that all of the buoys were inside the harbor, he rallied the desperate group to swim in that direction.

The tones of the bell rang out clearer and clearer, until at last a distant shape appeared in the fog. It took every last ounce of energy, but when they reached the buoy, the exhausted swimmers clung on for dear life. Half dead after nearly six hours in the water, they again shouted for help to no avail. With no one coming to save them, after a rest Bratton encouraged them to let go of the buoy and swim in the direction he thought the shore ought to be. Eventually, the white sandy beach of Sea Gate Point appeared, and soon they were collapsing safely onto its shores. His message to Charley: as long as you keep fighting, you too have a chance to survive.

Bratton could not speak for the regular members, but it seemed the few who even knew about Charley's presence in the club at all had yet to make the connection between the young swimmer and his notorious father. Neither Charley nor Dave, nor any of the watermen, could control what newspapers wrote about his family, or if friends decided to disassociate from him, or when the regular club members would realize his relationship to Tom Daniels and vote him out. Charley could control only his commitment to swimming. And that meant keeping at it as hard as he could for as long as he could, lap after lap, trying to uncover a glint of speed with whatever fleeting time he had left at the club. It wasn't in Bratton's nature to judge others harshly. He would not withdraw Charley's junior membership. And none of the watermen would say a word to any regular club member about his connection to Tom Daniels. However, none of that mattered if Charley failed to distinguish himself in the water by his nineteenth birthday. On March 24, his junior membership would expire, and he would be dropped.

WAHLE AND HANDLEY CONTINUED to focus on the herculean task of preparing the club's top watermen for the upcoming Olympiad, with no time for a noncontender junior member.

Keeping a low profile, Charley paid close attention to the champions' techniques and observed that no two of them swam exactly alike. Even if using the same stroke, the swimmers stylized their movements to their own strengths and physical attributes. A man with abnormally developed shoulders would have to strain to make an extreme reach, so a shorter one fit him better, while a slender, more proportionate man benefited from a longer stroke. And then there was the individual syncing of arms and legs and the various rates of speed of each swimmer's kicks. Charley concluded that a swimmer obtained the best results by adapting the various movements to one's attributes, so as to place no unnatural strain on any part of the body.

He also listened in on Wahle and Handley's conversations around the tank as they debated the latest techniques in speed swimming and continued to puzzle over Dick Cavill's mysterious "crawl." One afternoon, as the two were in the middle of one of their discussions about swimming, they spotted the club's instructor, Gus Sundstrom, performing a technique he called the "swordfish." Sundstrom had picked it up during his sailing days from a Pacific Native American swimmer named Big Red Fish. Swimming on his back, with his arms stretched out in front of him and thumbs linked together like a piercing lance, Sundstrom sped across the pool using only his legs, with a kick that was unlike any technique they practiced. His feet came out of the water, splashing straight up and down.

That's when Wahle's friend and fellow Austrian Olympic swimmer, Charles Ruberl, exclaimed, "Why, that's the Australian crawl stroke! Turn over and try it."

Sundstrom turned over on his belly, and with face submerged and arms pointed straight, he propelled himself with his legs beating up and down in narrow, alternating drives. That was the first time any of them had witnessed a conceivable version of Cavill's crawling stroke.

Handley, Wahle, and Ruberl endeavored to imitate it for possible use at the Olympics. For the most part, their efforts looked like a children's exercise to see how much water they could splash into the air. The crude kick appeared neither graceful nor scientifically sound. Each time they raised a leg out of the water their upper body sank. When they lifted their head to breathe, it threw off their balance and caused their hips and legs to sink, increasing drag. Handley expressed his skepticism, as they all struggled with buoyancy. Even Sundstrom failed to master the new movement with any degree of comfort or speed, and eventually they all dismissed it.

Charley stuck to sharpening his underwater scissor kick. The sidestroke offered the best vantage to look back and see what his legs were doing correctly or incorrectly. He experimented with the trudgen, but for a stroke of this type, where the swimmer faced forward, or even head down in the water, an outside observer was needed to critique his progress if he ever hoped to acquire proper mastery. His family's shame probably prevented Charley from reaching out to anyone, fearing being shunned or, even worse, told to leave. It was safer to remain invisible.

By early November, Charley saw his name posted for one of the final meets of the fall season. It is unclear if this was Dave Bratton's doing or if Charley had quietly requested it, but his moment of truth had arrived.

Wahle and Handley gave him a chance at both the hundred-yard century race and an intrasquad water polo contest where they positioned him at forward. As Joe Ruddy said, it was time to show if he was a persimmon or an athlete.

ON SATURDAY EVENING, NOVEMBER 14, butterflies fluttered wildly inside Charley's stomach. If he hoped to salvage his life, the first big step up the mountain to redemption would have to be tonight. The basement pool drew a decent crowd of spectators and watermen. Many of the leading college swimmers from Columbia, Yale, and Penn liked to attend the season's final competitions, including Columbia's celebrated champion, Joe Spencer.

Charley watched Spencer win the 300-yard invitational by an impressive fifteen yards. That past Valentine's Day in the same tank, Spencer had set just about every American record from 220 to 500 yards. The blond-haired Columbia man wore a dark blue full-bodied swimsuit, with a big white *C* emblazoned across his burly chest. His strong shoulders and arms looked as though he chopped wood for a living, especially in comparison to Charley, whose muscles were hardly pronounced. People around the pool that night began talking about Columbia's star waterman as a worthy challenger to the great Harry LeMoyne.

A field of thirty-two swimmers participated in the hundred-yard handicap, which was divided into four eight-man heats, making for a crowded tank. In the first heat, Charley watched his brawny twenty-year-old teammate, Budd Goodwin, edge out Lou Handley with a fast 66.4 seconds, the best ever recorded at the club. Then Charley took a spot in the second heat among the eight-man field. He tried to shake off the nerves that made him feel tight, while Otto Wahle, Lou Handley, and Dave Bratton looked on.

The gun fired. Charley dove. At the end of four laps, he touched the final wall behind the winner's uninspiring seventy-two seconds. Now his only remaining chance to prove he belonged was in the intrasquad water polo match—if he didn't get himself killed.

At the time, American water polo was described as the most dangerous sport next to bullfighting. Players used a partially deflated rubber ball, seven inches in diameter, which made it easier to hold underwater for long periods of time, leaving your other hand free to strangle your opponent. Proficiency at holding your breath underwater was critical. Unlike the more genteel European rules, as the sportswriter Arthur Daley wrote, "in the American style of play everything went except yanking out a bowie knife from your belt and slicing a rival's jugular vein. It was submarine wrestling, underwater rough-housing and aquatic mayhem all at once. If your opponent would rather drown than release his hold on the ball, he was being perfectly silly. You just drowned him."

Even certain choke holds banned in wrestling were allowed, and no one was better at them than Joe Ruddy. Able to hold his breath for more than three minutes, he never thought twice about dragging any ballcarrier to the depths until they turned purple and fish-eyed and released the prize.

"If a fellow sticks his thumb into your mouth to get a cheek hold on you, you try to get that thumb between your teeth and hang on," Ruddy instructed. "If he has a leg strangle on your neck, grab his big toe and twist it to make him let go. If he has a front hold underwater you draw both feet up and kick him in the stomach. If he has an arm strangle on you from behind, use jiu jitsu on his little finger to break the hold. And if you can't break it, go down to the bottom of the tank with him and wait to see who drowns first."

The rules did not limit the length of time a player could be held underwater if he possessed the ball or was within four feet of it. Unless the arm, leg, or neck you were clutching ripped off, there was no such thing as a foul. And even then, you probably would only get two minutes for roughing.

"If a fellow feels he's done up under water he just gives his opponent a little pinch—like that—and the fellow lets go. We call it the busy signal. It's a safeguard, you see, to keep fellows from really getting hurt under water," Joe explained, then added, "But it isn't done in the best water polo circles. You take your medicine and hope they'll miss you before it's too late." Joe Ruddy roared that when anybody could make him give the busy signal, that would be the day he retired.

When asked if anyone had ever drowned, Joe Ruddy just grinned.

"Once when I played with the Knickerbocker A. C. against the Boston A. A., back in 1898 . . . after the last referee's whistle," Ruddy recounted, he and Lou Handley were standing at the end of the pool, puffing and counting their arms and legs, making sure they were still in one piece, when Ruddy said, "Hey, Lou, where's Harry Reeder?"

At that very moment, a Boston player shouted frantically, "Where's Tommy Baxter?"

Joe recalled, "We found them gripped together and unconscious at the bottom of the tank." Both men were rushed to the hospital and recovered the next day.

Lou Handley might have been the water polo captain and coach, but Joe Ruddy was the undisputed king of hand-to-hand combat.

Probably the only thing that kept Charley from being drowned that evening was that Joe Ruddy wasn't playing against him. They were all so much stronger than the eighteen-year-old with his still developing body. When it was over, it was clear to everyone that water polo was not a good fit, which left Charley all the more on the outs with the watermen.

JOE RUDDY

AFTER THE NIGHT ENDED, Charley had to take a good hard look at himself and face the truth. His only chance out of the cesspool that had become his life was to swim through it. There was no longer time to worry about what others thought, all the judgmental eyes, condemning glares, and mockery. No more time to feel bad about being the elephant in whatever room he stepped into. And he wasn't about to use the "busy signal." He would make his body stronger. Whatever pain and anger he had crammed down deep inside himself so that his father's actions could not hurt him, he needed to find a way to use it for fuel.

With the last competition before the Thanksgiving holiday concluding, Charley's chances to impress Wahle and Handley by year's end were closing fast. Adding further angst, in order to salvage any last shred of honor, his mother was mulling over the difficult choice of filing for the "unthinkable measure." This, right on the heels of the 1903 Inter-Church Conference on Marriage and Divorce that called for churches to prohibit such an abomination, allowing the atrocity *only* if infidelity or abandonment could be proven. In Alice's case this was true on both counts, but even so, divorce promised to heap more disgrace on her family, and it would give the New York Athletic Club all the more reason to sever ties.

Alice and Charley's financial outlook wasn't good either. In a world where women remained second-class citizens, the employment options available for Alice were few. With Charley's graduation approaching that June, the feeling of duty to forgo college and start work to support them both loomed, even if Alice urged him to do otherwise. His window to become a champion swimmer was fast closing as each week the papers wrote about more people around the country who claimed to have been swindled by Tom Daniels.

FOR THE REST OF November, each day after school Charley continued to escape his shattered world by disappearing into the water. He worked hard, agonizingly so, to break seventy seconds.

As the snow and ice and frigid December winds screamed across Manhattan, he continued to make the two-mile trek north to Dwight and after school another mile farther north to the NYAC to repeat his slow, plodding sidestroke, lap after lap, hammering away, carefully making each movement and thinking all the time about what he was doing. No one was watching him as far as he knew. He slipped into the tank relatively unnoticed, swam anywhere from thirty to fifty minutes, and then left without incident.

The goal of a competitive swimmer back then was not to exhaust oneself by hours of training. Nor to transform muscles into bulging, knotty ones like a professional poser. Alex Meffert had espoused a daily regimen that would strengthen the muscles but not harden them. Swimmers needed to keep those clean, smooth arms and legs blessed with long, pliant, working muscles that never tired and didn't cramp or bind. They needed a routine that would improve their wind and help them hone their stroke, but not leave their muscles fatigued before a race. They believed swimming two quarter miles every day, with a fifteen-minute interval for rest in between, was enough to get a short-distance swimmer in the pink of condition yet still feel supple and free. Even a daily swim of three or four minutes, enough to cover two or three hundred yards, would increase any athlete's snap and dash. Thirty minutes a day of sprinting strokes was plenty.

With all the pressure that accompanied AAU-sanctioned races, Charley decided to take a chance before a totally different crowd. On Saturday, December 5, the New York Athletic Club held its fifty-second Ladies' Day. From 11:00 A.M. to 6:00 P.M., the club temporarily opened its doors to members' wives, daughters, and female friends. For entertainment, the men staged various sports exhibitions, including swimming, fencing, boxing, wrestling, and the standing jump, conducted by their three-time Olympic medalist Ray Ewry. Wahle, Handley, and the elder Gus Sundstrom gave exhibitions of various swimming techniques. Even at forty-four, the mustachioed Sundstrom looked fit enough to swim around the entire island of Manhattan as he had in his youth. For Charley, the day offered a pleasant distraction during a cheerless holiday season and one of the final few chances to prove himself.

Ladies watched from the pool's second- and third-floor galleries, high enough to save their long dresses from an unwanted splash. A relaxed atmosphere surrounded the event and perhaps helped alleviate Charley's usual nerves and stiffness. No one was competing for a trophy. It was just about having fun and putting on a good show for the "fairer sex."

The lanky eighteen-year-old stepped up to the pool's edge in the hundred-yard century handicap. Handicapping was used to make races more exciting. The method allowed officials to offset the varying abilities of competitors and equalize everyone's chance to win. With so few competitive swimmers, a noticeable gap existed between the handful of champions and the rest of the mediocre field. Rather than watch champions lead wire to wire, handicapping created exciting finishes by granting the lesser swimmers head starts over the favorite. The worse the swimmer, the greater his handicap.

Charley's poor record granted him a few seconds' head start over George Van Cleaf and A. R. Camp, and to everyone's surprise Charley held them off with his sidestroke to win by two yards. Moreover, if the timer could be believed, he had clocked a head-scratching personal best of 68 seconds. The following Saturday, in a handicap against Lou Handley, he swam a hundred yards in 67.6 seconds. Another personal best.

As Christmas trees went up and everyone was out buying presents for their loved ones, making plans with family and friends to attend jolly holiday gatherings, Charley continued to escape into the water every day. He worked alone on his sidestroke, perfecting his underwater scissor kick, strengthening his muscles, trying to work on the trudgen, when one day, while he was swimming laps, a voice called to him. When Charley looked up, the gray eyes staring down at him belonged to Otto Wahle.

Charley's time at the club appeared to have reached its end.

9.

STRUCK BY LIGHTNING

—

DECEMBER 1903-
FEBRUARY 1904

CHARLEY NEVER APPEARED TO BE EXERTING HIMSELF IN THE pool, nor moving all that fast, yet there seemed to be a rhythm and music in his swimming that a waterman who grew up in the town of Mozart and Beethoven could appreciate. Wahle loved classical music almost as much as he did swimming. And Charley's recent performance of 67.6 seconds intrigued him.

"Upper arm starts the recovery," Wahle pointed out, emphasizing the proper double-overarm technique that needed to be mastered for anyone hoping to swim the trudgen. "Then the under arm catches the water and begins another stroke."

Human beings weren't designed to move through water. We don't float very well. We cannot hold our breath all that long. Putting our bodies in motion in a horizontal position feels unnatural compared with how easily we walk upright on land. But we do know about science. And scientifically speaking, the trudgen is the superior speed stroke because each arm encounters less resistance in air than it does underwater. That's a fact. The key of course is proper execution.

Until that moment, the only Winged Footer to have taken any real interest in Charley was Dave Bratton. Wahle seemed more likely to evict him from the pool. Yet here he was, offering Charley a few pointers on the trudgen's one-two arm beat that he'd learned from watching the Brits at the 1900 Paris Games. Try to avoid large windmill arms that rotate in complete circles, he said. While this straight-arm technique pulls a lot of water, it pulls too soon, and the power used to do so quickly exhausts swimmers. Charley needed to focus on sustainable, more efficient high, bent elbows.

It certainly was a bit surprising that someone like Wahle would approach a pariah like Charley, and perhaps each was a bit skeptical of the other. Just about every man Charley ever trusted had abandoned him. He was wary.

Wahle, as a Jewish boy growing up in Vienna who was small for his age, could relate to those who were so hopelessly up against it and still fought gamely to defy overwhelming odds. He understood what it was like to be constantly told you couldn't do something. To be pushed aside because you were judged to be unacceptable or unworthy.

As the Jewish scholar Arthur Schnitzler wrote about growing up Jewish in Vienna during the years of Wahle's childhood, "It was not possible, especially not for a Jew in public life, to ignore the fact that he was a Jew." Jews were excluded from the popular turnvereins, youth gymnastics societies that were epicenters of the German community for both athletics and social activities. Jews were further stereotyped as nonathletes, since sport was predominantly Anglo-Saxon and not part of their culture. However, the city's public bath facilities, in order to promote good hygiene, health, and water safety, remained open to all. And so Wahle wasn't beholden to other boys' whims and prejudices if he wanted to participate. He need only rely on his own will. So he dedicated himself to swimming, determined to prove a Jew could be just as much of an athlete as anyone.

Vienna had a culture of public baths that dated back to the Roman Empire. The nearby communal bath along the Danube River accommodated twelve hundred visitors, with separate pools for men and women that were freshly fed with heated river water thirty times a day. Wahle's ambition soon put him in direct conflict with his faith, because many sporting events commenced on Saturday, the Jewish Sabbath, the day of rest. Traditional parents in his Jewish community of Leopoldstadt clung stubbornly to old-world habits and attitudes as they wrestled with watching many of their Austrian-educated sons, like Wahle, become more Anglo-Saxon in appearance, thought, and action. Aside from his fellow Austrian swimmer and friend Charles

Ruberl, a Catholic who had changed his first name from Karl upon arriving in America, Wahle found himself very much alone in his quest to become the Austrian champion. After he and Ruberl departed for the 1900 Paris Olympics, he never again returned to Vienna, not even for his only sister's wedding. He might well have had a falling-out with his family over disregarding the Sabbath and devoting himself to such an Anglo-Saxon sport as swimming.

The next time Charley showed up to swim during the Christmas and New Year's holiday, while most of the watermen were busy with family merriment, Wahle, being Jewish, and Charley, with little to be merry about, saw each other again. In fact, they were probably the only two at the pool.

Charley needed to keep the top half of his body square, facing forward, while awkwardly keeping his lower half twisted sideways to scissor kick. One scissor kick for each right arm pull, then another for the left. The fact the trudgen kept the face underwater most of the time necessitated a new breathing technique, which meant learning to lift the head straight up for a fraction of a second to gulp air and then exhaling slowly through the nose while the face was underwater. When Charley swam, Wahle offered more observations.

Charley listened closely to Wahle's instructions, observed his demonstrations, and then made adjustments as Wahle corrected him. When he seemed to gain some mastery of a particular aspect, Wahle offered a new component to work on, like how to use his arms to most effectively catch the water. This was not a formal coaching arrangement. Nothing like that was discussed. But almost every day during the holidays Charley showed up to train, and Wahle just "happened" to be there.

AN INCH OF SNOW fell a few days after Christmas, just enough for sledding in Central Park. By early January, temperatures dropped into the single digits. All through Christmas vacation, the lone teen made the trek north in cold and breezy weather to work on the trudgen.

Talk around the club that winter often centered on the upcoming World's Fair in St. Louis. The golden age of these extravagant international expositions had begun half a century earlier with the success of London's Crystal Palace Exhibition in 1851, followed by New York (1853), London (1862), Philadelphia (1876), Paris (1889), Chicago (1893), Brussels (1897), Paris (1900), and Buffalo (1901). The St. Louis exposition in 1904 was set to be the largest in history, twice as big as any previous world's fair. Tens of millions of visitors would be coming from all over the world to marvel at the latest inventions, art and history exhibitions, popular culture, entertainment spectacles, amusement park rides, and this time athletics. St. Louis planned an entire exhibition around sports, building a state-of-the-art stadium and gymnasium that Coubertin had dreamed about for Paris. What St. Louis didn't have, and wanted, was the Olympics.

The fight for the 1904 Games had begun when Coubertin was desperately trying to fend off the formation of Sullivan's International Athletic Union. With England and France having turned their backs on him, America was the only competent sportsman knocking on his door. And its sports authorities seemed determined to host the new Olympics with or without the IOC's permission. In an effort to discredit Sullivan's authority to hold the third Olympiad in Buffalo in 1901, Coubertin dispatched a cable to *The Chicago Times-Herald* announcing that he had received a request from the University of Chicago's president to host the third Olympiad there in 1904 and that the IOC looked favorably on awarding it to the city. His proclamation prompted the University of Chicago to throw a huge bonfire party, and Sullivan to throw a fit.

The next day, Jim Sullivan fired back with an angry open letter to the New York press, challenging the IOC's authority to make any decisions after the mess in Paris. "The Baron de Coubertin or his associates have no longer any power to name the place at which Olympian games or international athletic events of any character shall be held." He went on to tell the American press that the IOC no longer existed, that Coubertin had nothing more to do with sports matters, that the new International Athletic Union had been formed with the support of Europe's sports leaders, and that the next Olympic track-and-field competition would indeed be held at Buffalo's Pan-American Exposition, as previously announced.

At Professor Sloane's urging, Coubertin counterpunched by reaching out to another boisterous critic of the IOC, Caspar Whitney. It was a bold gamble. Whitney was an ally of Sullivan's. But he also operated a rival sports magazine and had long endured Sullivan's big personality. The Frenchman appealed to Whitney's ego. Rather than again play second fiddle to Sullivan on a new international union, why not take a leadership seat on the IOC? It was a brilliant maneuver. Whitney used his magazine to publicly affirm the IOC's legitimacy, discredit Sullivan's authority over the Games, and quash support for Sullivan's yet-to-be-ratified international union. The grave Sullivan had dug for the IOC was now one he found himself standing in. He had no choice but to mail Coubertin a mea culpa, hoping to make nice and gain a spot on the IOC.

"I am always willing, if I think I have made a mistake, to acknowledge it," Sullivan wrote. Coubertin still passed over Sullivan for an IOC seat. As the Frenchman later noted, "The fight was on!" But his victory proved short-lived.

When construction delays caused St. Louis to officially postpone its 1903 fair's opening by a year, the AAU Championships already scheduled to take place during the fair now precluded many of America's top amateurs from participating in a competing Chicago Olympics. Albert Spalding, as a member of the Chicago Olympic Committee, also saw St. Louis as the better alternative. St. Louis was spending a staggering thirty-one million dollars (one billion dollars today) to create a fair twice the size of Chicago's past Columbian Exposition. Railroads planned to add extra routes to St. Louis with specially discounted rates to draw folks from every corner of the country. At a time when 60 percent of Americans lived on farms or in small towns (versus 2 percent today), never venturing more than a few miles from home, with no telephone, no car, no radio, and a very isolated view of the world, the fair invited everyone to see, hear, smell, touch, and taste world culture, thus presenting the greatest audience to introduce the Olympic Games to America—and, of course, market Spalding athletic equipment.

Coubertin, however, loathed the idea of allowing another world's fair to swallow up the Games and chew them to bits. He feared it would be another disaster like Paris. Even with the powerful lure of a world's fair, Coubertin believed few European athletes would travel so far to compete, especially without the prestige and luster of England's top sportsmen. Lacking foreign competition, the American Games would be just a national championship. And England had already made it very clear that it wanted nothing to do with anything Olympic.

For months, Americans read about the two rival cities fighting over this strange international sporting festival with an unfamiliar Greek name. Newspapers fed the public's growing curiosity with articles explaining the origin of the Olympics. They touted the coming Games as "the greatest event in the athletic world on this side of the Atlantic during the present decade." The Olympic Games that until then had mostly only been known by East Coast athletic clubs and colleges were now making their way into the American zeitgeist.

In February 1903, unable to fight the momentum for the city named in honor of the sainted French king, the IOC voted 14–2 in favor of transferring the Games to St. Louis. It didn't matter. Coubertin, believing that whoever was hosting them, an American Olympics promised to be a disaster, assigned the organizational responsibilities of this doomed venture to the St. Louis World's Fair Committee. And who was the person whom the committee assigned to helm this ill-fated Olympic ship? None other than Coubertin's most hated enemy—Jim Sullivan.

A week before Christmas, all of the NYAC chatter and posturing about their chances at the upcoming Olympics took a backseat when two bicycle store owners from Charley's childhood home of Dayton, with no superhuman talents, little money, and nothing to distinguish themselves other than putting all their energies and resources behind one singular focus, shocked the world with their home-built motorized flying machine.

ON THE AFTERNOON OF Monday, January 11, around 3:15 P.M., Tom Daniels was enjoying a drink just a block from his former Wall Street office at the swanky Café Savarin, when a stranger approached. Before that moment, Tom had to be feeling quite pleased with himself. Sure, the prosecution had identified plenty of victims across the country who claimed he had defrauded them. Yes, detectives had amassed evidence showing exactly how his scheme had worked. And indeed, they had uncovered victims' written complaints to Tom, proving that he had been made aware of their concerns of possible fraud. But Tom had outfoxed them all.

The prosecution still needed proof that Tom Daniels had *intended* to commit fraud. Criminal intent, or what the law calls "having a guilty mind," was a key element to obtaining a conviction. The prosecution had nothing but circumstantial evidence. With none of Tom's co-conspirators willing to testify against him, Tom could claim his intent was always to do right by his clients, and the fact that he had zero success was just bad luck.

After months of gathering evidence and taking victims' testimonies, the prosecution had decided not to move forward. The cleverness of Tom's scheme and his dynamic duo of cutthroat defense attorneys had protected him for now, but the police and the district attorney's office would have their eyes on him. As would the U.S. postal authorities, who were put on notice about Tom's use of the mail to carry out his swindling operation. But Tom's biggest problem now was public relations. The whole country had been made wise to his confidence game, and newspapers had painted him as an unsavory character. No discharge would ever erase that, nor vindicate his disgraced name.

Tom was figuring out his next move when he heard the stranger address him. Tom looked up and tried to place the man's face. Then the man handed him a piece of paper. When Tom glanced down, his smile of greeting faded.

It was a divorce petition. Filed by Alice M. Daniels, accusing him of adultery.

LATE SATURDAY AFTERNOON, JANUARY 16, under a partly cloudy sky, Charley bade his mother goodbye, then walked out of their apartment to be greeted by a cold west wind blowing through the Washington Arch that often carried the foul stench of death from the Meatpacking District's 250 slaughterhouses less than a mile away. Dressed in his overcoat, suit, and tie, he hurried to catch the northbound train for what could be his last swimming race. Thirty minutes later, he arrived at the club and made his usual hasty walk down the basement steps to the natatorium, where he had one more shot at proving himself.

The challenge before him was one and a half times longer than any race he had ever competed in. The 250-yard length fell right on the borderline between sprints and mid-distances. For someone who focused his practices exclusively on sprinting, Charley's legs and arms promised to feel the strain. It was already daunting enough to be trying out the trudgen for the first time in competition, let alone the demands of its double overarm, which proved more exhausting than his one-arm sidestroke. Not to mention, this was a time before the invention of lane ropes or black lines on the pool floor to keep a swimmer on a straight course. Putting your head facedown in the water, as the trudgen required, even for a moment, took your eyes off the far wall, making a swimmer more apt to go off course. But Otto Wahle felt he was ready. What made the outcome even scarier was that if Charley somehow managed to finish in the top two of his heat, he would qualify for the finals, where Columbia's star swimmer, Joe Spencer, awaited.

Since Charley's limited track record made him unproven, the race official assigned him an unflattering handicap of nine seconds— a downgrade from his last outing. Charley lined up with the first heat of four and waited for the starter to call out his handicap number, then dove. Rotating his bent arms, right arm first, then left, palms slightly turned, fingers together, just as Wahle had shown him, he stabbed into the water with his hands at a forty-five-degree angle. Bringing his forearm down in a strong, steady pull, then working his underwater scissor kick, he traversed the pool for ten laps, periodically lifting his face straight out of the water to gulp air and catch a glimpse of where he was going. Observers said his stroke looked too relaxed, but when he touched the final wall first, his time, if it could be believed, was an astonishing 3:17—one second off Joe Spencer's American record.

No one in the entire pool believed it, not Otto Wahle, and especially not Charley. When he climbed out of the tank, still dripping and catching his breath, his fellow Winged Footers swarmed him, back-slapping and complimenting him on a crack swim. He was not accustomed to such a reception. Not since he'd won the National Sportsmen's Show's rifle contest had he heard others say his name with such enthusiasm.

Charley stood on the sidelines tingly and disoriented, almost in a dream. He would now take on Joe Spencer in the four-man championship heat.

Charley was a nobody. Until December, he had shown not the slightest talent for speed. He had brought no honors to the team. He certainly wasn't capable of breaking a record. Now his club mates cheered him on to do both.

Since Charley's handicap gave him a nine-second head start over Spencer, beating him to the final wall would not be enough to show up the champion. Otto Wahle and his club mates urged him to force the conversation by breaking the American record Spencer had set in the same tank last February.

Beyond the jitters and angst that always accompanied his races, Charley now had to face high expectations. He was competing against an unquestionably superior opponent. The challenge came with the fear of not stacking up.

"Ready!" called the official.

Three stopwatches set on Charley as he tried to stay focused through all the butterflies. He stared across the water. Everyone would be watching him.

Seconds before the official shouted out his handicap, Charley filled his lungs.

"Get set."

At the official's "Go," Columbia's Con Trubenbach started first with a twelve-second handicap, trudgening down the pool.

The official began counting. "One, two . . ."

Charley took off at "three." Another Winged Footer, Edgar Adams, dove in next. Spencer hit the water at "twelve."

Going from the sidestroke to the trudgen was like upgrading from a one-oar-powered canoe to two. Charley's arms and hands worked like two paddles pushing against the water while his inner buttock muscle that stretches over the hip bone worked his scissor kick, moving the legs away from the body sideways and bringing them sharply back together again with a propulsive motion. If the excitement of the race caused Charley to go at it too hard, he wouldn't be able to sustain the motion over 250 yards, not without his hip muscles and knees becoming painful and exhausted.

Charley made sure to stay in a straight line, keeping his head up as needed, anticipating Spencer's hot pursuit. He had several poor turns off the wall. When he finally settled into his stroke, he looked *too* relaxed, giving no impression of speed. Yet, over ten laps, he covered ground in a way that baffled spectators, eventually passing Con Trubenbach of Columbia. When Charley reached the final wall, he looked back to see Spencer trudgening almost an entire lap behind.

There appeared to be some uncertainty as the timekeepers huddled together, comparing stopwatches that showed three different times. The discrepancies varied by 1.4 seconds. To avoid further dispute in the face of Spencer's 3:16 record, officials agreed to accept only Charley's slowest figure. As Charley stood in the water, catching his breath, the officials announced his approved time and the Winged Footers exploded with cheers.

Three minutes and 15.4 seconds.

Charley had just swum the fastest 250 yards in American history.

Before he could even grasp the magnitude of what he'd done, he was swarmed by club mates as he stepped out of the tank. Their attention caught him off guard. Compliments were foreign to him. The spotlight uncomfortable. He hardly recognized his newfound speed. It had come to him so suddenly, like being struck by lightning; it didn't seem real. Yet the praise and hearty congratulations from his teammates filled him with warmth. His grin certainly stretched even bigger as he shared the victory with Otto Wahle. One of his first thoughts might have been that his father may well read about his record-breaking feat in the morning paper.

However, the next day's New York *Sun* attacked his performance: "Daniels's effort cannot be regarded seriously, as he started from a 'call' and not with the pistol shot, the one starting requisite in record breaking performances. He did not even wait for the call and was about dipping his head into the water when his number was sung out, and surely gained one second."

And indeed, because his time was made in a handicap race with a non-pistol start, Spencer's 3:16 remained in the books. But what proved more hurtful was the implied attack on his character. After the shame brought to his family name by his father's dishonest dealings, *The Sun*'s public condemnation of his own integrity cut deep.

10.

IN SEARCH OF AN
AMERICAN CHAMPION

—

1904

THE NEW YORK ATHLETIC CLUB AND COLUMBIA UNIVERSITY immediately announced a three-hundred-yard match race between Joe Spencer and Charles Daniels to settle the controversy. They sold it as a contest that promised to spur both young men to make a joint attack on the record. Behind the scenes, however, they saw Charley as nothing more than a stalking horse to push Spencer to new heights.

The race was set for Saturday, February 13, at the New York Athletic Club to commemorate the one-year anniversary of Spencer's 500-yard triumph at the same pool. During that race, each time Spencer touched the wall to make a turn, his time up to that distance was recorded. When he had finished, the timekeepers showed that he had set eight American records along the way, from 225 to 500 yards. This time, Spencer would not be tasked with swimming the full 500 yards, which would allow him to burn all of his energy over those 300 yards, virtually guaranteeing faster results.

The length favored Spencer's mid-distance sweet spot. It also marked one of E. Carroll Schaeffer's few remaining records that had eluded him. But for Charley, it would be the longest race he had ever attempted. For Joe Spencer, it offered the perfect way to celebrate the anniversary of his record-breaking feat by setting a new one that would pave the way for a match race against the great Harry LeMoyne.

Unlike running on a track, building momentum when you swim is difficult. Water resistance allows for minimal gliding. It pushes against you and brings you to a fast halt. A swimmer's shape and size, as well as his relative speed in the water, all affect the force pushing against him, or what they call drag. By maximizing arm reach, the swimmer can draw as much water back for as long as possible, increasing the pulling force and creating thrust to propel him forward.

Otto Wahle talked about the need to pace oneself. Charley had to find the fastest gait he could sustain over three hundred yards and not worry about what Spencer was doing. To let himself be drawn out by an early sprint, or to reserve energy for a sensational finish that would have been far better employed sooner, was folly.

Wahle timed Charley's practice laps, allowing him to gauge how evenly he held his pace. It helped him understand when to increase or slacken his speed. Over time, Charley worked on becoming a better judge of tempo.

A key trick to achieving the perfect stroke was to count the different movements in one-two-three periods, attaining the same length of time for each of the three. In the trudgen, his arm strokes counted one-two, his legs three.

Twelve days before the race, on February 1, Charley had to deal with the added distraction of his parents' divorce proceedings and the toll it was taking on his mother.

Tom's filed response had refused to acknowledge any wrongdoing, denying Alice's accusations of adultery, and asked the court to dismiss her petition. Witnesses testified. The attorney for Alice produced several individuals who swore to the fact that Tom had indeed been living with another woman on Staten Island for at least the past three years. They claimed that Tom referred to the woman as his wife and introduced her publicly as Mrs. Daniels. She was described as stout, about five feet four inches, with light brown hair. Until this divorce filing, none of the witnesses knew that Tom had another wife and son in the city. Other than the one time he had mentioned them to his groundskeeper, who testified before the court, Tom never spoke of their existence.

Alice listened to all of the humiliating and hurtful testimony, while Tom remained a no-show. His attorneys offered no witnesses on his behalf. He seemed incapable of acknowledging his own misdeeds or apologizing for any hardship he had caused Alice and Charley. He also did not challenge Alice's claim for full custody, nor did he even ask for any visitation rights to see his only child.

Divorce or not, the newspapers' nationwide coverage of Tom's swindling ring had ensured that Alice was destined to be a pariah the rest of her days. A divorce would at least allow her family to legally sever ties with Tom as an in-law, and perhaps save themselves socially. It allowed Alice to save her last shred of integrity. Unfortunately for Charley, Tom would always be his father, strapped to him like a bundle of dynamite, creating the constant anxiety that at any moment someone could light the fuse. Even though his teammates protected his secret, all it took was one person in their small swimming community to make the connection and he was done for.

THE REALITY OF SWIMMING a match race against America's mid-distance champion began to sink in. Charley had only one amateur victory to his credit and had never competed in a race this long. The opinion that he was being used to push Spencer to a record-breaking swim was now widely held. Some newspapers even called Charley a fraud. Nobody gave him a prayer.

On a snowy Saturday evening, Charley arrived at the club. When he reached his locker, hanging inside was the famed navy-blue swimsuit of the New York Athletic Club with the prestigious red winged foot sewn on the chest. The emblem, a separate piece of thick wool, was the same insignia worn by Wahle, Handley, Bratton, Ruddy, and the rest of the club's champion watermen. It meant he was part of the team. Not since Doc Seixas's junior branch scouts had he fully felt a part of anything, and he did not want to let his teammates down.

Spectators crowded around the NYAC's basement tank to watch America's mid-distance champion, Joe Spencer, set a new record. Charles Daniels would soon be another forgotten wannabe whose printed name would lie crumpled in yesterday's trash.

As was always the case, spectators were admitted by invitation only, ensuring the crowd not only was fashionable but adhered to gentlemanly standards. Enthusiastic invitees packed the club's second- and third-floor galleries, occupying every available vantage point surrounding the pool. The smartly dressed crowd comprised a mix of older members and their guests, some of whom were ladies, along with the collegiate men of Columbia, who cheered on their champion.

No evidence suggests that Alice attended. Perhaps Charley's status as only a junior member did not allow him to invite a guest. Perhaps Alice could not bear the thought of being in such an upper-society venue where people might stare, point, and whisper about her. The public humiliation over these last few months had gutted her. Watching her underdog son compete against the American champion only promised to spike her anxiety.

Charley grappled with his usual pre-race jitters, which twisted his stomach and made him feel sick. Otto Wahle, Lou Handley, Dave Bratton, and the rest of his teammates were all counting on him. Wahle preached that the best swimming was subconscious. Once you started thinking or worrying about the performance, it became mechanical and less fluid, slowing you down.

As the starter called the pair of them to the pool's edge, the natatorium erupted in applause that seemed largely directed toward the champion. The older, stronger collegian stood alongside the high schooler with his defined muscles mocking Charley's still maturing frame.

"Ready!" The starter raised his hand, holding a pistol.

The eighteen-year-old filled his lungs. Ahead of Charley loomed the longest competitive swim of his life.

The pistol cracked and both men dove.

When Charley's head came out of the water, he heard the cheers in the gallery as he focused on each movement that Wahle had helped him perfect: bent arms overhead; palms down into the water; use the forearm like a paddle; and a strong, even scissor kick. One, two, three . . . one, two, three . . .

Down the first length, the two competitors battled alongside each other. Charley's stroke looked steady and slow, almost too slow. At the turn, Charley counted off a lap, then dug in hard for another length. At some point, he lost track of Spencer's position, unsure if Spencer pulled ahead so far he couldn't see him. For twelve laps he counted, each stroke a plea that he belonged. When he hit the final wall, muscles burning and heart racing, completely out of breath, his eyes lifted out of the water to see who had won.

When he glanced to his side, Spencer was not there. The crowd looked stunned. He looked back and saw Spencer an entire lap behind.

The Winged Footers erupted. Charley looked as shocked as anyone as he watched Columbia's great champion finish a staggering twenty-four seconds later.

The great E. Carroll Schaeffer's American record for the three-hundred-yard distance was four minutes and 0.4 second. Charley had just swum it eleven seconds faster.

A rush of emotions hit him: elation, satisfaction, relief, a sense of the possible. Charley not only shattered the 300-yard record, but along the way he had broken seven other American records from 150 to 275 yards. When he climbed out of the pool, one wonders if his feet even felt the wet tiles as his teammates swarmed him with congratulations and cheers. Sharing the victory with his fellow Winged Footers, especially Dave Bratton and Otto Wahle, filled him with joy. He shook a lot of congratulatory hands, received backslaps, heard a wave of praise like "Well done!" "Great show!" and "Crackerjack swim!" The water polo guys even started calling him by a new nickname: Danny. The only missing voice was his father's.

As the spectators spilled out of the club's archway into the falling snow, they could not stop talking about the upset. One called Charley "a miracle."

The next morning, three New York newspapers posted a short paragraph about Charley's new American records. Page 9 of *The Sun* ran a small article headlined "New Swimming Records—Daniels Sets Up Fresh Figures in Match with Spencer." Page 14 of *The New York Times* ran a brief article headlined "Record Swim at N.Y.A.C.—C. M. Daniels Makes New Tank Figures from 150 to 300 Yards." A tiny article on page 7 of the *New-York Tribune* read, "Tank Records Fall—New York Athletic Club Swimmer Makes Fast Time," then printed his name as "O. W. Daniels." Even Harry LeMoyne's *Boston Globe* ran a blurb on page 2 that read, "Boy Breaks Records," then spelled his name "O. M.

Daniells." Overnight, Charley leaped from the bottom rung of swimmers to the top. Such an accomplishment would take time to sink in.

Alice was so proud she cut out every article that she could get her hands on. For the first time in more than three years, Charley and his mother got to experience a sense of pride.

Across the upper bay in Staten Island, if Tom Daniels read the *New York Times* article, he might have noticed that the *Times* made sure to emphasize that while Charley's record was nice, the three-hundred-yard world record, held by the legendary Australian Dick Cavill, was a whopping fifteen seconds faster.

With the Olympics less than seven months away, Charley's times did not bode well for America's chances. His eight new American records did not measure up against the superior times of Europe and the British Empire. The only swimmer who could give Uncle Sam a fighting chance against the Olympic foreign invasion remained the great Harry LeMoyne—that is, if any foreign champions even bothered to come.

CHARLEY'S SHOCKING UPSET OF Spencer suddenly made him the top contender in the East to challenge the great Harry LeMoyne. And as fate would have it, the New York Athletic Club's watermen planned to renew their heated rivalry with LeMoyne's Brookline Swimming Club on February 27. Last year, LeMoyne had set the American century record by scorching the Winged Footers' fastest short-distance swimmers. This year, as the much-anticipated contest approached, *The Boston Post* touted the upcoming matchup as follows:

> What in all probability will be the most important swimming meet of the year, with the exception of the international events at the St. Louis exposition, will be the annual dual swimming meet between the Brookline Swimming Club and the New York Athletic Club . . .
>
> Probably the event which will occasion the most interest will be the 100-yard match race between the American champion

for the distance, Harry LeMoyne, representing the Brookline club, and Daniels, the New York crack.

Although the Brookline boy holds the low mark for the way, the New Yorker has already swam the distance hazardously close to the record time, and the Gothamites are already loud in their predictions that their representative will lower the colors of the big Brookline collegian.

It is almost certain that the finish in the event will see a new American record for the distance, as it is known that when LeMoyne made the present record he was swimming well within himself, and has even improved greatly since then.

THE UPCOMING CENTURY RACE against LeMoyne turned into the closest thing to a heavyweight prize fight that the small East Coast aquatic community had ever seen.

HARRY LEMOYNE, BROOKLINE SWIMMING CLUB

By 1904, the heavily favored LeMoyne held just about every American swimming record from one hundred yards on down. When he had entered Harvard the previous fall, newspapers had hailed him as one of the greatest natural-born athletes this country had ever produced. Not only was he America's preeminent speed swimmer, but his first semester at Harvard he'd starred on the Crimson's gridiron squad as guard and punter, receiving an honorable mention for football all-American. In the winter, he'd captained Harvard's water polo team. A few days before Charley's record-setting three-hundred-yard victory against Joe Spencer, *The Boston Post* reported that LeMoyne had set a sixteen-pound shot put record with a throw of forty-six feet one inch, beating his nearest rival by eight feet. That spring, he planned to run track for Harvard and that summer compete as an oarsman. And yet despite all these extracurriculars, he still found time to swim competitively. Although a handful of Harvard students had recently started a swim club, they had only a small off-campus apartment pool in which to train and did not compete against any teams outside the Boston area. So on Wednesdays, Harry returned to Brookline to swim for his hometown, where the country's first municipal pool, and one of the biggest, had been established in 1896.

This lanky, Cinderella underdog named Charles Daniels who had come out of nowhere to claim eight American records was now about to face America's undisputed speed king. The match piqued the interests of all East Coast swimming enthusiasts, as well as sportsmen from the rival cities of Boston and New York. Tom Daniels certainly would be watching the results.

For someone as uncomfortable in the spotlight as Charley, this contest could not have rested easy on his nerves. He could not beat LeMoyne's natural athleticism or brute strength. His only chance was to focus on perfecting the finer points, the nuances of competitive swimming.

Beyond power, positioning, and stroke technique, there are other ways a swimmer can gain slight advantages in the water by reducing drag. The initial dive and turns off the wall all affect momentum. As Wahle pointed out, a well-executed wall turn can increase a swimmer's speed from one-fifth to four-fifths of a second over an opponent with faulty execution.

With no standard pool size during that era, shorter pool lengths necessitated more turns to complete the distance, and the more turns a swimmer made, the more speed boosts he gained from thrusting off the wall. Given that none of the strokes of the day could propel a swimmer faster than those first couple yards after a good wall thrust, the more turns off the wall a swimmer made, the faster his time.

Stretching his right arm out in front as he approached the wall, Charley worked on touching his palm just above the waterline, fingers pointing left in the direction he intended to circle. He then needed to twist his body around sharply so that the soles of his feet made contact with the wall a few inches below the surface. His arms then needed to extend forward as his legs straightened out with a snap, shooting him ahead at the push-off. Not until this burst forward slowed was he to take his first stroke, otherwise he was prematurely wasting energy better spent during the necessary stroke phase.

Charley's initial dive also required special attention because this is the fastest a swimmer travels in a race. During this short time, before crashing the water, a swimmer's airborne body encounters the least resistance. Air is more than eight hundred times less dense than water. The more distance one can cover diving through the air, the better. And the shallower a body can hit the water's surface, rather than making a deep plunge that takes more time returning to the surface, the better a body can remain more horizontal, minimizing resistance and reducing drag. However, too shallow a dive and the swimmer can create more frontal waves that push against the body.

Standing on the tank's edge, with his body bent forward ninety degrees at the waist, Charley practiced leaping outward, not down, striking the water with arms, body, and legs in a straight line that entered at such a shallow angle that he sank only inches below the surface. As Wahle pointed out, deep dives kill speed.

In the days leading up to the big race, Charley also became keenly aware that worrying about it was burning more energy than his intense practice sessions in the pool.

ON SATURDAY, FEBRUARY 27, the day's temperature reached a tolerable fifty-one degrees as crowds packed the second- and third-floor galleries overlooking the NYAC tank. Charley stood on the deck's cold wet tiles, his throat dry and face tense, hanging back from the rest of his teammates as he watched the American speed champion walk toward the edge of the pool to kick off the meet with a twenty-five-yard race.

The Greek gods could not have chiseled a more superior-looking athletic specimen than the dark-haired, ruggedly handsome twenty-year-old Harry LeMoyne. Newspapers reported that he stood any-where from six feet one to six feet two, but at that moment he seemed taller. He looked more muscular, too. In his thighs and upper body alone, his splendid physique easily boasted about thirty pounds more muscle than Charley's, and his hands and feet were huge. Though they were only a year apart in age, compared with Charley's boyish 150 pounds, LeMoyne was a strapping man. His exceptional athletic reputation, coupled with that body, made him a frighteningly intimi-dating opponent.

Like Charley, Harry LeMoyne came from a prominent family. His father, McPherson LeMoyne, was a wealthy Boston banker and a big man, with powerful shoulders, who was said to crush walnuts between his thumb and forefinger. They lived in a mansion in Brookline and belonged to the first established country club in the United States, the Country Club of Brookline, founded in 1882. Harry's mother too stood over six feet. Harry's older brother, Charles, was the amateur heavy-weight boxing champion of New England and fought several impres-sive exhibitions with the former middleweight champion of the world Tom Sharkey, and Harry was bigger than Charles. Before entering Harvard, Harry had excelled at the prestigious Stone preparatory school, setting just about every high school record in each sport he played.

As LeMoyne readied for his first battle in a short twenty-five-yard race, Charley watched closely, hoping to pick up any tips—or at least spot kinks in his armor. LeMoyne lined up against the Winged Foot speedsters Charles Ruberl and Joe Ruddy. At the gun, the Bostonian hit the water with a brilliant shallow dive, barely sinking beneath the surface. Its perfection was a rare sight, and Charley watched LeMoyne torpedo the surface farther and faster than Charley ever could. His powerful arms whipped up a froth with a long sweeping trudgen stroke as he tore down the lane and set a new American record. Ruddy and Ruberl, who both swam trudgens, never had a chance—not unless Ruddy put LeMoyne in one of his choke holds and let Ruberl make a mad dash for the finish. As elated teammates congratulated LeMoyne, he appeared bashful, exuding a quiet confidence and modesty, but his understated joy left no doubt that he competed to win. Now that he had warmed up, Harry LeMoyne took a quick breather to ready himself for the main event.

When officials called for the century, Charley had to have faced a moment of self-doubt. He admired the champion. The surreal experience both intimidated and supercharged Charley's competitive spirit. This was the race everyone had come for, and he was part of it.

The four-man field took their positions at the tank's edge, with Charley looking like a nervous sapling alongside LeMoyne's confident oak frame. Charley's teammate George Van Cleaf and another Brookline man rounded out the field.

"Ready!" The timekeeper lifted his pistol.

Charley filled his lungs, trying to maintain focus, his entire body tingling.

"Get set!"

The gun cracked.

Charley's nerves washed away the instant he hit the water and it became all about the race.

LeMoyne's dive was flawless. The Harvardian started fast with a powerful trudgen, each stroke embodying his raw strength and athleticism. The entire first length, he swam with his head facedown in the water, not taking a breath until he reached the other end. Approaching the first wall, Charley hoped to gain some ground off the turn.

LeMoyne touched first, making the turn look easy, fluid. His strong legs pushed off the wall with more power and skill than Charley could muster. Into the second lap, Charley saw LeMoyne's splashes several feet ahead of him. Charley fought to stay close, but by the second turn LeMoyne widened the gap further with another superior turn. Down the third lap it was LeMoyne and Charley, with the reigning speed king hammering out a pace that seemed certain to result in burnout.

Off the last turn, LeMoyne stretched his advantage and Charley tried to respond. With everything he had, as water roared in his ears, Charley battled down the last twenty-five yards, finishing an embarrassing ten feet behind.

Brookline erupted into wild cheers.

No celebration met Charley. There were no hearty backslaps, no congratulatory handshakes or praise. Teammates tried to lift his spirits. But Charley knew he wasn't just beaten; he was outclassed.

The night finished with Charley pitted against LeMoyne as competing anchors in the seven-man relay. When Charley entered the pool, he fought to make up his team's two-foot deficit over the final fifty yards but finished ten feet behind LeMoyne as he heard Brookline's cheers and watched them mob their great champion.

Ten days later, the New Yorkers traveled to Brookline, where Charley challenged LeMoyne in a fifty-yard race and was once again defeated by a record-setting performance. Charley watched his opponent carried off on the shoulders of his teammates as they chanted, "LeMoyne, LeMoyne, LeMoyne!"

ON MONDAY, A LEAP year day, Alice Daniels appeared with her attorney at the county courthouse in Brooklyn for her divorce hearing. Tom's attorney stepped before the bench, but Tom remained a no-show. Alice took the stand to testify. The whole experience was mortifying. She claimed that Tom's affair had been going on for some time before she had any knowledge or suspicion of it. Other than the one time she saw Tom in the street, she had not seen or spoken to him in four years.

The court-appointed referee, who acted as arbitrator, submitted his recommendation to the judge in mid-March to award an interlocutory dissolution of marriage, which required Alice to wait three months before the judge could legally issue a final judgment on June 21. The decree permitted Alice to marry again at any time she saw fit; however, the court proclaimed it unlawful for the adulterer to marry again until Alice was dead. Alice made no request for spousal or child support, probably because she knew she would never see a penny. The referee recommended that Alice receive sole care and custody of Charley until he reached the majority age of twenty-one. Tom's lawyer did not dispute it.

In the section of the newspaper reserved for scandal, *The Brooklyn Daily Eagle* reported,

MARCH 14, 1904

MRS. DANIELS GETS A DECREE.

Justice Dickey today granted an interlocutory decree of divorce to Alice M. Daniels from Thomas P. Daniels, upon the report of Referee Harry R. Lydecker. The custody of the 19-year-old son is given to the wife. The parties were married in 1884 and the plaintiff lives at 53 Washington Square, Manhattan. The allegation in the complaint was that the defendant lived with another woman at Tottenville and Eltingville, Staten Island.

With Alice listed as the one filing for divorce, many would view her as the guilty one. It didn't matter that Tom committed adultery. The public wasn't interested in the courage it took to throw him out. With divorce being so rare, all most people cared about was any little scandalous detail that could make them feel better about their own mundane lives. By listing her address in the article, the newspaper ensured that Alice and Charley would be readily identified by neighbors and receive an appropriate public shaming.

Fortunately for Charley, his name was never specifically listed. Other than his fellow watermen, none of the club's regular members appeared to know about his association with Thomas P. Daniels, and he hoped to keep it that way.

FIVE DAYS AFTER THE papers broadcast the Danielses' divorce and Tom's affair, the Winged Foot hosted the Amateur Athletic Union's annual swimming championships. Club members and others crowded the club's gallery, all under the watchful eye of Jim Sullivan.

With LeMoyne the clear favorite to represent America in the

Olympic sprints, Charley's chance to make the third Olympiad lay in the mid-distances, even though his heart never left the century. He competed in a 500-yard race, the longest distance of his young career, and broke four more American records. However, the 500-yard world record held by England's David "Boy" Billington was a whopping twenty-seven seconds faster. Australia's Dick Cavill beat Charley's 440-yard record by more than half a minute. Even Charley's 220-yard record was twenty seconds slower than Cavill's.

Reporters who watched Charley's seemingly effortless trudgen stroke asked him if he could exert himself further.

"The truth of the matter is that I swim just as fast as I can," he explained, "but my stroke does not seem to give the impression." With the Olympics quickly approaching, American swimmers were clearly not yet ready for a confrontation with the mighty Europeans.

England still remained unresponsive as to the St. Louis Olympic Committee's invitation. According to a report in *The New York Times,* however, the former British colony of Australia—only recently gaining self-governance as a dominion of the empire—sent Jim Sullivan word from the president of its Amateur Athletic Union that they were eager to raise funds to send four men to St. Louis—one being a swimmer. The *Times* speculated that the swimmer in question was the current century record holder, Dick Cavill, with his mysterious crawl stroke. However, until the Australians raised funds, such rhetoric was meaningless.

As for France, Sullivan had heard nothing about them sending athletes. Not even from Coubertin. There was also no word from Sullivan's Italian, Swedish, and Danish friends who had joined his failed attempt to start the International Athletic Union.

Charley continued to train and race while also competing on Dwight School's track team. With his daily swimming regimen strengthening his muscles, that season he ran an outstanding half-mile time of two minutes two seconds, prompting a letter from Columbia University's track coach inquiring about his plans for the fall. Charley's mid-distance running also received mention in the papers as being a nice fit for Harvard's track team. Not one college expressed interest in recruiting him for such an obscure sport as swimming.

Despite making two poor turns in a two-hundred-yard race, he set a new American record for that distance. Still, he longed to beat LeMoyne and continued to work hard on his short-distance fundamentals.

Wahle offered guidance, but questions from Charley sometimes fell on deaf ears—quite literally. Wahle had had a serious mastoid operation as a young man that had damaged his hearing. In the summer, when Wahle ventured to the New York beaches, he often swam past the waves and just kept on going. He was such a powerful swimmer that he felt confident going out quite far, but it would upset the lifeguards, prompting them to blow their whistles. Wahle could not hear them. Invariably, the guards would launch a boat and row until they caught up to him and turned him back.

ON A RAINY SATURDAY in early April, Charley had the opportunity to invite his mother to the club's fifty-third Ladies' Day, where she could enjoy the New York society that she had been denied. From late morning until 6:00 P.M., Alice could dine with other members' female guests and wander freely throughout the club, taking in the entertaining athletic exhibitions. She could watch Charley perform in the swimming program and enjoy the way he was featured as a kind of amphibious matinee idol. The event offered a taste of Alice's old life. But the disgrace of Tom Daniels still seemed too much to bear, especially at a distinguished event where she could be identified and shamed. Not to mention, it was indecent to scandalize proper ladies with the presence of a divorcée. She also risked casting a negative cloud over Charley that could jeopardize his situation. There was no evidence that Alice attended.

In the century race that day, Charley defeated the watermen from Columbia and Yale in a fast 63.6 seconds—2 seconds shy of LeMoyne's record.

The next morning, Alice riffled through the newspaper to cut out the article about Charley's victory. It was one of the few things in her bleak life that gave her joy.

———

IN MAY, AT A swimming exhibition to kick off the opening of a new free public swimming pool in Jersey City, Charley gave his mother another headline to clip when he smashed the West Coast's J. Scott Leary's 110-yard American record with a seventy-second time. Even though LeMoyne would still beat Charley with his turns, in an open-water straightaway Charley might give the Harvard flier a good fight come summer. However, when the college finished that June, America's only hope against the Europeans went missing.

Newspapers reported that the great Harry LeMoyne had been running into trouble. They published articles claiming that he was on academic probation for failing his midterm examinations. The chairman of Harvard's athletic committee denied any such probation, other than noting a misdemeanor for "an act of boyish indiscretion." However, it was later confirmed that LeMoyne had failed to pass his examinations in the spring for entrance into Harvard's sophomore class. Boston newspapers reported that his instructors considered him a bright pupil but said that he failed to take his studies seriously. The rigorous demands of playing football and water polo, swimming year-round, and then putting in a hard two-month season with the track team did not help his grades. If LeMoyne returned to Cambridge that fall, he would be on probation, having to repeat his freshman courses, which made him ineligible to join the football team that season.

Not only was Harry LeMoyne a no-show for the NYAC's regular summer swimming contests off Travers Island, but he vanished from civilization. Rumors circulated that he had retreated north where his French Canadian family had property in a northeastern frontier village of Labrador. In letters to friends in Boston, he reported that he weighed 205 pounds and was in splendid condition. To the swimming world's relief, *The Boston Globe* eventually reported that LeMoyne intended to return in time to compete at the Olympic Games in St. Louis.

In truth, Harry had skipped town to give himself a break from the stress of his academic troubles and took a summer job helping pilot lake steamers in Bay St. Lawrence, just as his ancestors had done for the past two hundred years. He lived on Crane Island at his family's manor house where generations of LeMoynes had grown up, including his father. Harry loved to dive in and battle the wash as he drafted off the sides of schooners. This clear open water is where he had loved to swim since he was six years old. Each summer, he perfected his skills by diving off the tugs in the St. Lawrence and swimming alongside, using the drag of the boat to make it more challenging. For Harry, it was pure fun and a good place to clear his head before the Olympics.

The upcoming Olympiad offered the perfect showcase for someone like the great Harry LeMoyne to shock the world with an American victory. Brookline offered to pay his way to St. Louis, where a swimming victory would not only bring the club great honors but finally inspire Americans to take up the aquatic activity, with the added benefit of saving lives. Unfortunately, the Olympics did not come soon enough.

NEWSPAPERS CALLED IT A "spectacle of horror." What began under a picture-perfect, sunny blue sky on Wednesday, June 15, would send shock waves across the country. That morning, the men of Kleindeutschland—Manhattan's Little Germany—bade goodbye to their families before heading to work, not realizing that for many it would be the last time they saw their loved ones. A few hours later, when the grand side-wheel steamship carrying more than a thousand of their wives and children for a church picnic burst into flames, the ability to swim suddenly mattered, and none of them knew how.

The few lifeboats on board the burning *General Slocum* were wired in place and unable to be lowered. The life jackets strapped to the ceiling of the ship's deck were out of reach for many of the women and children. Those who managed to grab them discovered most were so rotten they fell apart in their hands. The few life vests good enough to use were filled with nothing but pulverized cork that quickly absorbed water and sank into the East River.

The *Chicago Tribune* reported, "Mothers hugging their children to their breasts in love and terror were forced to choose between certain death in the flames and almost equally certain death in the water.

Some, made frantic by their sudden peril, threw their babes into the whirling waters . . . hoping doubtless for improbable rescue."

By the time the blazing steamer finally grounded sideways about twenty feet from North Brother Island, hundreds of bodies were floating in the water. Over the next twenty-four hours, bodies kept washing ashore. Some of the dead mothers still clutched their drowned children. Entire families were wiped out, fathers left alone to grieve. There was not a house in Little Germany that was not in deep mourning. The final death toll totaled 1,021, most of them women and children. A thousand lives that could have been saved had these victims known how to swim no more than fifty yards to shore.

It would be the worst disaster in the history of New York City for the next hundred years and a wake-up call to the nation. "Learn to swim" became the message to America, echoed by an editorial in the *New-York Daily Tribune* that urged, "That should be the resolve of every intelligent woman who does not already know how, upon reading the pitiful story of how woman after woman on that fateful June 15 was drowned within a few feet of the shore, in a few feet of water. The ability to swim a few strokes or even to keep themselves afloat for a few minutes would have saved their lives."

The question remained: How do women learn to swim when the cumbersome swimming gowns that Victorian modesty required them to wear were just as likely to drown them?

THE NEXT DAY, WHILE hundreds of the *Slocum* dead were still washing ashore and the men of Kleindeutschland wept for the loss of their wives and children, Tom Daniels reappeared in New York City at 141 Broadway, just a few blocks from his former Wall Street office. Dressed to impress, he strutted into the office of Alice's divorce attorney and collected a copy of the judge's interlocutory decree with, one imagines, a wink and a smile. At the time, Tom had a new pretty young girl on his arm named Lydia Sisson whom he introduced as his "fiancée."

Tom Daniels might have evaded jail time, but New York society cast its own judgment. Even if he could have afforded it, he could no longer dine in favorite restaurants without risking scorn or judgment.

Familiar social circles had become unwelcoming. Civil suits were still being filed against Tom Daniels for money owed. Federal authorities continued to watch his every move. He could no longer use his once impeccable family name to gain access to the pocketbooks of New York's wealthy. Ostracized socially and professionally, Tom couldn't return to business as usual.

A few days later, on Sunday, June 19, as New York schools kicked off a week of commencement festivities, marking Charley's graduation from Dwight, Alice made note of her last legal wedding anniversary. Twenty years earlier, she had walked down the aisle full of innocence and hope, with her father at her side and brother Fred as an usher. The day was made all the more somber by the nearly one hundred funerals across the city for victims of the *Slocum*. The horse-drawn processions blocked many of the city's streets, and in some cases two and even three hearses bore away the dead of a single family.

Two days later, the New York Supreme Court finalized the Danielses' divorce with a certified decree that forbade Tom to remarry. Alice was officially a divorcée. An affront to the sacred institution of marriage. The woman who had aspired to live a life of integrity and giving to others now broke the wedding vow she had taken before God, a choice that many society advice givers viewed as selfish. Tom, on the other hand, had no intention of being suppressed by the bench where for twenty-eight years his father had adjudicated. The very next day, he crossed the bay to Hasbrouck Heights and under the laws of the good state of New Jersey tied the knot with Lydia.

While Alice and Charley were forced to bear the stigma inflicted by Tom, he escaped nine hundred miles west to Milwaukee and assumed an alias, wiping away his past troubles back east, as well as his previous family. As far as his new community was concerned, he was Tom Cameron, an upstanding, trustworthy married man who ran a successful banking business in their city and had a beautiful young wife. A man to be envied and respected.

Now that Tom no longer lived in New York, the chance of Charley ever getting the closure or acceptance he needed seemed slim. There is no evidence that Tom showed up at Charley's twenty-five-student graduation or made any effort to say goodbye before he left. No evidence that he acknowledged Charley's accomplishments in swimming. Why would he? Alice and Charley were both liabilities, remnants of an incriminating past that had nothing to offer or benefit him. Even though his son was on the verge of competing in the third Olympiad, no one really knew what that meant. The Games were still an unproven enterprise with an uncertain future. Besides, there was only one American swimmer who had a prayer of not embarrassing himself if the Europeans decided to compete, and that was Harry LeMoyne. Charley couldn't even beat him, and Tom cared to associate only with winners.

What made it even sadder was that Tom knew the pain of being abandoned by a parent. He knew the need every boy has to be accepted by his father, which made his actions all the more cruel. Tom was five years old when the typhoid that took his mother's life caused his father to bury his grief deep in work, becoming physically and emotionally remote to his son. Even on their few short family vacations, the Honorable Judge Daniels busied himself by writing fifty-page briefs. The hard work that had saved the judge when he was orphaned as a boy was the only way he knew to survive the death of his wife. And so he turned over Tom's upbringing to a nanny at a time when nannies were hired not for their love and affection but to discipline children no matter what methods were used to accomplish it. And what did Tom do but repeat the only pattern he knew, by shutting the door on the needs of his son.

PART THREE

CRAWLING ON WATER

THE LOUISIANA PURCHASE
EXPOSITION, ST. LOUIS,
OPENING DAY, APRIL 30, 1904

11.

AMERICA'S FIRST
OLYMPICS

—

1904

L ONDON'S *DAILY NEWS* CALLED THE ST. LOUIS FAIR'S OPENING A "brilliant ceremony." On the morning of April 30, 1904, trains from around the country pulled into America's largest railroad terminal, dumping hundreds of people into St. Louis Union Station's midway every ten minutes. Close to a hundred thousand people passed through the terminal that day. By one o'clock, under sunny skies and a warm spring breeze, a sea of more than 200,000 people, the men in suits and straw boaters and the women in long dresses and big hats, gathered at the western edge of America's fourth-largest metropolis to behold a magical city of dreams. The legendary bandleader John Philip Sousa conducted his rousing patriotic march "The Stars and Stripes Forever." The fair's president, David Francis, and the U.S. secretary of war, William Howard Taft, gave inspiring speeches. Then, a thousand miles away in the White House's newly constructed West Wing, President Teddy Roosevelt pressed a golden telegraph key that flashed an electric current, triggering the fair's hundred cascades and fountains to bubble to life. The largest world's fair in history was declared open, and its boldness reflected America's ambition to step onto the international stage as a leader.

Over the next seven months, twenty million people would pour through the gates of this glorious white city that remained in a constant state of celebration. The fair captured the country's sense of pride, confidence, and optimism about what lay ahead. Visitors would stroll down the wide, crowded carnivalesque street of the Pike with barkers shouting through megaphones, surrounded by nearby screams of delight and laughter, by the smell of barbecue and sweets, and by the beat of a hot, new, peppy "ragged" piano rhythm that made listeners feel a kind of swing and musical looseness that threatened Victorian restraint. They called it ragtime. Considered the first distinctly American music to transcend all races, it rose from the African American community, rebelling against the stuffy opera and classical music of old Europe, conveying a new, modern energy.

No one who entered the fair's gates had ever beheld such wonders on this massive a scale, nor had most ever seen so many people in one place. Visitors called the fair "indescribably grand." With more than fifty different amusements along the mile-long Pike, for an extra ten to fifty cents each, one could take a trip to the North Pole, travel in a submarine to Paris, visit replicas of the Taj Mahal and Blarney Castle, explore the streets of Morocco and the walled city of Jerusalem, ride an elephant, sip tea with geishas, visit a Chinese temple, experience the simulated horrors of the Galveston Flood, travel back in time to watch an ancient Roman gladiatorial spectacle that featured two hundred persons and forty animals (including lions, tigers, and leopards), then have lunch in a German castle in the shadow of a hundred-foot-high replica of the snowcapped Tyrolean Alps. For another fifty cents, one could experience the view of a lifetime atop the tallest Ferris wheel ever built, gazing out at what seemed like the entire world.

Ten colossal exhibit-themed white palaces with names like the Palace of Electricity and the Palace of Transportation, each with lofty colonnades and ornate architecture, covered five million square feet of exhibit space. Sixty-two countries and forty-three of the then forty-five states had their own exhibit buildings, giving many visitors their first real sense of the vast diversity of the country and the world at large. They could marvel at the wizardry of wireless radio, motion pictures, X-rays, sound recordings, and air-conditioning. Fairgoers could witness airships trying to break new ground in manned flight and at night behold the not-to-be-missed spectacular of electricity, when the palaces and cascades were illuminated with more than a million lights.

The fair was a snapshot of the era, embodying both the greatness of mankind and the uglier side of humanity. Its popular anthropological exhibits would shock today's viewers. With social Darwinism all the rage and the Victorian practice of defining people by class and race alive and well, people from outside the so-called civilized world were paid to live in replicas of their native villages, offering fairgoers a rare glimpse into what they insensitively called "primitive societies." These exhibits mimicked the popular "human zoos" that had been featured in previous world's fairs and touring shows across Europe and America. The president of the American Anthropological Association even hoped to bolster his fledgling field—which had yet to be seen as a serious scientific discipline—by working with the fair's Department of Physical Culture to tie into the rising popularity of sports. Held in the main stadium was a two-day event called the "anthropological athletic meet" pitting Filipinos, Native Americans, and so-called "primitive" peoples working at the fair against each other for the professed purpose of studying the natural ability of these untrained "savages." The afternoon contests that included running, jumping, archery, baseball throwing, and pole climbing were not well attended. And despite David Francis wanting the fair to be enjoyed by people of all races, not all of the vendors and staff promoted that same agenda.

The fair's global kaleidoscope of cultures and inventions invited twentieth-century America to break from the Victorian ethos and create its own identity. Nowhere was this better illustrated than in the fair's culinary offerings, which gave birth to a distinctly American cuisine. For the first time, the mass public tasted hamburgers, hot dogs, and George French's yellow mustard; drank iced tea and Dr Pepper; sampled puffed rice cereal, peanut butter, and Jell-O; and delighted at one dentist's sugar-spun creation "Fairy Floss" (later called cotton candy) and a waffle vendor's novel ice cream cone. "The real legacy of the fair," the food historian Robert Moss wrote, "is that, for a few brief months in a single place, it captured an entire culture of eating that was being remade for the modern world."

Jim Sullivan set out to do the same with the Olympic Games.

———

THE AMERICAN PRESS HIGHLIGHTED the name "Olympic" with full-page articles and significant coverage. They ran headlines like "Modern Olympic Games to Outrival Originals" and "World's Fair Meet Will Be the Best Ever Held—Olympic Games Arranged on Lines Never Heard of in This Country." They reported on the construction progress of the fair's new state-of-the-art stadium and gymnasium—an Olympic first—fully outfitted, of course, with top-of-the-line sporting equipment from A. G. Spalding & Bros. Reporters touted what would be the Olympics' first modern-day cinder track, stretching one-third of a mile, proclaiming it "the fastest track in America." The athletic field was described as the most perfect ever built. Some articles claimed the stadium held fifteen thousand spectators, others more accurately stated twenty-five thousand, and Jim Sullivan proclaimed thirty-five thousand. They wrote about the country's record-setting amateur athletes who planned to compete against the best in the world. Boasted about the medals and handsome silver cups to be presented to individual winners. Reported on grassroots fundraising efforts in towns across the country to send local YMCA star athletes to the Games. From coast to coast, small articles captured the send-off of hometown Olympians as they boarded trains for St. Louis. But as for finding lodging once they arrived, the athletes were left to their own devices.

The concept of an Olympic village had yet to be conceived. Some athletes stayed in the limited housing on Washington University's campus or at the Missouri Athletic Club. Others rented rooms at boardinghouses, at hotels, or from St. Louisans who opened their homes during the fair. For $1.50 to $7.00 per night, athletes could stay at the world's largest hotel, the Inside Inn, the only lodging inside the fairgrounds, offering more than twenty-two hundred rooms and a restaurant that seated twenty-five hundred guests.

Athletes could train at the fair's stadium or gymnasium. If they belonged to a recognized club, the Missouri Athletic Club offered reciprocal accommodations. For gymnasts, the local German turn-verein societies operated practice facilities. As for the Games themselves, Jim Sullivan set out to make the events easier for spectators to follow in ways that seem commonplace today but back then were innovations.

Organizers placed signage on the field to mark the individual field events. Sullivan then initiated the use of white chalk lines to illustrate incremental distances so spectators could better follow throws in discus, javelin, and the hammer. He instigated the Olympics' first stadium announcer to call out times and performance results. "In a word," wrote the Olympic historian Charles J. P. Lucas, "the field arrangements and acoustics at the Olympic Games of 1904 were a revelation to Americans themselves." Then Sullivan and the St. Louis Olympic Committee initiated one of the greatest contributions to the Olympic legacy. While the victors in Athens had received silver and copper medals, and in Paris, silver, bronze, and a hodgepodge of other awards, St. Louis would introduce the gold medal.

Like the medals in Athens, its size was not much bigger than a silver dollar, one and a half inches in diameter. Designed and minted by Dièges & Clust of New York, the medal was inscribed "Olympiad 1904" on the front, with a depiction of a victorious athlete in a loincloth holding a wreath in front of the Acropolis. The back pictured a large standing Nike, the goddess of victory, and a small bust of Zeus, engraved with the event's name and "UNIVERSAL EXPOSITION, ST. LOUIS U.S.A." The medal was attached to a blue, white, red, and gold ribbon with a silver clasp engraved with "1904, Universal Exposition, Olympic Games, St. Louis." And it would be presented in a leather case, gilt stamped on the top with the legend "Medal for Olympic Games, Universal Exposition, St. Louis U.S.A., F. J. V. Skiff, Dir. of Exhibits, Jas. E. Sullivan, Chief."

For the first time, athletes finishing first, second, and third place would receive gold, silver, and bronze, forged entirely of the metal each represented. But the rather significant question remained: Which foreign champions, if any, were coming?

CHARLEY SPENT THE EARLY summer of 1904 with his mother at Rockaway Beach, the last vacation spot they had stayed at with his father. Each afternoon, he swam in the ocean, working hard to make the

Winged Foot's Olympic team. In between, he often stood on the sand and looked out at the ocean where he had watched his father swim half a mile out to sea and back.

One day, while he was on the beach staring off at sea, he overheard two bathers talking about him as they approached the surf.

"I see that fellow here every time I go in bathing," said one of them, "but I never yet saw him in the water. I'll bet you the dinners he couldn't keep his head up if he did go in."

Charley couldn't resist. He rushed into the water and swam with the speed of a shark out and around the farthest float, emulating his father's old feat. As he came ashore, he passed the same pair, standing in knee-high surf, gazing at him with dropped jaws.

Charley's weekly mid-distance practice routine alternated between swimming a relaxed half mile on one day and then a fifty-yard sprint on the next. Not until about two days from a contest did he swim the race's full distance as fast as he could. If he was training for a shorter race, he alternated between swimming about two or three hundred yards very slowly one day, and the next day sprinting twenty-five yards two or three times. This way he would not make his muscles sore by overtaxing them.

Sullivan had released his schedule of the stadium's track-and-field contests, designating the week of August 29 to September 3 as the third Olympiad. The other Olympic championships were left to each sport's individual committees to schedule, and Sullivan did not care whether they occurred during the specified dates for the Olympic Games or not. Track and field was the only thing that mattered to him. He had little interest in the swimming contests, which were scheduled over three days starting on Labor Day, September 5, two days after the official Olympics ended. If the international swimming championships at Buffalo's 1901 Pan-American Exposition offered any barometer, the three-day contests would be lucky to draw as many spectators as ducks around the lake.

Two weeks before the Games, Charley competed for the 100-yard Sackett Cup title in Philadelphia's Schuylkill River and set a new open-water American record of 62.8 seconds. The next Saturday, at Travers Island, with LeMoyne still a no-show, Charley broke the 110-yard American open-water record in 77 seconds.

Newspapers reassured the public that the country's outstanding all-around athlete, Harry LeMoyne, would indeed be in St. Louis to participate in both Olympic track events and swimming. But as the entire East Coast swimming community eagerly awaited his return, astounding reports from the West Coast began raising eyebrows.

Frank Gailey, the Australian who swam for San Francisco's Olympic Club, founded in 1860 as the first athletic club in the country, broke Charley's 220-yard American record by almost 7 seconds. Even more impressive was Gailey's teammate, J. Scott Leary, who reportedly swam the century in a breathtaking 60.2 seconds, over one second faster than LeMoyne. Because only one timekeeper clocked Leary's feat, it remained an unofficial record, but something was happening in San Francisco. Swimmers at the Olympic Club had been gaining unusual increases in speed over the year leading up to the St. Louis Games. Could this be explained by the fact that their coach just happened to be twenty-three-year-old Syd Cavill, the older brother of Australia's speed champion, Dick Cavill, who had shattered the century race's one-minute mark with his mysterious "crawl"?

As Charley prepared to depart for St. Louis, Aunt Flossie came to Rockaway Beach to keep Alice company. Perhaps Alice's battered psyche was too fragile to handle watching Charley perform on such a big stage. Nascent though they were, America's first Olympics were still a grand enough event to unhinge any mother's nerves.

ON SEPTEMBER 3, CHARLEY entered Grand Central Terminal with his fellow Winged Footers and boarded a westbound train that would take him to the new home of his old coach, Alex Meffert. Ever since Meffert had started his swim instructor job in St. Louis, he had developed quite a formidable team of watermen at the Missouri Athletic Club. He invited his former Knickerbockers to make the Missouri Athletic Club their headquarters during the Games, offering Charley the unexpected opportunity to reunite with his first coach and show him that he had indeed "stuck with it."

The water polo team consisted of its captain, Lou Handley, Budd Goodwin, Dave Hesser, Joe Ruddy, James Steen, George Van Cleaf, and Charley's gregarious sponsor, Dave Bratton. Rounding out the Winged Footers' Olympic swim team were Edgar Adams, Otto Wahle, and Charley. Absent was Wahle's fellow Austrian, Charles Ruberl, whose accounting job had kept him from being able to get in proper Olympic shape.

All of the athletes donned the colors and emblems of their club or college. There was no U.S. Olympic team, nor an official Olympic team from any country. Each athlete was sponsored by and competed on behalf of his club. Albert Spalding even donated a handsome two-foot-tall, five-hundred-dollar sterling silver cup to the club that scored the most points during the Olympic Games, which, judging by the void of foreign commitments, would certainly be American.

ENGLAND REMAINED A NO-SHOW. After suppressing the Boer farmers' uprising in their colony of South Africa with 400,000 troops and a scorched-earth policy, its soldiers were currently protecting its Indian borders by stamping out an insurrection in Tibet, pillaging its monasteries, and mowing over Tibetans with superior Western firepower. As one British lieutenant lamented, "I hope I shall never again have to shoot down men walking away."

With its focus on shoring up the empire, Britain did not consider sending its athletes to America a priority. The Paris Games had already left the Brits less than enthusiastic about the modern revival, such that England's powerful Amateur Athletic Association never even bothered creating an Olympic committee. Moreover, its superior swimmers deemed beating the lowly Americans a foregone conclusion. While a few U.K. newspapers devoted a sentence or two of ink to wishful words that England, or at least Australia, might send one swimmer to display its athletes' dominance in the water, it never happened. England's aloof attitude remained: if any Yankee believed himself worthy to swim against England, he could come to London—the center of the swimming universe—and embarrass himself at England's annual aquatic championships. After all, practically all of the world record holders swam for the British Empire. After they had dominated the Paris swimming contests in the river Seine, the London *Guardian* had boasted, "The results have confirmed the general impression that English swimmers are superior to all others." Why would any Englishman waste good money to travel across the Atlantic just to beat subpar Americans? There was no honor in that.

As for other foreign competitors, the Australians' optimism about raising the necessary funding fell far short. Sullivan's friends in Italy, Sweden, and Denmark sent no one. Not even Coubertin's home country of France sent a single athlete. As Charles J. P. Lucas wrote in his 1905 book, *The Olympic Games 1904*, "The French people showed their ingratitude by an entire absence of representation. America made the Paris games a success, and without American entries the second revival of the games would have been a farce."

Perhaps France's absence stemmed from its citizens' lack of enthusiasm for sport. Perhaps politics and petty jealousies within the IOC caused the lack of participation. But surely one reason was Coubertin's and Sullivan's hatred for each other. When Sullivan extended Coubertin a cordial invitation to hold the IOC's annual meeting in St. Louis during the Games, Coubertin declined, opting instead to convene the meeting in London. Three reasons stand out for Coubertin's decision. First, Coubertin had no intention of traveling so far away. Second, by his own words, he was still embarrassed to reveal his IOC to Sullivan. Of its impressive international roster of thirty members, only about six actually cared enough to participate. As Coubertin later recalled in his memoirs, "There would have been six or seven of us round a table prepared for thirty. And people would have said: 'What? So that's the famous IOC that makes so much fuss and trouble!'" However, the third and most compelling reason was that by convening in London, he saw an opportunity to ingratiate himself with the English.

A significant improvement in Anglo-French relationships occurred that April with the signing of the Entente Cordiale between the two governments, marking the end of almost a thousand years of Anglo-French conflict. In the spirit of extending the olive branch, Coubertin had received an invitation to hold the IOC's 1904 meeting at Mansion House, the mayor of London's traditional residence, under the patronage of King Edward VII. The invite offered a chance to finally bestow the incomparable prestige of Old England on his Olympic movement and, as he happily noted, "to add luster to our sessions." Even though the British amateur athletic establishment still had no desire to host the Games, they grew more interested in displaying their supremacy on a global stage and rolled out the red carpet for Coubertin.

In late June, IOC members assembled in London, and taking up a request from the president of Italy's gymnastics clubs, while dismissing a request from the Germans to host the next Olympics in Berlin, they awarded the 1908 Games to Rome. Coubertin estimated at most there would be four or five hundred total competitors and fifteen to twenty thousand spectators who would attend the various events. There would be no grand stadiums, rather smaller venues throughout the city. But the Games would be back in Europe. And England was giving every indication it would participate in 1908. "Now that [the Olympics] had just strengthened its position in Europe," Coubertin wrote, "the IOC wanted to draw as little attention as possible to the weaknesses of the American [Games]." There surely was also a part of him that wanted to see his hated rival fail as badly as Coubertin had in Paris.

However, what the Frenchman overlooked was America's melting pot of immigrants, coupled with the heavy German population in St. Louis with strong ties to the homeland. Germany announced it was coming to compete. As did the Austrians. The Hungarians. The Canadians. The Cubans. The Swiss. Even the Greeks reciprocated the 14 Americans who competed in Athens by presenting the same number of their countrymen to St. Louis. The Irish seemed the most excited about England's absence. For the first time Irish champions could compete under their own flag and not be forced to compete for the empire's. A few Irish expats living in the States competed for their home country. Some European athletes found local sponsorship or came on their own dime. The German team received an invitation from the beer baron Adolphus Busch, the German-born co-founder of St. Louis–based Anheuser-Busch, to stay at his mansion. And although Australia's Amateur Athletic Union failed to send an athlete, an Aussie living in San Francisco, Frank Gailey, who trained under Syd Cavill at the Olympic Club, made the journey with J. Scott Leary to compete. In all, 121 foreigners participated among the 651 Olympians, almost twice as many as in Athens. When it was all said and done, the St. Louis Olympic Games constituted the largest gathering of foreign competitors ever assembled on U.S. soil.

The Germans and Hungarians committed to sending their most powerful watermen, including Germany's most decorated mid-distance champion, Emil Rausch, and Hungary's speed champion, Zoltán Hal-

1904 OLYMPIC GAMES, STANDING HIGH JUMP
WITH RAY EWRY AND FOUR-HUNDRED-METER
HURDLES WITH GEORGE POAGE *(second from right)*

may. Like Wahle, Halmay had distinguished himself as one of the most formidable competitors at the Paris Olympics and now boasted a century time close to sixty seconds. Not even Harry LeMoyne had that type of world-caliber speed.

THE OLYMPIC STADIUM SAT upon Washington University's new hilltop campus at the fair's farthest northwest corner. From the fair's entrance at the Pike, it was a two-mile walk in long dresses or suits. If that sounded too daunting in the sweltering summer heat, three miniature railroads were provided to cover the distance. For those with sixty cents to spare, a rickshaw driver was at their disposal. Carriages pulled by oxen were also available for a fee, as were horse-drawn cabs and giant open-air motorized vehicles that carried more than a dozen people at a time.

Guests walking through the gates received the fair's daily program of events. The schedules also appeared each morning in the city's three major newspapers, which listed the day's sporting contests. Curious spectators could venture down the Pike to discover firsthand what these Olympics were all about. Some of the track-and-field events drew huge crowds, while others had yet to find a large audience.

As in the previous two Olympics, America's track-and-field men dominated. Out of a total of twenty-six contests, thirteen Olympic records and four world records were broken. George Poage, born a hundred miles up the Mississippi River in Hannibal, Missouri, a son of former slaves, ran under the colors of the Milwaukee Athletic Club to become the first African American to compete and medal in the Games, winning bronze in both the two-hundred-yard and the four-hundred-yard hurdles. Tom Kiely, one of Ireland's greatest athletes, refused to take British sponsorship and instead cobbled together his own funding to compete and win the inaugural Olympic decathlon for his home country. Frank Pierce, of the Seneca tribe, became the first Native American to compete in the Games as a marathon runner, paving the way for Jim Thorpe's dominant Olympic performance eight years later. One of the most remarkable athletes, the American gymnast George Eyser, broke barriers for athletes with disabilities by winning six medals (three gold), even though he wore a wooden prosthesis on his amputated left leg.

As with Athens and Paris before, the difficulties of foreign travel meant the host country had a disproportionate number of athletes, leaving certain Olympic events with no foreigners to compete against. But as Jim Sullivan told the press, "The contest also showed that America had developed the ideal athlete, the superior of the best men of other countries. All the important events were won by Americans, and the only foreign athlete who, in my opinion, would have won, is Alfred Shrubb of London. He could have won the long distance events." It was a clear shot at the rest of the British Empire's stable of world-class athletes, daring them to compete. It also showed how unimportant he thought swimming.

1904 OLYMPICS, ST. LOUIS. NYAC SWIMMING
RELAY TEAM FROM LEFT TO RIGHT:
BUDD GOODWIN, CHARLES M. DANIELS,
JOE RUDDY, LOU DE B. HANDLEY.

LIFE SAVING LAKE, SITE OF THE
1904 OLYMPIC SWIMMING EVENTS

The day after track and field ended, the Olympic aquatic events began.

NO ONE KNEW IF any spectators would show up. With the Missouri Athletic Club's basement pool area not big enough to accommodate a large crowd, St. Louis held the Olympic swimming contests in a man-made basin that also served as the fair's U.S. Life Saving exhibit. It was located directly to the west of the fair's most popular attraction, the 264-foot-tall great Observation Wheel, which dominated the western skyline, with its thirty-six school-bus-sized wooden passenger cars that made four revolutions per hour.

Alex Meffert helped arrange the matches, which included freestyle races for distances of 50, 100, 220, 440, 880 yards, and the mile, along with a 100-yard backstroke, as well as the first Olympic race exclusively designated for the breaststroke, the first Olympic relay race, and the inaugural Olympic diving contests. For the races' starting platform, Meffert designed a floating wooden raft buoyed by tin barrels. He set the course distance at 110 yards, with marker buoys along the sides, and constructed the finish line with a horizontal bamboo pole that rested on the water, supported in the middle by a small tin barrel and held on either side by two stakes that rose up from the lake.

On Labor Day, September 5, a clear Monday morning, the first day of Olympic swimming began in the pleasant seventy-degree heat, where a crowd began gathering dressed in their Sunday best. By the 10:00 A.M. race time, onlookers stood on fairgrounds' railcars, sat in the wooden bleachers, and lined several people deep along the water's edge. Newspapers estimated the attendance at eight thousand.

Charley was stunned. It was the biggest swimming crowd any of the U.S. watermen had ever witnessed. The public's interest had been sparked by the tragedy of the *General Slocum* and the growing awareness of swimming as an important lifesaving skill. For the first time, American watermen had a chance to grab the mass public's attention if they could beat some of Europe's top champions.

ZOLTÁN HALMAY, ST. LOUIS, 1904

As officials called for the start of swimming's most prestigious race, the century, there was still no sign of Harry LeMoyne. Something had clearly happened to their great sprinting champion. Without the short-distance swimmers from Britain or Australia, the only European entered was Zoltán Halmay, whose personal best of 60 seconds trumped any American record, including Charley's best time at 62.8 seconds.

TWENTY-THREE-YEAR-OLD HALMAY PROVED AN even more impressive male specimen than Harry LeMoyne. Standing six feet one and a half inches and weighing 180 pounds, he looked carved from steel. He was handsome, with deep-set brown eyes, broad-shouldered, iron-chested, yet still slender. He exuded strength. His neck stretched like a periscope. His muscular arms fanned out with an impressive wingspan. His powerful grasshopper legs stretched forever. When not wearing his swimming tank top and shorts, Halmay dressed straight from the front page of a fashion magazine, in an elegantly fitted suit and an ever-present straw boater that gave him an air of purpose and sophistication. In addition to his attractive features and powerful physique, his amiable and pleasant nature made him a great favorite wherever he appeared. And his shaved head said he meant business.

Born in 1881, Zoltán, at ten years old, moved with his family to Budapest, where he began swimming at a city pool. At age sixteen, he won Hungary's one-mile freestyle championship. By the time he finished high school around age nineteen, he was an all-around athlete, excelling at swimming, water polo, skating, and soccer. In 1900, he won the nationwide Speed Skating Championship in the five thousand meters. That same year, he medaled in three international swimming events at the Paris Games—all second and third place behind the British Empire.

Wahle remembered the Hungarian's impressive medal-winning performances in Paris and undoubtedly told Charley about him. It was rumored that Halmay came from a lot of money that allowed him to devote his life to training and travel, competing in all of the significant meets around Europe. Some newspapers even said Halmay was a count.

Without the great Harry LeMoyne to lead the home team into battle, America's field for the all-important century included five men: the West Coast phenom, J. Scott Leary, who had clocked the fastest indoor American century time at 60.2 seconds, making him America's best chance; the powerful Budd Goodwin; the twenty-three-year-old Chicago speed champion, Dave Hammond; the eighteen-year-old Philadelphia flier, Davey Gaul, who held the fastest American open-water time at fifty yards; and Charley, with his new American open-water century record.*

All five had the same vital objective: to beat Zoltán Halmay. And the enormous home crowd added further motivation—and anxiety.

Officials called the top three finishers from each of the two previous semifinal heats, triggering applause from the thousands of spectators who were eager to see if American swimmers could indeed score their first international victory. Charley had won his semifinal heat not long before in 67.4 seconds. Halmay had won his in an Olympic record time of 66.2 seconds and wasn't even winded.

Located near the U.S. Life Saving's boat slips, the starting pontoon was anchored on the east side of the oval lake. Charley and five other finalists crossed the narrow gangplank to reach the starting deck built of long wooden slats.

To Charley's earlier surprise, the West Coast champion J. Scott Leary walked with a noticeable limp. Leary's left leg looked withered and shorter than his right. Yet here, in the aquatic world, he redefined himself, his disability irrelevant.

As the six young men lined up, the weight caused the pontoon's slats to tilt toward the water. The swimmers' feet gripped the edge, their toes hanging over. Charley took the second spot from the end. Immediately to his right, on the far wing, stood the formidable Zoltán Halmay. To his left crouched J. Scott Leary, with his shorter leg causing an imbalanced left lean in his stance.

---

* Outdoor and indoor records were kept separately because of indoor's advantages. While outdoor was distinguished between swimming in still water versus salt water, the latter being slower due to waves and salt water's denser viscosity, indoor records were distinguished by how many turns one had to make.

1904 OLYMPIC SWIMMING HUNDRED-YARD CENTURY
FINALS, ST. LOUIS. FROM LEFT TO RIGHT: ZOLTÁN
HALMAY, CHARLES M. DANIELS, J. SCOTT LEARY,
DAVE HAMMOND, DAVEY GAUL, AND BUDD GOODWIN.

The smell of algae penetrated Charley's nose as he stared over the
murky green water. For five months, cattle from the fair's livestock exhibits had been wandering over and polluting the lake that was now far
from sanitary, carrying the added risk of catching a mouthful of deadly
bacteria. The officials had moved the bamboo pole to the hundred-yard
finish, where a rowboat of judges and timekeepers floated alongside,
ready to record the results.

Pre-race jitters provoked the six swimmers to peek around at the
competition or scan the crowd for a friendly family face. Charley, following an old habit, might have looked for his father.

Toes clinging tightly to the edge, Charley leaned over the green
water with hands on bent knees, his heart racing. There would be no

walls to worry about, no turns. However, the long open straightaway and the green water's poor visibility made swimming a straight line more challenging.

"Ready!" the official called out.

Halmay craned his neck to look over the field.

"Get set!"

The gun cracked.

As the men's legs pushed off, the pontoon slid backward. Leary's shorter leg caused an unbalanced entry that gave him a poor start, while Charley's shallow dive put him at the head of the pack, with Halmay right behind.

The foul, musty taste of algae filled Charley's mouth as the swimmers tore up the murky lake at a hot pace. Charley worked his scissors, while Halmay employed an unusual technique of letting his legs drag motionless atop the water while his long arms did all the work, a technique it was later said he learned from the Australian Freddie Lane in England. His head buried facedown in the water, the Hungarian did not take a breath during the first half of the race. At the fifty-yard mark, Leary recovered to claim the lead. His legs, like Halmay's, dragged behind him. However, while Halmay's legs remained close together and motionless, Leary's opened wider, vacillating at the surface to balance his body.

For the next twenty-five yards, Charley struggled to catch the San Franciscan and pull farther ahead of Halmay. He could hear and feel Halmay's splashes on his right and Leary's on his left. But the Hungarian, with his long arms and strange new kickless crawl, refused to let up. If anything, Halmay seemed to increase speed, while Leary, who had burned so much energy to come from behind, lost ground.

The last twenty-five yards turned into an all-out fight. Charley and the Hungarian passed Leary. Closing on the finish, Charley gained an edge. Cheers from the American side thundered. An uproar urged Charley to beat the European. His fellow Winged Footers were cheering his nickname: "Go, Danny!" That's when *The St. Louis Republic* reported that in the final ten yards the Hungarian did a "trick."

Most likely the "trick" referred to Halmay's surprise use of his legs, opening them wider and kicking them crawl-style. *The St. Louis Republic* reported that the "trick" produced a speed burst that shot him forward, catching Charley off guard and snatching the gold medal.

The Europeans followed their century victory by crushing the Americans in the mile. The German champion, Emil Rausch, using a powerful sidestroke, set an American record to win gold, the Hungarian Géza Kiss took silver, and the Australian Frank Gailey claimed bronze.

The next day's *St. Louis Post-Dispatch* ran the headline "Foreign Swimmers Take Main Events."

The rout vindicated the British Empire for not bothering to show up. While America just had its first bitter taste of the crawl.

12.

A GAME CHANGER

—

ZOLTÁN HALMAY'S IMPRESSIVE VICTORY LEFT AMERICANS struggling to find an answer to the crawl—and fast. Experts like Otto Wahle, Lou Handley, and Alex Meffert debated its superiority over the trudgen. The Californian J. Scott Leary offered a wealth of knowledge about the stroke, thanks to his training under Syd Cavill, who claimed to have invented this kickless version.

Syd had grown up swimming with his five brothers when Australia was still a British colony. His father ran the ocean baths near Sydney's Lavender Bay Wharf. In Australia, the only instructional materials on the sport were British handbooks that taught the racing sidestroke and trudgen. As Syd recalled the story, he was on his way to America in 1898, when the ship had a stopover in the city of Apia, on the Pacific island of Samoa. There he swam the trudgen against a local woman who gave him the toughest race of his life. She used an unusual technique, "not kicking her legs at all," Syd recalled. He immediately wrote home to his twenty-one-year-old brother, Arthur "Tums" Cavill, telling him how they could swim a faster trudgen with their legs tied than using the underwater scissor kick. That November, Tums challenged Sid Davis, a fast lad from Sydney's suburb of Balmain, to an unusual race. As reported by the Sydney *Referee,* before a very large crowd standing around the dock, Tums bet Davis five pounds that he could beat him over one lap, about thirty-three yards, with his legs tied together. When Tums won by a yard, it created a huge stir. Yet, unlike

Tums and Syd, their fourteen-year-old brother, Dick, remained unconvinced that a kickless stroke was the best approach.

Dick began to reason that every ounce of power, if properly applied, should increase speed; therefore, if doing nothing with your legs propelled one faster through the water than expending energy on a scissor kick, it merely proved the scissor kick was inefficient, and Dick set about trying to create a better one.

Around this time, Alick Wickham, a golden-skinned swimmer who was born in the Solomon Islands in 1886, relocated with his family to Sydney. A popular story about Wickham was that in 1898 he had astonished onlookers during a sixty-six-yard schoolboy race at Sydney's Bronte Baths with his unusual swimming technique. His head held high out of the water, Wickham used a double overarm, with his legs thrashing in a vertical plane, employing a kick that Solomon Islanders had been using for at least half a century. As he swam, an esteemed Sydney baths instructor reportedly shouted, "Look at that kid crawling over the water!"

It is debatable as to who deserved greater credit for introducing the kicking crawl stroke to Australia. Some suggest that Dick Cavill had already developed a similar vertical leg kick consisting largely of splashing, which earned him the nickname Splash. Other evidence suggests that Dick's kick was not perfected until after Wickham's arrival. Both swam at the baths run by Cavill's father, and each watched the other's leg techniques.

Eventually, with the involvement of the upstart Australian swimmer Cecil Healy, the crawl's leg action evolved into one big, pounding kick per each overarm cycle, with legs wide and the lower leg bending back high out of the water almost ninety degrees and crashing down with a huge splash. The opposite arms and legs moved synchronously together; that is, the right arm came up as the left leg went down and vice versa. Soon the top aquatic sprinters and coaches in Australia embraced the new stroke, dubbing it the crawl.

On September 24, 1902, Dick Cavill made history at Hornsey Road Baths in England when he unveiled his improved version to the English swimming establishment and shattered the world's 60-second century record set that July by his fellow Australian Freddie Lane, in a remarkable 58.6 seconds. The English swimming establishment thought Cavill's leg thrashing barbaric.

Back in 1844, the National Swimming Society of England had witnessed a similar "uncivilized" technique used by two Ojibwe who had been brought from the British Canadian territory of Ontario by a promoter of a touring human zoo. The two swimmers, Flying Gull and Tobacco, demonstrated a stroke that British newspapers called "totally un-European," exclaiming, "They lash the water violently with their arms, like the sails of a windmill, and beat downwards with their feet, blowing with force, and forming grotesque antics." The English establishment pitted their top breaststroker against the two Ojibwe. His easy victory over this "uncivilized" style proved the English breaststroke—and the Englishman—superior. Londoners felt equally repulsed by Dick Cavill's crawl. Despite its undeniably fast results, Cavill's inelegant-looking stroke found scant favor among the English establishment, who distanced themselves by dubbing it the Australian crawl. Otto Wahle, however, saw in it the future.

The moment Zoltán Halmay defeated America's fastest sprinters, Wahle finally grasped its working and realized its worth. The trudgen simply could not defeat it in sprints. Whether the crawl could be sustained over greater distances remained to be seen.

THE NEXT MORNING, ANOTHER large crowd watched the European watermen make fools of their American counterparts. First Zoltán Halmay set a new American record in the fifty-yard sprint, defeating J. Scott Leary and Charley, who respectively took silver and bronze. Then the Germans swept the hundred-yard backstroke, beating the three American finalists in another U.S. record-setting time and claiming all three medals. As the second day's contests drew toward a close, hope for a home victory faded.

For the day's last race, four men lined up for the finals of the 220-yard championship. Both Halmay and Leary abstained from the longer distance. The German mid-distance champion, Emil Rausch, took the line, as did the Australian Frank Gailey, who held America's 220-yard indoor record. Two Winged Footers, Edgar Adams and Charley, rounded out the field.

Charley's anxieties had built as the race approached and likely only increased as the four men walked onto the wooden float. Charley took his stance on the edge. In front of him loomed the open lake course—110 yards down, 110 yards back.

Nothing could prepare him for the emotions that pumped through his body as he stepped back onto the Olympic starting line. Nerves rattled all the contestants to some degree—the taste of bile, the queasy stomach, hyperventilation, and the terror of failure.

"On your marks," the official called to take their positions.

"Get set!"

The starting pistol's crack sent Charley flying into the cool, smelly water. Rausch followed, with Gailey third. Spectators watched them plow down the 110-yard course in a swirl of foam with Charley's blond head visibly forging to the front as he reached the pole and headed back. His long tan arms flashed in the sunlight, with the two foreigners battling to overtake him. At the 195-yard mark, Gailey switched back to the crawl. The Australian's legs dragged on the surface. With 25 yards to go, Gailey sped past the German champion, who was employing a powerful sidestroke. Legs dragging, the Australian locked on to Charley, ready to hand America another defeat. The two men pushed each other down the last 10 yards, fighting through the intensifying muscle burn. What happened next shocked everyone.

It was not the thousands of spectators erupting that proved so stunning, nor Charley's teammates' loud hoots of celebration. It was not even the exhilaration of Charley's hand touching the wooden float at the finish and winning U.S. swimming's first Olympic gold medal. What shocked everyone was that Charley's winning time not only broke E. Carroll Schaeffer's American record but broke David "Boy" Billington's English world record by almost two seconds.

Charley's head spun. As he climbed out of the water, his body tingled when he heard his nickname, "Danny!" Excited faces mobbed him with hearty backslaps and praise. He saw the big smiles on Otto Wahle,

Dave Bratton, Lou Handley, and Alex Meffert. His mother would have a great headline tomorrow to lift her spirits. But if Tom Daniels visited St. Louis that summer, there was no evidence he made any effort to see Charley at the Olympics.

The next morning, page 3 of *The New York Times* declared, "World's Record by N.Y.A.C. Swimmer." Page 6 of the *St. Louis Globe-Democrat* went so far as to print a picture of Charley diving off the pontoon with the caption "Daniels of New York makes new world's swimming record." Page 6 of *The San Francisco Call* touted "Daniels' Great Race." *The Daily Gazette* of Lawrence, Kansas, even ran a front-page story with the caption "Daniels a wonderful swimmer." All across North America, from California to New York, throughout the Midwest and South, down to the southern tip of Florida, as far north as Vancouver, Winnipeg, and Montreal, and everywhere in between, newspapers declared that Charles M. Daniels had broken the world record held by England's David "Boy" Billington. Youngsters in small towns like Anaconda, Fall River, Rutland, Oshkosh, Missoula, Tuscumbia, Ogden, and Galena—some who probably didn't even realize that swimming existed as a competitive sport—picked up the local paper and read that an American swimmer, for the first time in history, had slashed a world speed record and his name was Charles Daniels.

When word reached across the Atlantic, the Brits refused to recognize that some lowly American had usurped one of their world records. British newspapers noted that Daniels had merely set an "Olympic" record.

THE THIRD AND FINAL day of the swimming contests began with another rout by the Europeans. The Germans took the top two prizes in the breaststroke, but were caught off guard by a short, blond eighteen-year-old Chicagoan named Henry Jamison "Jam" Handy, who edged out their third swimmer for bronze, even though the fourth-place German, whom Handy described as "a big German beerhorse," kept grabbing Handy's ankle, trying to pull him backward to overtake him. Some of the Winged Footers watching from the dive tower began shouting and pointing at the foul, but no one intervened, other than

Joe Ruddy possibly plotting even more wicked choke holds to inflict upon the Germans when they met in water polo.

After that, three foreign swimmers swept the half mile, with Germany's Emil Rausch breaking the American record by sixteen seconds, Australia's Frank Gailey claiming silver, and Hungary's Géza Kiss taking bronze. Charley again saved the day for America when he beat out Frank Gailey and Charley's Austrian mentor, Otto Wahle, in the quarter-mile race, setting a new American record to win his second gold. After that, there was no more foreign competition.

In Olympic swimming's inaugural relay race, the Hungarians did not have enough men, and the formidable Germans were sadly ruled ineligible because they put forth an all-star team that comprised members from different clubs. It was an unfortunate sign of the times where individuals represented their athletic club first and their country second. The Winged Footers team of Budd Goodwin, Joe Ruddy, Lou Handley, and Charley beat the other clubs' teams to claim Charley's third gold, but without European competition the victory felt second-rate. Later, when the German water polo team discovered the matches would be officiated under America's no-holds-barred rules, they refused to play. Charley cheered on his fellow Winged Footers, who beat the Chicago and St. Louis teams to win gold, but Ruddy was certainly disappointed not to be able to put some choke holds on the Germans.

When it came time to award the medals, the ones handed out to the swimmers were not the special Olympic medals given during the stadium's five-day athletic competitions that Sullivan officially labeled the Olympic Games. Apparently, Sullivan only cared to manufacture enough to cover his favored track-and-field events. The Olympic victors in such a minor sport as swimming were given the standard gold, silver, and bronze medals that were awarded at AAU Championships, engraved with a standing Nike, the winged Greek goddess of victory, and the words "Amateur Athletic Union of the United States," with nothing to distinguish them as Olympic. Nor were any flags raised at the swimming contests to honor the victors, nor their national anthems played. Charley and Zoltán Halmay had congratulated each other like gentlemen, but somewhere, some way, Charley wanted another crack at Halmay's esteemed Olympic century title.

Charley returned from St. Louis with three gold medals, one silver, one bronze, and one world record—the most decorated Olympic swimmer in U.S. history, whatever that accolade in such a "minor" sport was worth. Tom Daniels would certainly have pointed out Charley's failure to beat Zoltán Halmay in the sprints, along with the fact that his world record meant nothing without a formal recognition by England. Even Charley's three gold medals were won against a field that did not include Halmay or the fastest watermen from the British Empire. He had not even beaten the best sprinter in America—Harry LeMoyne—whose reasons for remaining in the Canadian wilderness and missing the St. Louis Olympics had yet to be revealed. And while newspapers across the country unanimously agreed that America's first Games had brought tremendous awareness of the Olympic movement to this side of the Atlantic and elevated their esteem, competitive swimming still had a long way to go.

Fred Wenck, one of the Winged Foot's water polo players, wrote an article summing up the post-Olympic state of American swimming and the enormous mountain that lay in front of them. "For years this country has been beaten in the water by Australians, Hungarians, Austrians, Englishmen, and others, and even at the World's Fair in St. Louis, a German won the half and one-mile American championships, while a Hungarian won the fifty and hundred-yard events, proving that the fastest sprinters as well as distance men belonged not to the United States."

And Wahle too lamented that without the top watermen from England and Australia competing, "the international competition was very inferior, thus robbing the races of a great deal of their importance."

Given that Charley's new world record remained unacknowledged by the English establishment, besides the possibility that the newspaper coverage it received inspired a few American kids to think more about swimming, it was merely a nice victory for the New York Athletic Club in an obscure sport that quickly became yesterday's news. Still, for the first time, Wahle saw that American swimming might have a chance to pull off the impossible.

They would need to overcome a series of obstacles. First, they needed to devise and perfect the most optimal crawl stroke. Next, since the British Empire's watermen refused to come to America, an American champion needed to cross the pond and rip the English century crown right off their head. They would need to do it under the scrutiny of British watches and British officials, breaking their world records in British waters. That would leave the Brits no ability to dispute such an American's claim to the title of "Champion Swimmer of the World." And with the right crawl, Charley might be the American champion to do it. The task would defy all odds. But Wahle saw something revolutionary in the crawl and something special in Charley—if Charley could conquer his own demons.

13.

INTO THE LAIR
OF GIANTS

—

OCTOBER-NOVEMBER 1904

NO MATTER HOW MANY OF CHARLEY'S TRIUMPHANT HEADLINES Alice clipped into her scrapbook, she appeared to still be suffering under the weight of the public humiliation and bleak social prospects that went with being a divorcée. Tom Daniels had taken everything from her: her youth, her marriage, her place in society, her good name and identity, and any chance of returning to Buffalo, the only refuge she knew. She was a lone female pariah in a man's world.

For Alice's sake, and perhaps for the whole family's, Grandmother Meldrum and Aunt Flossie thought it best to get far away from all of the condemning eyes of New York, to a continent that had never heard of Tom Daniels. The last twelve months had brought nothing but more disgrace and humiliation. Even with Charley's success in St. Louis, his fame in swimming's small circles had yet to resonate with the wider public. Even at the New York Athletic Club, Charley told a reporter, not more than twenty men took any interest in swimming, and there still appeared to be no general wish of the public to learn more about it. And the Olympics remained a new concept that Americans were just awakening to. Outside the tiny aquatic world, the shadow of Tom Daniels still kept Charley and Alice in darkness.

During this difficult time, it is not known but likely that Alice suffered serious depression. Just that fall, Grandmother Meldrum's esteemed neighbor Frank Goodyear had suffered a nervous breakdown under the pressures of his vast business empire and embarked on a six-week European rest with his physician. Alice's late father had once done the same. That same remedy offered the perfect escape for a dishonored family. Grandmother Meldrum began making plans to leave on November 5 for a year abroad. She booked passage to London for herself, Aunt Flossie, and Alice and asked Charley to accompany them. Charley was still eager for a match race against Harry LeMoyne, who had yet to resurface. Otto Wahle and Lou Handley wanted Charley to stay in New York and continue his training.

"Nothing worthwhile is accomplished without effort," Handley said. "Real results are attained only through faithful and painstaking work."

Charley still had not managed to beat LeMoyne's century record—let alone the British Empire's—and Cavill's new crawl stroke might be just the answer. Wahle and Handley wanted to spend the winter working with him on the crawl in preparation for the next summer's American championships at Travers Island. Perhaps Charley could enroll at Columbia University that fall. Charley still kept the letter from Columbia's track coach, inviting him to join the team, which Alice had added to her scrapbook, but no college had written to him about his more obscure sport.

While just about every university had a track team, only eleven had swim teams, and most of them were small student-organized clubs without a designated campus pool. After Penn and Columbia became the first to start official teams in 1896 and 1897, Yale and Harvard followed in 1898, then in 1901 Cornell, the University of Chicago, the Armour Institute, and Wisconsin, and finally Princeton, Brown, and Washington University in St. Louis. Vassar Female College had a swim program in 1890, but because Victorian society worried that if competitions became too strenuous, a female's frail constitution could suffer "nervous fatigue," intercollegiate competition among women was forbidden. By 1904, the first intercollegiate swimming league had yet to be formed, and college teams competed against local athletic clubs or amateur teams rather than each other. The personal expense and time required to travel made visiting other colleges impractical.

On October 5, after months of speculation and rumors about the fate of Harry LeMoyne, reports appeared in newspapers from Boston, New York City, Washington, Philadelphia, Buffalo, Pittsburgh, and as far west as Salt Lake City that shocked the sporting world.

Harry had been dealing with more behind closed doors than anyone could have known. He had grown up in a very formal household. His father, McPherson LeMoyne, was a husky Victorian man who was never seen without a coat and tie and adhered to the Puritan belief that athletics were borderline sinful and a waste of time. In *From Harvard to Hagerman,* Myron Finkbeiner's biography of Harry LeMoyne, his father was described as never one to hug or kiss: "Seldom was there an expression or use of the word 'love' from father to children." Harry's older brother, Charles, had graduated from MIT and run off to Idaho, rebelling against McPherson's plans to one day run the family bank. His father never spoke his name again, and now the mantle fell on Harry. Harry's poor academic performance at Harvard did not sit well with McPherson, who was furious over his son's athletic frivolities and lack of academic focus. Not wanting to stoke his father's anger with more athletic obligations, Harry had escaped to Labrador that summer, hoping the time away would cool his father's ire by the time the Olympics started.

Like Charley, Harry was happiest when he was outdoors, hunting or trapping in the woods, playing sports, and swimming. He hated crowds and big cities. School was never for him. Nor was running a bank. When Harry told his father that he wanted to defer his sophomore year at Harvard to spend a year working on his older brother's sheep ranch in Idaho, McPherson threatened to disown him. If Harry went to Idaho, he would be dead to him, just like his older brother.

Harry did not return to Brookline until the first week of October. Shortly after his arrival, he told an inquiring local reporter that he was walking away from Harvard, from college athletics, and from fame and glory to spend his life under a big wide-open Idaho sky. The New York *Sun* wrote that his "loss will be severely felt," and McPherson LeMoyne forbade anyone to speak Harry's name in his presence.

Harry never again saw his father. Yet he did not regret his decision.

Harry would remain in Hagerman, Idaho, start a family, live until the age of ninety-nine, and die with one lament—passing up the 1904 Olympic Games.

The idea of chucking it all to disappear into the outdoors certainly appealed to Charley. He was as much a child of nature as LeMoyne. But he and Wahle had started something that remained unfinished. The water called to him as it did to a newly hatched sea turtle. Charley would need to find another way to break from LeMoyne's enormous shadow.

As Harry LeMoyne boarded a train headed west, Charley prepared to sail in the opposite direction. Any aspirations he had for college no longer mattered. He was the man of the house now. Alice had helped him through some of his anxiety by taking him to his first swimming lessons and exposing him to the great outdoors. Now it was his turn to see her through this dark time.

With the Olympics behind him and no Harry LeMoyne, Charley needed to find another challenge to immerse himself in or risk granting his mind idle time to ruminate over his internal demons. As President Teddy Roosevelt said about his depression, "Black care rarely sits behind a rider whose pace is fast enough." And Charley wanted to keep the demons that chased him well in his wake.

ON NOVEMBER 5, A chilly gray Saturday morning that at any moment threatened to pour, Charley arrived by carriage at Pier 39 on the Hudson, or what some old New Yorkers still called the North River. Seagulls squawked overhead. The river's cross breezes brought a reprieve from the city's ever-present stink of garbage and horse manure, with a musty, earthy, fishy-smelling wind laced with sea salt. Charley had with him a steamer trunk stuffed with a year's worth of clothes and personal effects. Accompanying his grandmother, aunt, and mother, he was warmed by the excitement of his first ocean excursion as he looked up at his home for the next ten days. They did not book passage on one of the more popular, luxurious liners like the RMS *Baltic* where they were more likely to sail with members of New York society who could associate them with Tom Daniels. As an added precaution, forty-year-old Alice sailed under her maiden name with her sister Flossie—two spinster sisters traveling together—while Charley accompanied Grandma Meldrum, who registered herself as "Anna Daniels," in order to distance their association with Alice and Flossie. The ruse seemed intended to keep Alice from being identified as Charley's mother and a divorcée—a label she couldn't bear. They hoped the charade would keep the other sixty-two first-class passengers from asking too many questions over the next ten days at sea.

They checked in their trunks with one of the ship's porters and walked up the ramp of the large transatlantic steamship, the *Minnehaha*, with its six-hundred-foot-long black steel hull, four masts, and a singular red smokestack that would transport them to the biggest city in the world and the birthplace of competitive swimming. Charley had heard Wahle's stories about London's glorious nautical palaces and their superior watermen and now would see them for himself.

Around 3:30, the *Minnehaha*'s loud foghorn blew. Passengers crowded against the railings, waving to loved ones as the ocean liner pulled away from the pier. Soon the nineteen-year-old Statue of Liberty saw them off, triumphantly holding her torch as if raised to bid them Godspeed. Through the mist, Charley soaked up his last views of lower Manhattan.

While passengers waved farewell to America, Charley's goodbyes with his Winged Foot teammates were behind him. He portrayed his extended leave as an opportunity to take on Britain's top swimmers. America's David to Europe's Goliath—a Jack the Giant Killer of sorts—which did not sit well with Wahle. The Austrian wanted him to stay with the club and work on the crawl and not be so eager to rush into the lion's den. The pressure of swimming in England would prove unlike anything Charley had yet experienced, especially if he were to come up against the new stroke that he was still trying to perfect. His failure would set America back even further—not to mention what it would do to Charley's confidence and reputation. It was naïve and foolhardy and too soon. And Wahle wasted no time looking to train a new American champion to replace him. Someone willing to take up the crawl and not run away on some half-baked crusade that promised to destroy everything they had built the past year. It was as if Charley were now dead to him. Judging by Wahle's subsequent actions, one doubts Charley divulged the real motivation behind his departure or shared his concerns about his mother. Charley was always a man of few words and avoided talking about his troubled personal life.

As Charley departed, *The New York Times* proclaimed, "Daniels will at once challenge Billington and Derbyshire, the leading English tank swimmers, and will meet them or any others in as many matches as may be arranged." The December issue of the *New York Athletic Club Journal*, the club's monthly magazine, published a similar rationale for Charley's long absence abroad.

London smelled a lot like New York with more than six million residents and just as many horses. The capital of the greatest empire in the world was crowded, vast, and a panorama of abject poverty and unrivaled displays of wealth and ostentation, with the occasional surprising roar of an underground electric train. The four of them stayed at London's luxurious eight-hundred-room Hotel Cecil, located between the Strand and the river Thames, where they could look west along the river and see the distant spires of Westminster and the tower of Big Ben and look east to see the dome of St. Paul's.

They had barely been there a week when word came from back home that had caused the New York Athletic Club to lower its white rooftop flag to half-mast. Charley's sponsor and friend, Dave Bratton, had died. The news was shocking. Apparently, Dave had been on a business trip in Chicago when he fell ill with typhoid, leaving behind a widow, two young children, and endless beloved friends. His body was transported to his home in New Jersey, where a funeral service was held on December 6 before a big crowd of heartbroken friends and Winged Footers. The next day, per Dave's last wishes, his cremated remains were scattered in East Hampton's Fresh Pond, one of his beloved swimming holes.

Dave's death hit Charley hard. Like every prominent male role model in his life, he was now gone. Charley once again found himself very much alone against the world—or, more precisely, the British Empire.

THE SUPERIORITY OF ENGLAND'S swimming culture surpassed Charley's highest expectations. There weren't just infinitely more public pools than in America; each facility was a spectacular water temple. Many pools were housed in huge atriums with glass ceilings or enormous skylights, the likes of which Charley had never seen. It made the New York Athletic Club's basement tank seem like a flooded mine shaft. Just about every community in London enjoyed its own facility that housed not just one but multiple indoor pools and baths.

In districts where people were not of the same social plane, the local bathhouse often offered first- and second-class pools. According to *Modern Sanitation*, the difference was not so much in the quality of the facility as in the admission price. As a rule, though, the first-class swimming bath was typically larger than the second-class tank. When demand for pools increased among the growing number of local swim clubs, all of the first-class baths were supplied with diving boards, water chutes, and water polo equipment. Charley saw firsthand how far swimming in America lagged compared with the wonderful popularity swimming enjoyed in England.

Shortly after his arrival, a reporter from *The Sportsman* of London interviewed him. "According to Daniels," the article stated, "swimming in America is not a great sport." Charley pointed out to the reporter that only three first-class baths existed in all of New York, and only two of them were open to the public. He further noted that the public baths' expensive half-dollar admission prohibited most working-class New Yorkers from going and kept the sport from becoming popular, and there appeared to be absolutely no national impetus to encourage Americans to become interested. The country was professional baseball and college football mad. The lone glimmer of encouragement had occurred during the Olympic swimming contests in St. Louis, which drew a surprising crowd of eight thousand.

Charley concluded the interview by saying he hoped to see swimming wake up in America and then praised Harry LeMoyne for pushing the American century record to 61 seconds. Of course, that time already seemed an ocean behind the world record of 58 seconds now posted by the British Empire's Dick Cavill and Cecil Healy.

UNFORTUNATELY FOR CHARLEY, HIS late-November arrival in London was poorly timed. The swimming season had ended. If he wanted a special out-of-season match race with Derbyshire, Jarvis, or Billington, he needed to find an English promoter to arrange it.

The most well-connected promoter was William Henry, the co-founder and honorary secretary of the esteemed Royal Life Saving Society. An Olympic medalist on Britain's victorious water polo team in Paris, Henry taught swimming to the British royal family and had vast connections, including most important to King Edward VII and to one of England's most accomplished sportsmen, Lord Desborough. But Charley would discover that Henry had no interest in arranging a race with an inferior American champion. Nor did any other English promoter. Such a contest held no appeal to the mass public, except maybe to give them a good laugh.

Back home, Charley's status was faring no better. Along with Handley, Ruberl, and Sundstrom, Wahle began experimenting with various crawl techniques in the NYAC's basement pool. For the same reason that caused racing yachts to be built with a shallow underbody to reduce resistance, they tried to develop a technique that threw as much of the body on top of the water as possible. They tried strokes with their legs stretched astern, with no movement above the knee and little above the ankle. They experimented with Gus Sundstrom's swordfish kick, which resembled the leg action of pedaling a bicycle.

They applied Archimedes's ancient principles of buoyancy. With the center of buoyancy in the chest, they needed to press it down below the surface to cause the hips to rise, allowing the swimmer better flotation. When the hips and legs came up, however, balance and weight had a natural tendency to dunk the face. The tricky part was finding a way to keep their heads above water to breathe and, equally important, to see where they were going.

Having only seen Syd Cavill's initial kickless crawl executed by Leary, Gailey, and Halmay in St. Louis, they had no idea that that kickless version used by Cavill and Wickham had evolved into a timed two-beat high kick synced with each cycle of the arms. By November, the four had devised a two-beat crawl that, unlike Australia's, exhibited kicking independent of the arm stroke. George Van Cleaf, Budd Goodwin, Ted Kitching, and a junior member of the Winged Footers named Jack Lawrence set out to adopt it. Goodwin, the two-hundred-pound water polo center, developed a lazy-looking pedal motion. The teenager Jack Lawrence employed a vertiginous up-and-down wiggling of the lower legs. Ted Kitching adopted a rapid pedal-like kick. Even the Olympian Jam Handy, after getting his ankles pulled by the Germans, started experimenting with his own kickless crawl like Zoltán Halmay's. No two men seemed to follow the same rule. Their style of vertical kick seemed to evolve according to whatever allowed their type of body to stay buoyant. Lifting their legs high out of the water like the Australians seemed to sink them. Legs fanned out wide on the surface gave them a little more balance and stability. Yet to everyone who abandoned the underwater scissors—or added one or two small flutters between scissor kicks—the results were similarly positive. If one kept as much of the body above the surface as possible, the resistance through air was far less than one encountered moving through liquid, and one surged through the water like a motorboat.

"The crawl is not pretty to look at," reported American newspapers, which had begun seeing it in swimming contests. "The onlooker merely sees a great splash tearing over the water without any sign of its cause." Someone justly compared it to "the antics of a wounded shark." But in a couple of months, every swimmer who adopted it had clipped several seconds off his short-distance times. Now the question was, which of the many crawl kicks was the best?

In December, at the club's Ladies' Day, Jack Lawrence made an attack on Harry LeMoyne's twenty-five-yard American record. Young Lawrence was not previously considered a fast aquatic sprinter, yet with the newly acquired crawl he matched LeMoyne's 12.4 seconds. Later that winter, Lawrence clipped three-fifths of a second off LeMoyne's fifty-yard record. Budd Goodwin used his crawl in a hundred-yard race and emerged as the new American indoor century champion. And apparently the husky swimmer's crawl looked so erratic—with arms swinging wildly and legs tailing behind listlessly—that one of his fellow Winged Footers remarked, "If Budd should ever learn to swim, he will be a world beater." Even Charley's old coach Alex Meffert began boasting that his outstanding seventeen-year-old protégé, Marquard "Mark" Schwarz, at the Missouri Athletic Club, would break Charley's records by the next summer's AAU Championships. Out west, J. Scott Leary and a new crawler from Honolulu, Dan Renear, both recorded an open-water century time of one-minute flat.

CHARLES M. DANIELS, 1905

Speculation that this magical new stroke was too taxing to sustain over long distances was disproved once Jam Handy's leg-dragging crawl broke the American mile record.

Otto Wahle declared to the press that "anyone not using the crawl will have to take a back seat when it comes to racing."

With Charley three thousand miles overseas, his status as American champion began to wane.

CHARLEY'S FAMILY SPENT THE first part of the winter in Paris. Most likely under Grandma Meldrum's patronage, they traveled throughout Europe, down to the warmer parts of Spain, and even ventured along the Mediterranean Sea to visit French-controlled Algiers and British-occupied Egypt. In that era, letters to secure proper lodging had to be mailed in advance to the hotel managers, written, if possible, in French, German, or the language of the country, or in the clearest possible English using the politest terms. Over the next five months, Alice introduced Charley to the Old World, just as she first experienced it around his age. These memories were of a time in her life before her unhappy marriage, when she was still full of hope for the future. Perhaps she might rediscover some of that spirit. They took in all of Europe's magnificent sights, experiencing Napoleon III's beautifully renovated Paris and marveling at one of mankind's greatest engineering feats, the sixteen-year-old Eiffel Tower, which stretched twice as tall as any New York skyscraper. They laid eyes on the great pyramids of Giza, created to inspire awe and reverence, as they pondered how these astonishing wonders were built block by fifteen-ton block. Five-hundred fifty miles south in the mountainous Gilf Kebir plateau of the Sahara lay what would later be dubbed the Cave of Swimmers, with pictographs, dating as far back as eight thousand years, depicting the oldest images of people appearing to swim. Charley did not see the cave, because it would not be discovered for thirty more years by the Hungarian explorer László Almásy.

By the time Charley returned to London in May, he had learned the sad news that his fellow Winged Footer the twenty-five-year-old George Van Cleaf had died of typhoid that past winter, just like Dave

Bratton. And Lou Handley had fallen ill with the disease as well.[*] Charley had also heard about young Jack Lawrence's new American records in twenty-five and fifty yards using the crawl, and most likely read Wahle's statements to the press about trudgen swimmers like him being antiquated.

All the news weighed on him as he tried to decide whether to enter Britain's open-invitation championships come late August and September or return to New York at that same time to defend his American titles. If he stayed overseas, he forfeited his American titles. If he left England before its swimming championships, the English might accuse him of running scared. His only other option was to force an earlier match race in England. For that, he needed a promoter like William Henry. And to make that happen, he had to convince Henry that a contest between himself and an English champion would draw a large crowd. To establish himself as a top contender would take a string of victories over some of England's best university swimmers and local champions. For Charley to even participate in those races, he would need to become the first Yankee to earn a spot on one of the British Empire's elite swimming teams.

The prestigious Otter Swimming Club was the second oldest in London. Founded in 1869, it boasted more than 150 members. Donning their traditional black-and-white colors, the all-male team regularly competed against universities and other local clubs. They used St. George's Baths on Buckingham Palace Road as their home base, and each summer their coveted captaincy was swum for in a one-mile race in the river Thames. Charley's unassuming nature and undeniable speed persuaded the members to take a chance on their first American.

Over the next several weeks, Charley beat the sprinting champions

---

[*] Newspapers blamed these tragedies, all the victims being 1904 Olympic water polo players, on the St. Louis fair's ironically named Life Saving Lake. Some papers claimed the manure runoff from nearby livestock had contaminated the lake. Other newspapers claimed the water was polluted because seals swam in it. If the men indeed contracted typhoid in St. Louis, given the usual incubation period is six to thirty days, they would've shown symptoms by October and struggled for months until death, when death usually happens within thirty days. This scenario could neither be confirmed nor refuted.

of the cities of Cheltenham and Swindon. Defeated the watermen of Cambridge University. Embarrassed the swimmers at Oxford, which English newspapers promptly tried to dismiss by claiming that three of Oxford's top men were absent. He eventually won the Otters' mile-long swim in the Thames to become their first ever non-English captain. But he still had not produced the record times he had posted in America. England's newspapers impugned Charley's claim as a legitimate contender, voicing skepticism about the times he was alleged to have swum in America, given that his times in England proved much slower. When no match race came about, Charley grew frustrated.

His fellow Otters tried to offer some good cheer by introducing him to one of England's favorite pastimes—sports gambling. Taking him to Epsom Downs for England's biggest horse race, they purchased "the Pink 'Un" tip sheet and used its advice to place bets with Joe Welch, a bookie who conducted business from the back of his horse-drawn wagon. It was a much-needed distraction for Charley, proving a great day for followers of "the Pink 'Un" and a lousy one for bookies. Charley won four out of five races. When the Otters went to collect their winnings after the last race, Welch had already skipped town. Charley later recounted the tale to American reporters and remarked how the bookie Joe "certainly Welched us," forever solidifying into the American lexicon "welching on a bet."

Charley's victories had ruffled a few feathers, but Henry and the British swimming establishment remained uninterested in organizing a match race with the American champion, especially given the imminent arrival of the "Champion Swimmer of the World."

14.

THE AUSTRALIAN
INVASION

—

SUMMER 1905

THE TWO FINELY DRESSED MEN LOOKED LIKE FATHER AND TEEN-age son when they passed under the second-floor balcony that circled the dance floor beneath the enormous overhead glass dome. The restaurant Frascati, located in London's trendy West End, billed itself as "the World's Rendezvous." Celebrated for its cosmopolitanism and unrivaled French cuisine, Frascati was the place where Londoners went to spot royalty and be seen, and that Saturday evening, June 17, Charley was dining with his mother, grandmother, and aunt at one of the nearly hundred white-clothed tables when the father and son walked in with the five heads of England's powerful swimming establishment who had all been ignoring his victories.

The seven-man entourage walked across the thick red carpet, through the forest of palm trees and its fashionable clientele, who dined and mingled and danced to operettas and classical piano waltzes played by its ten-piece orchestra, while savoring the mouthwatering aroma of freshly baked bread, cheeses, seafood, meats, and buttery sauces. Most of the ladies at Frascati emulated the latest fashions with their hair piled high upon their heads, wearing dresses of lace and ruf-fles and, underneath, the newest corsets that bucked the old hourglass figure for the trendy new S curve, thrusting the hips back and the bust forward. Gentlemen diners as a rule wore evening tailcoats, white waistcoats, white ties, white gloves, black cloaks, and silk hats. The ex-travagant new Edwardian era, which had erupted in reaction to Queen

Victoria's death in 1901, was epitomized by Oscar Wilde's witticism "Nothing succeeds like excess." Someone like Charley, whose American idea of appropriate formal dinner attire was a lounge suit and tie, would be deemed déclassé. No Edwardian socialite would dare think about wearing something as common as a lounge suit.

Besides the father and son, the distinguished, middle-aged group included the country's famed swimming promoter and secretary of the Royal Life Saving Society, William Henry. Henry, aged forty-five, was a big man with a hearty mustache. The group also included the president of England's powerful Amateur Swimming Association, the vice-chair of the RLSS, the ex-president of the ASA, and the honorable treasurer of the RLSS. Like all British men of their class, they had been raised to build an empire with stout hearts and sharp swords and exuded an imperial swagger. Charley had seen that same self-assuredness throughout England. There was a righteous air of purpose and destiny in its citizens that despite its arrogant undertones was undeniably magnetic. That aura was amplified in its aristocracy, who constantly displayed their love for high ceremony and showiness, which somehow still cast a powerful spell over the tens of millions of English men and women whose lives bore no resemblance to theirs.

Amazingly, Charley somehow mustered the courage to walk over and formally introduce himself.

To these men, the so-called Champion of America was no more than a fly buzzing around the table. The American's claim of setting the 220-yard "world record" in St. Louis was doubted by all of them. Yet, when Charley walked over, they surprised him with a cordial greeting and even invited him to pull up a chair for a moment, most likely for their own amusement.

After a round of introductions, Charley met the father and son, who were not father and son at all. They had both arrived from Australia that morning after a six-week ocean journey. The "father," W. Hilton Mitchell, was a sublieutenant and schoolmaster of the *Sobraon* clipper, a reformatory ship out of Sydney Harbor for vagrant and delinquent boys. The bright-eyed "son" was one of his incarcerated vagrants: Bernard "Barney" Kieran, whom Australia was billing as the "Champion Swimmer of the World."

Barney was muscular, like Harry LeMoyne, but when he stood up to shake Charley's hand, the top of his head did not reach Charley's nose. With a dark complexion and a manly appearance, he looked older than his eighteen years, no doubt a result of his rough upbringing on the mean streets of Sydney. His former life of vagrancy and petty thievery began after his father had died in a train accident when Barney was not yet five. When the court sentenced him to the *Sobraon* at age thirteen, on his first day aboard they gave the neglected street urchin a bath, nursing care, a haircut, and a sharp new naval uniform. Then they handed back his old bundle of rags and ordered him to cast them over the side of the ship into the harbor as a symbol of rejecting his past. It was on the *Sobraon* that he learned to swim.

Twelve months earlier, Barney Kieran had been virtually unknown, just like Charley. Now he held every world record from two hundred yards to the mile, with the century, held by his fellow Australian Cecil Healy, being the only one that so far eluded him. And according to the promoter William Henry, Kieran grew faster with each race. Touted as a shining example of the power of British sports to reform delinquent youths, the boy with no future had risen to become an inspiration that ordinary people could relate to. His success prompted Henry and the Royal Life Saving Society of Great Britain to invite Australia's newest hero to participate in the upcoming English swimming season.

The society paid half of Kieran's expenses, and the Kieran Fund Committee from Australia had raised the remaining 170 pounds. The British swimming establishment gave the teenager top billing during his time in England, expressing the hope that Kieran would not only stimulate English competitive swimming but help bind the colonies to the mother country in this brotherhood of sport. William Henry hoped that Londoners would make Barney feel right at home with his English kith and kin. The same hope was not extended to Charley. That was the thing about the British, as Charley was fast discovering. They would rather say nothing than pay an insincere compliment.

When a reporter approached their table, Charley watched him ask Kieran all sorts of questions about his upcoming series of matches against the English champions, about whether he thought England's practice of not using a pistol start as they did in Australia would cause him trouble. "I can only say that I shall do my best," Kieran answered in a shy, humble, but happy tone. "One cannot do more." The reporter had nothing to ask Charley.

However, before Charley departed the table, William Henry offered him the shot he had long been making a case for. Three weeks out, at the Royal Life Saving Society's upcoming King's Cup swimming gala in Blackpool, the society had scheduled a six-hundred-yard open invitation race with Kieran. If Charley felt so inclined, he could enter. Charley jumped at the chance.

"It is hopeful that this youthful American will be able to give our best men a good fight," wrote the reporter from England's *Athletic News*, "as swimming in the States is far from healthy." The reporter concluded, "Whether successful or not, Daniels will have a chance of seeing a high type of British sportsmanship," which was the gentlemanly way of saying Charley was about to be humiliated.

BARNEY KIERAN, CIRCA 1903–1905,
"CHAMPION SWIMMER OF THE WORLD"

———

EIGHT DAYS AFTER THE chance meeting at Frascati, Barney Kieran made his English debut at a highborn gathering at London's Bath Club. Hosted by the acting president of the Royal Life Saving Society, Lord Desborough, a renowned athlete himself, the evening saw the men dressed in tailcoats and white ties, the women in elegant gowns. All the white-gloved lords and ladies gathered around the swimming pool, which had a makeshift, three-foot-high screen around its edge to protect them from unwanted splashes, while Kieran put on a special trudgen exhibition, slashing twenty-one seconds off England's six-hundred-yard record and putting to shame Charley's American record by a whopping forty-three seconds, inciting one spectator to proclaim, "He is a fish, not a man!"

The next evening, Kieran appeared at a special Otters' swimming exhibition with Charley at St. George's Baths. Everyone was eager to see the "Champion Swimmer of the World" in action. Charley just hoped to stay relevant.

Before the large crowd, under the white-tiled pool's glass roof, Charley demonstrated his textbook trudgen in the twenty-yard-long pool and exited to polite applause. Kieran wasted no time showing him up.

Wearing the red, white, and green colors of the North Sydney Club, Kieran demonstrated his speedier trudgen, which made Charley's look pedestrian. Disregarding the traditional teaching to "keep steady," Kieran rolled from side to side at every half stroke. Every time his arm shot forward, he turned almost completely on his side. The action enabled him to reach farther forward, increasing the length of each arm stroke by probably nine inches and generating more power than Charley was capable of.

Young Kieran also had a brilliant way of inhaling. He breathed sideways. Unlike lifting the head straight out of the water to gulp air, this innovation did not slow momentum. Kieran incorporated a heavy rolling motion that allowed him to bring his mouth above water on both sides, enabling him to take two inhalations for every one of his opponent's. As Charley knew, a greater intake of oxygen was especially advantageous on longer swims, where oxygen insufficiency played a big part in muscle fatigue. Breathing more increased endurance without extra exertion.

If Kieran's trudgen demonstration made Charley's look outdated, his next one made him look archaic. After a short rest, Kieran reentered the pool using a different stroke. Facedown, with his body flat and legs wide and outstretched, he lifted his left calf off the surface to about ninety degrees. As his right arm came up, the leg crashed down, splashing water, according to witnesses, seven feet high. Then the opposite arm and leg repeated the sequence, each leg timed to alternate with the opposite arm. It was the first time Charley observed the actual Australian crawl (as opposed to someone's interpretation of it). Straining to see through all the splashing, he tried to analyze each component of Kieran's technique with the intensity of a scientist. The stroke was ugly, but Kieran moved fast. Much faster than Charley could. And it surely left him with a sinking pit in his stomach and an ominous realization: How was he ever going to beat this man? Even with Kieran's willingness to share his secrets, Charley could not adopt them all in two weeks, not even if Wahle were there to help.

The prospect of losing certainly heightened Charley's anxieties. He was over his head and he knew it. He harked back to being tossed into Gebhard's pool by his father, only to flail and sink and swallow water. As he stood on the pool deck of St. George's Baths alongside the formidable Australian champion, awaiting the program's last featured exhibitionist of the evening to appear, Charley needed another distraction like Epsom Downs to calm his nerves. What entered the natatorium next made him forget all about his impending doom.

Her name was Annette Kellermann. Hailing from Down Under, Annette had been introduced by her parents to swimming at age four to overcome a painful disability that forced her to wear leg braces. At age fourteen, she became the champion amateur female swimmer of Australia, in a world totally unfamiliar with women athletes. At fifteen, she won the amateur mile championship, beating the prior women's record by almost four minutes. She then earned a reputation for climbing up the fifty-foot high dive where "no woman had ever gone before" and drawing huge crowds with her fearlessness and graceful plunges, all the while continuing to claim just about every major swimming championship. After her parents, both music teachers in Sydney, fell on hard times, the eighteen-year-old shed her amateur status, hoping to cash in and improve her family's dismal finances.

The swimming mecca of London offered such an opportunity, but success in England was not coming easily after Kellermann arrived that May of 1905. Billing herself as the "Australian Mermaid," she aspired to make a name for herself in England by becoming the first woman to swim the English Channel. She hoped the hype around her Channel swim later that summer would generate some lucrative exhibition bookings, but, as she put it, "high society was not going in for mermaids enough that season to keep the wolf in his den." The charming Australian beauty and her father were in such desperate financial straits that they were close to being out on the street as she began her long-distance training in the Thames River. It seems British high society did not approve of a mermaid whose bathing costume affronted Victorian morality.

For Victorian eyes deprived of seeing the contour of the female figure in public, when the eighteen-year-old walked into St. George's Baths that evening, she might as well have been naked. Jaws dropped. Mouths gasped. Eyes practically popped from their sockets. Her shocking, tight-fitting men's swimsuit provided an unprecedented opportunity to gaze upon every lovely curve and contour of her well-proportioned figure.

Charley admired her boldness and self-confidence. Annette was single-handedly taking on the era's morality that had banished Charley and his mother from proper society. Unapologetic, she refused to give in to the unequal standards Victorian culture imposed on women. As Kellermann explained to the press about her risqué choice of costume, "I can't swim wearing more stuff than you hang on a clothesline." The one concession she made for Victorian eyes was sewing black silk stockings onto her suit to cover her bare legs. If she couldn't get any more bookings because of her choice of bathing costume, then so be it. She could still make her fortune if she became the first woman, and only person besides Matthew Webb, to swim across the English Channel.

Her odds of succeeding seemed about as good as Charley's chances of beating Kieran. If she failed, newspapers would say women were not capable of such feats. If Charley failed, newspapers would point to it as proof of American watermen's inferiority. Both had perhaps foolishly staked their reputations on lofty goals. But backing out was not an option for either of them.

ANNETTE KELLERMANN,
"THE AUSTRALIAN MERMAID"

TWO WEEKS LATER, OVER the clickety-clack of the train, Charley had six hours to think about the upcoming race as he traveled north across the English countryside on that early July day. After 250 miles, the squeal of rails and the loud whistle broke his thoughts as his train chugged into the large bustling station of Blackpool, the most popular beach resort town in the kingdom. Fourteen train platforms served the three million visitors who came each summer to enjoy the healthy seaside air and show off their latest fashions. It's hard to imagine that Alice, Grandma Meldrum, and Aunt Flossie would not have accompanied him to this fashionable destination.

Dressed in his suit and tie, Charley stepped off the train to be greeted by a cool ocean breeze and the overhead squawk of seagulls. Not far in the distance, along the beach, rose the town's mini replica of the Eiffel Tower. Soon he was among the throngs of people traversing up and down the entertainment-lined promenade, alongside horse-drawn buggies, bicyclists, and one of the world's first electric trolley lines. Men in hats and women armed with sun-shielding parasols took in the shops, theaters, restaurants, hotels, entertainment palaces, zoo, and amusement rides, including a 220-foot-tall Ferris wheel. Faint orchestra music poured out of the lavish ballrooms. All around were smiles, chatter, merriment, the roar of the ocean, and the smell of fish-and-chips. When Charley finally reached the seven-mile stretch of beach, he saw the ocean course where he would be swimming. The water looked cold and the waves rough.

On July 8, two days before the six-hundred-yard race, a reported fifty thousand spectators lined the beach and promenade for the start of the Royal Life Saving Society's weekend swimming gala, while a contingent of the society looked on, including William Henry and the dapper, forty-nine-year-old Lord Desborough.

Charley participated that day in the society's prestigious lifesaving race, the King's Cup, where the swimmers raced fully dressed in three pounds of clothes—a shirt, collar, tie, trousers, and leather shoes—to retrieve a "drowning victim" in the ocean and carry him ashore the last forty yards. A dozen international champions competed, including several of Britain's giants. Newspapers billed the high-profile contest as a battle between England's mid-distance champion, David "Boy" Billington, and the Australian phenom, Barney Kieran. No one considered Charley a legitimate challenger, and he was determined to prove them wrong.

LORD DESBOROUGH   WILLIAM HENRY

At the signal, the dozen men rushed down the beach in their clothes and heavy shoes and splashed into a shock of cold sea. The 440-yard race was set over four laps of the 110-yard ocean course. Never having practiced anything remotely like this, Charley struggled with his apparel's weight and the frigid water. At the first turn, Kieran emerged as the clear front-runner. By the last lap, Charley was far behind in fifth place. Up ahead, he watched Kieran struggling to secure his "drowning man," while Billington's man practically swam into his arms, allowing the English champion to take the lead and race for shore. Charley finished fourth, doing nothing to change the British opinion of American swimming nor giving his mother anything to uplift her spirits or a headline to cut out for her scrapbook.

Two days later, Charley's moment of truth arrived with gray skies and intermittent drizzle. An official rowed the five-man field out to the ocean start. Per ASA rules, one large rowboat of officials floated just outside the makeshift starting line, carrying a judge and five timekeepers. The judge addressed the swimmers and described the six-hundred-yard course down the promenade shoreline to the spot where the race terminated, marked by another rowboat with a judge and five more timekeepers.

Charley and Kieran lined up in the cold sea with the three others at a floating start. It was not only Charley's first real swimming test against a top champion of the British Empire; it was America's. During that unforgiving minute as they treaded the frigid water while awaiting the starter's call, the cold sea caused him to breathe quicker and his heart rate to quicken, his endorphins and adrenaline pumping. The judge called, "On your marks," "Are you ready?" and when he was satisfied that all five men were indeed ready, he simply said, "Go!" and the starting line erupted with splashes.

The swimmers thrust forward. Charley's arms dug in, his legs working a tight scissor kick. Kieran used a combination of his powerful crawl and novel trudgen to traverse the long straightaway. Charley fought to keep up. Every hundred yards Kieran drew farther away, until a second-place Charley watched the Australian cross the finish seventy yards ahead. The defeat was worse than he had ever imagined.

Afterward, *The Sportsman* of London snickered at Charley's chances in England's upcoming August championships. "It will certainly be surprising if [Daniels] is successful," the reporter wrote, noting that "Daniels does not appear to be quite up to championship form." It was the gentlemanly way of calling him second-rate.

Charley's status back home was slipping as well. A wave of American crawlers began to clip his home records. If he returned to defend his title, the Brits would definitely accuse him of running scared now. And there was also his reluctance to leave his mother.

PART FOUR

SPEED SWIMMING

CHARLES M. DANIELS,
TRAVERS ISLAND, 1905

15.

THE AMERICAN
CRAWL

—

AUGUST 1905–
JANUARY 1906

ALICE WAS NOT READY TO RETURN TO HER BLEAK LIFE BACK IN the States. She opted to stay with Grandma Meldrum and Aunt Flossie in Europe until the three of them returned for Thanksgiving, which certainly caused Charley some reservations about leaving. But his title was the one thing that kept him from being looked upon as no more than the son of a Wall Street swindler. Alice had little hope of making a bright future back home, neither as a woman nor as a disgraced divorcée. In Europe, where no one knew about her divorce or Tom Daniels, she did not have to feel bad about herself or worry about being judged. Her only offense in England was being a woman.

Picture Alice seeing off her twenty-year-old son on a hot August day with a tearful goodbye. He had already given up his chance to attend Columbia University the past year in order to remain at her side. He gave up a year of training at the club, letting down Wahle and his teammates. Perhaps Charley apologized to Alice for failing to make any good English headlines to add to her scrapbook. But it was time for him to return to New York. If he ever hoped to beat someone like Kieran, he needed to train under a trusted instructor. And that was back at the Winged Foot.

When Charley arrived in New York, he soon discovered that he had become a target. Every upstart swimmer wanted to dethrone him. What made things worse, Charley returned in miserable condition. The excessive heat of London, the constant competing, and a poor passage home had reduced him to a shadow. "I was weak, listless and several pounds under weight," he recalled. And predictably, his times were hopelessly below form.

Charley sought out his family's past vacation sanctuary at Rockaway Beach to recuperate and train. He went alone to his old resort, Avery's cottages at Arverne by the Sea. Walked on the same beach where he'd once sat as an anxiety-ridden boy. He gazed at the ocean where he'd last watched and admired his father swimming out to the far buoy. Perhaps Charley even crashed through the surf and swam to that same buoy, hoping to regain some sense of self-worth as a defeated champion and a son whose father still wanted nothing to do with him. Or maybe, like Barney Kieran tossing his old clothes over the side of the *Sobraon*, it was his way of trying to cast off his past—and his father.

TOM DANIELS WAS NOW operating a network of "banking" businesses in Milwaukee and Chicago under the alias Thomas E. Cameron. Barely married a year to his second wife, Lydia, he was already rumored to be driving around town with a new beautiful young mistress in a fancy new touring car. It was even reported that Tom possessed several automobiles at a time when owning even one was considered lavish and that he showered his mistress with diamonds and furs.

Once again, Tom advertised across the country for investors willing to pay large amounts of cash to bankroll companies wanting to expand—all for an up-front fee of three hundred to a thousand dollars. It seemed just a matter of time before his scheme erupted into another national scandal that would destroy all of Charley's hard work to salvage his own name. Only now, with Charley being a bit of a swimming celebrity, the fallout for him would be much worse and much more public. If the Brits caught wind of it, the disgrace might preclude him from swimming against the "gentlemen" of the British Empire. Whatever Charley hoped to accomplish, he needed to do it soon.

CHARLEY'S DEBILITATED STATE MADE his chances for the upcoming Amateur Athletic Union Championships shaky. Dave Bratton was no longer there to offer a helping hand or cheerful pick-me-up. In Charley's absence, Otto Wahle had become a zealot about the crawl and put no faith in the future of anyone who did not take it up. He now focused his efforts on training Budd Goodwin, Jack Lawrence, and several other Winged Footers who had become fellow crawl disciples.

Charley still found the crawl unnatural, opting instead to focus on adopting Kieran's trudgen techniques. History does not tell us what exchange Charley and Wahle had upon his return, if any, but Wahle could not have been happy that Charley had taken on the British Empire before he was ready.

Now twenty, Charley no longer had junior membership status with the club. After being away nearly a year, he was probably uncertain about where he stood, especially now that his sponsor, Dave Bratton, was dead and his relationship with Wahle unsettled. For a week, he practiced alone in the waters off Rockaway, feeling listless and slow. Then a cordial letter arrived for him from a fellow Winged Footer, Dr. Dave Hennen.

Doc Hennen, a prominent surgeon, had been one of the best all-around athletes ever to attend Harvard and Columbia. A big advocate of swimming, Doc invited Charley to prepare for the AAU Championships at his camp in New Hampshire, where several Winged Footers were already training.

"I cannot promise you excitement or a gay life," Doc Hennen wrote, "but air such as you will find nowhere else, good food, comfortable quarters, every facility for training . . . and our friend Handley will look after the coaching."

Lou Handley, the Winged Foot's water polo captain, had survived his bout with typhoid and was the most likely impetus behind Doc Hennen's invitation. Lou still believed in Charley.

"Coming at the time it did," Charley recalled, "this letter seemed a message from heaven. Here was the very thing I needed, with a healthy outdoor life, a medical adviser, and a good coach all thrown in."

LOUIS DE BREDA HANDLEY, or L. de B. as the younger swimmers called him, was a truly gifted all-around athlete. Besides being one of the

LOU DE B. HANDLEY,
CAMP MOWGLI, 1905

foremost water polo players in the country, he rode horseback, canoed, sailed, cycled, hunted, played football, trained hunting dogs, and possessed a deep passion for anything aquatic. He developed his love for swimming under the shadow of the dome of St. Peter's Basilica in the river Tiber. Lou grew up in the Vatican, where his American father worked as a sculptor and private butler for two popes. After Lou's English mother died when he was seven, he saw his two sisters sent away to convent schools while he was placed with the Christian Brothers in Rome. Unlike his sisters, both of whom became nuns, Lou failed to find his calling in the Catholic Church and moved to the United States at age twenty-two.

Handsome, slim, muscular, with kind blue eyes and an equally kind heart, Lou was especially meticulous in his grooming and appearance.

He parted his brown hair neatly in the center, dressed impeccably, and often sported a fashionable homburg or straw boater. Women found him attractive, yet despite their affections Lou curiously remained a bachelor all his life. He worked as a freelance journalist, writing out of his apartment, which afforded him the flexibility to pursue his passion for swimming and water polo, as well as other self-determinations. Like Charley and his mother, he lived in the avant-garde community of Greenwich Village, with its progressive acceptance of outcasts and its growing gay population, who otherwise lived under constant fear of being harassed, shunned, and more recently, with the police's anti-gay-establishment raids around town, arrested and sent to prison.

Lou lived at 80 Washington Square, in what was advertised as a bachelor's apartment, with artists, playwrights, and other unmarried men, overlooking the park on the opposite side from Charley and his mother. He, too, saw the groups of immigrant women each morning crossing the park, only to disappear into the Triangle Shirtwaist Factory building not three hundred feet past his apartment. It is unclear what his fellow watermen knew about his personal life, or how much they cared to know. Certainly Charley saw him around the neighborhood and perhaps glimpsed some of the company he kept. Lou was a damn good waterman, and maybe that's what mattered to his teammates. After all, he was one of them. As long as anyone presented himself as a true manly gentleman (the heterosexual criterion being understood), there should have been no problem. But it's hard to imagine his association with the club was not without its challenges.

Lou always held a special place in his heart for the marginalized, the oppressed, second-class citizens, and women's suffrage, which most of the regular club members did not share. The water became his battleground for equality. Proficient in Italian, English, French, Spanish, Latin, and Greek, Lou was a master communicator and used his talents with the pen to promote swimming for all. He wrote books and articles about it, reported on competitions in the leading New York papers and magazines, volunteered his time lecturing, teaching, and giving speeches on swimming—anything to create awareness and tout its benefits. If this outcast sport ever gained the respect it deserved, he believed it would elevate those within it, especially women, immigrants, the poor, and all those searching for a place of equality. The movement just needed a great champion to capture America's imagination. While Wahle went looking elsewhere, Lou put his chips on Charley.

A GRATEFUL CHARLEY LEFT on the next available train for New Hampshire's wilderness. The following evening, after changing trains in Boston, he arrived at the lakeside station on Lake Winnipesaukee's most southern point, Alton Bay, where he boarded the *Mount Washington*, a beautiful side-wheel steamship that ferried him twenty-two miles north to Center Harbor, which was a two-mile canoe ride to camp. Charley had not seen his fellow Winged Footers since his departure for Europe and was excited to reunite with them in the great outdoors.

When he arrived in Center Harbor late that evening, it was the first time Lou Handley had seen him in more than eight months. Charley indeed looked only a shadow of his former self. He was not the confident, robust young man who had won five Olympic medals. He was ten pounds underweight, drained, unsure, and anxious. The British had certainly had their way with him.

Handley wanted to know only if Charley had done his best while he was over there. Had he given everything he had against the British Empire? As far as Handley was concerned, losing mattered naught as long as you gave your all. And Charley had. It just wasn't good enough.

"Do not become discouraged if you fail to succeed at once," Handley said, trying to put his experience in perspective. "Keep going." But the humiliating loss to Kieran was still in Charley's head and left him full of self-doubt.

Doc Hennen's Camp Mowgli, named after Kipling's *Jungle Book* hero, rested alone on a quiet shore, surrounded on all sides by dense pine groves and miles of mountains and forests as wild as Mowgli's jungle. The camp's rustic wood cabin was a long, one-story bungalow, with a front porch overlooking the lake, where the friendly faces of Doc Hennen, Ted Kitching, and Lester Crane welcomed him. The long day's journey ended with Charley falling asleep on a bunk to an outdoor serenade of frogs, crickets, and owls. The next day, a new journey would begin.

Charley's first morning at camp started early with a brief dip in the cool lake. Breakfast was served; then Handley allotted everyone an hour to take care of correspondence before they began training.

With the transatlantic telephone line more than twenty years away and domestic calls still a novelty, letters offered the only way for Charley and his mother to keep abreast of each other's well-being. Separated loved ones were expected to write not less than once a week, and some made it a rule to write a brief letter at the close of each day. It was often part of one's daily routine, especially for women, to devote an hour or two to letter writing. Schools taught classes on this essential art. According to the popular *Hill's Manual of Social and Business Forms*, in writing to loved ones, you gave all the news, with all the little particulars, just as if you were talking, including minute details and bits of gossip about friends and loved ones. Those "little tidbits," *Hill's* noted, "are often the sweetest morsels of the feast." Undoubtedly, Charley wrote to Alice, Grandma Meldrum, and Aunt Flossie about days at the camp and his upcoming races, while they relayed their goings-on in Europe, extending distant kisses and wishes of luck, and perhaps updates from his grandmother and aunt about Alice's well-being.

After Charley's morning letter writing, his training began with a two-mile canoe trek to the closest village to drop off the mail. When he returned, Handley put each man over the racing course.

"Try smiling," Handley would advise his team during their swims. "The more you smile the faster you swim."

Handley touted the benefits of the crawl, but was still not convinced that it was the breakthrough Wahle believed. Charley felt the same, at least for himself, insisting, "What was good for one might not suit the other at all." The crawl's leg work still felt awkward. He had experimented a little with Barney Kieran's Australian version, but the wide-open legs and high, out-of-water kicks made him sink, making it more difficult to execute Kieran's side breathing without swallowing water.

Morning practice ended with the call for lunch, followed by a choice of activities: walking, fishing, chopping wood, or similar muscle-building endeavors. Although Charley enjoyed the excellent lake fishing, he had no intention of taking it up as a regular hobby. "The fish have to do too much and the man too little to supply real entertainment," he said, preferring action.

Around five o'clock, drill was called again, and under Handley's direction there was either some sprinting or easy, long swims.

Charley soon embraced the camp's routine. Having a lake right out his front door recalled wonderful memories of the Hiawatha Lodge. The cool fresh water was therapeutic. There, in this liquid world, he discovered that Kieran's trudgen innovations were beginning to work for him. However, breathing from side to side, with the constant twisting of the head—left-right, left-right—made him feel a little dizzy.

After their evening swim, Handley promoted a healthy dinner that consisted chiefly of thick, generous slices of roast beef, potatoes, baked beans, and eggs, with bread and butter, and forbade sodas, sundaes, candy, and fancy pastries. "They play havoc with condition." Then Handley encouraged a good night's sleep for all. "Few things impair physical fitness more than insufficient sleep," he said, asserting that swimmers "require at least eight hours in every twenty-four, but will profit by enjoying nine regularly."

During the evening swim before dinner, and sometimes at dusk, Charley experimented with various breathing techniques, hoping to create one that best suited him. In the cool waters under the waning golden light, he tried different ways of rolling from side to side. Yet Kieran's rolling technique seemed to create some resistance that was detrimental to speed. It remained to be seen whether the advantage gained by breathing more frequently made up for the increased resistance, but Charley ultimately settled on hardly any rolling, only taking a breath every two or three strokes by a quick side twist of the head as his upper arm was brought down, and only turning to his left side to avoid the dizzying back-and-forth. His head twisted just enough to get his entire mouth above the surface so as not to inhale water. When night fell and the stars twinkled to life, he heard the familiar call of a loon.

Charley gained back the ten pounds he'd lost in London and felt a reinvigorated joy for swimming. As the weeks flew by, he realized that Doc Hennen's camp and Handley had turned his life around.

The American championships promised to bring a wave of crawlers. And Charley's decision not to adopt the new stroke certainly caused some concern that he would be swimming at a big disadvantage. As they closed up camp to head for Travers Island, it felt as if America's champion was about to defend his title using a horse and buggy while everyone else showed up in an automobile.

(From left to right): LOU HANDLEY,
TED KITCHING, CHARLES DANIELS, LESTER CRANE,
CAMP MOWGLI, 1905

The *Chicago Tribune* best captured the upcoming championships by stating,

Not in years have swimmers kicked up such a fuss as they have been doing the last week or so over the national championships.

As a rule these events are held so quietly . . . but this year the swimmers really have succeeded in getting themselves talked about and are arousing a lot of interest in the races. The contests will be a duel between the Trudgeon stroke and its new rival, the "crawl," as C. M. Daniels, who recently returned from Europe, will stick to the trudge, while some of his foes who have developed the new Australian stroke during his absence will endeavor to convince him of its superiority. A mite from Chicago is going to give some of our swimmers a surprise in the championships. His name is Handy. He certainly is with his hands and feet. Western experts predict he will make our lads look like a bunch of crabs.

On Saturday, August 26, sailboats and yachts enlivened the wharf around the New York Athletic Club's thirty-acre island. All morning, the club's automobile enthusiasts ventured up the sixteen miles of unpaved roads in their open-air vehicles and arrived covered in dust. Every hour at a quarter to the hour, crowds of members arrived by train at the nearby Pelham Manor Station, where the club's horse carriages shuttled them to the man-made causeway that connected the mainland to the island.

By noon, the crowds covered the island's banks overlooking Long Island Sound, not far from the tennis courts and cinder track, where nearby the club's palatial new summer home was nearing completion, with magnificent dining facilities, lounges, and overnight bedrooms, to replace the original mansion that had burned down in a 1901 fire. Most of the men brought ladies with them, which, *Scribner's Magazine* pointed out, was done "in order that athletics might be made as respectable as they were in England." More spectators watched from a flotilla of canoes, skiffs, motorboats, and yachts, as well as from the overlooking bluffs. The racecourse started from the dock of the majestic boathouse and stretched 110 yards, marked off by buoys, into the bay's placid waters, which were shielded from the wind by a surrounding cluster of islands.

It is not known if the reunion between Charley and Otto Wahle was awkward or friendly. Wahle certainly evaluated how Charley looked after nine months, what his confidence was like after Europe, and whether he still possessed the fire to take the hits and keep coming. And most likely he would have chided Charley for not taking up the crawl.

Over the next week, Charley prepared to face most of America's best crawlers in a grueling gauntlet that included distances at the century, 220 yards, half mile, and mile. Not even the great Harry LeMoyne had been versatile enough to win both speed and mid-distances. And Chicago's Jam Handy, the 1904 Olympic bronze medalist, had secretly developed his own side-breathing technique, unaware of Charley's efforts. In July, it helped him crawl his way to victory in the quarter-mile, half-mile, and mile Western Championships in Oregon against his fellow Olympians J. Scott Leary and Frank Gailey. Handy was now eager to do the same against Charley.

The two men squared off in the final field of the half-mile championship. Using Kieran's wide trudgen kick and his own left-side breathing technique, Charley battled Handy and the rest of the crawlers in the saltwater bay, fighting Handy down to the wire as he set a new American record. Afterward, Handy accused Charley of somehow spying on him and stealing his side-breathing innovation. The false charge did not sit well with Charley. He beat Handy again in a tight mile race, breaking away from the kickless crawler in the last hundred yards to set another American record. He also won the 220-yard championship in near-record time. But the century posed the greatest threat. The crawl was ideal for shorter distances, and the century's adrenaline-pumped field of crawlers was ready to avenge their earlier defeats.

At the pistol, the Hawaiian champion, Dan Renear, took the early lead. At fifty yards, Charley had fallen behind three crawlers—Renear, Goodwin, and Kitching. Down the final stretch, Mark Schwarz, who got sandwiched at the start, was now surging at Charley's heels, threatening to push him into fifth place. A cry went up from the crowd, "Daniels is beaten!"

Charley plunged his head underwater like a warhead, not breathing until he broke through the pack and crossed the finish in a new course record of 63.2 seconds.

Cheers and applause resounded for several minutes. Otto Wahle was undoubtedly impressed, though he certainly wondered how much faster Charley could've swum if he'd used the crawl. The Austrian became determined to make a convert out of him. In its coverage, *The Boston Globe* wrote that the only person with a chance of beating Daniels was Harry LeMoyne. What the *Globe* meant to say was the only *American* . . .

Across the Atlantic, Barney Kieran avenged an earlier loss to Billington in England's Mile Championship by winning the Quarter-Mile Championship, setting a new world record that was forty-eight seconds faster than Charley's best time. Kieran then beat Billington in the Half-Mile Championship, setting yet another world record with a time that was almost two minutes faster than Charley's. In England's Century Championship, Charley's Olympic vanquisher, Zoltán Halmay, used his kickless crawl to defeat England's top trudgen sprinter, Rob Derbyshire, with an impressive fifty-nine seconds (a second off the world record shared by the Australian crawlers Cecil Healy and Dick Cavill). But the biggest headlines that summer came from Annette Kellermann.

Annette's attempt to become the first woman to cross the English Channel captured the attention of both the British and the American press, and journalists could not stop writing about her swimsuit. They also loved her innovative use of automobile goggles; she was the first person to wear them swimming. Just as Matthew Webb had been given tea and roast beef sandwiches during his epic Channel swim in 1875, the accompanying boats fed Annette hot soup from a straw, tiny sandwiches, and, unfortunately, chocolate that upset her stomach. Even when the choppy waters made her seasick, she kept swimming, egged on by the fact that her sponsor, the *Daily Mirror,* was paying her by the mile. When writing about Annette, reporters for once tied female beauty not to the usual Victorian virtues of frailty and fairness but rather to strength and power. Annette's third and final attempt lasted more than ten hours, getting her three-quarters of the way to France before seasickness again stopped her. She never made it across, but undaunted, she announced plans to perform in America the following summer.

Annette rolled with defeat, able to confidently move on to the next big thing. For Charley, the thought of failing or disappointing anyone was terrifying. Even with his proven American victories he still seemed to grapple with self-doubt. The British Empire's watermen were clearly so much better. Why couldn't he take failure more in stride like Annette? But then again, Annette had a loving father who not only managed her but stood by her side every step of the way.

IN SEPTEMBER, NEWSPAPERS ANNOUNCED a surprise Olympiad to be held in Athens the following April. The 1906 Games, scheduled to commemorate the tenth anniversary of Greece's first modern-day Olympics, offered Charley a unique opportunity.

In truth, Coubertin was far from excited about this off-year Olympiad. Greece's dubious finances and political turmoil had finally stabilized enough to enable the government to demand that the Games return to Athens. At this point, however, the Frenchman was focused on Rome and offered no personal support for these off-cycle Games. Coubertin accused those nine or ten IOC members planning to attend of momentarily losing their heads, insisting this "session" in Athens could not be considered properly representative of the Olympics. Still, the rest of the world embraced the idea.

This time England's and Australia's top watermen planned to compete. It was Charley's chance to try to avenge his losses against Barney Kieran and Zoltán Halmay, as well as test his mettle against such greats as Derbyshire, Billington, and Australia's reigning speed king, Cecil Healy. Unfortunately, limited funding prompted the newly formed American Olympic Committee to focus on sending only their track-and-field men. They had no intention of squandering good money on a "minor sport" like swimming, especially just to watch the Americans get embarrassed by the Europeans and Australians. It was up to Charley to prove U.S. swimmers belonged.

One way to get the American Olympic Committee's attention was to accomplish what only the Australians and Zoltán Halmay had done: break the sixty-second century barrier. Otto Wahle insisted that Charley's only chance was to take up the crawl, but Charley still felt more comfortable with the trudgen. Since he was breaking records regularly and steadily improving, he thought it was wise to leave well enough alone.

But Wahle kept badgering: "There is not a man who has not improved decidedly on his changing from the trudgen to the crawl."

Nowhere was Wahle's point better illustrated than in the success of Chicago's Jam Handy, whom newspapers nicknamed the Little Water Devil. In late October, using his own version of Zoltán Halmay's kickless crawl, Handy beat Alex Meffert's protégé, Mark Schwarz, in a quarter-mile match race in Chicago and along the way broke Charley's 330-yard record. In November, during another Chicago race, Handy broke five American records from 300 to 600 yards, two of them being Charley's. In mid-December, Handy broke two more mid-distance American records. But what Handy really wanted was to defeat not Charles Daniels's records but Charley himself.

ON NOVEMBER 18, a week before Thanksgiving, Grandma Meldrum, Aunt Flossie, and Alice returned from Europe, happy to reunite with Charley. Hoping the storm created by Tom Daniels had somewhat diminished during their yearlong absence, they all made plans to spend Christmas with their family in Buffalo before Grandma Meldrum and Aunt Flossie headed west to spend the winter in Pasadena. When they arrived for the December holidays, Charley's swimming accolades had made him a notable curiosity in town. Both the *Buffalo Times* and the *Buffalo Evening News* named him 1905's top national swimmer. Perhaps as a result of Charley's accomplishments, Alice felt empowered to break her exile and attend a small gathering at Buffalo's swanky Twentieth Century Club, one of the first private clubs for women. The wife of a U.S. foreign diplomat was giving a talk about her experience living in Turkey, and the thought of attending the intellectual discussion at the exclusive club certainly excited her. However, Alice's sister-in-law Louise, her younger brother Herbert's wife, who was a member, apparently felt the need to keep a safe social distance from Alice, at least publicly, and did not accompany her.

Despite the uncertainty about how she would be received, Alice braved it alone, hopeful that she would not be shunned. The next day, her name appeared in the Buffalo society pages for the first time since the arrest of her husband. Both the *Buffalo Courier* and the *Buffalo*

Times made sure to list her among the event's guests as "Mrs. Thomas Daniels of New York, formerly Miss Meldrum," ensuring that her connection with Tom would not be overlooked. There is no indication that Alice was ever permitted to return.

TWO DAYS BEFORE CHRISTMAS, Charley received the devastating news that he would not get to rematch Barney Kieran in Athens—but not for the reason he thought. Buried on page 12 of the *Buffalo Morning Express* was a small headline, "Australian Champion Swimmer, B. B. Kieran, Is Dead." Charley was stunned. Just a week earlier, the nineteen-year-old world champion had blown away the two-hundred-yard record beyond anything America could touch. A few days later, it appears, he had complained of feeling ill. By the time doctors rushed him into surgery for an emergency appendectomy, it was too late. Swimming had lost its greatest champion.

Newspapers on both sides of the Atlantic reported on Kieran's subsequent funeral in Sydney, which drew thirty thousand emotion-filled countrymen. The once petty criminal who'd been imprisoned in the government's floating reformatory had used swimming to resuscitate his reputation and become a national hero. He was the best Charley had ever seen. He'd set an almost impossibly high bar to pursue, but Charley saw what he wanted to become if he kept chasing his dream and following his heart. As a constant reminder, Charley clipped a newspaper article about Barney's death and kept it with him for inspiration. The best way to honor Barney Kieran was to keep pushing himself and aspire to one day stand in Barney's wet footprints as the "Greatest Swimmer in the World." However, Barney's final record-breaking performance only reinforced the American Olympic Committee's inclination not to sponsor its own watermen, who had yet to prove they could compete against the British Empire.

When Charley returned to the pool after the holidays, Wahle wasted no time pestering him about taking up the crawl. Charley later recalled Wahle being so insistent that in self-defense he had to give the stroke a trial. The problem was there were as many versions of the crawl as swimmers using it. No two men swam it alike. Halmay and Handy dragged their legs motionless. J. Scott Leary rocked from side to side, using his legs like balancing rudders. Budd Goodwin used a lazy, continual pedal motion of one kick per arm stroke. The late, great Barney Kieran deployed a wide, two-beat high kick that synced with each arm movement.

Otto Wahle offered pointers as Charley, the nonbeliever, attempted to incorporate these variations into his own workable crawl. Lying facedown in the water, legs extended, with heels peeking above the surface, he bent his knee, lifting back his lower leg, and gave a vigorous kick, first with one foot, then the other. The action did not generate as much propulsion as when his legs snapped together at his scissor kick. But Wahle pointed out that every time he opened his legs to snap underwater, it was the equivalent of opening a parachute behind him, stunting momentum. Furthermore, the trudgen required the body to maintain a forty-five-degree angle, while the crawl kept the body on *top* of the pool's surface, creating less water resistance.

"In the Australian crawl," Wahle pointed out, "all the motion is positive."

Charley admitted later that he didn't pretend to know anything about the principles of applied mechanics, but he kept on practicing in the club's tank, perfecting his own version of the crawl. One day, a fellow Winged Footer, Jack Lawrence, probably goaded by Wahle, challenged Charley to a friendly fifty-yard race. Before Jack adopted the crawl, his performance had warranted little attention. Now he swaggered around the pool as America's reigning fifty-yard speed king.

The fifty-yard contest comprised one pool length down, a turn off the wall, and back. Most likely Wahle held the stopwatch and gave the signal. It was the first time Charley had attempted the crawl in an actual race, and Jack Lawrence was ready to take down the American champion.

At Wahle's "Go!" the two competitors dove in. Charley's crawl-like leg action looked awkward, strangely out of balance, and lacked adequate propulsion. Yet, into the turn, Charley and Jack remained even. Cleaving down the last lap, Charley took a breath on his left side, while Jack lifted his head straight up, as the two men battled neck and neck. Rather than trying the Australian version's short choppy arm movement that Lawrence used, Charley stayed true to his trudgen's long-reaching overarm that he'd learned from Kieran. At the wall, Charley won by a touch.

If Wahle was indeed holding the stopwatch, a grin must have split his face as he looked down at the second hand and saw a new American record.

CHARLEY CONTINUED EXPERIMENTING UNDER the guiding eyes of Wahle, Handley, and Sundstrom as they sought to create the perfect speed stroke. He compared the crawl's effectiveness to a flat stone that has been thrown hard along the surface of the water. "So long as the flat side strikes the water," Charley said, "it bounces on without a check until its momentum ceases. But let even the smallest portion become immersed and it is brought to a sudden stop ... no matter how great its speed." Their task entailed eliminating as much drag as possible and increasing speed, which soon unearthed a bigger problem.

It started by expending more energy with Charley's arm strokes. When observed from above, his arms mirrored the Australian's bent elbows that looked like a V-shaped chicken wing rotating through the air, but when plunging through the surface, rather than stabbing his fingers at a sharp downward angle he discovered that an extended reach forward let him catch more water that he could pull back longer, generating greater propulsion. To stay more horizontal, he sucked in his belly and tightened his glutes to avoid any bending through the waist. Then, after he eliminated the wide Australian leg stance by holding his knees closer together and swapped out the Australian's rigid ankles with toes pointed down, for rotating his ankles down and back, which one observer likened to the rolling foot action of a swan, he modified the Australian's high ninety-degree kick to one that lifted his calves no more than forty degrees, pushing the kick from two beats to four, which burned even more energy to generate greater velocity. But somewhere during the century race, around sixty to ninety yards, it felt as if a baby grand piano dropped on his back. It damn near paralyzed him.

His arms suddenly felt as though they were encased in thirty pounds of concrete, and his back, shoulders, arms, and legs screamed with burning pain. This new stroke's demands deprived the muscles of sufficient oxygen, which forced the body to find fuel through lactate metabolism. However, its lactic acid by-product made the muscles acidic and hampered their ability to contract. The result was paralyzing fatigue and a burning sensation that besieged the body. The only way to make it go away was to stop; otherwise it just grew worse. Go too fast and hard early and you awakened the monster too soon, making it impossible to finish the race.

ON NEW YEAR'S DAY 1906, eight hundred miles west, in front of a large crowd at the Central YMCA of Chicago, nineteen-year-old Jam Handy broke Charley's 770-yard American record and along the way shattered American records at 330, 550, and 660 yards. When a reporter asked why nineteen seemed to be the average age of swimmers in their prime, Handy commented, "I think that it is due to the fact that the young swimmer has not lost the suppleness which is bound to occur when he matures more fully. As soon as a man begins to get over twenty years of age, he loses his speed in the water." Charley would turn twenty-one that March.

ON WEDNESDAY, JANUARY 10, the American Olympic Committee held its first meeting at the Waldorf Astoria to assess the feasibility of sending men to that year's Olympic Games in Athens, scheduled to take place from April 26 to May 2. Presided over by Caspar Whitney, the twelve-member committee included men from across the country, including the consul general of Greece in New York City, who had extended the formal invitation to the United States to compete, and an enthusiastic but somewhat bitter Jim Sullivan.

Sullivan's efforts to make the 1904 Games a success had earned universal praise across the country. Newspapers had applauded his unparalleled organizing skills. Even Coubertin could not deny his rival just praise. In October 1904, Coubertin had sent a letter extending his warmest congratulations and informing Sullivan that he would be awarded a special gold medallion at the following June's IOC meeting in Brussels to commemorate his "wonderful work" in organizing and reviving the Games. Sullivan was deeply touched, until his invitation to the IOC's meeting never came, nor was that promised gold medal ever awarded. But what Sullivan wanted more than anything and believed he had earned was a seat on the IOC.

For the first time at that January meeting, a few of the members of the American Olympic Committee raised the idea of sponsoring athletes not only from track and field but from other, "minor" sports as well. They agreed for that to be an option they would need to raise at least twenty-five thousand dollars. At a minimum, the committee expected to send twenty-five of its finest track-and-field athletes. Beyond that, it remained unclear which "minor" sports the committee would include, and if they would include swimming.

American watermen needed to prove they belonged.

THREE DAYS LATER, ON a gray Saturday that hovered just above freezing, Charley walked out of his Greenwich Village apartment in a trench coat, suit, and tie, mentally preparing himself to implement the crawl for the first time in an official AAU-sanctioned century race. Just as he had eschewed his old trudgen stroke, he was no longer obliged to take the old, coal-choked elevated train. For a five-cent fee he could experience the revolutionary engineering marvel of the city's new subway, with its olive-green cars that whizzed through underground tunnels, through the darkness and unfamiliar air, suddenly shooting into beautiful stations with white-tiled walls that bore big signs telling the location, which the elevated never had.

When Charley arrived at the club's natatorium that evening, all eyes were upon him. His fellow Winged Footers were probably betting among themselves as to whether their devout trudgen champion would flip religions. As he lined up at the scratch position in the century handicap race, with all of his opponents assigned head starts, some as much as ten seconds, Otto Wahle readied his stopwatch as one of the official timers.

At the referee's signal, the men started diving in at their assigned handicaps. One by one, Charley watched his competition make their way farther and farther down the tank until he was the last man dry. Finally, the official fired his pistol and Charley dove.

It was a poor start. Both feet fluttered, and one person reported he used a scissor kick. Once he found his groove, one lower leg splashed about forty degrees out of the water, then the other. Two kicks—left, right—with each arm stroke, taking no more than two breaths each twenty-five-yard lap. Handley remarked later that "Daniels seemed to positively crawl over and above the water." The next morning's edition of *The New York Times* would report that he plowed through the pool as if propelled by a motor. But at some point after fifty yards, he knew he would face the monster. At seventy-five yards, he had passed everyone and now the lactic acid buildup in his tightened muscles screamed for him to stop. The last lap was a fight between himself and the pain

CHARLES MELDRUM DANIELS, 1906

and heavy arms that no longer wanted to work. When Charley hit the final wall, a commotion broke out among the four timers, who began frantically comparing watches. Wahle looked up from his stopwatch and down at Charley with delight. He had just swum the century two-fifths of a second faster than Healy's and Cavill's fifty-eight-second world record.

The crowd exploded with a thunderous ovation. Charley was stunned.

A week later, Jim Sullivan officially entered Charley's time into the American Amateur Athletic Union's record books as the fastest ever swum by a world amateur.

The English swimming authorities took exception on the grounds that it was made in a handicap race. Therefore, under England's Amateur Swimming Association rules, they refused to acknowledge it.

16.

IN ROUGH WATERS

—

JANUARY–APRIL 1906

CHARLEY BECAME AN OVERNIGHT EVANGELIST OF THE NEW STROKE. Interviewed by the New York *Sun* under the headline "Daniels Praises the Crawl," he made an open confession, almost as if he'd lost a bet with Otto Wahle.

"I am firmly convinced that Wahle is right when he says that the crawl will supersede every other racing stroke," conceded Charley. "The crawl has improved the speed of every man that adopted it. This admission should bear all the more weight as until quite recently I was an enemy of the new stroke."

As Charley would recall about his sudden conversion, "To see is to believe. I had to give in in spite of myself."

After offering further explanation for the superiority of the new stroke, he concluded, "My advice to those having championship aspirations is to take up the crawl without hesitation. Results have proved to me beyond the shadow of a doubt that it is a better stroke than the trudgen. There is no doubt about it, the crawlers will lead the world."

ON FEBRUARY 15, JIM SULLIVAN received notification from the New York Athletic Club that they had unanimously voted to appropriate a thousand dollars toward the Olympic fund to send our greatest athletes abroad to Athens. J. P. Morgan and several other wealthy donors also pledged donations to the fund. However, the fundraising efforts remained well below the twenty-five-thousand-dollar minimum goal, which left the fate of American watermen in doubt.

OVER THE WINTER, JAM HANDY had broken nineteen American indoor records, and his coach, Frank Sullivan, was boasting, "Now for Daniels and the rest."

Handy and the Chicago newspapers even started touting that Handy had set a handful of "world's records"—more than the great Charles Daniels.

When the international swimming community caught wind of this off the wire, Richard Coombes, the father of amateur athletics in Australia and president of the New South Wales Amateur Athletic Association, published a sharp rebuttal picked up by many American newspapers stating, "This is absurd. Such records are merely *records* because no one else has been clocked over these odd distances."

Without a uniform international governing body, the British Empire's established swimming records were the only acceptable distances to make international comparisons. For the most part, records were recognized at increments of twenty-five yards. And as Coombes pointed out about Handy, "He claims 420 yards in five minutes thirty-seven seconds as a new world's record. Why, Kieran swam 440 yards (twenty yards farther) in five minutes nineteen seconds. This is merely one case. By the way, Handy's friends claim his 280 yards in 3:35.4 as a world's record, whereas Kieran and [Dick] Cavill of this country have both swum 300 yards in faster time."

Every one of Handy's claimed "world records" was indeed over an unrecognized distance. Coombes's public reprimand put an end to Handy's boasting. Coombes's published rebuttal concluded by firing a shot at Charley.

"We do hope your great crack, Daniels, will be at Athens with his 100-yard world's record honors thick upon him," Coombes stated. "If he goes it is my opinion that Healy will outswim him at all distances."

——

IF AMERICAN WATERMEN WERE to rise to the Australian challenge, they needed to prove their "minor sport" worthy of Olympic sponsorship. The way to bring the matter forcibly before the public, as *The Philadelphia Inquirer* noted, was by competitions in the form of speed races. Speed races were exciting. Setting records made headlines. "Every one of these contests," the *Inquirer* correctly observed, "helps very much to accomplish the object of increasing an interest in this health-giving and useful acquirement." And Charley intended to make a lot of excitement at the February AAU Swimming Championships in New York.

San Francisco's J. Scott Leary, who had just set the American century's open-air record of one-minute flat, planned to make the five-day journey by train to challenge Charley at these New York championships. Charley's old coach, Alex Meffert, even claimed that his St. Louis protégé, Mark Schwarz, was better than ever and coming east for Charley's scalp.

"I think Schwarz has an excellent chance to defeat Daniels," voiced Meffert. "Daniels is good. Nobody knows it better than me. It is only a matter of time till I am able to beat him, however, with Schwarz."

One champion noticeably absent from the upcoming competition was Budd Goodwin, who had suffered a severe case of blood poisoning that called for the amputation of his left arm. Fortunately, Doc Hennen, the Winged Foot watermen's guardian angel, refused to accept the prognosis. In a dramatic and unprecedented eighty-minute surgery, Hennen dissected Goodwin's entire left forearm from the elbow to the fingers to stop the toxin from spreading, then reassembled the veins, muscles, and ligaments. For four days, Hennen stayed at Goodwin's bedside until the crisis subsided. The ordeal left Budd with a long ugly scar and without the use of his little finger, but his arm was saved. Budd was recuperating down in Palm Beach, with no expectation to swim competitively for at least several months.

ON WEDNESDAY, FEBRUARY 21, seventy of the country's best swimmers gathered at the New York Athletic Club to compete in the three-day

AAU Championships, including San Francisco's J. Scott Leary and St. Louis's Mark Schwarz. Oddly absent was Jam Handy. There were rumors that since Handy's New Year's Day record-breaking performance, the nineteen-year-old had fallen out of peak condition due to his demanding workload at the *Chicago Tribune*, where he worked in the advertising and newsreel divisions. Others suspected that in the wake of Charley taking up the crawl, the Little Water Devil had gotten cold feet. His coach announced that Handy needed to rest: "There is such a thing as swimming too many races, and that is what Handy has been doing the past few months."

In the event, Charley beat all comers, including Schwarz and Leary, who finished second and third, respectively, and in the process broke thirteen American records. He also tied Dick Cavill's and Cecil Healy's world century record of fifty-eight seconds. The most important witness to Charley's victories that day was Jim Sullivan. However, at that evening's celebratory dinner, where congratulatory remarks were made and prizes handed out by Sullivan, he gave no word about the U.S. watermen's fate for the upcoming Games. With Sullivan already planning to leave for Athens on March 15, Charley's window of opportunity was fast closing. And the American Olympic Committee had raised only $14,864.

WHETHER CHARLEY WAS READY or not, he had to move out of his comfort zone for the sake of his sport and step into the spotlight. Like it or not, he was the face of American swimming. He was America's first century world record holder (even if England refused to acknowledge it). No one could advocate for his fellow watermen the way he could, and his position required him to use his normally silent voice.

Taking a page from Lou Handley's playbook, Charley submitted an article to the *New-York Tribune*. He addressed all the cynics who constantly heaped criticism on American swimmers, as well as any skeptics who questioned sponsoring swimmers for the upcoming Olympiad.

"Unthinking persons often smile at the poorness of some of our records," Charley wrote, "but [our records] are really remarkably good, when everything is taken into consideration." He decried America's lack of swimming facilities as the reason the country lagged so far behind England and Australia.

"Previous to 1900 progress had been desultory," Charley wrote, "then some of the universities became interested and immediately the forward trend began. We have made greater proportionate progress since 1900 than any country in the world, Australia not excluded."

Charley then took a cannon shot at all the naysayers. "Sneering critics, professing to write for the benefit of American sport, have of late been belittling the performances of some of our best men, on the grounds that, while they might be American records, they were so far behind those of other nations as to be ridiculous. Such is not the case, but even were it, the system is wrong. To encourage the man who shows ambitions and possibility is the only way to make him attain his best form. Success is not achieved in a day, nor can we expect miracles, but more will be accomplished by a little judicious praise than by all the sneering on earth."

Charley continued to make his point. "In writing, I have the history of swimming before me, in three pages, containing the annual records of Australia, England and America," Charley noted. "They speak pretty plainly. We are slowly but steadily crawling up on the others. We have already taken the 100 yards world's record, and expect soon to get the 220, which Lane set at 2:28.6, and which the great Kieran tried vainly to replace. Others will follow, for new champions are cropping up on every side, and it will not be many years before American names will have crowded all others off the list of the world's swimming records."

With those bold words, Charley put the U.S. swimming program on his back. "We may have been their laughingstock in years gone by," he wrote, "but I think this time we will show that the progress we have made is not altogether on paper." Charley was essentially promising Jim Sullivan and the American Olympic Committee a gold medal. It was a last appeal to send American watermen to Athens.

At the beginning of March, Sullivan's committee met at the Waldorf Astoria to make its final selection of athletes. A week later, a letter arrived in care of the New York Athletic Club to "Mr. C. M. Daniels" from the "American Committee of the Olympian Games at Athens,

Greece, 1906." It read, "Dear Sir: I beg to advise you that at a meeting of the Committee on Team Selection of the American Committee, Olympic Games, 1906, to be held at Athens, Greece, you were unanimously selected to represent America." After providing some logistical information about traveling to Athens, the letter concluded, "You are now in a responsible position for the eyes of the American public will be on you." It was signed, "Yours truly, James E. Sullivan."

The boy who a decade earlier had read about this mythical place across the world and dreamed about competing in the ancient stadium was actually going.

When Charley told Handley and Wahle, they rejoiced. For the first time, America would finally send worthy representatives to compete in the aquatic events. As later noted by the *New York Athletic Club Journal,* Charley's performance "will be watched with breathless interest by Americans." It was their chance to prove themselves. "We have been a good deal of a joke to the swimming world," Lou noted, and now it was on Charley to show the world otherwise.

WHEN NEWS ABOUT THE American Olympic Committee's decision to send swimmers hit the wire, *The Philadelphia Inquirer* best summed up America's reaction:

A year or two ago, even the very suggestion of including our swimmers in a representative American team at the Olympic contests would have been frowned down upon as almost an insane suggestion. Besides, swimming had never been recognized on the same plane as other branches of sport, and interest in such competitions were [sic] of a mediocre character. But ... by dint of hard training, study of strokes and keeping everlastingly at it, our swimmers have at last compelled the athletic authorities of this country to take notice of their work and recognize it accordingly, with the result that three men have been selected to compete for the stars and stripes against the pick of the world, the selection being Charles M. Daniels and Joseph W. Spencer, of the New York Athletic Club, and Marquard Schwartz [*sic*], of the Missouri Athletic Club, of St. Louis. Daniels now stands in a class all by himself.

But the reporter quickly pointed out, "His most dangerous competitors are Zoltan Halmay, the Hungarian who won the last English 100-yard championship . . . and Australia's best representative, Cecil Healy, of Sydney, who shares the world's 100-yards record with Daniels."

J. Scott Leary was unable to take so much time away from his business interests to join the Olympic team, so Columbia's Joe Spencer, who had graduated and was now a member of the Winged Footers, earned the third spot. A fourth waterman, the Chicagoan Frank Bornamann, was selected for diving, but the Olympic Committee refused to fund one more swimmer. The snub did not sit well with Jam Handy, who could have represented the United States in the distances and helped the relay team.

The hard reality was that if American swimmers failed to make a good showing in Athens, the critics at home and abroad would show no mercy—especially to Charley, as America's No. 1 swimmer. Everything they worked so hard to build would fall like a disgraced house of cards, just like the Daniels family name. And as Sullivan told the press right before his departure, "We all look to Daniels to score several victories." The pressure on Charley could not have been greater.

Before Charley sailed for Athens, his final bit of training entailed heading west on the week of his twenty-first birthday to compete against the top swimmers in Chicago and St. Louis, including Jam Handy and Marquard Schwarz, and perhaps see his father. Charley's uncle, Charles Daniels, Tom's older brother and a Buffalo attorney, was still trustee of whatever remained of Tom's inheritance and would have known his brother's current address.

Tom's Milwaukee home was only a ninety-mile train ride from Chicago. And Charley would be twenty-one. No longer a minor. He and his father could finally talk man to man. However, three weeks before Charley was due to arrive in the Midwest, Tom moved out of his home leaving his second wife, Lydia. Tom accused her of disregarding her marriage relations and duties, using obscene and abusive language toward him, and possessing a violent temper that resulted in Lydia's slapping him across the face, hurling a plate at his chest, and throwing a vase at his head "without any provocation whatsoever."

Lydia accused Tom of adultery. She said Tom stayed away from their Milwaukee home two or three nights a week, and sometimes a week at a time, always claiming to be away on "business." Tom often dined with business associates in Chicago and after drinks and dinner would suggest they take a cab ride down south to "sport," hitting the red-light district on Dearborn Street and visiting half a dozen "sporting houses." At some point he took up with one of the girls. Where Tom was at the moment, Lydia was uncertain. He still had his banking office in Milwaukee, although she suspected he was in Chicago sleeping with lewd women or holed up somewhere with his mistress. What no one realized was that U.S. postal detectives in Chicago had begun watching Tom's every move, as well as his fellow conspirators', making it just a matter of time before his latest fraud ring blew up in Charley's face.

TOM DANIELS COULD NOT have opened a Chicago newspaper without reading about the arrival of the famed "C. M. Daniels." For a week leading up to the races, the *Chicago Tribune* wrote about Charley and the upcoming competitions at the Central YMCA and the Chicago Athletic Association.

When Jam Handy again proved a no-show, rumors swirled that he was not in proper shape. In his absence, Charley broke England's 110-yard world record. There is no indication that Tom Daniels made any effort to see Charley or wish him a happy twenty-first birthday. Then again, Charley had yet to prove himself in head-to-head competition against the world's best, so perhaps Tom was waiting to see if his son could score a victory in Athens before getting in touch.

The next evening at the Missouri Athletic Club's basement tank, in a race to the wire against Mark Schwarz, Charley seemed to unleash all of his pent-up emotions as if pounding his father with each slashing stroke. The burning in his limbs that intensified over the last fifty yards

MARQUARD SCHWARZ AND ALEX MEFFERT

he endured like his father's belittling, using it for fuel, battering one hundred yards of water in an astonishing fifty-six seconds.

The aquatic fraternity stood breathless. Teammates swarmed him. His old coach Alex Meffert congratulated him. The next day, Charley celebrated his twenty-first birthday and became the recipient of his namesake grandfather's gold watch and chain—a fitting gift for America's speed king.

When news of Charley's fifty-six seconds hit England, the English swimming establishment refused to believe it.

AMERICAN NEWSPAPERS WERE CALLING the upcoming Olympic Games in Athens the "Year's Most Important Event in the World of

Sports." On April 2, a rainy Monday evening, thirty-two elite athletes from across the country assembled in the boardroom of the New York Athletic Club, with Charley and Mark Schwarz noticeably absent. The American Olympic Committee called the meeting to welcome the men who would be representing the country in Athens. Giving them instructions left by Jim Sullivan, committee members implored the athletes to adhere to the same good sportsmanship displayed during the 1904 Olympic Games. They were informed that unlike in the prior Olympiads, they would no longer be permitted to wear their athletic clubs' jerseys. Instead, the committee introduced a white jersey with an embossed hand-sized shield on its chest of the Stars and Stripes—the first official U.S. Olympic team uniform. The four aquatic men were to wear dark blue swimsuits with the same patriotic emblem (because white would be a little too revealing once wet).

After a few more encouraging words, the team let out a cheer for "Old Glory."

Neither Lou Handley nor Otto Wahle would accompany the swimmers. The Olympic Committee extended no extra funding for a swim coach. The team's success or failure rested solely on Charley.

The next morning, April 3, the American Olympic team arrived at the docks in Hoboken, New Jersey, and boarded the North German Lloyd steamship *Barbarossa* amid the cheers and good wishes of their relatives, friends, schoolchildren, and former champions. At 11:00 A.M., the U.S. team's thirty-four athletes sailed for Athens. That is, everyone except Mark Schwarz and Charley.

Charley had learned from his previous voyage to Europe how the ten-day transatlantic crossing took a physical toll. There was the potential for seasickness that could leave one malnourished. And while runners could trot up and down the decks, swimmers faced the irony of being surrounded by water yet having no ability to swim in anything larger than their own bathtub. Swimmers needed to train right up to the day of the race to keep their muscles limber. With so much pressure upon him, Charley wanted a few more days to recover and whip himself back into shape, so, upon receiving Sullivan's approval to leave early, he and Schwarz had departed the previous Saturday, March 31. It was a good thing, too. On the U.S. team's second day at sea, as the men assembled on deck for their daily workout routine, a fifteen-foot rogue wave broke over the bow, scattering six unlucky Olympians about the deck like bowling pins. The runner Harry Hillman and weight thrower Jim Mitchell were violently thrown and suffered serious leg injuries. The team hoped the unfortunate incident was not an omen of things to come.

Prior to his departure, Charley had received well wishes from the Winged Footers and bidden Alice goodbye, and then, with Mark Schwarz, he boarded the American Line steamship *New York* for an eight-day journey to England. On Thursday, April 5, while both Charley's steamer and the U.S. team's ship were somewhere on the Atlantic, the earth around the U.S. team's destination port of Naples trembled with a massive volcanic explosion. The legendary Mount Vesuvius that destroyed Pompeii in AD 79 spewed a column of ash and gas that reached a height of eight miles. Fumes from subterranean fires and volcanic slag choked the nearby inhabitants, who fled for open air, while lava flowed and deadly projectiles of molten rock shot from the crater, some weighing as much as a ton.

Upon making port on April 8 in Southampton, England, Charley and Schwarz traveled to London for a few days of swimming practice with the Otters, then took a boat across the English Channel and a train to Paris, and then boarded the Rome Express for a thirty-hour journey to the ancient capital, changed trains, and headed five hours south to Naples, unsure if the ship that was scheduled to take them the rest of the way to Athens was even able to make port amid all the destruction.

When they arrived in Naples, lava dust clouded the air. Gray ash covered the streets and rooftops like snow after a winter storm. More than one hundred people had perished in the eruption. Roads around the volcano were impassable. Rooftops had collapsed under the weight of the volcanic debris. There were reports that three nearby villages had been buried under three feet of ejecta, and the town of Boscotrecase had been enveloped by lava streams.

Under the dark polluted sky, they made their way through the ghostly seaside town, where most of the shops were eerily closed. An occasional coughing figure moved through the gray fog. Others walked with umbrellas to shield themselves from the snow of falling embers. When they finally made their way down to the port, they saw their steamship, but the destruction made one thing clear: the repair costs to the Italian government would be overwhelming. Funding a luxury like the 1908 Olympic Games no longer seemed feasible. It felt like another bad sign about what lay ahead.

By Easter Monday, after weeks of sleeping on rocking boats and rickety trains, and trying to keep down barely digestible food, Charley and Schwarz finally made port in Piraeus, about seven miles southwest of Athens's city center, ready for a good meal and great night's sleep, only to discover the Greeks had other plans for them. A reception committee greeted them. A band played "The Star-Spangled Banner." They were then taken by a horse-drawn carriage into town for another reception at the Athens Olympic Committee's headquarters. When they finally returned to their carriage, they were whisked away to another obligatory meet and greet. They again traveled over newly paved asphalt streets, passing freshly painted government buildings, an endless array of white-and-blue-striped Greek flags, and signs in strange Greek lettering. High above them, the distant hilltop ruins of the Acropolis and Parthenon came into view. The horse came to a stop at a long yellow two-story building with an iconic front colonnade of white pillars. Above its entrance was inscribed the name Zappeion. It looked like a hall of government, yet if they understood their Greek hosts correctly, for the next two weeks it was to be their home.

The vast building had been constructed by the late Evangelis Zappas, a rich businessman who, in 1865, hoping for a future revival of the Olympic Games, bequeathed his fortune to establish an Olympic trust fund. He left further instructions and money to construct a building designated to serve Olympic needs. For these Games, it had been transformed into the first Olympic Village.

Their Greek hosts led them into the Zappeion's great exhibition hall, where inside they passed a beautiful open-air rotunda surrounded by colonnades on their way to the adjoining rooms that had been converted into dormitory housing. Rows of small, curtained cubicles had been erected with partitions about seven feet high. The spaces were akin to stalls, offering an uncomfortable mattress and little privacy, let alone any chance of a quiet night's sleep. The daily menu consisted of unfamiliar goat meat and poor-quality water. Charley and Schwarz smiled, thanked their hosts, and then quickly walked out to find a hotel. Four minutes from the Zappeion they froze in their tracks.

Whatever their concerns were about finding a hotel, or thinking about the upcoming competitions, or whatever was on their minds vanished that instant. Nothing they had ever before encountered or seen applied to this moment. What once seemed like a fairy tale to Charley now manifested itself in full glory. Across a bridge, over a narrow river, past an impressive colonnade of arched entrance gates, their eyes gazed upon what would be the epicenter of the athletic world for the next twelve days. Nestled between the twin pine-covered hills of Ardettos and Agra, the two-thousand-year-old Panathenaic Stadium arose in its white marble splendor, with its horseshoe-shaped arena opened toward the river. They stood motionless, without words, their senses of observation heightened as they absorbed every detail of its sheer size and magnificence. This was a stadium.

The following day, they met up with Jim Sullivan, who had arrived a few days earlier, and attended a reception where Edward, king of the United Kingdom and Ireland and emperor of India, was introduced to the athletes. Having assumed the throne five years earlier, upon the passing of his iconic mother, Queen Victoria, this short, gray-bearded, portly, middle-aged king—rumored to have an insatiable appetite for food, drink, gambling, and other men's wives—represented the golden age of the British upper class, an era defined by the new Edwardian morality of excess, entitlement, and discreet sexual debauchery, so long as, according to Edward, it didn't "frighten the horses."

Under Edward's encouragement, this golden age was fueled in part by an estimated billion dollars in American bridal dowries. Debutantes of America's *nouveau riche*, longing to increase their social status with prestigious royal titles, readily entered into cash-for-title marriages with insolvent British lords desperately looking to maintain their extravagant highborn lifestyles and shore up their crumbling castles. While these English lords eagerly took Yankee dowries, they still thumbed their noses at American society. Even America's richest man, William Waldorf Astor, who had attended Alice and Tom's wedding, abandoned the United States for English citizenship and his own castle, announcing that America was "no longer a fit place for a gentleman to live."

Charley, Schwarz, and Sullivan were presented to the British monarch, who did not shake hands as Americans were accustomed to doing. British noblemen resisted such affections. Nor did the British highborn remove their hats to someone of lower class. They expected

AMERICAN OLYMPIC TEAM, ATHENS, 1906
(CHARLES M. DANIELS IN SECOND ROW,
SECOND FROM RIGHT)

PANATHENAIC STADIUM, ATHENS,
OPENING CEREMONIES, 1906

to be addressed by lofty titles such as "Your Royal Highness," "Your Grace," or "Your Lord." The Yankee trio bowed to "His Most Excellent Majesty, King Edward," but Jim Sullivan had no love for any self-important royal who thought his blue blood made him superior to Americans. Charley agreed with him, thinking that people who put on such airs reminded him of his father.

17.

AWAKENING ZEUS'S THUNDERBOLTS

—

APRIL-JUNE 1906

W HEN THE BULK OF THE AMERICAN TEAM ARRIVED THE NEXT day, they brought with them devastating news from back home that rattled Charley's ability to focus on the upcoming contests.

The previous day, April 18, at 5:12 A.M., a 7.9-magnitude earthquake had shaken San Francisco to the ground. It toppled buildings, ignited fires that ravaged the city, and claimed three thousand lives. When it ended, 80 percent of the city sat in rubble, including the premier clubhouse of the Olympic Athletic Club, where the champion swimmers J. Scott Leary, Frank Gailey, and Syd Cavill belonged. Over the next two days, newspapers continued to stoke fears of another big quake out west, with reports of aftershocks and earthquakes as far north as Oregon and as far south as Southern California, where Grandma Meldrum and Aunt Flossie were still wintering. Charley had no means of knowing if they were all right or how his mother was handling the news and uncertainty. With communication lines down across the West Coast, Buffalonians were still anxiously awaiting telegrams from loved ones in California confirming their safety.

Already the long journey and lack of nutrition had taken a toll on Charley, and now he was distracted. His daily swims were short, extending only the time necessary for him to negotiate his distance in the freezing Greek sea. In the days before the Games, Charley seemed listless, not focused, and far from his usual form.

———

SUNDAY MORNING, APRIL 22, Charley awoke to the day he had dreamed about since he was eleven years old. All roads leading to Athens saw a constant procession of wagons and citizens. Excitement swept the city, resounding with an occasional cheer from the gathering crowds. Hours ahead of time, carriages and individuals began making their way through the throngs of street revelers leading toward the stadium, as an indescribable spirit electrified the air. The feeling was something more than being among the ancient ruins. More than the awestruck impression Charley felt upon first laying eyes on the glorious ancient stadium. Something else made the opening of the 1906 Olympic Games remarkable.

Around two o'clock, Charley and his U.S. teammates walked across the bridge over the river Ilisos to the stadium's arched gates, where all the teams began assembling, awaiting the anticipated three o'clock arrival of the Greek and British royal families. Most of the Olympians wore hats, suits, and ties. The U.S. team all wore suits and white newsboy caps and lined up in rows of four men across.

Charley spotted several of his competitors among the other teams. His old St. Louis vanquisher, Zoltán Halmay, stood with the Hungarians. Another St. Louis gold medalist, Emil Rausch, appeared with the Germans. The team from the British Empire included aquatic giants like Rob Derbyshire, John Jarvis, the rising distance champion, Henry Taylor, and from Australia, the formidable Cecil Healy. Conspicuously missing was David "Boy" Billington, who had unwittingly lost his amateur status the prior year by entering a race against a professional, barring him from Olympic competition. But the biggest void was the late Barney Kieran, whose name occupied just about every world record in England's Amateur Swimming Association's books.

A swell of distant cheers erupted north of the stadium. All heads turned as the din grew louder and closer and the nearby crowds pushed toward the stadium's entrance, obscuring the athletes' view. Suddenly Greek military personnel stretched out in two long parallel lines from the entrance's arched gates, forming a ten-foot-wide lane between them as they faced each other. As the cheers grew deafening, the Greek royal family's procession of open-air carriages appeared from their half-mile journey from the Royal Palace to the stadium. King George stepped out first, wearing an admiral's uniform and accompanied by his sister Queen Alexandra of England. Next came her husband, King Edward VII, accompanied by Queen Olga of Greece, followed by the Greek crown prince and the Prince and Princess of Wales.

When committee members escorted them inside the stadium, the explosion of applause drowned out the band. The mad cheers eventually ceased just enough for King George to address the crowd. The instant he proclaimed the Games open, organizers signaled the athletes to begin the first ever parade of nations.

They entered in alphabetical order, according to their French names, except for England, who for some reason stepped ahead of America. First came the Germans, then the English, the Americans, the Australians, the Belgians, the Danish, the French, the Hungarians, the Italians, the Norwegians, the Swedes, and last, the host country. One bright spot resulting from Coubertin's absence from these Games: the Danish featured the first female team—a group of women, parading in white dresses, there to perform an exhibition of gymnastics.

The United States led with a row of their four biggest men, shocking spectators with the size of these giants. Charley marched in the second row, right behind the hulking (for the era) six-foot-three Martin Sheridan. Words could hardly describe the impression the stadium made on the athletes as they entered the gates: tiers of white marble seats rising to the clouds, its unsurpassed size and dimension, its fifty thousand euphoric citizens on their feet. As the overwhelming applause reverberated in his chest, Charley felt giddy. The moment exceeded anything he'd imagined as a young boy.

Charley saw thousands of Greek soldiers atop the stadium lining the entire upper row, their heads dotting the sky as they stood shoulder to shoulder to prevent the fifty thousand more people on the hills from stepping over the marble wall. Dressed in traditional kilts, white wool jackets, and red fezzes, the soldiers, called evzones, made for an imposing if not peculiar spectacle, especially when one imagines how many there must have been, considering the stadium's upper outer wall measured more than one-third of a mile in circumference.

Jim Sullivan could not imagine another place in the world to hold an Olympic Games. Having refused to attend the Olympiad's inaugural revival a decade earlier, he was a reformed sinner ready to rejoice "Amen!" The Greeks' enthusiasm elevated these Games to a magnitude not felt in Paris or St. Louis. "The people seemed enthused over something that meant more than sport," he commented. "To them these Olympic Games were a sacred festival . . . reminiscences of the days of the Greek splendors and supremacy."

The teams rounded the narrow arena track with the intensity of troops marching into battle, but Charley could not stop smiling.

As each team passed in front of the royal box, members saluted according to the custom of their own country and marched to their reserved seats in the stadium's left wing.

Never before had any of the participants witnessed such a fervent celebration. To Charley, marching in the opening ceremony at Athens was one of the biggest thrills of his life.

"Where in the world could one collect an audience of at least 100,000 to witness the sight?" Sullivan later recalled, quickly concluding, "Nowhere but at Athens; classic Athens."

AFTER THE OPENING CEREMONY, a reception for the athletes commenced in the Zappeion's rotunda, attended by the royals and all the foreign ministers. The most highly anticipated events, track and field, would not begin until Wednesday, giving those athletes a few more days to train, relax, and explore the city's ancient ruins and surrounding countryside. Swimming commenced on Tuesday, with those men under greater pressure from home to prove that the American Olympic Committee had made the right decision, spending good money to send its watermen to Athens.

ON WEDNESDAY MORNING, APRIL 25, Charley awoke knowing that in just a few hours his fate would be decided. When he returned to his hotel later that day, he would either be Olympic century champion or a huge disappointment.

1906, ATHENS, OLYMPIC SWIMMING CONTESTS,
BAY OF PHALERUM

A picturesque cobalt sky greeted him when he walked out of his hotel around 7:00 A.M. and climbed aboard a horse-drawn carriage for the forty-minute journey to the Bay of Phalerum, where the final hundred-meter race was scheduled for nine o'clock that morning.

The previous day's events had gotten the American swimmers off to a disappointing start. Joe Spencer had taken on a twenty-seven-man field in the one-mile freestyle, finishing a disappointing tenth.

Today, Charley faced the fastest men in the world. The all-star field included his former St. Louis Olympic rival, Zoltán Halmay, Australia's Cecil Healy, England's Rob Derbyshire, the rising English star Paolo "Raddy" Radmilovic, and Charley's scrappy teammate, Mark Schwarz.

Charley felt the pressure and expectations after winning his preliminary heat the day before. The *Chicago Tribune* touted "Daniels Picked to Win Finals." The *Spokane Daily Chronicle* headlined, "One American Shows Class." *The New York Times* proved a little less enthusiastic, proclaiming on page 12, "Olympic Contests Begin—Minor Sports Occupy the Day—Swimmers Compete." If Charley lost, there would be a lot of "I told you sos." As *The Philadelphia Inquirer* correctly observed, Charley faced "dangerous competitors."

Fred Wenck, the Winged Foot water polo player, best summed up the overall outlook regarding American swimmers' chances in Athens.

"We have ever been a joke to the rest of the world when it came to swimming races. Therefore, few people thought very seriously of our entrants at the world's championships at Athens, and confidently expected that either the Australian, Healy, the Hungarian, Halmay, or the men from England would win out."

When Charley arrived at the dock, the first rival he spotted was Zoltán Halmay. A fierce competitor, he looked even stronger than he had in St. Louis.

Next he saw the twenty-four-year-old Australian Cecil Healy. Of medium height, stocky, with powerful arms and shoulders, a kind face, and the intense eyes of a warrior, Cecil was only fourteen when his father had died, the same age as Charley when Tom Daniels had walked out on them. The death of Cecil's father put too much of a financial strain on the family to allow him to attend university, so the boy had used his talent for swimming to make a name for himself. In 1901, he was selected for the "Flying Squad," a five-man relay team with the legendary Freddie Lane, and won the New South Wales championship. He perfected a two-beat Australian crawl and in 1904 joined Dick Cavill and Alick Wickham as one of only three people in the world to break a one-minute century. The following year, he equaled Dick Cavill's world record of fifty-eight seconds, which remained one of the few records Barney Kieran had failed to better.

Lou Handley had forewarned Charley to watch out for both Halmay and Healy. "Healy is one of those phenomenal all-round swimmers who can tackle anything from the 'hundred' to the mile with equal success." And "Halmay," Lou had noted, "has improved greatly since [St. Louis] and won the hundred-yard English championship last summer in fifty-nine seconds. He is said to have done even better during the winter."

Charley also noticed twenty-seven-year-old John "Rob" Derbyshire, short and trim, sporting a mustache. One of England's greatest speed champions and record holders, Rob was the son of a Manchester baths superintendent and was a natural. Until Dick Cavill's crawl hit the scene, Derbyshire was the fastest century swimmer on the planet.

Due to organizational snafus, the men stood around for several hours, and the boats did not ferry them to the starting line until closer to 11:30 A.M. Few spectators attended. Greece's naval fleet lined up side by side to mark off the course, together with rowboats and sailboats filled with officials and spectators.

Charley surveyed the ocean and saw that the conditions were not good. In addition to the naval fleet having dumped their garbage into the water, Charley judged the course as bad a one as could have been picked. It was laid out where winds had an unchecked sweep and the water was so rough as to make victory as much a question of brute strength as of speed, which is hardly a fair test of swimming.

Ocean swimming was more difficult than in fresh water. The turbulence hindered the body's ability to slice through the sea. Salt water's density made it slightly thicker and rather sticky, which slowed the body and stung the eyes.

There was also no float to dive from as at the St. Louis Games. Charley and the field of Olympians were taken out in boats to the start of the course and told to jump in and wait at the starting buoys. Easier said than done. The water was so cold the men had to brace themselves to willingly inflict such pain upon their bodies. No one can ever be prepared for such a shock. When Charley plunged into the freezing bay, he felt hit by a thousand needles. Soon, his teeth began chattering and his body shivering as he treaded water at the starting line, hoping to hear the pistol before hypothermia set in. Officials and spectators stood in rowboats that lined the course. The current was already stretching the marker buoys apart, lengthening the 100-meter distance to about a 106-meter straightaway, which made this metric course more than sixteen yards longer than the 100-yard century Charley was used to.

The frigid sea made Charley's lungs contract, triggering breathing problems. His muscles tightened, his arms and legs felt heavy, and the cold slowed his heart rate as much as 25 percent, constricting blood flow to his extremities. His body burned precious energy trying to stay warm, which meant the monster would come sooner.

As if the cold weren't bad enough, waiting for the call of the race was psychological torture. Charley struggled to control his nerves and insecurities. He needed to push aside the weight of the moment, the global ramifications of the outcome, and try to boil it all down to a one-hundred-meter race—which was growing longer by the minute.

The starters called the athletes into position in Greek. Charley hoped to settle his nerves enough to avoid a false start.

Halmay looked intense, as did Healy and Derbyshire.

"Etoimos." The starter called them to *get ready*.

"Etoimasou!" *Get set!*

Off the pistol's crack, the water turned into an instant boil. The salt water burned their naked eyes. Charley's muscles stiffened in the cold, making swimming painful.

Healy jumped out with his Australian crawl and his two-beat kick syncing with each arm stroke. Halmay shot forward with his kickless crawl. Derbyshire relied on the trudgen. Mark Schwarz drew a bad course and swam crooked. Charley's American crawl broke through the pack. A spirited battle ensued down the last half of the straightaway between Charley and Halmay. Charley fought through the waves, the cold, searing eyeballs, constricted breath, and eventually paralyzing muscle pain, awaiting another of Halmay's last-second speed bursts as in St. Louis. The current continued to push the finish-marker buoys farther and farther away, prolonging the agony as his arms felt as if they no longer worked. Other than stopping or backing off, the only way Charley could endure the intolerable burning was to try to block out the pain by concentrating on his stroke, kicking harder to finish sooner, and tricking the mind into believing there was less distance to the finish than there actually was. *Only five more seconds of pain.* He crossed the finish to resounding cheers. His enthusiastic countrymen whooped and hollered from the docks, waving the Stars and Stripes. He had clipped Halmay by a meter. Cecil Healy finished a distant third. Charley's teammate, Mark Schwarz, who had shown such promise back in the States, finished last.

Back home, *The Buffalo Commercial* exclaimed that Charley's victory marked "a new era in American aquatics," reporting, "Daniels is the first Yankee to win in open competition against the best swimmers in the world." His victory, the paper continued, "will give to the swimmers of the United States a prestige which they have not hitherto enjoyed."

The English swimming establishment promptly dismissed Charley's victory. Beyond the poor conditions of the Athens sea, the current that pushed the end-marker buoys to a course length of 110 meters they claimed made the race illegitimate.

The English newspapers mentioned how the favorite, Cecil Healy, who took third, was "anything but satisfied with the result of the Athens race, and thinks that the general conditions on that occasion were anything but conducive to a fair trial of strength." And in fact they had a point. Healy had arrived in Athens after a long sea voyage shortly before the contest and had no time to acclimate to the venue. The rough seas had Halmay coughing up water the entire race. Further, the Hungarian team's lean financial situation gave them no choice but to accept the less-than-ideal living accommodations at the Zappeion, which did not allow for the good night's sleep the Americans had. They also ate goat's meat, which was unfamiliar to the Hungarian diet, and drank poor-quality water that upset their stomachs. All of it took a toll on their physical condition.

The ghost of Barney Kieran loomed large as well. Nothing short of Charley breaking a world record would have dissuaded the British Empire from insisting that Kieran would have claimed gold had he been alive. And even then, they probably would insist that Kieran also would have broken the world record.

Things unraveled further from there. To give the American team the best chance to win the 4 x 250 relay (four men swimming 250 yards each), both Charley and Joe Spencer decided to save their energy, withdrawing from the 400-meter freestyle scheduled immediately before the relay. They agreed that a team victory would bring more glory to America than an individual one.

However, to their dismay, storms postponed the afternoon 4 x 250 relay to another day. Their best-laid plan proved a missed opportunity, leaving them on the sidelines for the 400 meters while they watched Austria's sixteen-year-old Otto Scheff win gold and England's Henry Taylor and John Jarvis claim silver and bronze. *The Evening World* of New York best summed up America's disappointment at their American champion with the simple headline "He Didn't Start."

After the Europeans outclassed America's Frank Bornamann in diving, U.S. swimmers had one last chance to prove their worth. Because the American Olympic Committee had balked at sending a fourth swimmer like Jam Handy, Bornamann had to round out the relay team. Although the modern relay strategy is to place the two fastest swimmers at the first and fourth relay legs, they opted to put their slowest, Bornamann, at the front.

"[Bornamann's] opponents set a fast pace from the start," recalled Charley, "and, although he responded nobly, swimming a hard and gritty race, he was quite exhausted by the time he had covered 150 yards, and trailed to about forty yards behind the field. We did our level best to pick this up, but it wasn't in us."

Halmay avenged his earlier loss to Charley by leading the Hungarian relay team to an impressive victory. Twenty-six seconds later, the Germans claimed silver. The bronze went to Britain. The United States finished a disappointing fourth.

"Universal regret was expressed that H. J. Handy had not been chosen a member of the team," lamented Charley, believing he not only would've helped them in the relay but might have had a good chance at medaling in the mile and quarter-mile races.

Their relay defeat evoked more haughty grins from their critics at home and abroad, as did Charley's teammates being completely outclassed in their individual events.

Back home, Jam Handy made his own statement about being left out of the Olympics by breaking twenty-seven American records from five hundred yards to the mile, with eight of those records being Charley's.

AMERICAN TRACK-AND-FIELD ATHLETES DOMINATED the medal podium. Participating in twenty events, they won twenty-three medals— eleven gold, six silver, and six bronze—"while England," crowed Sullivan, "with all her possessions," took home only three gold medals.

In Coubertin's absence, Sullivan, with his prior Olympic organizing success, became the person Greek officials looked to as the ultimate sporting authority. When a problem arose in the competition, the royal officials in Athens turned to Sullivan for advice. Three IOC members in attendance even voiced their opinion that they hoped Sullivan would become an IOC member himself and encouraged him to write Coubertin expressing his interest. Their support filled him with excitement.

Lord Desborough, the flag bearer for the British Olympic team in the opening ceremony's parade of nations and winner of the silver medal in fencing, was also working to gain a seat on the IOC. The fifty-year-old sportsman was the epitome of British manliness. With a broad chest and beefy arms that looked as if the lord split rails for a living—which he most certainly did not—he was as fit and strong as any man half his age. In his youth, Desborough had sculled for Oxford's champion crew team. He had rowed across the English Channel, twice swum the rapids at the base of Niagara Falls where Matthew Webb met his demise, three times climbed the Matterhorn, hunted big game all over the world, held a seat in the House of Commons until being elevated to the House of Lords upon his bestowed lordship in 1905, and was a firm believer in the strength of the British Empire. Now, as a proud Olympian, he began worrying about the Italian government's inability to fund the 1908 Games and the devastating effects it would have on the Olympic movement.

CHARLEY'S LONE VICTORY IN a "minor sport" had added one more gold medal to America's coffers. Back home, Alice Daniels clipped out a headline from the *Buffalo Courier* that read, "Americans Win at Athens Games—C. M. Daniels, Well Known in This City, First in Brilliant Swimming Contest." The article went on to say, "He is a grandson of former Judge Daniels and a nephew of H. A. Meldrum." It made no mention of either of Charley's parents.

On the final day of the Athens Olympics, sixty thousand cheering spectators shook the stadium for the closing ceremonies. As his name was announced, Charley departed from the ranks of standing athletes and walked to the royal box, where His Majesty King George presented him with the classic olive branch and a gold medal, just as he had read about as a boy.

The medal was about two inches in diameter, made of gilt silver, and felt the weight of about two slices of bread, with the front featuring a giant head of Zeus, along with the Greek letters for "Olympia," and the back showing the Acropolis and Parthenon with more Greek words and the year "1906."

During a reception given by the American foreign minister, once again attended by a flotilla of royals and many prominent Americans, Mark Schwarz fell asleep at the post-dinner dance and awoke to discover his jokester teammates had turned him into a walking autograph collection, with all their signatures inscribed across the front of his nicely pressed white button-down shirt.

At their final dinner in Athens, packed into their hotel dining room, Sullivan read a cablegram dispatched from President Roosevelt upon hearing the news of their dominant performance in track and field. "Hearty congratulations to you and the American contestants. Uncle Sam is all right." Three long cheers went up for their athletic president. But in swimming, Uncle Sam was not all right.

While the rest of America's victorious Olympians eventually returned home to be greeted in New York Harbor by a steamship carrying a welcoming party led by Albert Spalding, Charley's work in Europe had just begun.

CECIL HEALY, AUSTRALIA, 1906

18.

TAKING ON THE EMPIRE

—

JUNE-JULY 1906

EﾠNGLAND'S AMATEUR SWIMMING ASSOCIATION SPONSORED SEVEN annual championship races: the Long-Distance Championship swum in a river over a distance of either five or six miles; the Mile and Half-Mile Championships swum in a lake; the Salt-Water Championship swum in the ocean over a distance of 440 yards; and the 500-Yard, 220-Yard, and 100-Yard Century Championships, all swum in a pool. The ASA required that each contestant submit an official entry form with his five-shilling entry fee no later than five days before the race, with the ASA reserving the right to refuse any entrant without providing a reason. Charley planned to compete in the Century Championship in July.

Rather than start training right away, Charley followed Handley's advice to put more smiles on his face and took the next month to travel Europe, enjoying the sights, replenishing his soul, so that, come June, he would be excited to swim again. He read the groundbreaking news out of Finland that made it the first European country to give women the right to vote. When he finally arrived in London on Sunday, May 27, he discovered that Healy and Halmay had been training there for nearly a month.

Funded by the NYAC, he took up residence at the Thackeray Hotel in central London, opposite the British Museum, where a night's lodging cost around $2.50. The place was also a temperance hotel, which meant no booze allowed, even though Charley was known to take an occasional drink and smoke.

Charley's return to London was no longer as an inconsequential American champion. He was the Olympic gold medalist in the one-hundred-meter race and current world record holder of one hundred yards, even if the Brits disputed both.

Unlike his last visit, where he struggled to schedule races with top contenders, this time the promoter William Henry, who'd helped England's freestyle relay team take bronze in Athens, took Charley under his management and arranged good side matches leading up to the championships.

The British Empire's watermen proved eager to avenge their loss against the American under more favorable swimming conditions than the tempestuous Athens sea. Now that Healy had two months in London to prepare, he would be ready. Halmay, too, anticipated much better performances in ordinary tank contests.

As for England's best sprinters, they began to awaken to the uncomfortable reality that their resistance to adopt the crawl had left them at a disadvantage. After Derbyshire's disappointing performance in Athens, *The Manchester Courier and Lancashire General Advertiser* wrote, "It must be confessed that England is quite out in the cold when mention is made of champion short distance swimmers. J. H. Derbyshire is our best man, much better than all the rest in Great Britain, but he is only fourth."

This deficit forced the English to turn to the British Empire's colonial Australians. Even a win from the Hungarian would be better than an American victory; at least Zoltán Halmay was a fellow European. By attracting Halmay and Healy to the English Championships, the British swimming establishment anticipated seeing the upstart American put back in his rightful place.

English newspapers, as well as the European swimming community, continued to doubt the validity of Charley's fifty-six-second world record. When dealing with his American performances, reporters often wrote, "Daniels claims," or "It is said," or "If this be true," implying that they had only Charley's word for it, which was particularly irritating to Charley, having worked doubly hard to build a reputation of the utmost integrity to counter that of his father. But in reality, Charley's speed frightened England's swimming world, and they hoped Cecil Healy would put an end to the matter.

In anticipation of the 1906 English Championships, which included races from a hundred yards to the mile, the British Empire's *Ottawa Journal* wrote, "The presence of the late Barney Kieran served to make last season a memorable one to swimmers, but this year may prove even more interesting. Australia has again sent up a great swimmer in Cecil Healy, whose home records prove him to be a wonder. He hardly did justice to himself at Athens, but hopes to be in record-breaking shape for the 100 yards English championship, which will be decided at Nottingham on July 12 . . . We can hardly expect J. H. Derbyshire to prove equal to the task, so must hope that Healy will be able to score for the honor of the Empire."

The *Manchester Evening News* was even more blunt about England's prospects: "As it is unlikely that Derbyshire will turn out we will have the sorry spectacle of the first three positions being filled by visitors to our shores—a fear unknown in the annals of English swimming."

THE PRESSURE WAS MOUNTING on Charley. Unlike the prior year's English Championships, the spotlight now shone white hot on him. Newspapers back home, in Europe, and in Australia would be covering his every stroke. Without the nearby support of his mother, aunt, and grandmother that he enjoyed last time, and with his Olympic and Winged Foot teammates an ocean away, he had to face this daunting challenge alone.

Charley had no one to help correct his stroke, make adjustments, or assist him in returning to peak racing form. With the rest of the U.S. Olympic team back in America, he found himself the lone gunslinger riding into town. But when he reached London, ready to check in to his hotel by himself, Otto Wahle was waiting for him.

———

WAHLE WAS NOT ABOUT to let the fate of U.S. swimming be decided without some say in the matter. And Charley's previous stint in the U.K. had clearly proven he needed all the help he could get.

Charley had never been happier to see his twenty-six-year-old coach.

Wahle was a systematic trainer. Not being a natural swimmer, he had relied on persistence and hard work to climb to the top. His method was to first figure out the time he needed to win a race and then proceed to train down to it.

Charley and Wahle trained together at the Otters' home swimming pool. They planned to focus strictly on sprinting. If Charley took care of himself and stuck to the training schedule, Wahle believed he could go under fifty-six seconds. Wahle also believed there was much to learn about swimming from Mozart and Beethoven.

Music trains the power of imagination. One must understand how a certain note should sound in order to play it. When musicians see a note, they hear its sound, and their hands or their fingers or their lips go where they need to play that note. Practice gives them muscle memory. They practice so their hands know precisely where to go. When one plays a piece of music, there are many notes to understand, so the musician must anticipate, practicing diligently so that each note is hit in perfect sequence until the piece is over. Similarly, in swimming, it isn't enough to learn a fast stroke or a good wall technique. One has to understand the entire course, the entire composition, the entire race. Each pool, like every musical composition, is different. Each has its own personality. The water varies in temperature and clarity. Most natatoriums at the time were not well ventilated. Many were not well lit, which could make swimmers feel lethargic. Most important, without any standard dimensions, the various lengths, widths, and depths created different ripples and waves in the water that affected momentum. A competitor had to have a plan and know exactly how many strokes it would take to reach the wall so he could anticipate the strokes leading up to it.

If a swimmer had not acquired a knack for anticipating the wall and turning quickly in that particular tank, he would be beaten every time. To do this well, he had to be intimate with the pool and know exactly how many strokes would carry him the length of it. Then he would know just when to prepare for the turn and when to kick off. Most swimmers negotiated turns by swimming right up to the end of the pool, which slowed them down. And depending on the length of the pool, he needed to be able to touch the wall with whichever hand hit it first and turn accordingly. There was no such thing as being right-handed or left-handed. A well-executed turn and kick off the wall provided a critical advantage, and practice was the only way to earn it.

Charley needed to work on perfecting his turns, and Wahle knew that the best way to go about it was to train him to swim as if he were blind. If it took twenty strokes to reach the end, he should know after the nineteenth to execute his turn. He should be able to swim the race in his mind long before he stepped onto the starting edge. Close his eyes, start the watch in his head, know how many breaths, how many strokes, and which hand he'd use to make the turn, and know exactly where his opponents would be without ever needing to look.

"You should not care about what your opponent is doing until the final stretch," Wahle said, emphasizing the need to be true to your pace. "The only time to sprint is at the finish, when every ounce left may be expended."

Several times a week, Charley's training schedule allowed for competitions around England. British reporters noticed that his once skinny physique looked considerably more toned than it had the previous year. During one race at the Nautilus Club, when Charley broke the 150-yard English record and then clocked a record-breaking century of 57.6 seconds, the Amateur Swimming Association of England refused to recognize either. In discounting his fast time, the association pointed out a technicality. True, the 25-yard tank he swam in complied with the minimum racing length. Yes, the timekeeping was conducted by a bona fide ASA committeeman, and another half a dozen competent men verified the official's stopwatch. However, as *The Manchester Courier and Lancashire General Advertiser* commented, "the only thing wanting was a little forethought of the Nautilus Club members to have written the governing authorities for the appointment of specially appointed watch-holders in anticipation of a great effort by our Yankee visitor, and then all would have been well."

According to the rules, the secretary of the district association must receive the names of the timekeepers and judges prior to the race. Because the Nautilus Club failed to comply, Charley's remarkable times did not qualify as official records. A week later in Richmond, Charley and Wahle made certain to comply with all necessary record-qualifying protocols for the century, and Charley clocked a jaw-dropping 57.4 seconds, even faster than the previous race.

The next morning, Charley's record appeared as a simple mention on page 8 of London's *Daily Telegraph and Courier*. On page 11, almost just as buried, was a report that certainly sickened Wahle. Another Russian pogrom had resulted in the massacre of eighty-two Polish Jews. All his life, Otto Wahle had used swimming as a way of challenging anti-Semitism. The brilliance of sport was that it gave outsiders like him and Charley a chance to prove they belonged. The water was the ultimate equalizer. Society might be able to shun them, but no person could hide behind their prejudices and "superior" pedigrees in the gladiatorial arena.

And in what seemed to be yet another effort to rattle Charley, England's *Evening Star and Daily Herald* reported that back in the States, Jam Handy was "taking further advantage of the absence of C. M. Daniels," noting how Handy had smashed eight of Charley's American records. In a country that rarely bothered to report what the lowly American swimmers were doing across the pond, this seemed deliberately orchestrated to throw Charley's status as American champion in dispute and shake his confidence.

TEN DAYS BEFORE THE Century Championship, the Royal Life Saving Society's Annual Gala at the London Bath Club called together all the contenders in the evening for a 120-yard scratch race. The heads of England's swimming establishment were all there, as well as what looked like the entire House of Lords and their ladies. A waist-high curtain ran along the side of the pool to protect the spectators' fancy clothes against splashes.

"This was more a social than athletic club," Charley recalled. "Most of the members were titled. The Earl of Sussex was the president and the Duke of Gloucester was honorary president. Black ties and evening gowns were worn by the spectators." Lord Desborough presided over the evening's program. To a young American like Charley, it was another education in the British upper-class social hierarchy, which was divided into three rivalrous subcategories: the royal family being the upper upper; the aristocracy, as the middle upper, who of course had a hierarchy of their own; and finally the lower upper, made up of citizens who had earned their wealth.

Down at the poolside, the competition was equally fierce. Charley found himself surrounded by champions. On one side of him at the start were George Dockrell and Herman Meyboom, champions of Ireland and Belgium. On the other side were Cecil Healy, champion of Australia; Zoltán Halmay of Hungary, the European champion; and John Derbyshire, champion of the British Empire.

Charley familiarized himself with the thirty-yard tank, which was ten yards longer than his practice pool at the Otters' St. George's Baths. The race comprised four laps. Charley would later say that swimming during this unusual black-tie affair made it one of his most memorable races. He appeared very nervous on the starting platform, yet he edged out Healy with a record-setting time. The upstart American had now officially snatched two British speed records. But the big prize, the century, was just ten days away.

THE CENTURY CHAMPIONSHIP WAS scheduled for July 12, 130 miles north of London at Nottingham's Victoria Baths. Its exhibition pool was said to be the largest in the kingdom, stretching an astounding 110 feet, longer than any pool Charley had ever swum. Its unfamiliar length meant that Charley would have to practice timing his strokes to the wall. Unfortunately, his English promoter, William Henry, had scheduled an exhibition at St. Marylebone Baths in London on the evening of July 10, which would keep Charley from departing London until a day before the championship race. Perhaps that was precisely Henry's intention.

If Charley and Wahle objected, Henry persuaded them to honor the commitment. It was already being promoted as the American champion's attempt to break the century record. For Charley to renege at this point would make him appear unreliable, and he was loath to gain an untrustworthy reputation like his father's. But what Henry certainly knew, and Charley and Wahle might not have been aware of, was that Cecil Healy and Zoltán Halmay planned to skip the event. Instead, they had already traveled north to Nottingham to spend the entire week training and familiarizing themselves with the long pool.

In the days leading up to the Marylebone race, after a workout at St. George's Baths, Charley was toweling off when an English gentleman asked if he wouldn't mind getting back into the water. Two well-dressed boys about ages twelve and ten who'd heard about the new English records set by the American champion asked to see him swim. Charley obliged. He gave an exhibition and then was asked to give the boys some pointers. He happily agreed. As it turned out, the admiring young boys were the Prince of Wales, later King Edward VIII, and his younger brother the Duke of York, later King George VI, the future father of Queen Elizabeth II.

On Tuesday, Charley's century swim at the St. Marylebone Baths posted a disappointing 60.2 seconds.

The next morning, Wahle and Charley took a three-hour train ride to Nottingham. From the station, it was a mile to the city center at Sneinton Market, where one couldn't miss the two-story redbrick natatorium's landmark clock tower. The magnificent complex housed four separate pools the likes of which the United States had never dreamed of, decorated with stained glass, terra-cotta, mosaic floors, and beautiful skylights. Its main exhibition tank was the longest Charley had ever laid eyes on. Sunlight poured in through the overhead glass atrium, creating a cheery atmosphere. A second-floor balcony surrounded it. At one end, embedded in the wall, was a giant electric fan, providing the perfect ventilation. The water felt clear, warm, and smooth. Its broad thirty-five-foot width allowed for six men to swim unobstructed in the same heat, with fewer waves bouncing off the sides than one encountered in tighter pools. Everything seemed ideal, except Charley appeared to struggle to get his stroke count to the wall.

The next evening, a large crowd packed the natatorium. The event was billed as "THE RACE OF THE YEAR." Spectators paid a shilling for a balcony seat and two shillings for a reserved poolside seat.

The five-man field consisted of Charley, Halmay, Derbyshire, Healy, and the local champion, G. H. Carlisle. Halmay was ready to defend his title. Derbyshire wanted to reclaim it for England. Healy intended to win it for Australia and the empire. All of them hoped to avenge their recent Olympic loss to the American.

As the starter announced each competitor, loud cheers resounded, with Halmay, the current titleholder, and Derbyshire, the hometown favorite, receiving the greatest ovations. This was the moment when nerves were most intense. Halmay and Carlisle drew the two side lanes. Charley, Derbyshire, and Healy drew the three in the middle.

The five men stepped up to the pool's edge. Charley's fingers and toes tingled. He tried to push aside his nerves to focus.

W. T. Kerr, vice president of the Amateur Swimming Association of New South Wales, who accompanied Cecil Healy, reported that Charley "appeared very nervous on the starting platform." The pressure seemed to be getting to him.

Using a non-pistol start, the caller shouted out, "Take your marks." Then "Are you ready?"

Halmay's eagerness to get the jump caused him to make two false starts, the second time being accompanied into the pool by a nervous Charley. The third attempt achieved a clean entry and all five men took to the water. They swam down the first length practically in a line.

According to Wahle's account, Charley drew away from the rest of the crowd by the end of the first length, holding a lead of three and a half yards. Only Charley misjudged the number of strokes to the wall, which caused a bad turn that cost him time.

British newspapers reported that the trio of Charley, Healy, and Derbyshire came off the first wall together. Wahle reported the front three as Charley, Healy, and Halmay, with Charley in the lead and Derbyshire half a yard behind. Healy seemed to lose ground at the first turn, but then pulled about even by the time they reached the second turn, with Halmay a yard behind Healy, and Derbyshire a foot farther back.

Charley's second turn was a thing of beauty. He started before he reached the wall, barely touching it with his fingertips to qualify, both legs drawing well under him as he straightened with a brilliant push off the wall and glided forward with scarcely a ripple, while Healy again lost ground at the turn. The Australian's weakness at this crucial skill was apparent to British reporters and the attending Australian official, W. T. Kerr, who noted that "nearing the end of each lap he just made up what he'd lost in the kickoff and looked to be forging ahead, when he had to turn again, and fell behind once more."

Going into the third and final lap, Charley led by no more than four feet, with Halmay coming on and Healy again closing the gap in the straightaway. Then a strange thing happened: at seventy-four yards, at the second turn, Halmay unexplainably stopped. Newspapers later reported that Halmay found the tank too shallow for him to turn properly, while other reports said he pulled up with a leg cramp. Most likely the monster hit him too hard.

The race was now between Healy and Charley.

Down the third stretch to the finish, the Australian went after the American over the final twenty-seven yards. He put on a magnificent spurt and rapidly reduced Charley's lead. The burning in Charley's back, shoulders, chest, and arms began as Healy increased speed down the final stretch. Charley fought to keep his heavy arms working as the monster intensified and made him doubt if he'd be able to sustain his speed. A loud cheer resounded from the crowd as the colonial overhauled the American. Healy splashed up alongside him, coming on like a shark as they approached the rope that ran about a foot above the surface to mark the hundred-yard finish line.

The English spectators leaned at the edge of their seats as Healy put his very soul into the last spurt. The two rivals battled to a close finish, reaching to touch the rope in a rush of white water.

One British reporter proclaimed it a "dead heat."

Officials compared watches. There was certainly some English hand-wringing. The Australian newspaper *The Referee* voiced the overall sentiment: "Another stroke and the 100-yard world's championship would unquestionably have come to Australia. [Healy] had the sympathy of the great onlooking crowd almost to a man, because all could see plainly that the faster swimmer had been defeated."

Healy's time was 59 seconds. Charley's was 58.6—the new English champion.

In spite of the close finish, it was a huge victory for Charley and Wahle.

THE NEXT DAY, SOME of the empire's newspapers still proclaimed Healy the faster swimmer, stating that Daniels only edged out the Australian champion with his superior turns. *The Referee* of Australia stated, "It was the opinion of a good many that Cecil Healy [would] have won in two more strokes," reiterating that Charley's off-the-wall pushes were the only reason Daniels won. "We Australians had to console ourselves," the paper opined, "with the knowledge that kicking-off was not swimming." And the English establishment refused to accept any of Charley's "alleged" times under his 58.6 seconds. London's *Athletic News* called such claims startling, which was the polite British way of saying "no one believes it." As far as they were concerned, Cecil Healy and Dick Cavill still held the world century record at 58 seconds. As *The Australian Star* wrote, "As soon as we have evidence that [Daniels] did 100 yards in 56 seconds, under proper conditions, it will be accepted in England—but not before." And with the aim of setting up those "proper conditions," W. T. Kerr extended an invitation from Australia's governing swimming body for Charley to compete in their upcoming season.

Otto Wahle did not think it a good idea. He told Kerr that Charley had done a great deal of traveling during the previous several months and badly needed rest. He added that Charley's mother was ill back home and that he needed to return.

In Charley's long absence, Alice had most likely slipped back into a deep depression. While her previous European sabbatical had given her a welcome respite, once she returned home, she realized her status hadn't changed and would likely remain that way for the rest of her life.

When Charley and Wahle set sail for America on July 18, British newspapers commented that Charley had made up his mind after escaping with a "very narrow victory" to leave well enough alone and "skipped home" as quickly as possible. And both the British and the Australian press continued to insist that "Healy had proved himself the better swimmer." W. T. Kerr even stated that "the young American was afraid of having to meet Healy again." Even Alice Daniels clipped one of the belittling articles with a headline that read, "Swimming Officials Refuse to Recognize the Superiority of Daniels over Healy."

Not only was America's lone champion a target of taunts and ridicule abroad, but back home the Daniels name was again about to be dragged through the mud.

19.

MUDSLINGING

—

JULY-NOVEMBER 1906

AMERICAN SWIMMING STILL HAD A LONG WAY TO GO. WAHLE knew it, too. But one thing was for sure, they had gotten the British swimming establishment's attention.

After four months abroad, Charley returned to New York on July 26, 1906, and soon thereafter took a ferry out to Long Island to spend some time relaxing and recuperating at Manhanset House, a luxurious six-hundred-guest resort on Shelter Island. Whether Alice joined him is unclear, but one of the most special moments for Charley was bringing his Athens Olympic gold medal home to his mother. It was the same medal the Greeks had awarded at the first modern Olympiad in 1896, except for the engraved 1906 date and the fact that his gold medal was actually gilded in gold this time rather than silver.

Alice certainly loved to hear Charley describe the whole spectacle, how the Greeks presented the medals at the closing ceremony, about the mind-boggling Panathenaic Stadium with its gleaming white marble that stretched to the sky, the more than fifty thousand cheering Greek spectators, and how, one by one, each gold medal winner was called to the royal box, where he was given an olive branch plucked from the storied city of Olympia and presented his medal by none other than His Greek Majesty King George I.

Even though 125 years had passed since America's successful rebellion against the Crown, British and European royalty still retained a fascinating hold on American society, with all of their inherited celebrity and fancy titles. American newspapers constantly reported on the comings and goings of European royals, and readers couldn't get enough. Perhaps it stemmed from a desire to live in that enchanting fantasy world so unlike their own. Charley regaled Alice with stories about meeting kings and queens, princes and princesses, lords and ladies, dukes and duchesses. He even told her about teaching his crawl stroke to the future king of England, which undoubtedly pleased her, considering how her social set had shunned her.

Charley brought her back a handful of his press clippings—some in Greek—to add to her collection. Alice showed him all of the articles she'd clipped while he was away that now spilled into a second scrapbook. But she went further than that. She had gotten ahold of Charley's monthly New York Athletic Club magazines and cut out images of the red Winged Foot symbol to paste throughout the book for added flair. She had cut out pictures of him from newspapers and headlines. Had inserted photographs. Clipped depictions of him from newspaper cartoons. Posted handbills of his swimming contests. Attached letters from fans and lists of his records and statistics. The love she poured into the book shone on every page.

Charley's victories gave Alice something to look forward to, gave her hope and a sense of pride. Any time her exiled existence made her depressed, her two scrapbooks offered a window to a happier place where she didn't feel like a complete failure. There, in bold headlines, from newspapers across the world, was proof that she must have done something right to raise a son like Charley.

As for Charley, he only wished that he could somehow remove the black mark inflicted upon her by his father. He had seen her be a loyal friend to an elderly widow whose family no longer cared for her welfare. Alice was a devoted daughter, a supportive sister, and a loving mother, as well as a strong woman at a time when society frowned upon the latter. She deserved better than the hand life had dealt her. And all this time, Tom made no effort to reach out to her or give the slightest acknowledgment of Charley's overseas success.

———

IN OCTOBER, NEWS BROKE that shot the Olympic Games' profile into the stratosphere. Suddenly it moved from a novel international competition to *the* international contest.

When the financial devastation of Mount Vesuvius forced Italy to abandon hosting the 1908 Games in Rome, Lord Desborough formed the British Olympic Association to step in as the new host. As Baron Pierre de Coubertin enthusiastically noted, "Quietly the curtain fell on the settings of the Tiber and lifted again over those of the Thames."

The Olympics would finally be embraced by the world's most powerful empire and cradle of modern sports. For Coubertin, this meant his Olympic dream would at long last be legitimized. It would raise the Olympics to an international profile no sporting competition had ever known.

Lord Desborough reached out to the organizers of the 1908 Franco-British Exhibition, who were in the process of constructing a large white city on 140 acres in west London. This pseudo world's fair was meant to celebrate the new treaty between the two countries that had significantly improved Anglo-French relations. It was the largest exhibition of its kind in Britain, and Lord Desborough persuaded the fair's organizers, in exchange for a lucrative share of the Olympic ticket receipts, to build alongside their white city the biggest, most advanced stadium the world had ever seen. At a cost of sixty thousand pounds, the Olympic stadium would be a modern-day wonder to fully embody the supremacy of the British Empire, capable of holding 140,000 spectators, which would put America's 1904 Olympic stadium to shame. Newspapers across the United States proclaimed the upcoming London Olympics would be the greatest ever held. The British Empire confidently viewed these Games as the perfect world stage to reassert its athletic superiority.

In Lord Desborough's acceptance speech as host, he praised Coubertin and acknowledged the prior Olympic Games in Athens, Paris, and St. Louis, deliberately eliminating any mention of the 1906 intermediate Games. His omission would carry deeper ramifications.

Coubertin had long hated the idea of these off-year Games. Now emboldened with the British Empire's full support, he would eventually move to have the International Olympic Committee forever remove the "Olympic" designation from the bastard "Second International Olympic Games in Athens." The IOC would declare them "intercalated games" and refused to recognize the medals distributed to their participants. Charley's gold medal in Athens would no longer qualify as Olympic, and he was deprived of the title "Olympic Century Champion." That honor remained with Zoltán Halmay as reigning victor from the 1904 St. Louis Games.

Jim Sullivan also felt the sting of these latest developments. After returning home from Athens, he wrote a long letter to Coubertin, baring his deep wounds and making his case to join the IOC.

"I propose to be frank with you," Sullivan wrote, noting that the IOC members he'd befriended in Athens encouraged him to share his feelings. After voicing his regret that the Frenchman was not in Greece to see the pronounced success of the Games, Sullivan acknowledged that Coubertin did not like him. He also pointed out that Coubertin had yet to present him with his promised medal and wondered if he'd rescinded the honor. Sullivan then went on to chide him for single-handedly and repeatedly striking his name from membership to the IOC, accusing the Frenchman of being a man who "could not stand opposition." Finally, Sullivan recounted the wishes of his three new IOC friends from Athens to appoint him a fellow member. "I told them that I felt very highly honored, but that before I could accept anything like this I certainly would want a letter from you."

Coubertin responded with a calculatedly dismissive correspondence, stating that there was not one single word of truth to any of Sullivan's statements.

Sullivan angrily wrote back, "Well, I think that settles it! I guess I must have taken a lot for granted. I am thoroughly convinced, from the attitude which you take, that we had better cease writing."

In 1907, Coubertin would be elected to a second ten-year term as president of the IOC, and Sullivan would ascend to the presidency of the powerful AAU. In a move that certainly drove a knife into Sullivan, Coubertin again passed over arguably the most qualified sportsman in

America, if not the world, and appointed a fellow aristocrat, Lord Desborough, to the IOC. He also did not give Sullivan his promised medal.

FOR A YOUNG MAN like Charley about to turn twenty-two the following spring, the 1908 Olympics was an unrealistic commitment. Most men his age had already begun careers, entered into marriage proposals, and planned to start families. That's what had happened to the great E. Carroll Schaeffer, who had been around the same age as Charley when he walked away from swimming to start a law career. It also befell Otto Wahle's fellow Austrian speed champion, Charles Ruberl, another exact contemporary of Charley's, who couldn't get in shape before the 1904 Olympics due to his work commitments. Even the great Harry LeMoyne, at age twenty, had quit what promised to be one of the greatest amateur athletic careers his country had ever seen. And Charley had his mother to support.

Yet the 1908 Olympics had the potential to be the tipping point for the American swimming movement. In the two years leading up to it, Charley would need to build a case to claim the late Barney Kieran's mantle of "Greatest Swimmer in the World." It had to be so airtight that not even the Brits could deny him. In fact, for it to be legitimate, the British swimming establishment would have to proclaim him as such. To even have that chance, for the next two years Charley could not lose one race. Not in America, not in Australia, not anywhere. Any defeat would give them an excuse to question his fortitude and point to someone who was better, even if just for that one race. That's all they needed to refute any claim that an American was the world's No. 1 swimmer. To stay unbeaten would involve an enormous commitment to training. He would need to defend his English championship title in 1907 when all of Europe would be gunning for him. Even at home, some of the Winged Footers doubted it was possible.

Fred Wenck, one of his fellow watermen, published an editorial in American newspapers, which Alice cut out, noting quite point of fact, "Although Daniels is far and away the best man in this country at any distance, compared with the world's best he ranks purely as a sprinter, and it is doubtful if he could at present accomplish the remarkable times for long distances now on the record books to the credit of the late B. B. Kieran of Australia."

For Charley to have a chance, it would take an incredible sacrifice that not even Otto Wahle or Lou Handley had the right to ask of him. The executive committee at the New York Athletic Club even voted against funding a long trip for Charley to Australia, believing that a young accomplished man like himself, at his age, would do better focusing on more profitable pursuits. Charley had made a respectable name for himself in the amateur athletic world and brought honors to the club, whose members hailed from some of the country's most established families and captains of industry. Such admirers could open doors for him. One fellow Winged Footer had already offered him a lucrative job selling insurance. Marquard Schwarz was trying to persuade him to attend Yale with him that fall. For the first time, a promising future seemed possible.

Charley allowed himself to think more and more about a better life. The ocean of fog he had been swimming through the past two years had finally given way to land.

CHARLEY'S NEW STATUS AS not only America's champion but the English century champion, and champion of the international century race in Athens, brought on a whole new set of responsibilities, expectations, and woes that he was unprepared to face, making trading it all in for a lucrative career that much more enticing. After a newly recovered Budd Goodwin threw Charley a big dinner party at Travers Island to celebrate his unbroken list of European victories, Charley found himself the target of national criticism.

The firestorm began shortly after he stepped off the train in St. Louis for September's National Swimming Championships at Laughlin's Lake. The twelve-acre, spring-fed lake (now called Lake Sherwood) was located in Overland Park, a twelve-minute streetcar ride from the city. The woodland lake offered grandstands and a tall wooden diving platform that rose thirty feet from the water.

The *St. Louis Post-Dispatch* promoted the championship by touting its benefits to the public: "Not one in one thousand swimmers really knows how to swim." The championship offered a way to watch "the great swimmers of the world" so "we can learn how to swim, not only easily, but correctly." The article served as a reminder that despite the sport's progress, it still had a long way to go to inspire the American public.

Top swimmers from the New York AC, Denver AC, Chicago AA, and Chicago Central YMCA rolled into St. Louis to meet the local champions and compete for national titles. Everyone wanted to test their mettle against America's first English champion. None of them was more eager to compete with Charley than twenty-year-old Jam Handy.

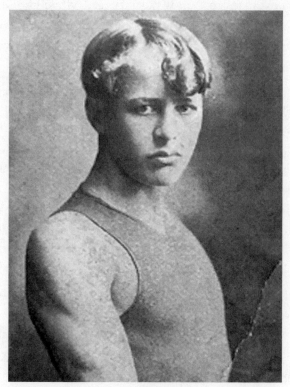

HENRY JAMISON "JAM" HANDY

HANDY HAD ARRIVED IN St. Louis a week ahead of Charley, boasting about the new American mid-distance records that he had taken from Charley and broadcasting his avowed determination to wrest whatever distance titles Charley still held. The Chicagoan had gained a reputation as a bit of a troublemaker. After being kicked out of the University of Michigan for poking fun at a professor in a *Chicago Tribune* article, he was hired by the *Tribune*. Every night, Handy put the paper to press at 2:30 A.M., then headed to the Chicago Athletic Association, where he'd made arrangements with the night watchman to sneak into the pool and experiment with innovative breathing techniques and crawl strokes.

In the week leading up to the races, Handy was literally living at Laughlin's Lake, where he pitched a tent and practiced daily in the water, swimming late under moonlight. Reporters who saw him training claimed he had more than his usual speed, while Handy told them he never felt in finer physical condition. The *St. Louis Post-Dispatch* published an article claiming that several Chicago men with bundles of money wished to wager on Handy beating Daniels in the upcoming mile race.

Otto Wahle and Lou Handley both discouraged Charley from competing against Handy. They believed the longer-distance training would lessen his sprinting ability. When Charley withdrew from both the 880 yards and the mile championship, the newspapers accused him of running scared.

"I would rather win the hundred yards than any other championship," Charley responded, explaining that he swam the crawl stroke in short races, the trudgen in long distances. And felt that mixing the strokes and distances would dull his speed. Nevertheless, the media quickly jumped all over him, accusing him of not living up to his duties as America's only international champion.

Charley didn't know whether to take these accusations to heart, unsure of his responsibilities in a role no American had ever held before. There was no precedent. No one to learn from. Before, he had just concentrated on swimming. Now he found himself in unfamiliar waters, with the new added weight of success causing him more doubt and distractions.

Charley explained his intentions to retire from long distances altogether, but to appease his critics, he agreed to swim the quarter-mile race—the dividing line between sprints and distances—which presented a fair test for both men. Charley even approached Handy.

"I have been training for the 100 and you have been training for the half and mile. Now here is a race at a quarter mile, just between both our specialties, why don't you come in and have it out with me?" Handy refused to meet Charley at anything less than six hundred yards.

When Mark Schwarz refused to swim any distance races as a sign of solidarity and support for Charley, the *St. Louis Post-Dispatch* snapped back: "It must be that Daniels and Schwarz admit Handy's superiority or that they are fearful of tackling him in far waters. The latter would be most unbecoming of the champion of America."

After Charley won the century and 220-yard races in record time, and Handy won the half-mile distance, Charley refused to indulge critics who tried to shame him into swimming the mile against Handy. Instead, he sat up in the stands, crouched forward with his chin on his hands, and watched the Little Water Devil dominate the distance. Charley tried not to let it bother him as Handy obliterated the field, finishing an impressive full lap ahead and making good on his boast.

Joe Ruddy leaned over. "Never mind, Danny. Wait until we get him in our saltwater."

And indeed, Handy's win was less impressive than it appeared, falling two minutes short of the record. From the stands, Ruddy knowingly shouted out, "Who's the current American record holder?" When the announcer replied, "C. M. Daniels," the Winged Footers responded with a loud cheer. Reporters later wrote that those cheers would have been better provoked by Daniels's actual performance against Handy rather than by a mere memory of figures Charley set "in the dim and distant vistas of the past."

As the news spread about Charley's refusal to compete, the *Chicago Tribune* wrote, "There is much dissatisfaction here with Daniels' action in declining to enter the long-distance races against Handy." Some newspapers went so far as to question Charley's sportsmanship, calling him a disappointing champion. As a *St. Louis Post-Dispatch* reporter wrote, "I do submit that the honorable office of champion calls for more than sitting in a stand while another man is plucking your laurels and while spectators are cheering the things you did—last year."

Without any hindrance from America's so-called greatest swimmer, Handy strutted away with two national distance titles that until then had belonged to Charley. *The Buffalo Commercial* best summed up the swimming world's dilemma: "Now the West will brag of its Handy and the East of its Daniels, each claiming the honor of having the fastest swimmer in America and each alleging that the other's man is afraid." It also made sure to point out that Charley's American mile record was still three minutes slower than the late Barney Kieran's world record.

The criticism hurt. The ever-present shame about his father made Charley hypersensitive to the slightest attack on his integrity. The whole ordeal seemed to stir repressed personal pains buried deep within the twenty-one-year-old.

Otto Wahle and Lou Handley were dead set against the idea of Charley's swimming longer distances. After a week of the newspapers' attacking Charley's integrity, Handley penned an article defending the champion's position: "Is it not, rather, decidedly imprudent to allow our great sprinter, the only world beater we have ever turned out in swimming, to risk hurting his magnificent speed by training for a grueling distance race that will surely make him slower?"

Handley went on to say: "Swimmers know only too well that sprinting is injurious to distance swimming just as distance swimming is to sprinting, and now that there are promising men to fill all classes we should devote every effort toward encouraging specialization, instead of stupidly criticizing those who, having acquired wisdom, refuse to compete out of their classes."

Sprinting was all about power. Distances up to 220 yards were all about going as fast as you could with as minimal breaths as possible so as not to disrupt momentum. It was anaerobic, which meant relying on less oxygen and increasing your lactic threshold before the muscle burn and pain slowed you down. Sprinting was also less forgiving than distances. Because the race was so quick, one mishap in your entry dive, one ill-timed turn, and you were done for.

Distance races over 440 yards (quarter mile) required more endurance training and pacing. They were more aerobic, requiring consistent breathing and superior cardiovascular strength. The key was efficient use of energy, maintaining the same even stroke over long distances to generate the greatest propulsion with the least amount of exertion. Greater distances required more mental stamina, staying focused for extended, repetitive periods.

Wahle and Handley believed it critical for the U.S. swimming movement's success that Charley spend the winter training to defend his century title in the next year's English Championships. The British establishment would do everything in its power to prove that his previous performance was a fluke. Already rumors circulated that Zoltán Halmay had adopted Charley's four-beat crawl stroke with great success. But they couldn't stop the press from continuing to take shots at Charley, calling him afraid and making sure to publicly downgrade him as the *former* mile and *former* half-mile champion. And some continued to call him a coward.

Wahle and Handley urged him not to take the bait. If swimming was ever going to catch on in America, it needed to be a team effort. Charley's part was to focus on defending his titles at the 1907 English Championships. If he could pull that off, his two trainers were already lobbying to send a complete swimming team to the 1908 London Games. But the more Charley saw his name besmirched in print, the more he felt compelled to defend his honor.

When he visited Buffalo after St. Louis, Charley noticed that he had begun to gain some notoriety beyond the tiny aquatic community. The *Buffalo Courier* noted his arrival in the social pages. Almost every day during his stay, one of the papers ran an article on him. The *Buffalo Evening News* published a picture of him in his NYAC swimsuit with the caption "C. M. Daniels—captured all swimming events at Olympic Games Greece." The *Buffalo Commercial* ran an article speculating that the much-anticipated match race between Daniels and Handy was practically a certainty. The *Buffalo Sunday Morning News* ran a page 6 story with the headline "World-Famous Athlete Here—He Is C. M. Daniels, Champion Swimmer at Olympic Games." The article identified Charley as the nephew of Herbert Meldrum and a grandson of Mrs. Charles Daniels, his grandfather's second wife and widow, whom he barely knew. Once again, his parents were not mentioned.

Before Charley returned to Manhattan, his uncle Herbert asked him to meet one of his store clerks, Matt Mann, a twenty-two-year-old English immigrant who loved swimming and wanted to race his boss's famous nephew. Charley obliged, met Matt at Buffalo's YMCA pool, gave him a seven-second head start, beat him soundly, and then showed him how to swim the American crawl.

"It was quite a nice thing for him to take up his time to come down from the visit with his uncle and swim the young punk that I was," Matt recalled, impressed by Charley's graciousness and commitment to both swimming and clean living, which Matt wanted to emulate and pursue. Years later, Matt would become a Hall of Fame swimming coach of thirteen NCAA championship teams at Michigan and Oklahoma and coach of the U.S. men's team at the 1952 Summer Olympics that won four gold, two silver, and one bronze.

Charley was becoming a national curiosity. For some, a rising hero. Perhaps even a role model. He was realizing that he had the ability to inspire others. And running from a fight was not a message he wanted to convey.

To Wahle and Handley's dismay, Charley informed the press that he would accept a match race at any distance Handy liked. Four hundred and forty yards was considered the dividing line between sprints and mid-distances. Handy insisted on no less than twice that distance. A match race for half a mile was scheduled for February 8. A month later, a week before Thanksgiving, the positive example that Charley strove to represent in and out of the water was threatened by his father.

ON NOVEMBER 21, PAGE 4 of *The New York Times* reprinted a special report from Milwaukee that Thomas P. Daniels, operating under the alias Thomas Cameron, had been arrested. Tom's latest million-dollar swindle was again based on defrauding small corporations by charging a fee to issue their bonds and then making no real effort to sell them. This time he had a co-conspirator in Chicago posing as a "buyer" who agreed to purchase the stock while providing an examination by "experts," whereby another accomplice from Chicago acted as the "expert," who also shook down the businessmen for a large fee and then found some flaw or *pretended* flaw in the company and declared the whole deal off. It was reported that Tom had made the equivalent of what in today's dollars would amount to $1.5 million. Upon his arrest, newspapers noted that Tom told police that his real name was Thomas P. Daniels, that he was forty-five and the son of the New York Supreme Court justice Charles Daniels, and that he once ran a store in Dayton until he figured out that he could make more money on Wall Street. The only thing he didn't mention was his relationship to American swimming's first international celebrity.

Fair or not, Charley's renown had risen to the point that he would no longer be afforded privacy. And if the drama-hungry press made the connection between him and Tom Daniels, the positive image that Charley worked so hard to build would suffer a terrible fall from grace that not only promised to hurt the U.S. swimming movement that was starting to build momentum under Charley but would certainly end his association with the image-conscious New York Athletic Club and most likely his swimming career and any chance at a real future.

Since the tight-knit East Coast swimming scene was reported in the newspapers almost exclusively by Lou Handley, Otto Wahle, and Fred Wenck, these three fellow Winged Footers protected their champion's image by keeping his relationship with Tom Daniels out of their reporting and away from the general public's knowledge. Whether Tom found it of any value to publicly acknowledge Charley as his son remained to be seen. But what posed the greatest threat to being linked to Tom Daniels was how the story was reaching the broader public.

At the time, news spread across the nation in two ways. The largest newspapers, like those in New York City, Philadelphia, Boston, Chicago, and St. Louis, often supplied one another, as well as some of the country's twenty thousand smaller publications, with courtesy subscriptions so editors could peruse and republish any articles of interest. Almost a hundred papers also belonged to the Associated Press, whereby stories investigated and reported by the major papers would be shared by telegraph wire to all AP members. With Tom's criminal case based in Chicago, the paper covering the story and sending its reports out on the wire was none other than Jam Handy's *Chicago Tribune*. Charley certainly worried about how much Jam knew about his background. All it would take to connect the dots was knowing that Charley's grandfather was the late Judge Charles Daniels.

CHARLEY COULD NOT CONTROL whether his name would one day appear in the papers linked to Tom Daniels, but that didn't make his anxiety or the distraction any easier. While newspapers across the country continued to republish reports out of Chicago about his father's upcoming criminal trial, Charley channeled all of his emotions and energy into preparing to race Handy. He put on several exhibitions and in the process enabled more people to see firsthand what this obscure sport was all about. The enthusiasm he was creating saw the teams at Penn, Harvard, Yale, Princeton, Columbia, and Brown form the first intercollegiate swimming league that year. YMCA branches across the East Coast and Midwest began organizing swimming teams, and all of the rowing clubs in New York followed the YMCA's lead into the swimming boom.

On January 26, 1907, the Veteran Association of the New York Athletic Club honored Charley as the year's top amateur athlete. Jim Sullivan gave a speech in his honor, noting the Europeans' and Australians' distrust of his records. The club's veterans called Charley up to the front for a toast. With characteristic modesty, Charley begged to be excused after a few remarks.

A few days before the anticipated February 8 match race, Handy claimed he had made a previous promise to compete at the Evanston water carnival on that same evening and backed out. Newspapers questioned the truth of his excuse: "We don't say Handy is a liar, but we don't trust him as far as we could throw him up a ladder."

The match race was rescheduled during the February 23 meet against the Chicago Athletic Association at the NYAC, with Handy insisting on a farther distance of a thousand yards.

Otto Wahle and Charley shifted their training to prepare for the longer race. It was all about finding the right tempo for that exact distance, about discovering how hard Charley could go before he brought on the burn, then ride that razor-thin line on the safe side of collapse. Consistent breathing, consistent strokes, all helped keep the monster at bay. It was important to time each inhalation with the rhythm of his arms to make turning his head to breathe as seamless as possible, creating the least amount of drag. His stroke needed to be moderated to maintain it for the longer distance. At times he might vary his kicks from two beats to four beats to allow himself to ease up when he felt the burn coming on—a luxury he did not have in all-out sprints. For a thousand yards, his mental focus had to sustain itself for more than thirteen minutes while he kept an ongoing lap count in his head. If his concentration wavered, so too would the control over his stroke, and the piano would drop on him early. Otherwise, he could hold it at bay until sometime during the last few laps, but it *would* drop. And then it came down to a battle of wills between himself and the pain.

Perhaps Handy's strategy throughout was to keep them off balance. The sudden shift in gears gave them only three weeks to train for the lengthier swim, as opposed to the optimum six weeks, which Handy had probably been training for the entire time.

Rather than let his shorter distance training go to waste, on February 2, Charley lined up for a 500-yard handicap race at the NYAC and smashed records at 250, 300, 350, 400, and 450 yards and clipped eight and one-fifth seconds off Handy's 500-yard figure. The drums of war began to beat.

NEWS OUT OF CHICAGO reported that U.S. postal authorities were on the lookout for the "Diamond Queen," Tom's secretary and mistress, Clara Heder, who was a key witness to prove Tom's intent to defraud. Before authorities froze Tom's bank account, Clara, bejeweled in diamonds, managed to withdraw what today would amount to half a million dollars. She then rendezvoused with Tom, who was out on bail, in Indiana, where they applied for a wedding license. Having just been divorced from Lydia in October, Tom ignored a court order forbidding him to remarry, hoping to avoid the problem by crossing another state line. After a preacher refused to wed them upon learning of Tom's recent divorce, they stood before a justice of the peace. Tom gained something more valuable that day than a beautiful young bride who looked radiant in her diamond necklace, bracelets, and rings. Now as his legal wife, Clara could no longer be forced to testify against him under spousal immunity. With this accomplishment in hand, the newlyweds returned to Chicago and walked boldly into the office of the chief postal inspector, the man who had spearheaded Tom's arrest, and asked him to congratulate them on their marriage.

THE MATCH RACE WAS billed as a battle between East and West. Speed versus endurance. A clash of America's champions. While easterners claimed that Charley was America's best swimmer at any distance, westerners swore Handy could show his heels to the Gothamite at any distance above a furlong.

On Saturday, February 23, Charley and Jam Handy met at the Winged Footers' tank for the match race that had been the talk of the swimming world for the past six months. Finally, the question as to who would claim American swimming supremacy would be decided that evening.

The Washington Times reported that when the match was finally arranged, Handy wrote a long letter to Daniels, in which he berated the Winged Foot swimmer for "taking advantage" of him. Then the Chicagoan went on to say that he knew he couldn't be in proper shape for the race but that he would swim anyhow, essentially saying that if Charley won, the match proved nothing. However, Handy's excellent condition contradicted his posturing. A few days before the race, Handy took on three of Penn's top swimmers in a six-hundred-yard race, in which he allowed his opponents to swim the distance in a relay with each man swimming two hundred yards. Handy defeated the trio soundly. So the letter was most likely another ploy to keep Charley off balance and perhaps lull him into a false sense of security.

Charley made no comments leading up to the match, preferring to let his performance speak for itself.

A large, enthusiastic crowd packed into the New York Athletic

Club's natatorium. When Charley and Handy were introduced, each received a rousing reception.

The two rivals lined up on the pool's edge, sporting their clubs' swimsuits, with Charley standing more than a head above the five-foot Handy. Nerves plagued both men.

"Ready!" called the starter.

"Get set!"

The young men crouched down with eyes focused on the stretch of pool before them. Forty laps lay ahead.

At the pistol's crack, they launched.

At the midpoint, Charley had a commanding lead. At six hundred yards, he shattered Handy's record by almost twenty-five seconds. At eight hundred yards, he destroyed Handy's record by over thirty seconds. At the half mile, Charley obliterated Handy's mark by over thirty-four seconds. When he touched the final wall, he scorched Handy's thousand-yard record by forty-three seconds and left his opponent four laps behind. The race ended with Charley claiming sixteen new American records and every title Jam Handy held under a thousand yards. Even if Handy was out of form as he claimed, Charley left him no sanctuary for excuses, having broken *all* of his top times. The new thousand-yard champion received one of the greatest ovations of his life.

Handy's western supporters insisted the race proved nothing. They pointed out that Handy remained the superior distance swimmer. He still held every American indoor record from a thousand yards to the mile. Such distances, Charley's critics agreed, exceeded the sprint champion's limitations.

Two days later, the New York Swimming Association scheduled a special one-mile match race at the new Hell's Kitchen Public Bath House, inviting Charley and Handy, and even offered Handy a small head start. While Handy remained a no-show, Charley clipped all thirteen of Handy's remaining records, erasing the Little Water Devil from the record books. Charley's new American mile record still fell twenty-four seconds short of the late Barney Kieran's. But Kieran had never broken sixty seconds in the century. The fact that a sprinter could go out of his class and obliterate the American mile record left the country's swimming community in awe.

By the time February turned the page, Charley held every indoor American record from twenty-five yards to a mile. He was now America's undisputed champion. Jim Sullivan even commissioned him on behalf of Spalding's American Sports Publishing Company to write an instructional book with Wahle and Handley titled *Speed Swimming*. But he still had yet to earn the respect of the British swimming establishment, whose view was the only one that mattered.

PART FIVE

SWAMBLING

SWAMBLE—a rugged combination of
swimming and scrambling

ANNETTE KELLERMANN AND
CHARLES M. DANIELS, 1907

20.

THE ENGLISH
CHAMPION RETURNS

—

1907

ON APRIL 28, A DENSE FOG ENVELOPED NEW YORK HARBOR, AND somewhere in the whiteout one of Charley's Australian swimming acquaintances was trying to make port.

The dynamo from Down Under had been staging a successful vaudeville and swimming act at London's wondrous Hippodrome. The show opened with her playing a violin and performing ballet, gradually stripping down to her tight-fitting swimsuit and diving into the theater's eight-foot-deep, 100,000-gallon circular tank, where she performed an exquisite water ballet that became the inspiration for synchronized swimming. It was even reported that she could hold her breath for three and a half minutes at a time. When word of her show's popularity crossed the Atlantic, America beckoned.

A large crowd awaited Annette Kellermann's American debut at the new Hell's Kitchen Public Bath House at 232 West Sixtieth Street while she remained delayed in the harbor. When it became apparent the fog would not permit her ship to make port on time, a story arose that Annette, sick of waiting, had donned her bathing suit, ready to swim the remaining eighteen miles to shore until the captain forbade it. When reporters caught wind of this, the news made her a media darling.

For the past two months, Charley had been traveling through Pittsburgh and Chicago and swimming venues throughout the East, setting records and hoping to inspire the American public. Annette was in town for only a week before she boarded a train for Chicago for an extended four-month summer engagement at the White City Amusement Park, which required a demanding fifty-five shows per week.

Shortly after her arrival, she published an article that was syndicated nationwide, calling for American women to liberate themselves from their cumbersome bathing skirts in favor of a cheap, sleeveless, ordinary stockinette suit, which clung close to the figure, and the closer the better. "There is no more reason why you should wear those awful water overcoats—those awkward, unnecessary, lumpy 'bathing suits,' than there is that you should wear lead chains," she declared. "Heavy bathing suits have caused more deaths by drowning than cramps."

On Saturday, May 4, Annette rescheduled her missed exhibition at the same Hell's Kitchen Public Bath House where two months earlier Charley had shattered every last record of Jam Handy's. The evening's special program also included a hundred-yard AAU handicap in its thirty-five-by-sixty-five-foot pool. Charley was competing and made a point of reconnecting with the dynamic Australian beauty.

A REPORTER SNAPPED PICTURES of Charley and Annette posing in a locker room after the swimming exhibition. One photograph captured the two sitting on adjacent benches eyeing each other, with flirtatious smiles and sparks apparent between the two attractive young swimming stars. They had common interests, and Annette liked tall men. However, with the Australian performing all summer in Chicago and Charley training in New York for the English Championships in August, fate seemed to be working against any potential romance that summer. They had both come far since their last encounter. Both had struggled to break free from their personal darkness.

When Annette reflected on the childhood leg braces that drove her to try swimming, she said, "My early physical misfortune has turned out to be the greatest blessing that could have come to me. Without it I should have missed the grim struggle upward and the reward that waited at the end of it all."

One wonders if Charley felt as positive about the struggles with his father.

CHARLEY INTENDED TO COMPETE in England's 220-Yard Championship on August 19 and its Century Championship on September 7. When asked by American reporters what he hoped to accomplish as he departed for England in late July, Charley modestly said, "I just want to show them that the results last summer weren't a mere accident."

The British Empire hoped to show him otherwise. In April, Cecil Healy had posted a century time of fifty-seven seconds, which the British swimming establishment acknowledged as the new world record. Unfortunately, Healy lacked the funding to make the long journey from Australia, so Charley's most formidable competitors were Zoltán Halmay, Rob Derbyshire, and the promising twenty-year-old Welsh champion, Paolo "Raddy" Radmilovic, all of whom now swam Charley's American crawl. Halmay had just won Austria's 220-yard Championship in near-record time and was rumored to be posting century times close to Healy's. Otto Wahle and Lou Handley hoped the five months Charley had devoted to training for Handy's long-distance race wouldn't come back to bite him. This year, Charley would be going it alone, because Wahle could not afford to make the trip.

When *The Brooklyn Daily Eagle* asked Wahle what he thought about the London *Referee*'s prediction that Daniels would need to swim close to Barney Kieran's 220-yard record to have any chance against Zoltán Halmay, Wahle bullishly responded that he hoped Halmay would be at his best so that he might push the young New Yorker to his utmost.

On the day of the 220-yard English Championship, Wahle and Handley eagerly waited at the club for a telegram containing the results. London was five hours ahead. When the dispatch arrived, their jaws dropped.

The next day, newspapers across North America and Europe reported the outcome: "Human Fish Beaten."

The Buffalo Commercial proclaimed, "America's Best Swimmer Beaten by Speedy Foreigner."

The Province of Vancouver headlined: "Zoltan Halmay Won World's Swimming Match."

The New York Times exclaimed, "Daniels Was Third."

"It is hard to comprehend the brief cable dispatch which told of the defeat of the great Daniels," reported the *New York Athletic Club Journal.* "We had come to think of 'Danny' as invincible, it has been so long since he lost a scratch race at any distance. He certainly could not have been in form."

English scoffers who refused to acknowledge Charley as the "world's greatest swimmer" now gloated. They concluded that at age twenty-two Daniels's best days were clearly behind him. British newspapers proclaimed that the Yankee's great speed was on the wane. The era of Charles M. Daniels and American swimming appeared to be over as quickly as the bad joke had begun.

FOUR DAYS AFTER HIS defeat, Charley failed to show up at a 150-yard race against Halmay. The Hungarian not only won but made a big statement by beating Charley's record by two-fifths of a second. When word reached Wahle and Handley, their hearts and heads sank. Their dream of watching the British Empire bestow their long-held swimming crown upon an American had all but vanished.

AFTER CHARLEY'S TEN-DAY OCEAN voyage left him with only a week to prepare, supporters speculated that the American champion's third-place finish resulted from his inadequate time to train for the distance. However, another possible explanation arrived by mail from England a few days later. According to one eyewitness account, Halmay and Radmilovic did not beat Charley to the line, as earlier cables suggested. The later dispatch claimed that British officials cheated him. As the men closed in on the finish, Charley's hand missed the pole, and it was not until his shoulder went over the line that he touched it. The judges refused to count him finished until some part of his body came into contact with the pole. Halmay and Radmilovic both touched out before that happened, allowing the judges to negate Charley's American victory on a technicality. If those were the rules, it was a fair call, yet it was far from the resounding defeat that the British had crowed about.

CHARLES M. DANIELS

While Halmay hunkered down for the next two weeks to train for the century, Charley made the risky if not ill-advised decision to go on an exhibition tour, believing the best training was to actually race.

Lou Handley espoused tapering. Constant swimming keeps the body exhausted and the muscles broken down. To reach peak performance, you need to reduce the amount you swim in the days leading up to a big race. It gives the body needed recovery time and positions the athlete to give maximum effort. It was exactly what Handley forced Charley to do back at Camp Mowgli, but neither he nor Wahle was in London to train him. In the four days leading up to the English Century Championship, Charley swam an invitation race each night, traveling outside London and up to Nottingham, and did no better in the century than 60.8 seconds, while Halmay was turning in practice times of an even 57.

ON SATURDAY, SEPTEMBER 7, an all-star field of swimmers prepared to gather fifty miles southeast of the popular seaside resort of Blackpool for England's Amateur Century Championship in Manchester. After competing at Nottingham's Victoria Baths the night before with a less than stellar century performance, Charley took an early two-hour train ride, hoping to familiarize himself with Manchester's pool prior to the evening's race. From the city's Central Station, it was a three-mile carriage ride to the new Victoria Baths, which Rob Derbyshire's father managed.

Dubbed Manchester's Water Palace, the luxurious new redbrick complex housed three separate pools, with the main one, the men's first-class bath, stretching seventy-five feet long by forty feet wide. An innovative system of boreholes, pumps, and tanks filtered sixteen thousand gallons of fresh water throughout the day. Under a long skylight,

VICTORIA BATHS, MANCHESTER,
MEN'S FIRST-CLASS BATH

a second-floor gallery surrounded three sides of the bath, where spectators, many of whom were women, began to crowd into the seats an hour before race time until there was hardly space to move. On display was the sterling silver Century Challenge Cup, a handsome, two-foot-tall trophy with exquisite side handles that would be awarded to the winner for one year.

The six competitors hailed from all parts of the globe. Charley was the current titleholder with his time of 58.6 seconds. The tall Zoltán Halmay was the former champion. Rob Derbyshire had won the title six times before being beaten by Halmay in 1905. The field was rounded out by Paolo "Raddy" Radmilovic, the Welsh champion; the short and swarthy Theo Tartakover of New South Wales, Australia; and George Dockrell, the Irish champion, who looked more like a rugby forward than a sprinter.

The six men were greeted with tremendous applause as they entered the bath. Led by Radmilovic, they took their spots on the starting board. Charley lined up in the fourth lane, with Halmay next to him in lane three and Tartakover in lane five.

The fight-or-flight adrenaline flooded Charley's body as he tried to bridle his nerves.

At the call "Take your marks," the champions crouched into starting position.

Charley bent at the torso ninety degrees, upper body parallel to the water with arms outstretched and eyes locked on the course. The green water beneath him looked as still and smooth as a giant billiard table.

"Are you ready?" called the official.

Charley filled his lungs. What no one in the baths knew was that Charley had a secret.

"Go!"

The men exploded off the deck, hitting the smooth water in one huge splash. They surged beneath the surface for a good ten yards and emerged with six pairs of arms churning the tank into a froth. Halmay's powerful legs pounded the water seething white with a version of Charley's four-beat American crawl, as did Derbyshire's in lane two. But Charley seemed to glide atop the surface. His arms speared the water with hardly a ripple, in nice, smooth rotations, while his calves and feet cut the pool like a propeller blade. What no one knew was that Charley had been secretly working on a new six-beat crawl—three kicks to each arm stroke. The added two kicks between strokes made him feel as if he were swimming downhill, as opposed to flat, or uphill as you'd feel without using the legs, but it also demanded more energy, which would bring on the monster sooner.

He reached the first wall just ahead of his two great rivals and, thrusting off the turn, torpedoed at least twenty feet. By the halfway mark, he came into the wall maybe a yard ahead of Halmay. Another strong push off and Charley again shot twenty feet underwater, resurfacing with a bit more of a lead.

The awestruck spectators saw only Charley's blond hair and white shoulders amid the froth with the tall Halmay coming on like a tidal wave, as the two men pushed each other to their limits.

Charley's forearms continued to pull him like paddles through the water as he felt the monster coming on. He once again showed his great skill off the turn, rocketing beneath the green surface and emerging in a cresting whitecap. Fighting through the white-hot burn in his muscles that screamed for him to stop, he battled his way down the final length. At the wall, his blond hair and shoulders emerged. Halmay finished four yards behind, with Derbyshire three yards after that.

The crowd stood speechless.

Charley raked back his wet hair, heart palpitating, catching his breath. His wide eyes looked up at the excited officials who compared watches and conferred.

Derbyshire clocked his fastest century ever at a flat minute. Halmay broke the English world record with 56.8 seconds. Charley hit 55.4.

The English aquatic world was stunned.

Charley's entire body tingled. A smile split his bewildered face.

All at once, the walls of the natatorium shook with a tremendous ovation. Charley had just swum faster than any human on Earth.

"Fifty-five and two-fifths," Charley muttered, shaking his head in disbelief. "Good golly!"

21.

TO SWIM OR
NOT TO SWIM

—

THE NEXT DAY, LONDON NEWSPAPERS BUZZED WITH THE NEWS: "It was appropriate that Manchester, the original home of fast swimming, should have been the scene of the greatest performance ever accomplished over a short distance in water," wrote *The Sportsman*, declaring, "Extraordinary Feat by Daniels." *The Athletic News* even posted a headshot of Charley with the caption "Whirling in the water world—Daniels' wonderful win." *The Yorkshire Post* was a little more balanced: "Sensational Swimming by Daniels and Halmay."

The London *Daily News* best summed up the overall British sentiment of Charley's shocking performance: "The race proved one thing, namely, that Englishmen need to take up the crawl stroke seriously. It is undoubtedly the stroke of the future."

Back in New York, the Winged Footers' monthly journal proclaimed, "If there are any admirers of Charles M. Daniels, the club's greatest athlete, whose faith in his ability to dispose of all comers was shaken by the cabled news of his defeat at the hands of two foreigners . . . those souls of little faith may cast away their doubts and fears. Not only is 'Danny's' great speed not on the wane but he is faster than ever. English scoffers who refused to credit Daniels' great performances since his last trip abroad are ready now to believe the wonderful amphibian capable of anything."

A transatlantic telegram arrived for Charley from the elected manager of the New York Athletic Club's athletes, Captain E. F. Haubold, that read, "Well done. Hearty congratulations, Haubold."

Charley saved it for his mother's scrapbook.

When a reporter from the London *Evening News* prodded him for insights into his unique crawl, Charley happily obliged, just as Barney Kieran had done for him. The next day, the paper published a full-page exposé on Charley's stroke, while the rest of the British press urged the empire's short-distance men to read Daniels's *Speed Swimming* if they hoped to have any chance at next year's Olympics. The English Amateur Swimming Association, however, was less enthusiastic about Charley's victory and refused to let him take their Century Challenge Cup back to America.

Charley barely had time to soak in his historic win when English reporters began asking him about his plans for the upcoming 1908 Olympics in London. Some newspapers reported that Charley stated he would not visit England again as a swimmer. *The Echo* of London remained unconvinced, speculating that "it will be surprising if he is not found amongst the American athletes that visit this country next year for the Olympic games." The day before he departed England, Charley entered a 150-yard race to reclaim the world record that Halmay had set a few weeks earlier and beat it by two seconds.

Back in New York, Charley returned to the club to a joyful shower of congratulations. With his characteristic modesty, he had little to say of his performances. When pressed, he would change the subject. He laughed off his swimming ability, seemingly one of the few people not in awe of his talent.

"I don't know how I get speed," said Charley. "I simply kick my feet up and down as fast as I can and pull my arms out and dip them in again as rapidly as possible."

Asked by reporters what he thought about the U.S. swimmers' chances in the next year's London Olympics, Charley said it was hard to tell at this early date. "The colleges are very active, though," he noted, "and it would not be surprising to see them turn out a few good ones, but at present our material is only fair." Charley made no commitment as to whether he would swim in 1908, much to Wahle's and Handley's dismay.

CHARLEY DIDN'T MAKE ANY money from swimming as an amateur. There were no sponsorships or advertising deals to be had. No lucrative performance contracts of the kind that were enriching Annette Kellermann at a rumored twelve hundred dollars per week. Charley's amateur status actually prevented him from charging for appearances or giving swim lessons. As a twenty-two-year-old young man who had accomplished almost all he'd set out to do in the water, like Schaeffer and LeMoyne before him, it was time to think about his future beyond swimming. There were not enough hours in the day to both forge a successful career and stay in peak racing form. It was an either-or proposition. It's why the great E. Carroll Schaeffer walked away at the top of his game to start a law career. It's why Charles Ruberl and Jam Handy struggled to return to their top shape.

Perhaps, like Schaeffer, it was better to walk away on your own terms than to become less of a swimmer, unable to maintain peak performance, and sully your legacy with avoidable defeats. Yet Charley still had not fully accomplished what he set out to do. Barney Kieran's 220-yard record still eluded him. His recent defeat by Zoltán Halmay in the 220-yard English Championship had cracked his invincible persona. He would fall short of achieving the goal he'd set with Wahle and Handley to become the undisputed champion swimmer of the world.

Certainly, one of Charley's biggest regrets was that he had not become a popular enough champion to liberate his mother from the black mark of his father. Outside the swimming world, his sport was still a mere curiosity with the American public. But inside, he had built up enough goodwill and respect among New York's athletic community to perhaps finally step out of his father's shadow and build a successful life for himself.

For starters, the moment the club heard about the Brits' refusal to relinquish the Century Challenge Cup, they went to war for Charley. When England's Amateur Swimming Association demanded a bond of $125 to insure the cost of the trophy, the club furnished it. When British authorities then refused to send their precious cup on the grounds that the American bond signers were "unknown in England," the gloves came off. The fact the Brits deemed representatives of the leading athletic club of the United States, which owned property valued at more than $1 million, not sufficiently responsible for a bond of $125 seemed absurd and insulting. The club tapped into its esteemed social network to acquire signatures from Ogden Reid, the son of the U.S. ambassador to England, and H. Bigham, a nephew of Sir John Bigham, justice of the King's Bench of England. British authorities had no choice but to accept the bond and begrudgingly ship the coveted trophy to America. When it arrived, the Winged Footers displayed it as if it were the very head of King Edward VII, parading it around the club while offering toasts to their conquering hero, Charles M. Daniels.

Charley's fellow watermen honored his great triumph overseas by purchasing a hundred tickets for themselves and fellow club members on the steamer *Monmouth* for a two-hour trip up the Hudson River for the Yale–West Point football game. Joining them in the stadium was Doc Seixas, now married and the father of a newborn. He had watched Charley's swimming career over the last few years and took great pride in helping set the nervous young boy on a path to becoming a world-class swimmer. Doc still headed the junior branch scouts of the National Sportsmen's Association, but with a family to look after, those magical summers of running camp had ended. For Charley, the visit certainly triggered fond memories of the man who helped bring him out of his shell at a time when he'd desperately needed a father figure. It now seemed time to take the next step into manhood.

CHARLEY COMMITTED TO A full-time position at the fire and liability insurance firm of a successful NYAC member. The opportunity promised a financially stable life for himself and his mother.

Before he started, two hundred Winged Footers gathered to give him a send-off into the working world with a raucous fraternal "beefsteak" dinner involving bibs, beef, and lots of beer. They rented out the Morgue, a Manhattan tavern decorated with skulls and crossbones. Winged Foot emblems and championship banners flanked its walls, while a band played music throughout the rollicking party. Charley was congratulated for the thousandth time on his brilliant triumph in England, where he'd spread the fame of the club as no one ever had before. Everyone wished him as much success in selling fire and liability insurance as he'd achieved in the pool.

At the height of the evening, Captain Haubold lifted his towering six-foot-six frame toward the rafters and said, "The purpose of our gathering tonight is to pay homage to Daniels. Anyone who can achieve a world's record and achieve it in England is surely a 'phenom' athletically. For if there are any doubting Thomases in the world, they are in England, no matter how often they get 'trimmed.'"

Amid wild cheers, Haubold presented Charley with a world championship medal for breaking both the century and the 150-yard world records. Charley humbly thanked the captain and the club members for the medal and the rousing reception but admitted that speechmaking was not his forte.

One of the highlights of the night was a song written about Charley that was sung by a solo Winged Footer with all the club members joining in on chorus. It was sung as the band struck up the tune of Will Handy's popular 1902 peppy Dixieland composition "Oh, Didn't He Ramble," which appropriately was often played down in New Orleans after a funeral to celebrate the deceased's life, suggesting he should have no regrets since he'd rambled all around town.

———

DANIELS WENT TO ENGLAND JUST TO

SHOW WHAT HE COULD DO,

AND WHEN HE WENT HE REALLY THOUGHT

HE KNEW A THING OR TWO,

BUT AFTER HE HAD REACHED THE PIER

AND STEPPED UPON THE SHORE,

THE BLOOMING ENGLISH SHOWED HIM WHAT

THEY HAD FOR HIM IN STORE.

———

CHORUS:

DIDN'T HE SWAMBLE, DIDN'T HE SWAMBLE,

HE SWAMBLED IN THE TIDE,

FOREIGNERS DEFIED.

DIDN'T HE SWAMBLE, SWAMBLE,
HE SWAMBLED AND HE'S NOW THE NATION'S PRIDE.

———

**SO IN HE WENT TO WIN A RACE AND
ALL THE RECORDS BREAK,**
HE WON AND THAT'S ACKNOWLEDGED,
BUT THEY CALLED IT A MISTAKE,
THOSE ENGLISHMEN WERE ON THE GAME AND
WITH A SUBTLE GRIN,
THEY SAID HE WON, BUT BY THEIR
RULES HE COULDN'T CLAIM THE "TIN."
(CHORUS)

———

**THIS HUNDRED YARDS HE HAD TO WIN OR
ELSE HE HAD TO LOSE,**
HE LOOKED IT OVER THOUGHTFULLY AND
THEN HE QUIT THE BOOZE.
HE DID THE TRICK IN JUST A FRACTION OVER FIFTY-FIVE,
AND THAT YOU KNOW IS GOING SOME AS SURE AS YOU'RE ALIVE.
(CHORUS)

———

**WELL, CUT IT SHORT AND CALL A HALT ON
ALL THIS SORT OF THING.**
OUR CHARLEY DID THE JOB AND
OF THE WATER HE'S THE KING.
SO HERE'S A HAND TO "COTTON TOP"
THE LOYAL, LUSTY "SWEDE,"
NONE EVER WILL DISPLACE HIM FOR
THEY'LL NEVER HAVE THE SPEED.
(CHORUS)

———

**BUT NOW HE'S HOME AND STARTING IN
TO EARN A PILE OF DOUGH,**
INSURANCE HE HAS CHOSEN AND HE'S SURE TO MAKE A GO.
FOR ALL HIS FRIENDS WILL WHOOP IT UP
TO HELP HIM WIN SUCCESS,

AND DON'T FORGET HE ALSO HAS
THE BACKING OF THE PRESS.

JOE RUDDY OFFERED ONE piece of advice. "Never quit athletics. It's the quitting that does the harm—not the keeping on." Joe went on to talk about running into ex-athletes, friends with successful careers, who somewhere along the way had stopped competing.

"Some of these ex-athletes were rich men who controlled big corporations down in the financial district," Ruddy said, "but a good many of them were men who no longer could control the corporations under their belts. That's nature's curse on the athlete who quits—fat! Now, personally, I'd a lot rather wake up in the morning with thirty cents in my vest pocket feeling like a million dollars, than to wake up with a million dollars in the bank and feeling like thirty cents. Not that keeping fit physically means that you can't be successful in business. It's just the other way around. Physical fitness pays big dividends in any branch of professional business life. And physical fitness is worth more than money." No doubt Ruddy's words hit home, because Charley was torn between training for the London Olympics and putting all his energy into his new career.

IN NOVEMBER, THE AMATEUR Swimming Association of New South Wales reached out to the NYAC and again invited Charley to compete with Cecil Healy and their top watermen. They offered to pay all of Charley's expenses for a six-month championship tour of the antipodes. It involved races in the principal cities of New Zealand and Australia, including Annette Kellermann's and Barney Kieran's hometown of Sydney, where seven miles outside the city, under a Celtic cross, in a squared gravel grave, a marble tombstone bore the inscription "In Loving Memory of Bernard Bede Kieran, Died 22nd December 1905, Aged 19 Years, Champion Swimmer of the World."

The club again advised against it. It was their opinion that a young man just starting to make his way in the world should not give so much of his time to athletics, time that should be used to further his business interests. Charley knew it was the right advice, but he wanted to compete. However, so much time away would interfere disastrously with his new job. He would also not be around for his mother. The Australians would of course accuse him of running scared. He was torn, but as Times Square dropped its first ever electric ball on New Year's Eve, ushering in 1908, Charley made plans to move into one of the residential apartments at the club and hunker down to a life of selling insurance.

Neither Wahle nor Handley could blame him. Charley deserved a successful future. He had made a name for himself, had achieved more than any of them thought possible. How far he had come from that nervous, gangly boy they first met. To accomplish what he'd done so far had taken pure grit. On the strength of it, he had finally gained acceptance from the club's upper set, who could certainly open a lot more of society's doors than a bunch of basement water cutters.

THE 1908 OLYMPICS WERE shaping up to overshadow all the previous Games. Scheduled the following summer from July 13 to July 25, the opening competition was attracting worldwide interest. Americans as a whole had not fully understood the significance of Charley's English Championship victory as had the athletic clubs, but got caught up in the excitement about the Olympics nonetheless. The young upstart nation was eager to show it belonged at the table with the old-world powers. With the 1906 Athens Games reduced to non-Olympic status, the London Games would be the first Olympics at which athletes would represent their countries instead of their individual sports clubs. Nations would compete against one another for points and medals. This battle for national pride was something both the American and the British publics were fully behind.

In that pre-world-war era, the "special relationship" between England and the United States had yet to become special. Many Americans felt it patriotic to dislike the British. Not even a century before, the British had burned down the White House. Only forty years earlier—and still a barb in many northerners' minds—England's immense appetite for southern tobacco and cotton and its desire to weaken America had led it to secretly outfit the Confederacy with warships, helmed by mostly British crews, who enjoyed a little too much success sinking Union vessels.

On the other side of the pond, Britishers thought Americans rude and overbearing, especially the British ruling class, who saw Americans as a threat to their way of life. Many in England despised the intrusion of wealthy American women marrying English lords for their titles. And Americans in turn didn't like the millions of U.S. dollars leaving the country in bridal dowries to shore up these highborn husbands' estates and excessive lifestyles.

America's huge new wave of German and Irish immigrants brought their own history of anti-British sentiment. Although America's upper echelon still admired England and its class-based society as the ideal civilization, the majority of regular Americans were ready to break free from Britain's dominant cultural influences and Victorian values to create a new, uniquely American identity.

Faces of this new twentieth-century America included a melting pot of people who wanted more for themselves. They included German immigrants like Henry and Gertrude Ederle, who ran a butcher shop in Manhattan and tried to teach their three girls to swim in horribly oppressive Victorian swim dresses. Or Peter and Elisabeth Weißmüller, newly arrived Hungarian immigrants in Chicago, whose eldest son, Johann, suffered polio and turned to swimming to help strengthen his legs. Or seventeen-year-old Duke Kahanamoku, who was one of Hawaii's few remaining wave riders with his hundred-pound longboard. The ancient Hawaiian sport was close to vanishing in part because of a century of missionaries who subscribed to the British colonialization mantra to "civilize" indigenous peoples and eradicate local leisure activities like surfing. Rather than see it vanish, Duke wanted to make surfing part of the new American culture.

Earlier in December 1907, President Roosevelt launched his Great White Fleet—sixteen new battleships, all painted a glorious white, that embarked upon a fourteen-month goodwill tour around the globe to build friendly relationships, reestablish treaties, and display America's growing naval power, which now equaled Germany's and was second only to the fleet controlled by the British Empire. Supremacy on the water was key, reiterated by Roosevelt's strategic ongoing construction of the Panama Canal. Now that the United States saw the possibility of breaking out as a global power on equal footing with the British, the two sports-crazed cultures viewed the 1908 Olympic Games as the perfect bloodless battlefield to have it out. Neither could afford to show inferiority.

IRONICALLY, AS CHARLEY COMMITTED to a full-time career, America's budding swim culture was now demanding his leadership more than ever. As 1908 began, newspapers across the country proclaimed how Charley held every American swimming record from fifty yards to the mile. The *Los Angeles Times* even printed a list of each of his records, their times, and dates they were set, and then noted how the University of Southern California had been inspired to construct a campus swimming pool.

As U.S. swimming's only world champion and marquee ambassador, Charley was bombarded with requests for appearances. He did his best to accommodate, stretching himself thin between work and swimming. He traveled the East, drawing crowds, putting on exhibitions, promoting the opening of new swimming facilities, and signing autographs for both young and old, girls and boys. In the New York *Evening World*'s "School for Athletes" symposium, Charley contributed an article on "how to swim," citing the most important ingredients as "knack and confidence." When he appeared at Madison Square Garden's National Sportsmen's Show to swim against his old rival Jam Handy, he jeopardized his amateur status.

Because the show's swimming exhibitions were being run by the U.S. Volunteer Life Savings Corps and not the Amateur Athletic Union, the AAU threatened to suspend the amateur status of anyone who participated. But Charley wasn't about to disappoint the junior branch scouts. Nor was the Little Water Devil. The two rivals stood together, and Charley's fellow Winged Footers Budd Goodwin and Con Trubenbach joined them. Amid loud cheers from the kids, Charley broke his previous 80-yard record, tied his 120-yard record, and beat Jam Handy in a century race in a blistering 56.2 seconds. Hundreds of fans tried to shake Charley's hand, voicing their hopes that he would represent the country at the upcoming Olympics. The crowd so overwhelmed him that Trubenbach and Goodwin had to force a passage for Charley to reach his dressing room.

The strong solidarity among these four friends and rivals certainly moved Charley. Their united front made the AAU eventually back down from issuing any suspensions. And it was becoming clear that their community of watermen was bigger than all of them, transcending nationalities and genders. They all shared the goal of promoting swimming for all, and from that standpoint they had each other's backs. Perhaps that is why the *Chicago Tribune* was never informed by Jam Handy about Charley's connection to Tom Daniels.

AS AMERICAN NEWSPAPERS BEGAN touting the upcoming London Olympics "as certain to eclipse all of its predecessors," Tom Daniels cut a deal with the prosecution to turn state's evidence against his fellow bond swindlers. Several of his accomplices received sentences of fifteen months to two years in the federal penitentiary at Leavenworth, Kansas. Tom pleaded guilty in Milwaukee and received a sentence that merely required him to pay a fine. Once again, the smooth operator managed to avoid prison and wasted no time setting up another lucrative banking and bond operation in Pittsburgh.

It seemed that just as Charley was finally getting established, professionally and socially, his father was preparing to bring him down again.

ACROSS THE POND, ALONGSIDE the Franco-British Exhibition in west London, the newly constructed Olympic stadium at Shepherd's Bush was being heralded as "the largest structure of its kind ever built." Constructed in just under a year, at a cost of about ten million dollars in today's money, the oval-shaped stadium seated seventy thousand people, with standing-room accommodations for seventy thousand more. It was so large that Athens's entire Panathenaic Stadium could be placed inside the running track. Its exterior cement walls rose to a height of sixty feet, housing one hundred rooms that included numerous dressing rooms to accommodate each team, equipped with lockers, cots, showers, baths, rubbing tables, and every other training apparatus. Electric bells and signboards were installed in every room to notify competitors of their approaching events.

The stadium's enormous field also surpassed anything of its kind, stretching 235 yards long by 100 yards wide. Its inner perimeter was ringed by a third-of-a-mile running track and its outer perimeter by an even larger cement bicycle track with banked turns. But for watermen, its most notable innovation was one of the largest concrete swimming pools ever built, which, the press said, "will be the center of interest for many days during the great athletic carnival." Located in the infield directly in front of the grandstand and king's royal box, the rectangular pool was framed by a well-defined concrete lip like the reflecting pools at Versailles. Its depth at each end was four and a half feet, sinking to a middle depth of twelve and a half feet, where a collapsible tower mechanically lowered below the surface of the pool when not needed for the high-diving competitions. An advanced filtration system replaced the water every twenty-four hours.

Designed by William Henry, the English swimming promoter, in conjunction with England's Amateur Swimming Association, the pool stretched a staggering 100 meters long (109.3 yards), almost four times longer than any man-made pool Charley had ever swum (twice as long as what would become the standard 50-meter Olympic pool length). The distance eliminated any need for turns in the 100-meter race. They had effectively taken away Charley's greatest advantage and seemed to be daring him to compete.

WITH ONLY TWO YEARS to prepare to host the fourth Olympiad, Lord Desborough had set about organizing London's first Olympic Games with as much vigor and determination as he brought to his other personal conquests. Sir Theodore Cook, a fellow organizer of the London Games, said, "His own sheer force of personality and prestige enabled Lord Desborough to carry out a task which no one else would have attempted." An overjoyed Coubertin said, "Left in the care of such men, the fourth Olympiad could not fail to be a brilliant success." Every inch the proud Briton, Lord Desborough summed up his motivation to the press: "As this country has been the cradle of so many forms of athletic sport, it is absolutely essential that the Olympic Games, if they are held in England, should be carried out in a manner worthy of a great athletic nation."

These Games seemed finally to have achieved the international partnership that Coubertin had long sought for his Olympics. For the first time, British organizers insisted on submitting details of their Olympic program to the IOC before publishing it. They provided Coubertin with a 190-page book compiling all of the rules and regulations of sport to be enforced at the London Games. When Coubertin made comments or wanted changes, they complied. They all agreed that for the first time they would hold a separate Olympics in October for winter sports like skating and hockey. When the organizers wanted to begin the marathon race at Windsor Castle so that the Princess of Wales could watch the start with her children, and then finish the race at the stadium in front of the king's royal box, Coubertin agreed, even though it would elongate the marathon's historic distance of 24.85 miles to 26 miles 385 yards, unaware that this concession would forever standardize this longer distance.* And to avoid the recent situation at the Athens Intercalated Games, where the international referees were not fully abreast of the sporting rules and customs and had to turn to Jim Sullivan for all final rulings, both the Brits and the IOC agreed that the obvious solution was to use only seasoned officials from the country that had invented officiating—England. Jim Sullivan was furious.

This Camelot that Desborough and Coubertin had created was almost perfect, except for three thorny issues. The first was the problem of which measurement system to use, the French metric or the English imperial, which was a point of pride for both countries. The British imperial system was used by the two leading sports nations, England

---

* The marathon originated as a race during the first modern Olympics at Athens after Michel Bréal, a friend of Coubertin's, suggested that a long-distance run from Marathon to Athens should be organized to honor the fabled run of the Greek soldier who ran from the Battle of Marathon to Athens to carry the news of victory.

and America. It had evolved from the thousands of various Roman and Anglo-Saxon measurements in the Middle Ages and been officially adopted by the empire in 1824. The metric system, derived from the Greek word *metron* (a measure), was invented by the French, whose scientists had long declared it superior. It offered a more consistent system of units, the decimal made for easier calculations, and, well, it was French. Coubertin insisted its use was "absolutely vital" for Olympic contests. In his memoirs, he later recalled, "Though changing the 100-yard race into the 100 meters (which made it 109.3 yards) was not a catastrophe for Britain's athletes technically speaking, many of them felt it to be a sort of national humiliation." Lord Desborough conceded, which forever solidified the metric system in international competition, but drew a line in the sand on an issue more sensitive to Britain—the "Irish Question."

Some of the greatest athletes on both the American and the British teams were from Ireland. With a fourth of the world population part of the British Empire, there was the touchy and complex issue of deciding who could compete under what flag. For example, could Irish athletes, as a country under British rule, compete under their home flag, or would they be required to compete under the Union Jack? Would an Irish citizen living in America be free to join the American team? As a member of the House of Commons, Lord Desborough had long opposed Irish self-rule. And being that Irish athletes had won most of the British track-and-field medals in Athens, Desborough insisted that Ireland was not a nation and must compete under the British flag. He further sent a communication to America notifying them that American contestants must be American citizens, which would exclude several of America's top Irish athletes. Jim Sullivan, as former head of the Ancient Order of Hibernians, was irate, as were most Irishmen, some of whom boycotted the Games rather than compete under the British flag.

One final sticky matter was whether to allow women to compete. Coubertin vehemently opposed the idea, emphasizing that he restored the Olympics for the solemn glorification of the male athlete alone and insisting that the only suitable place in sports for women was to cheer men on. However, British suffragettes were growing more vocal. Less than a month before the opening ceremony, up to half a million men and women would march through London for women's right to vote. Against Coubertin's wishes, the organizers decided to allow women to compete in athletics that emphasized graceful movement rather than strenuous competition, sports that would preserve a woman's femininity, where they could still wear leg-covering skirts and dresses and stockings, not sweat, and not jeopardize their health and ability to become a mother. Archery, lawn tennis, and figure skating were selected as official events.*

IN DECEMBER, THE AMERICAN Olympic Committee announced its intention to raise fifty thousand dollars to send a team to London. With the nation's reputation on the line, it was reported that after the American watermen's abysmal showing in Athens, if Charley did not swim, there was no need to send any other U.S. swimmers, who could surely not bring credit to the country.

"That our swimmers will have a hard task in winning from the water experts abroad is a foregone conclusion," the San Francisco Chronicle wrote, "as swimming in England can almost be classed as the national sport. In England nearly 10,000 competitors have taken part in the races during the past year, witnessed in many cases by a crowd of over 100,000 spectators." It concluded by noting the absence of any organized attempt to develop swimmers in America beyond a few athletic clubs, and said, "Indeed, the victory of Uncle Sam's swimmers, if such be the case, will be remarkable."

For the first time, rather than selecting athletes based on past performance, the American Olympic Committee planned to hold simultaneous regional tryouts. Penn's Mike Murphy, the beloved track and football coach, was named the Olympic team's official trainer over all

---

* Gymnastics and diving were selected as demonstration events in 1908, which were put on as exhibitions, but were not recognized as official Olympic events at the London Games.

athletes. They allocated no money to fund a swim coach. Swimming trials for the West were scheduled to take place in Chicago and for the East at Travers Island. Both would be held on June 4.

The swimming contests scheduled for London included the hundred meters, four hundred meters, fifteen hundred meters, hundred-meter backstroke, two-hundred-meter breaststroke, and four-by-two-hundred-meter relay, which made each race almost 10 percent longer than the Americans were used to swimming under the shorter yard distances. The water polo contests were placed under the tamer English rules, which to hardcore players like Joe Ruddy seemed downright sissified. No allotment was made to send an American water polo team.

IN MAY, NEWSPAPERS REPORTED that Cecil Healy turned down the Australian association's request to join the 1908 Olympic team, regretfully citing his business obligations. Perhaps this was a sign that Charley should be focusing on his own business.

Healy's withdrawal only made Australian newspapers more vociferous in their claims that their man could beat Charley over one hundred yards if the two met in an open-water straightaway. They pointed out that in establishing his world century record of 55.4 seconds, the New Yorker had the advantage of three turns, which, according to present standards, meant a benefit of about 3 seconds. The Australians argued that this would make Charley's open-water century time 58.4 seconds: more than a second slower than Healy's straightaway mark of 57.2 seconds made in February. In addition, with British Olympic officials decreeing meters the official measurement of the Games, the shorter hundred-yard century now seemed passé, and the twenty-eight-foot-longer hundred-meter distance was looked upon as the true test of the world's fastest swimmer, for which Healy held the world record of 67.2 seconds.

AMERICA WAS CALLING FOR Charley to compete in the London Games. Handley and Wahle were both part of the selection committee for an Olympic swim team. The *Los Angeles Times* heralded Charley as one of the four greatest amateur athletes in America, along with Martin Sheridan (discus thrower and jumper) and the tennis players Jay Gould II and May Sutton. Gould's father, George Jay Gould I, a wealthy railroad scion, a fellow Winged Footer, and an honorary vice president of the American Olympic Committee, set out to entice Charley to compete. In the spring, he invited Charley to the fashionable town of Lakewood, New Jersey, where Charley could enjoy the fresh pine air on Gould's two-hundred-acre country estate, stay at their palatial forty-bedroom mansion, and train in one of the first residential pools in the country, while Gould's Olympian son, Jay, trained on the estate's tennis courts.

The offer was meaningful beyond just affording Charley his own Olympic training site. The Goulds were members of New York society's elite Four Hundred. Not to be overlooked, however, was that George Gould's late father, Jay Gould, had amassed the family's $100 million fortune (more than $2 billion today) the old-fashioned way: through hard work, dishonesty, bribery, stock manipulation, and squeezing his workers dry. The most despised of all the robber barons, Jay Gould earned the nickname the Mephistopheles of Wall Street. Apparently, he wasn't much different from Thomas P. Daniels, except that he was more successful and didn't get arrested. George and his wife, Edith, made it a priority to be nothing like the senior Gould, becoming well-liked socialites and associating with only the most upstanding company. The fact that George invited the son of Thomas P. Daniels to be his guest was socially significant.

As Charley thought about Gould's offer, reports came from California that J. Scott Leary was unable to leave his business to compete at the Olympics, nor was he in good enough form to swim on the British stage. Mark Schwarz's college demands and Jam Handy's grueling newspaper schedule at the *Chicago Tribune* also took their toll, leaving both watermen out of form with not enough time to ready themselves for international competition.

A few up-and-coming teenagers showed promise, like seventeen-year-old James Reilly, sixteen-year-old Harry Hebner, and twenty-year-old Les Rich from Brookline, but they had yet to crack the century's sixty-second mark.

To properly train and compete in the London Olympics would take Charley away from his insurance job for more than two months. If he left the agency for that length of time, there might be no job to come back to. Especially if he went over to London and lost. His legacy would never regain its luster. He would no longer be a hero; no more would he be the English champion. He would just be Charles Daniels. Never in his life had that been enough.

OLYMPIC FEVER BEGAN TO sweep both sides of the Atlantic. In the months leading up to the London contests, articles appeared in newspapers detailing the history of the modern Games. The public devoured news about London's ongoing preparation and the construction of its unprecedented stadium. American journalists speculated about the current college athletes who might make worthy Olympians. They posted pictures of the top track-and-field stars, whom Jim Sullivan publicized as the nation's finest specimens of athleticism. Given the winning history of American track and field, the press devoted most of its coverage to them. The American public was eager to hear about their impressive performances at the American Olympic trials and the ultimate team selections. On both sides of the Atlantic it was shaping into a showdown. One newspaper wrote that America's track-and-field men were like two fists ready to hit England in the solar plexus. Swimming seemed more like a tap on the shoulder.

The American Olympic Committee set May 29 as the last day to register for the Olympic swimming trials, to be held in June. To meet the deadline, an athlete needed to mail his signed intent to compete to the head of the AAU's swimming committee, Otto Wahle.

Charley continued to spread himself thin between his job and his swimming appearances. Fortunately, he did not have to train exceptionally hard to keep beating the American field. International competition was different. It would require him to be at the top of his game, and that meant he had to take a leave. He also faced the difficult reality that no aging athlete can stay at his peak forever—a reality that was clearly on his mind.

"An athlete in any line can never know when he is going to hit the chutes," Charley told *The Buffalo Commercial*. "You may start to go back any minute, and not be able to account for it." But no other U.S. prospects had emerged to take his mantle. Without a clear contender to send to London, the American Olympic Committee saw little point in sponsoring any swimmers.

On May 10, *The New York Times* ran a story that Charley had gone to Mr. Gould's Lakewood estate to train. On May 20, *The Buffalo Commercial* confirmed the report, saying that Daniels "has made no trials under the watch, but is satisfied with the way he is moving." A few days before the registration deadline, Wahle was thrilled to receive a letter from Charley announcing his plans to compete.

On June 4, Charley appeared at Travers Island and swam a hundred-meter century. Although he finished about 9 seconds ahead of the next man, his 69.2-second time was 2 seconds behind Healy's world record, and already there were rumors that Halmay was posting world-record times in practice. Yet Charley remained America's best chance. Beyond him, Lou Handley best summed up the performances of the other prospective watermen in an article. "It was disappointing to see the tryouts for the Olympics result in such a fizzle," he lamented. "The tryouts showed nothing."

On June 8, the American Olympic Committee gathered at the Hotel Astor in New York under the chairmanship of Jim Sullivan to sift through the list of potential Olympic athletes and their tryout results. After a daylong session, the committee announced they agreed to send seventy-six men to represent the United States.

A week later, an official letter arrived for Charley notifying him of their decision to send eight U.S. watermen, with Charley leading the way. Selected to accompany him were his fellow Winged Footers Budd Goodwin and Con Trubenbach; Les Rich from Brookline, Harry Hebner from Chicago; the long and lanky Gus Goessling from St. Louis, who'd won the hundred-meter backstroke and two-hundred-meter breaststroke at the Chicago trials; and two other swimmers from Chicago and St. Louis. Little faith was given to any of them succeeding other than Charley.

Alice Daniels added the Olympic Committee's letter to her third scrapbook and bade her son a heartfelt good luck. She certainly would have gone to London to see Charley swim if she had had the means.

As for Otto Wahle and Lou Handley, without the Olympic Committee sponsoring a swim coach, neither of them could afford to make the trip. The two of them and Charley had come so far together. There were no more words, no more nuggets of advice to impart. The time for big speeches was over. Wahle and Handley would be with Charley in spirit, eagerly awaiting the cabled results back home, but Charley needed to walk into the lion's den alone.

FOURTH OLYMPIAD, OPENING CEREMONY,
SHEPHERD'S BUSH STADIUM, LONDON, 1908
(outdoor stadium pool on upper left)

22.

DANIELS IN THE
LION'S DEN

—

JUNE-JULY 1908

AMERICA'S GROWING ENTHUSIASM FOR THE OLYMPICS SUPERSEDED even the 1908 presidential campaign. A political cartoon in *The Brooklyn Daily Eagle* depicted a giant Uncle Sam waving off the two tiny presidential candidates, Taft and Bryan, like bothersome children as he intently pressed his ear to a candlestick phone marked "Direct Wire to the Olympic Games." Newspapers across the country, from cities to small towns, continued to run articles about the upcoming Games, whetting the public's appetite. Not only was this shaping into an epic battle between England and America, but newspapers were calling it "the most remarkable athletic gathering ever witnessed." *The New York Times* reported that even France, which always disregarded athletics "with great disfavor . . . proposes to send a large and representative team to London for the coming Olympic contests."

The American public was still not sure what to make of Daniels and his obscure sport, but they loved a winner. Charley needed to claim the gold medal in the hundred-meter century to complete his Cinderella story. All of America was watching. Anything less than victory would reduce him and all of his previous heroics to the wastebasket of history.

Charley had received several invitations from swimming clubs in England to compete in century races a week prior to the Olympic contests: one against the Belgian champion and another against Rob Derbyshire, who was rumored to be using Charley's crawl to swim his fastest times yet. Wahle and Handley insisted that tapering training the week before the race was the best approach to keep muscles fresh. It would let his body heal and his muscles return to optimum levels. But Charley's gut was telling him to push himself. And competition was the best way to do that.

On June 17, two weeks before the rest of the team set off for England, Charley set sail for Liverpool on the huge British luxury liner the RMS *Lusitania*. Newspapers across the country ran headlines about his departure: "America's Greatest Swimmer First to Leave for England." A few days before he boarded, the *Lusitania* itself made headlines by breaking the Atlantic-crossing record from Ireland's Daunt Rock to New Jersey's Sandy Hook Lighthouse with a time of four days twenty hours and eight minutes. The grand turbine steamer would make bigger headlines seven years later when a German U-boat sank it off the coast of southern Ireland, killing 1,100 of its 1,900 passengers, including more than 120 Americans. As Charley departed, one of the final headlines read, "American Swimmers Face Hard Task to Defeat Foreign Stars in Meet." And by "American Swimmers," they meant Charley. As *The Manchester Courier* would somewhat overstate upon his arrival in London, "Daniels stands for everything in America."

For the fourth time in as many years, Charley set off for England to do battle. As the great ship left New York's Upper Bay to pass through the narrows and into the Atlantic, to the west of him lay Staten Island and on the east lay Brooklyn's Bath Beach. He could see the waters where his father used to swim out to sea and the island where his father left him to start a new life. Then a loud boom from artillery shells exploded on both sides of the ship. Brooklyn's Fort Hamilton and Staten Island's Fort Wadsworth fired two more shots from their twelve-inch coastal defense guns that whizzed over the ship's British flag, abruptly stopping the British liner caught in the crosshairs of what was later described as a war game. After a twenty-minute delay, the *Lusitania* forged ahead, but the ruckus between these two countries was an omen of things to come.

Around midnight on Saturday, the ship stopped again. This time for crewmen to throw lit buoys overboard after a second-class passenger climbed the railing and took a fatal plunge, never again to be seen.

A few days later, after five days at sea, the *Lusitania* made port in Blackpool early Tuesday morning, June 23, in the very waters where Barney Kieran had dealt Charley a resounding defeat.

When Charley arrived in London the following day, he checked in to his hotel and eventually made his way to the Olympic stadium to see the pool that his former promoter, William Henry, had designed to defeat him. Charley had made special arrangements with the Olympic organizers to familiarize himself with this beast of a tank and use it for training.

Its hundred-meter straightaway proved daunting. The length and width made it easy to swim askew, especially if they had to race on a day the water was green and murky. Already the extra twenty-eight feet that the hundred-meter length added to the century was intimidating. In all of Charley's earlier victories in the English Championships, Healy and Halmay had both been coming on fast at the end. Halmay was exceptionally strong, much stronger than Charley. Had either opponent had an extra ten yards to make up the distance, especially on a straightaway with no turns, the swimming world might never have heard of Charles Daniels.

In the weeks leading up to the opening ceremony, often under gray skies, sometimes in the rain, Charley practiced daily in the stadium's long, cold tank. He had no coach to tell him what he was doing wrong. No one to clock his times. Until his American teammates arrived, he was alone with the water. This was a time when Charley couldn't help but face his demons—the demons of his childhood and adolescence. About the boy who could never meet his father's expectations. The boy who wasn't worthy enough for his father to want to be in his life.

On the morning of July 6, seventy-three of Charley's Olympic teammates arrived on the steamship *Philadelphia*, and the ship's grizzled captain, Mills, could not have been more thrilled to see them leave.

"If the American Line had to carry a team of athletes every trip it would either have to double its rates or go into bankruptcy," said Captain Mills. "I expected them to have big appetites, but the way some of those big fellows ate made the kitchen look as though a band of pirates had struck it. If we had had just a few days of real rough weather it would have sent a lot of the fellows below with some real seasickness, but I couldn't find a storm on the chart or I think I would have steered into it."

Charley was happy to see the friendly faces of Budd Goodwin and Con Trubenbach and, to his surprise, Joe Ruddy. The feisty Irishman was not about to miss Charley's chance to take the swimming crown from the Brits.

ON TUESDAY EVENING, JULY 7, Charley boarded a train alone for a 220-mile trip north, arriving at the Hyde Baths after 8:00 P.M. He immediately stripped, donned his blue bathing costume bearing Mercury's red-winged sandal, and lined up for a century race against the Belgian champion, Herman Meyboom. Even though the Hyde tank was one of the most ill-suited baths in England, it was the venue chosen for Charley to attempt to break his century record of 55.4 seconds. Watching in the gallery was the only living man who had ever defeated Charley in international competition, twenty-seven-year-old Zoltán Halmay, who was eager to see how his American rival fared.

At the official's call "Ready," "Set," "Go!" Charley won the race, but fell 2.6 seconds short of his record.

The next day, about eight miles west of Hyde, before a distinguished gathering at the High Street Baths in Manchester, Charley proceeded to break his own 150-yard record by three-fifths of a second and received a great ovation. Halmay, who opted to save his energies for the Olympics, stood in the crowd watching once again, carefully clocking Charley's splits.

What these splits revealed was that Charley was four and a half seconds slower in the second fifty yards than in the first fifty, and eight and a half seconds slower in the last fifty yards. His endurance fell short of where it should be, and he was still relying on his wall turns to make up speed.

As he continued his journey, on Saturday evening, July 11, about thirty-five miles west in Liverpool, Charley's speed improved against Derbyshire, his time falling just 0.8 second short of breaking his hundred-yard, 55.4-second world record. But he still needed his wall turns to make it close, and the hundred meters was almost ten yards longer.

ALL THIS TIME LEADING up to the Games, the English proved extremely hospitable to Charley and his teammates. In fact, Charley observed, the English were eager to treat us "a little too fine."

"We were invited to ten dinners before and during the events," Charley recalled. "When the boys politely declined to eat or drink, dozens of young Englishmen came to our quarters and chided us for not being sociable. We had every reason to drop our condition quickly if we had accepted their hospitality."

During one of these social gatherings, a beautiful, tall, stately blonde from Buffalo asked to be introduced to Charley. Their lives had always danced close to each other but, until now, never intersected. She had grown up on Delaware Avenue, practically next door to Charley's grandmother. When Charley was practicing at the Goulds' Lakewood estate, she was wintering down the road. And it appears she had sailed for London a day before Charley had departed from the same New York port. Funny their paths should finally cross on this side of the Atlantic.

Charley instantly recognized her name. Six years earlier the Buffalo newspapers had declared her the belle of the season's debutantes. She hailed from one of the city's most prominent families. When her father, Frank Goodyear, had passed away the prior year, flags throughout the city were lowered to half-mast. Besides the family's enormous Delaware Avenue residence, they owned a winter home at the most exclusive vacation club in the United States, Georgia's Jekyll Island, whose members included the Rockefellers, Morgans, Vanderbilts, Pulitzers, and Fields. She was the embodiment of high society, so of course she knew about Charley's father and their shameful family scandal. Yet she very much wanted to meet the famous American waterman who was vying to become the champion swimmer of the world.

She was introduced to Charley as Mrs. Florence Goodyear Wagner, and it was not long before Charley learned that the "good match" she had married into at age eighteen had proved anything but. Shortly after Florence had received an enormous inheritance upon her father's death, her well-bred, Cornell-educated, tennis-obsessed husband quit his engineering job at her late father's railroad company to join the semiprofessional tennis circuit, eventually abandoning Florence and their two very young daughters to take up with his mistress—a fellow tennis player. Wanting to avoid the scandal of divorce for herself and her children was the only reason she remained legally married, a decision Charley understood all too well.

The two enjoyed each other's company. Florence was chic and sophisticated, funny and entertaining, worldly and well traveled, and exuded a bit of a devil-may-care attitude. They shared a love for automobiles. Florence hadn't appeared to have any previous interest in competitive swimming but was fast becoming a fan.

DAYS BEFORE THE OPENING CEREMONY, British officials informed all twenty-two teams that during the parade, as they passed the royal box, the flag bearer was required to dip the colors in homage to King Edward VII.

"The American team was made up mostly of Irish," Joe Ruddy recalled. "To them the King was a symbol of oppression and tyranny." So, the night before the opening ceremony, the American team held a meeting. "We selected Ralph Rose, the 280-pound shot putter, to carry the Stars and Stripes," Ruddy said, and then "we told Rose if he dipped the colors, we would throw him into the swimming pool on the spot."

Ruddy grinned. "Rose knew we would do it, too. There were three or four other fellows on the squad just as big and strong as he, and they were to march immediately behind him in the parade."

On Monday, July 13, the morning of the opening ceremony, Charley opened his hotel room's curtains to dark clouds and a heavy rain. The storm would keep many spectators away, not to mention some of the athletes, who did not want to subject themselves to possibly catching a cold or getting sick.

By 2:00 P.M., as the men waited in their assigned locker room beneath the stadium, preparing to march onto the rainy field, the sun came out as if to smile on the British Empire. By three, nobles began filtering into the royal box. A little before four, the band struck up "God Save the King," signaling the royal family's arrival at the gates. Lord Desborough and a group of dignitaries in top hats and tails, including representatives of the British Olympic Association and the Franco-British Exhibition, greeted King Edward VII and Queen Alexandra, along with their royal entourage. Then Desborough presented Baron Pierre de Coubertin, who bowed to their majesties, and, in turn, introduced his IOC members to the king and queen.

The U.K. had a formidable team of 513 athletes. France produced the second-largest showing with 219. Sweden came third with 169 athletes and then Hungary with 154 men.

Once the royal family had settled into their seats, a bugle sounded, the red and gold lions of the Royal Standard were unfurled, and the stadium's gates swung open to commence the parade of the twenty-two participating nations. The European teams entered first, the arena's cavernous space making the crowd of thirty thousand look sparse. When the Danish women gymnasts marched in wearing salacious knee-length pants, Coubertin was appalled. The crowd, however, greeted them with loud applause. When the U.S. team entered the arena, they saw the array of fluttering world flags decorating the top of the stadium with one noticeably absent—the Stars and Stripes.

"And do you know what happened when we passed the King's box?" Joe Ruddy asked with a grin. "Rose held the flag as high as his arms would reach."

Lord Desborough later apologized for the "oversight" of not flying the Stars and Stripes, but the omission wasn't helped by the fact that the flags of Japan and China, neither of which sent athletes, flew proudly. Rose's snub of the British Crown also did nothing to help advance international relations. The first of many shots had been fired between the Americans and the British, and although Joe Ruddy might not have directly pulled the trigger, he certainly was behind the scenes handing out bullets and telling people where to shoot.

——

AFTER KING EDWARD DECLARED "the Olympic games of London open," American watermen prepared for their first event, the four-hundred-meter freestyle. The British champion, Henry Taylor, won gold. Australia's replacement for Cecil Healy, seventeen-year-old Frank Beaurepaire, captured silver. The eighteen-year-old Austrian who won the four hundred meters at Athens, Otto Scheff, took bronze. Budd Goodwin and Harry Hebner failed to advance from the nine preliminary heats. The British flag went up the victory pole to thunderous applause and "God Save the King." For the American watermen, it only got worse from there.

In the fifteen hundred meters, the British Empire swept the field, with Henry Taylor again taking gold, Great Britain's Thomas Battersby silver, and Australia's Frank Beaurepaire bronze. Once again, the Union Jack flew up the victory pole. In the two-hundred-meter breaststroke, the Brits took gold and silver, and the Union Jack was raised up the pole once again.

Otto Wahle and Lou Handley, receiving cable updates back in New York, lamented that the other American watermen "did not," as Handley put it, "rise above mediocrity." None of them made it out of their preliminaries. The American swimmers had proven themselves a laughingstock. The pressure on Charley to save face intensified.

FOR CHARLEY, THERE WOULD be no pistol start as he was accustomed to back home. British officials opted for the traditional English caller. This made the start much harder to hear with swimming caps and cotton earplugs, especially if you were "randomly" assigned the farthest lane as Charley was.

Jim Sullivan had already lodged complaints about the British officials' refusal to allow any American or other representative to be present when they secretly drew the positions of contestants' heats—especially when the British athletes seemed to repeatedly end up with the most favorable spots and the Americans the worst. Throughout the London Games, all contests were being exclusively overseen by British judges,

British timers, and British-made stopwatches. Unless an athlete won a race by a visible margin, the opportunity to rule in someone else's favor was ever present.

English officials also had the ability to call a foul to disqualify a winner, as happened in the four-hundred-meter track race, accusing the American leader of "bumping" a competitor and ultimately awarding the gold to the British runner-up. The incident nearly brought both sides to blows. The *Academy* magazine of London perfectly expressed the officials' hierarchical attitude: "A more disgraceful exhibition of foul running has never been seen on an English track and it is becoming increasingly obvious that in the future American 'amateurs' will have to be debarred from taking part in athletic contests in this country, which are supposed to be reserved for gentlemen." Mike Murphy, the U.S. trainer, best voiced America's outrage: "English officials will do anything to prevent an American or anybody besides their own people from winning a race." Jim Sullivan went so far as to accuse the British of cheating. In the marathon, when the Italian front-runner, Dorando Pietri, collapsed from exhaustion upon entering the stadium for the final lap, the moment British officials saw that the next runner was an American, they ran out onto the track to lift the rubber-legged Italian onto his feet and carry him half-conscious across the finish.

"The pulling of the Italian, Dorando, across the line was outrageous," noted the eight-time U.S. gold medalist Ray Ewry. "There is no doubt in my mind that if the spectators had seen that the man following this runner had been an athlete of the United Kingdom they would sooner have hit Dorando over the head than help him over the tape."

The American press wrote, "It was simply a case of pursuing their land-grabbing tactics—athletically—to prevent anyone but themselves from acquiring the world's Olympic athletic championship."

From his seat in the stadium, Coubertin observed, "Sports passions became raised to a pitch never reached before. The huge amphitheater, sometimes black with people gone wild with enthusiasm, gave off a feeling of organic power which I have never come across since." But what was happening between the British and the Americans concerned him. This was not his romantic idea of bringing the youth of the world together to compete in peace and understanding. "There seemed to be a direct confrontation between the two Anglo-Saxon nations creating, within the Games, a sort of muscular duel between their champions," observed Coubertin. "Both teams showed so much keenness and determination to win that one might have thought that all their historic rivalries had been roused and that their national honor was definitely at stake."

RAIN FELL SO HEAVILY during the early hours of Friday, July 17, that it turned the pool into a murky swamp. With no lane separations, the poor visibility made it more difficult to navigate a straight line. As Charley stepped off the track onto the grass infield, mud squished beneath his feet. A sweet, earthy post-rain fragrance pleasantly surrounded him as he walked to the pool in his long white robe.

The morning swim schedule included nine qualifying five-man heats for the hundred meters, with the winners of each heat advancing, as well as the man who swam the fastest time among all the losing swimmers. When competition began, poor weather hampered attendance. But by lunchtime, the summer showers subsided, and the nine qualifying heats for the hundred-meter century kicked off.

Zoltán Halmay swam fast enough to win his heat in a speedy 68.2 seconds but was clearly saving himself for the finals. His practice times were rumored to be regularly breaking Healy's 67.2-second world record. Some even said by as much as a whole second.

In the fourth heat, during the final few yards, the poor visibility caused a Belgian swimmer to crash into the English champion, Rob Derbyshire, costing Derbyshire the win. Oddly, Derbyshire took no action to file a protest and failed to advance to the semifinals. Charley's teammates Harry Hebner and Les Rich both won their heats. But it was Charley's qualifying performance in the fifth heat that made England shiver.

At the official's "Take your marks," Charley stepped onto the pool's starting deck, constructed of wooden planks, where five white towels lay along the pool's edge, spaced about five to six feet apart to mark each swimmer's starting position. He wore a navy swim cap tied around his chin and removed his long white robe in the cool sixty-three-degree air, a bit daunted by the hundred-meter straightaway that denied him any turns.

At the official's call "Are you ready?" the swimmers crouched into their diving stance. When they all looked set, the official called, "Go!"

Charley hit the water with a shallow dive and quickly took matters into his own hands, tearing down the tank to touch the final wall in a breathtaking 65.8 seconds—a new world record.

English officials stood shocked. Finally, they could no longer refuse to believe his record-breaking times, having seen him do the impossible with their own eyes.

CHARLES DANIELS,
1908 LONDON
OLYMPICS,
100-METER
FREESTYLE

ZOLTÁN HALMAY,
1908 LONDON
OLYMPICS,
100-METER
FREESTYLE

———

THREE DAYS LATER, ON Monday morning, July 20, the century's two semifinal heats, each with a field of six, commenced, with the two winners and both second-place finishers advancing to the afternoon's four-man finals. Temperatures remained in the lower sixties, and in true English fashion showers started falling as the first contest began. The pool again was green and cloudy, making visibility in the water difficult.

In the first heat, the U.S. swimmer Harry Hebner swam off course after a solid start, taking himself out of contention as Halmay claimed first and Harald Julin from Sweden took second. Charley won the second semifinal heat, but clocked a slow 70.2 seconds, perhaps swimming a little askew himself, and the American Les Rich nabbed second to advance.

Everyone knew the battle for gold was a match race between the American and the European champions. If Halmay was indeed putting up practice times of 66.2 seconds, Charley needed to maintain a straight course and somehow repeat his earlier world-record speed of 65.8 seconds. That would give him a visible margin of victory of a couple feet, just enough not to be cheated by the finish-line judges in a "close call." But there was no room for error.

The weather cleared as the day matured, and it grew warmer than at any time since the opening of the Games. With ticket prices lowered all around with the hope of increasing attendance, about fifteen thousand people came to watch that afternoon's events, scheduled between three and four o'clock. The British press had ramped up excitement about the hundred-meter freestyle finals as a battle of champions. At the stadium's far end, a section of Americans brought their miniature flags and noisemakers, much to the Brits' annoyance, whose hope for the race's outcome was "anyone but a Yankee."

One of Charley's Olympic teammates, Gus Goessling, from St. Louis, said, "One of the big points of controversy in those races grew out of the British custom of starting the races by shouting 'Go!' instead of using a gun. The swimmers wore colored caps for identification and had cotton in their ears, so those on the far side of the pool not only had to swim through the horrible chop that bounced off the sides, but also couldn't hear the starter's call." British officials had again "randomly" assigned Charley to the farthest outside lane.

Charley had been competing in Europe for three summers. At all meets the starters alerted swimmers to the line with "Take your marks!" Then they gave the intermediate warning "Are you ready?" Sometimes they asked it twice if swimmers were still preparing themselves before they called, "Go!" The London Olympic officials used the same three-step procedure in every race. However, unbeknownst to Charley, this time something untoward was afoot.

The two European swimmers competing in the hundred-meter finals—the Hungarian and the Swede—appeared to have been forewarned by the English officials that an unconventional two-step— "Take your marks!" and "Go!"—would be used for the championship race. Unbeknownst to them, the same officials failed to offer the Americans the same courtesy.

Four years of climbing this impossible mountain came down to the next sixty seconds. If Charley lost, the Brits could finally dismiss him as the fraud they claimed him to be. And back home, he would be a disappointment, quickly fading from memory, as would his efforts to gain acceptance for himself and his mother.

Charley stepped up to the outdoor pool's wood-planked starting deck where a white towel marked his position at the far end. The musty stench of algae rankled his nose. Three of the fastest swimmers on the planet readied to take their starting positions alongside him. They wore unitard wool swimsuits that stretched neck to knees, with different-colored swimming caps secured by a string around their chins to distinguish them amid all the splashing. Charley's was navy, as was Rich's. Halmay wore black and Julin white. Europe's towering Halmay lined up six feet to Charley's right. Beyond him stood Julin and Rich, all spaced about six feet apart from the other.

A hundred-meter straightaway of green water lay before them. There were no roped-off lanes or black lines on the bottom of the pool to guide them. Swimming the shortest distance possible in a dead straight line was key to winning the race. This was the time when Charley was most on edge—his heart racing, his palms sweating—before the competition made him forget everything but swimming.

When the mustachioed British official, Mr. Hudson, called, "Take your marks!" the swimmers dropped their robes, and Charley began removing his as he stepped onto the platform, awaiting the intermediate warning "Are you ready?" But the next word that came out of Mr. Hudson's mouth was "Go!"

His two European opponents hit the water and disappeared. Some reports even said Charley's robe was only half drawn off when the call came. His head practically spun off his neck, only to see the British officials' smirks. As he realized what was happening, his confidence dropped. In his gut, he felt that sick, sinking feeling. Then an inside voice, perhaps that of his father, told him, "It's over." Charley saw all that he had worked for racing away with the pack.

The British crowd cheered as they saw the European champions get off to a tremendous start. The American section did not know what they were witnessing as their lone champion stood at the line. Everyone in the stadium knew that Charley had already lost.

Then the voice that always urged Charley forward called to him once more.

No time to argue, Charley exploded into the air. A second later, the smash of cold water instantly blurred his vision as the rush of liquid roared against his ears. He felt the water speeding up on his skin as his dive propelled him forward. The world beneath the surface was so much

CHARLES DANIELS, 1908

calmer and quieter than above. Somewhere ahead and to his right, in this green odorless realm, he heard the loud vibrations of his competitors churning up the water like machines. When he felt his momentum off the entry dive starting to slow, he pulled the water back with his left forearm in a perfectly straight line and ignited his six-beat kick.

The British officials' trick had given the Europeans a seemingly insurmountable two-meter head start.

With his feet beating the water with the regularity of a propeller, Charley kept his head facedown, not breathing, not looking, making it easier to swim askew, but he had no other choice. He hoped that his weeks of familiarizing himself with the pool would keep him on a straight line. There was no room for error. No walls to gain an edge off the turn to make up for lost time. As his legs churned, he moved through the water like a long, low motor craft with his head acting as plow, trying to make up almost a seven-foot deficit.

No longer having the luxury to set a sustainable pace, he was already pushing his body to its extreme limits just to get back into the race, not taking a breath, which ensured the burning in his upper body would start sooner than normal. Charley surged after the field at a tremendous rate. His extended arms stabbed the water, his feet fluttering a fierce three kicks between each stroke, incinerating lactate energy, as he fought to make up ground. At ten meters he trailed. At twenty meters he trailed. At thirty meters he felt Halmay's legs splashing on his right side.

A great battle ensued between Halmay, Julin, and Charley as he drew close to even, already feeling the burn that sought to shut him down. The three competitors swam side by side as they reached the halfway mark, when Charley turned his head sideways for a quick breath and heard the crowd's cheers. The pain in his arms came fast now, tightening his muscles.

As he passed the halfway mark, it soon became apparent that the race was between Charley and Halmay. Halmay's long arms churned up the water like a paddle wheel. The Hungarian worked magnificently to hold off his rival as Charley struggled through the physical pain and exhaustion, fighting to maintain his impossible pace with the singular goal of reaching the far wall before he gave out.

The two rivals fought down the last twenty meters to the finish, Charley's entire body screaming. The last ten meters he felt it trying to shut down as he fought through the murderous pain, willing his paralyzed arms to move, as both men reached for the wall in a rush of white water and an eruption of cheers.

Charley's muscles went limp, his chest heaving for oxygen, as he lifted his head out of the murky water to see who won—or rather whom the officials declared the winner. He had thought himself beaten before he even started, but saw the officials frantically comparing watches. He knew it was close. Other faces standing around the pool's edge looked stunned. He had touched the wall a yard ahead of Halmay in a blistering 65.6 seconds—a new world record.

The far section of U.S. fans exploded with uproarious applause, rattles, noisemakers, and a flurry of miniature American flags. Smiles abounded, and probably none bigger than Mrs. Florence Goodyear Wagner's.

On the field, Joe Ruddy, Budd Goodwin, Con Trubenbach, and the rest of his teammates went wild with euphoric shouts and backslaps.

Once he'd begun to recover his breath and his pained muscles allowed him to move again, Charley climbed out of the pool to a rousing reception. Blue eyes twinkling, his face lit up with a big, joyful grin of both disbelief and relief. A whole battalion of photographers rushed to take his picture. Even the British officials could not deny his brilliance.

More than thirty-five hundred miles away, the results of the race came over the transatlantic cable. Otto Wahle and Lou Handley rejoiced, along with the rest of the Winged Footers.

The next day, Alice Daniels's scissor-happy hands awoke to a windfall of press clippings, and she did not have to look hard to find them. Newspapers across the country carried Charley's victory on the front page—a first for swimming. Page 1 of *The Buffalo Enquirer* headlined "American Wins Swimming Victory—C. M. Daniels Captures Final Event in 100-Meter Swim and Ties World's Record," making sure to identify him as a Buffalo boy. From his childhood home, the front page of *The Dayton Herald* proclaimed, "Daniels Equals World's Record." Front pages from *The Washington Times* to *The Boston Daily Globe* to *The Sacramento Star,* and even small-town newspapers like Nebraska's

CHARLES DANIELS, 1908 LONDON OLYMPICS,
IMMEDIATELY AFTER CENTURY WIN

Kearney Daily Hub, heralded his incredible victory. The article in Handy's *Chicago Tribune* noted how "Daniels made a grand win after a miserable start," blaming his poor start on England's use of the spoken word instead of the pistol. The full reason behind Charley's poor start would not be revealed to America until the athletes returned home and Ray Ewry and several other teammates told the press. Now the only thing that mattered was that Daniels had won.

The Brooklyn Citizen declared Daniels the "now undisputed world champion." *The Buffalo Express* proclaimed, "Daniels, World's Best

Swimmer," saying, "A Buffalo boy is now admittedly the greatest exponent of aquatics in the world today."

Lou Handley penned a syndicated article that appeared in newspapers across the country titled "C. M. Daniels, American Winner in Great Olympics, Is World's Greatest Swimmer." He wrote, "An athlete of such marked superiority is seldom born and when we consider that just one man alone was able to lift American swimming from the bottom of the ladder, where it was the laughing stock of Europe, to the top rung, we cannot but admit that we owe a great debt of gratitude to the one who accomplished that arduous task."

The British swimming establishment was silenced. No more did they offer excuses or dispute Daniels's supremacy as the world's great-

CHARLES M. DANIELS, 1911

est swimmer. *The Sporting Life* of London called Daniels "the finest sprinter in the world." They also pointed out that the rest of U.S. swimming again proved laughable, because the American relay team, despite a brilliant performance by Daniels, finished a distant third behind the British and the Hungarians.

It didn't matter. With this triumph, Charley had conquered his Mount Everest. He stood atop the swimming world with nothing more to prove. As he proudly watched the American flag run up the victory pole inside the world's largest stadium, with wild cheers from the American section and ample applause from the British fans who could not help but commend his gritty win, he thought about everyone who had helped him reach this moment and everyone who'd told him he would never make it. He was America's undisputed champion from fifty yards to the mile, the world record holder of all short distances, the English and Olympic century champion, the undisputed champion swimmer of the world, and soon to be named the Amateur Athletic Association's "Athlete of the Year." His father could belittle him no more.

23.

THE LAST CENTURY

—

ON CHARLEY'S JOURNEY HOME FROM LONDON, WHITE STAR'S new steamship, the *Adriatic,* the first ocean liner equipped with a pool, seemed to honor its famous passenger, the great Charles Daniels, by engaging in a transatlantic race against the British Cunard liner the *Umbria* and defeating it in a new ship record of six days eighteen hours and fifty-eight minutes. The race made for a fun diversion for the passengers, although, for Charley, a much greater diversion was found on board in the person of Mrs. Florence Goodyear Wagner.

America's new conquering heroes returned to New York for the modern world's first ever national victory parade of athletes, escorted in a procession of automobiles. Across the parade route along Broadway and Fifth Avenue, the raucous crowd stood ten people deep. Afterward, President Roosevelt invited the Olympians to a reception at his Oyster Bay home. Upon their arrival, the enthusiastic president greeted each athlete with a hearty congratulations and then asked, "Where is Daniels?"

Charley was three hundred miles north at the Hiawatha Lodge, enjoying the peace of his beloved Adirondacks. He had skipped the parade, avoiding all the pageantry and limelight, which never made him comfortable. There, among the pines and mountain lakes, he had a chance to finally soak in how far he had come since he had first heard the call of the loons.

In the wake of Charley's inspirational Olympic triumph, the East

Coast press noted that the beaches saw more people swimming that summer. At Bath Beach it was said the number of swimmers quadrupled. People from seven years of age upward, boys and girls alike, began to take to the water, the more serious among them trying to imitate Charley's six-beat American crawl—or what we now call the freestyle.

The following year, Charley asked Florence to marry him. She went to Paris, where she could obtain a quick and discreet divorce for what the Paris courts deemed "outrageous abandonment," and ironically, it was Charley's good name that kept Florence from being scandalized back home. The *Buffalo Times* reported that when the Episcopal church refused to marry them because of Florence's status as a divorcée, Charley would not let this unfair stigma cast a pall on his fiancée as it had upon his mother. On June 7, 1909, the two married at the Plaza Hotel before a small gathering of friends and family presided over by a Unitarian pastor. They spent their honeymoon in the Adirondacks, and the following year Florence gave birth to Frank Henry Goodyear Daniels, named after her late father. Florence's two young daughters, Grace and Florence, aged four and six at the time of her marriage, also took the prestigious last name of the famous Charles Daniels, and Charley raised them as his own. In 1910, Charley's name and Florence's inheritance prompted Buffalo's Social Register to recognize the newlywed couple as members. Their position allowed Alice Daniels to finally be welcomed back into Buffalo society and shed the black mark of association with Thomas P. Daniels.

TOM DANIELS NOW HELD himself out as a prominent Pittsburgh businessman. The fifty-five-year-old was still a tall, handsome, dapper gentleman, with what little hair remained on his bald head now a distinguished white. He ran the Bankers' Bond Company, which occupied attractive offices at the Magee Building downtown. The company ran regular newspaper ads in every major city around the country, offering to handle the financing of good enterprises and creditable projects. People who knew him claimed that besides his luxurious five-room suite at Pittsburgh's Hotel Lincoln, Tom kept a secret apartment with oriental furnishings for his beautiful Japanese mistress, Kiki Fujiwara. While on paper he remained married to Clara Heder, who lived back in Milwaukee, Tom's friends said that his infatuation for Kiki approached madness. He loved escorting her to restaurants, to theaters, and on motor trips. Tom seemed to love showing her off. He also liked to brag that he was the father of the champion swimmer of the world, Charles Daniels, and made sure to mention that he had taught his son everything he knew.

When Charley came to town with his old rival Jam Handy to make another attempt at Barney Kieran's 220-yard record, the one sprint record that eluded him, *The Pittsburgh Press* interviewed Tom Daniels before the race. "[Tom] says," the journalist wrote, "that in the personal letters which his son writes him, he dwells at length upon the special preparation he has been making to accomplish the task set before him, and he also declares that he never was as fit for any trial as now."

Perhaps Charley and his father were indeed corresponding. Maybe Tom Daniels was genuinely trying to rectify his past actions and connect with his only child. Or maybe these were just the bogus words of a smooth operator trying to capitalize on his son's good name, just as Tom had with his honorable father, the late Judge Daniels. Based on his behavior over the years, it was evident that, other than using his paternal relation to impress friends or business associates, Tom had no use for Charley. One can conclude that rather than taking pride in his son's success, Tom most likely resented the fact that it far surpassed his own.

That night of March 26, 1909, with the help of being challenged by Jam Handy, Charley went ahead and broke Kieran's elusive 220-yard record. The crowd said he looked as if he were shot out of a cannon. But there was no evidence that Tom witnessed it, or indeed ever bothered to meet up with his son.

Not long after, Pittsburgh authorities raided the handsome offices of the Bankers' Bond Company and after an ensuing search arrested the fugitive Tom Daniels in Cleveland. Newspapers across the country reported on the latest fraud by the legendary swindler. In addition to associating him with his reputable New York Supreme Court justice father, this time papers noted that Tom was the father of Charles Daniels, champion swimmer of the world. The public association of Charley with such a notorious criminal certainly raised eyebrows and outrage among some of the NYAC's members, but the swimmer's name and reputation had sufficiently supplanted his father's so that the bad deeds of Tom Daniels could no longer drag Charley down or result in his expulsion.

Before a federal judge passed sentencing, Tom skipped bail and with a reported thirty thousand dollars in hand (close to one million dollars today) fled the country. A few years later, a report emerged that an American man, going by the name J. A. Dent, who looked a lot like Tom Daniels, was running a similar swindling scheme out of London, offering to make investments in Oregon lands and other businesses. It was the last Charley and Alice heard of Tom Daniels.

In the four scrapbooks Alice filled with Charley's swimming accomplishments, the only mention of Tom Daniels was the clipping from *The Pittsburgh Press* where Tom bragged about his son.

CHARLEY HAD ACCOMPLISHED EVERYTHING he set out to do and now wanted to give back. Although he kept his insurance job, he mostly spent the next three years promoting swimming by giving exhibitions and breaking world records around the country, trying to inspire the next generation of Olympic swimmers. If American swimming was to thrive, the country needed to prove that it had more to offer at the next Olympics than just a one-horse show.

A year before the 1912 Stockholm Games, the seeds Charley had planted and cultivated over the previous seven years bore fruit. In 1911, finding it increasingly difficult to keep to a regular swimming schedule, Charley decided to commit to training himself into top form one last time to compete in the AAU Championships that spring and hopefully draw out a successor. Having never been defeated in the American championships, he was willing to put his unblemished record on the line. He planned to compete in the 500-yard, 220-yard, and his last AAU century. Up-and-coming swimmers who had been inspired to take up the sport by Charley's astounding feats now wanted to catch their hero like an elusive trophy fish. The most formidable proved a pack of young wolves from Chicago: eighteen-year-old Richard Frizelle; nineteen-year-old Harry Hebner; nineteen-year-old Ken Huszagh; and the five-foot-nothing seventeen-year-old Perry McGillivray. All had been making names for themselves. Otto Wahle, too, did not plan to make it easy for Charley, training his own set of wolves from New York: twenty-year-old James Reilly and seventeen-year-old Nick Nerich.

Returning to Pittsburgh, Charley would be forced to equal his own world record in the 1911 220-yard AAU Championship to avoid a narrow defeat by the young wolves. Three days later, before two thousand spectators at St. Louis's Crystal Natatorium, Charley eked out another tight victory in the 500-yard race. But the wolves smelled blood.

On March 24, his twenty-sixth birthday, at the New York Athletic Club, Charley lined up for his last AAU Century Championship against three of them: Frizelle, Hebner, and McGillivray. At the gun's crack, they dove as if one man. Charley quickly found himself at the rear. At the final turn, Charley was still fighting Frizelle for third place, and for the first time since the London Olympics he was afraid of losing.

Down the last twenty-five yards, Charley never looked up. Five feet from the finish he was still a foot behind his opponents, any one of whom had a better chance to touch first. But Charley knew exactly where he was without having to look. With one last champion's effort, he extended his arm to its limit. The crowd erupted. The four men were a fraction of a second apart. Until that moment, never in the aquatic world's history had one race witnessed four men together covering the century in 57 seconds or less. Charley's 56.8 seconds won. It was the narrowest victory of his career.

Responding to Charley's new world records and the speed posted by the wolves, Australia's *Sydney Morning Herald* noted, "The improvement shown by American swimmers since the advent of Daniels is truly remarkable, as prior to this man's appearance in the Olympic Games of 1906, where he defeated Zoltan de Halmay and Cecil Healy, Americans were not considered as exponents of [swimming] at all. Since their champion's success several first-class men have come to light, and the improvement no doubt is due to the success mentioned."

Six months before the 1912 Olympics, when all of America was clamoring for their great champion to lead the Stars and Stripes into battle, Charley reached out to the press. "I have decided to retire from competition before I am beaten," Charley said half jokingly. "There has been wonderful improvement in speed swimming among Americans. Whereas a few years ago speed swimming was confined to a few experts, now there are hundreds throughout the country." He noted, "I have been doing speed swimming for nine years and that is long enough for anyone."

When pressed to reconsider, Charley said, "The only time that I am going to swim . . . is for pleasure. After I retire, if there are life preservers enough to go around I shall simply crawl into one and float until some kind hearted soul picks me up. No, sirree; I won't even swim ashore."

Rumors kept swirling about the great Charles Daniels joining the Olympic relay. Even Otto Wahle, who was working with the twelve-man American Olympic Committee to select the swimmers, asked Charley to reconsider, since Wahle was planning to go as a coach. In April, Charley wrote to him asking that his name be scratched as a candidate for Stockholm. No one could understand it. Charley was still at the top of his game. His fellow watermen at the New York Athletic Club said he was swimming as fast as ever.

Newspapers ran headlines like "Olympic Team to Lose a Big Star" and "Team Crippled in Swimming," commenting, "Daniels absence likely to deal death blow to this country's chances." But if Charley participated in the 1912 Olympics, his legacy would overshadow the team. Charley wholeheartedly believed if U.S. swimming was to ever come into its own, it needed to do so without Charles Daniels.

Charley retreated to a remote part of his beloved Adirondacks that summer, overseeing the construction of a family home on a two-hundred-acre lake called Bear Pond. As the Stockholm Olympics began with reports of incredible feats on the field by the Native American Jim Thorpe, Charley eagerly awaited the results from the Olympic swimming pool, which, for the first time, included women. Although, regretfully, not from America.

The request to allow women swimmers to compete came from England, perhaps believing they might help recapture its swimming prowess. In one of the rare instances that Sullivan and Coubertin saw eye to eye, both men opposed the idea. British representatives had raised the issue at both the Fédération Internationale de Natation, the first international swimming governing body formed during the London Olympics, and the IOC's annual meeting. As for Victorian sensibilities, swimming was one of the few sports where women were not seen sweating. With the IOC hovering around forty members and no longer an autocracy, for the first time it voted against its founder's wishes in favor of including women swimmers. In April 1912, a few months before the Games, the American Olympic Committee met in New York to discuss whether to send some of its leading women swimmers, and Sullivan vetoed the matter.

Twenty-seven female swimmers from eight countries competed in the hundred-meter freestyle and four-by-hundred-meter relay. They all wore Annette Kellermann swimsuits, much to the revulsion of Sullivan and Coubertin, and swam Charley's American crawl. Wahle successfully filled Charley's vacant spot on the Olympic team with an impressive twenty-year-old Hawaiian "wave rider" named Duke Kahanamoku, who was also a first-class swimmer.

Each morning, before he opened the newspaper for the latest Olympic results, as the July sun broke over the glassy lake and his wife and children still slept, Charley walked from the Adirondack house to the lakeshore. He removed his robe, revealing the body of a world-class athlete, and waded into the water among the ducks and loons. Surrounded by the Great North Woods, he dove into the refreshing lake and embarked on his daily mile-long swim to the far shore, just as he did as a boy at the Hiawatha Lodge and scouting camp. There were no stopwatches, no opponents, no accolades for a great performance, no yearning to win the approval of his father. He did it for the pure joy of swimming.

EPILOGUE

—

CHARLEY HAPPILY FADED FROM THE SPOTLIGHT HE HAD NEVER wanted. Over time, his name, once synonymous with every world record from fifty to three hundred meters and every American record from fifty yards to the mile, disappeared from the record books.

In Stockholm, Duke Kahanamoku defended Charley's hundred-meter century title for America, this time getting a fair start and winning gold over Cecil Healy in a time that clipped half a second off Charley's world record, with Ken Huszagh claiming bronze. The American four-by-two-hundred-meter relay team of Huszagh, McGillivray, Hebner, and Kahanamoku took silver behind a world-record performance by the Australians anchored by Cecil Healy.

In the first women's appearance at Stockholm, England and Australia dominated. When World War I canceled the 1916 Games, the situation would be rectified at the 1920 Olympics in Antwerp. By then, Lou Handley had been volunteering as the first U.S. women's swim coach, fighting for equality along with the founder of U.S. women's swimming, Charlotte "Eppy" Epstein. In the three female swimming contests, the American team, led by an eighteen-year-old phenom trained by Lou Handley, Ethelda Bleibtrey, swept the hundred meters and three hundred meters and took gold in the four-by-hundred-meter relay. The American men, again coached by Otto Wahle, and led by Duke Kahanamoku and Stanford's Norman Ross, swept the hundred meters, took gold and silver in the four-hundred-meter freestyle and hundred-meter backstroke, and claimed gold in both the fifteen-hundred-meter freestyle and the four-by-two-hundred-meter relay. Four years later, at the Paris Games, Lou Handley was named the first U.S. Women's Olympic Swim Team coach. The 1924 U.S. Olympic Swim Team was led by Duke Kahanamoku and a speedy young Chicagoan, Johnny Weissmuller (born Johann Weißmüller and later of *Tarzan* fame), along with Lou Handley's newest protégée, eighteen-year-old Gertrude Ederle. The team won nineteen Olympic medals, five more than all the other teams combined.

Two years later, Gertrude Ederle, in a Kellermann swimsuit, became the first female to swim the English Channel—and did it two hours faster than any man—returning to U.S. shores to become the first woman honored with a ticker-tape parade down New York's Canyon of Heroes.

Annette Kellermann continued to promote greater women's freedoms through swimming. After a Harvard study on ideal female physicality voted her the "Perfect Woman," she went on to Hollywood fame, starring in the first million-dollar-grossing picture, 1914's *Neptune's Daughter.* Two years later, she broke more ground by not only starring in the first film with a million-dollar budget, *A Daughter of the Gods,* but also becoming the first actress to pose nude, creating quite the scandal—and even better publicity for her film. She married her manager and never stopped pushing the envelope for women's rights.

Lou Handley remained a volunteer coach of the women's swim team until his death in 1956, never receiving a penny. He penned five books on swimming, published countless articles, wrote the swimming section in the *Encyclopaedia Britannica,* and was the first and foremost swimming journalist and its original public relations machine.

Otto Wahle compiled and maintained swimming's official records for more than fifteen years and wrote most of the AAU swimming rules. His love for the sport and for classical music never waned. He compiled an extensive collection of 78 rpm records and could be seen far off Jones Beach swimming back and forth with his head bobbing in the surf until his death at age eighty-three in 1963. In addition to coaching Charles Daniels and Duke Kahanamoku, he taught swimming to a young George S. Patton training for Stockholm's Olympic pentathlon, who thirty years later played a commanding role in defeating the Nazis.

In 1924, at age thirty-eight, Jam Handy made history when he won bronze on the U.S. Olympic Water Polo Team, becoming the first Olympian to compete in the Games twenty years apart. However, Handy's biggest contribution lies at the bottom of the swimming pool. During his competitive swimming days, leading up to the Central AAU Championships, when the pool was being drained to be refilled with clean water for the contest, the Little Water Devil induced the night janitor to paint a single black stripe down the length of the pool's bottom in the lane he would use. While everyone else was swerving all over, Handy swam a straight line and won. Soon afterward, the practice of painting black lines in racing pools became standard.

Joe Ruddy played water polo into his fifties and would be compared by reporters to Jack Dempsey, Superman, and Milton Berle. He and his wife raised all five of their children to be excellent swimmers. His son Ray became a three-time Olympic swimmer and water polo player (though under English rules). The rough-and-tumble American play that Joe thrived on met its end in 1911. After a murderous match between New York and Chicago resulted in a huge free-for-all brawl and four men being hauled out of the pool unconscious—all before the first half ended—the AAU eliminated the no-holds-barred American version to conform to the Olympics' far-less-lethal English rules of play.

Duke Kahanamoku went on to popularize surfing throughout California and Australia. The beloved Hawaiian came to be known as the Ambassador of Aloha.

Johnny Weissmuller became the first swimmer to break the one-minute mark in the hundred meters and found greater fame starring in Hollywood films.

Cecil Healy died six years after the 1912 Olympics, killed fighting in France during World War I.

Zoltán Halmay and Charley never swam against each other after London. Decades later, in the 1950s, when Halmay was ill in Budapest, it was reported that Charley sent his old rival money and needed medicines.

Jim Sullivan never made it onto the IOC and would never see another Olympics after Stockholm. Those Games were a culmination of
the previous two decades of evolution when the Olympics truly became the international sports festival that Coubertin always dreamed
of, with wonderful venues, good sportsmanship, and a genuine cama-
raderie among the athletes. Sullivan was excited to watch the Native
American Jim Thorpe excel in Stockholm, establishing himself as the
greatest athlete at the 1912 Games by winning gold in both the pentathlon and the decathlon. After that, Sullivan's animosity toward
Coubertin began to mellow, and in fact he dedicated his book on the
1912 Games to "Baron Pierre de Coubertin, to whose perseverance and
zealous work for thirty years is due the revival and final success of the
Olympic Games." Coubertin's ire toward Sullivan also softened. In
May 1914, he invited him to Paris, where he finally awarded the American his long-promised medal in appreciation for his achievements in
promoting the Olympics. Sullivan would call it one of his proudest
moments. Four months later, on September 16, he died of a heart attack at age fifty-one.

The year after Stockholm, Coubertin had an epiphany, much like
his late father's inspiration to paint *Rétablissement des Jeux Olympiques*.
On top of one of his letters, he drew five interlinking rings, making
each a different color: blue, yellow, black, green, and red. The rings represented the five parts of the world now won over to Olympism. The
colors, including the white background, were those that appeared on
all the national flags of the world at that moment. In August 1913, he
introduced the rings to the public in his Olympic magazine.

Coubertin would live to the age of seventy-four, long enough for
his earlier stance against women athletes to evolve with the times. He
would hear of the glorious introduction of the Olympic torch relay and
lighting of the cauldron in Berlin in 1936 after declining an invitation
to attend the Games as Hitler's guest of honor. The following year, he
would die penniless, having used his entire fortune to promote the
Games. He spent his last years in Lausanne, the city of the Olympic
headquarters, living off the good graces of others. His body would be
buried in the Swiss city, save for his heart, which, according to his last
wishes, was buried by the ruins of Olympia.

For thirty years, Charley and Florence split their time between a home in Buffalo and their Adirondack estate along Bear Pond. During both world wars, Charley volunteered as a lieutenant and taught swimming and lifesaving skills to soldiers. He made a successful living on their Adirondack estate as an award-winning silver fox breeder, earning ten thousand dollars for a pair, and became a skilled golfer. In 1921, he set the golf endurance world record for playing 228 holes in one day. In his sixties, he twice won the California Seniors Golf Association Championship. By then, his and Florence's thirty-two-year marriage had sadly come to an end. In 1957, their beautiful Adirondack estate was sold to the Boy Scouts of America to use as a summer camp.

Charley moved to Carmel-by-the-Sea, where he bought some cheap land on a floodplain along California's Carmel River, building a tiny one-bedroom ranch with his own two hands. He made a very modest living as a woodcrafter, making chessboards and walnut cigar boxes to sell. He sold off many of his trophies and medals to make ends meet. Most of his Carmel friends had no idea he was a famous Olympic swimmer, nor that the six-beat "freestyle" crawl many of them swam in the ocean was his invention. He never spoke of such things.

Instead, they knew him as a shrewd cardplayer who frequently showed up at local watering holes to play for beer money and usually won. To his two granddaughters back east in Buffalo, whose father died when they were seventeen and ten, he was known as a kindhearted grandpa who visited once or twice a year, wrote regularly, and telephoned to make sure they knew they were loved. None of them ever heard him speak of his extraordinary accomplishments. Then again, he was a man of few words, with a visceral reaction to braggarts.

In his later years, the Olympics became more sentimental to Charley. Decade after decade, he watched America's unrivaled Olympic dynasty triumph, eventually accumulating more gold medals by 1972 than all other countries combined. During those Olympics, at the age of eighty-seven, Charley watched Mark Spitz achieve the greatest Olympic feat of any swimmer in history, winning seven gold medals, all in world-record time. Since Spitz had already won four medals in 1968, Charley's sixty-four-year record that he shared with Zoltán Halmay of having the most Olympic medals of any swimmer (although Charley had two more golds than his old rival) was finally surpassed. But for Charley, it had always been about the journey.

He continued to swim regularly in the cold waters of the Pacific Ocean. His lithe six-foot frame, long arms, broad shoulders, and narrow hips still hinted of that former great athlete. Yet, when he looked at his aged face and bald head in the mirror, he no longer resembled the handsome teen with the sun-bleached blond hair who graced posters, trading cards, magazines, marquees, record books, and newspaper headlines around the globe. Nor did his quiet, tortoise-like nature suggest his once dynamic speed.

During one bout of nonstop stormy weather, when the swollen Carmel River spilled over its banks and fanned out across the woods behind his home, advancing ever closer to his back door, rescue crews showed up to evacuate everyone in the area to higher ground. Charley stood at his front door, facing the young men who certainly had no clue whose blue octogenarian eyes they stared into, and with a sly grin and a twinkle in his eye he said politely, "If I can't swim to safety, the water can have me."

ACKNOWLEDGMENTS

———

I'VE ALWAYS LOVED A GREAT UNDERDOG STORY. MY WIFE AND KIDS laugh at me because no matter how many times I watch *Rudy, Miracle*, you name it, without fail, by the end I'm all tears. It gives hope. It's rocket fuel to take on whatever life throws at you. My family can tease me all they want. I'll never change.

What drew me to the story of Charles M. Daniels was pure luck. To paraphrase J. M. Barrie, author of *Peter Pan*, it's the kind of luck when you open a crammed drawer looking for something you will never find and something falls out the back that is even more interesting. As chairman of the St. Louis Olympic Legacy Committee, I was researching the 1904 St. Louis Games and unearthed this athlete who, during those Games, won the first gold medal for U.S. swimming. Then I learned that his seven recognized Olympic medals stood for more than six decades as the most Olympic medals won by a swimmer until Mark Spitz broke it in 1972. I was stunned not to have heard of him until that moment. The more I looked into his story, the more amazed I became. Instigator of the first U.S. Olympic Swim Team. Inventor of the freestyle stroke—are you kidding! I thought that had been around since humans began swimming. Then to discover that his dad turned into a Bernie Madoff of sorts and what Charley and his mother had to overcome: this narcissistic patriarch, crippling anxiety, public shaming. Their perseverance and grit to keep moving forward and ultimately triumph against impossible odds made it as relevant today as ever—and one hell of a great story.

All of the facts, events, and characters are true. This book was exhaustively researched and cross-referenced through newspapers and magazines, the *New York Athletic Club Journals*, interviews, court records, passenger lists, files, legal documents, historical records, unpublished manuscripts, and dozens of books and accounts about the early Olympic Games and the era. I read through early books on swimming, books about Buffalo and New York society. Many articles had inaccuracies and embellishments that needed cross-checking. Lou de B. Handley was not only a swimmer at the time but a great advocate of the sport who contributed countless articles on the subject. James E. Sullivan, the head of the AAU, kept copious statistics and published annual reports about sports in America and the Olympics. Charles Daniels's book *Speed Swimming*, which he wrote with Otto Wahle and Lou Handley, proved insightful, as did other books by Otto Wahle and Annette Kellermann. Photographs of certain swimming events helped visually put them into context, as did conducting numerous site visits.

It was invaluable to have exclusive access to the Daniels family scrapbooks, letters, baby books, photo albums, and stories. For this I am forever grateful to Charles Daniels's two granddaughters, Mary Ellen McCormick and Grace Murphy, who carry his grit and love of swimming and embody his kind, humble spirit. I also conducted extensive research at the rich archives of the International Swimming Hall of Fame in Florida and thank Bruce Wigo for being my enthusiastic research guide and friend and a great historian. I also thank Hillel J. Kieval, professor of Jewish history at Washington University, for shedding some light on Jewish life in Vienna at the turn of the century. A special thanks to my fellow colleagues at the International Society of Olympic Historians and Yvan de Navacelle de Coubertin, whose labor of love and extensive writings offered a guiding light and sometimes a helpful shovel in my research.

The story further demanded the full understanding of what Olympians and Olympic swimmers endure to compete at such high levels, and I would like to thank John Naber, Debbie Meyer, Rowdy Gaines, Matt Biondi, and Mark Spitz for their invaluable insights, and just being wonderful people and great ambassadors of their sport. A special thank-you to Jackie Joyner-Kersee—friend, role model, GOAT—they don't come any better. And to Bob Costas, the brilliant voice of eleven Olympic Games, who supported this project from the start.

Some aspects of the story were difficult to know with 100 percent certainty. As inevitably happens with events that unfolded more than a hundred years ago, there is an incomplete narrative. No matter how hard you dig, or how many obscure dark places you search, you never fill in all the gaps. Since none of the people in this book are alive, I could not interview them, making it impossible to know all of the subjects' exact thoughts, motives, fears, secrets, and complex relationships. They will forever remain elusive, no matter how close you are to touching them. In focusing on what drove Charles Daniels to achieve the impossible and understand what he battled internally, I relied on the difficult relationship with his father. I recognize that other motives might well be possible, but my research into his life and the human psyche when dealing with a narcissistic parent strongly suggests my position. In this area, I conducted extensive research on mental health, relying on several psychiatrists, along with reading countless articles and interviews on survivors of narcissistic parents and/or spouses. Franz Kafka's *Letter to His Father* provided an insightful resource to understand the thoughts and feelings of a son struggling under a narcissistic father. Sometimes the Danielses' divorce documents, which under New York law had been sealed for a hundred years, provided a good road map in this area. Other times I had to use accounts of what typically happens in these tough situations to paint an appropriate picture of what Charles M. Daniels withstood, as well as understanding the mind and behavior of a narcissist.

The crippling anxiety he struggled with in his youth we know from reports of Lou Handley. There are other observations by coaches and reporters during his swimming career that indicate his continuing struggle and how anxious he became before a big race. Again, to paint an accurate picture, I conducted extensive research and interviews into anxiety, as well as understanding the era's knowledge of and approaches to mental health, in addition to interviews with Olympic gold-medal swimmers and the emotional roller coaster they must manage. I worked very hard to convey this as accurately as possible.

With some of the bigger races Charles Daniels swam, he later spoke about what he was thinking during the race. With others, I filled in the gaps as truthfully as possible with insights gleaned from other accomplished Olympic swimmers. In a few circumstances where we will never know exactly what the characters were thinking or feeling, I exhausted every bit of research at my disposal to capture the moment and agonized about achieving factual authenticity.

Everything in quotation marks was said by the person quoted. There are numerous instances where I took quotations from an individual and added them to a scene where I felt they were appropriate and truthful to the moment; however, I cannot say for certain the character spoke those exact words at that exact instance, even though the character did say them at one point. In these cases, I erred on being true to the story and the character who said them.

There are two instances I could not confirm to a high degree of certainty, so I relied on the evidence at hand, or, more appropriately, the lack thereof. The first is when Charley initially went to the Knickerbocker Athletic Club. I could not confirm that Doc Seixas accompanied him—even though I believe he did—so I kept him out of the scene. Given that the club did not allow anyone under nineteen, especially a youth who was not the son of a member, I'm pretty sure Doc was there, but the lack of evidence could not push it past a strong hunch.

The other instance was during the summer of 1901. I could not find a specific listing that named Charley as one of the boys who attended Doc Seixas's National Sportsmen's Association's junior branch camp on Bluff Island that summer. However, we do know that Charley attended the Madison Square Garden show just about every day the following February where the scouts put on a daily reenactment of outdoor life and that he competed in the scouting riflery events. We know he attended the summer camp in subsequent years. We know Charley also fondly recalled spending repeated summers in the Adirondacks during his youth. Lou Handley reported that Charley was a great outdoorsman and tracker before he became a competitive swimmer and cited his outdoor experience as helping him through his nervousness. In this instance, while I did not have definitive confirmation, I felt that given the strong circumstantial evidence at hand, it would be less factual not to place him there. If for some reason my timing is inaccurate, I apologize.

I'd like to thank my agent, the marvelous Mackenzie Brady Watson, whose New Year's resolution to get through her sludge pile that first week of January I'll be forever grateful for. Every writer should be so lucky to have someone as wickedly talented, passionate, kind, patient, savvy, enthusiastic, and hardworking as Mackenzie. She is a dream maker. Thanks to her vigilant assistant, Aemilia Phillips. I'd also like to thank my incredible editor, Susanna Porter, whose spot-on notes were a master class, pushing me to dig deeper and elevating the material to its full potential. She wields a brilliant scalpel, and I would happily go under her knife any day. And thanks to her assistant, Sydney Shiffman, and all of the talented copy editors and marketing and sales reps at Penguin Random House who worked tirelessly to make this book the best it could be. A special thanks to Jessie Bright at PRH for her amazing cover art. To the multitalented Jocelyn Seagrave for her author photograph. I'd like to thank early readers of various excerpts and encouragers—Bart Baker, Paul Guyot, and my parents, Bob and Jenni Loynd—for their enthusiasm and guidance. To Joe Reinkemeyer, friend and mentor. To Katie, my best friend, loving wife, and partner in crime, for putting up with me in my writer's cave and knowing when to break me out to share a bottle of wine. This dream would not have happened without you. And last, to my kids, who know I'm ADD and are always game to strap on their packs and climb the next mountain with me. I'm so proud of you all.

NOTES

A NOTE ON SOURCES: AS I RESEARCHED MY SUBJECTS FOR THIS BOOK, Mary Ellen McCormick and Grace Murphy, the granddaughters of Charles Daniels, generously gave me access to the private scrapbooks and baby book that Alice Daniels fashioned for her son. These books included a wealth of newspaper and magazine clippings, photographs, event posters, telegrams, and letters, many of which do not include complete publishing information. In the notes, I indicate these incomplete annotated sources with the abbreviation "IS" (incomplete source).

PROLOGUE

3 **Fifteen thousand British:** The number of British spectators was noted in U.K. newspaper accounts such as "The Olympic Games," *Aberdeen Daily Journal,* July 21, 1908, 6. The report as to the exact number of fans was most likely an eyeball estimate. Two days earlier, newspapers reported the crowd for Saturday's events between forty thousand and fifty thousand spectators.

3 **human fish:** "World's Swimming Mark Shattered by Daniels," *Pittsburgh Daily Press,* April 24, 1907, 2.

3 **dark blue swim cap:** Daniels's attire that day was based on the U.S. swimmers' uniforms and a photo of him at the 1908 London Olympics in a white robe. Courtesy of Topical Press Agency/Getty Images. The official swimming rules at the 1908 London Games required swimmers to wear black or dark blue. There are conflicting reports as to whether Daniels wore a white robe or a white sweater that day as he stepped up to the start of the race. Photos taken at the stadium show him wearing a sweater at one time and a robe at another. However, the most likely scenario is a robe.

3 **almost no one in America swam:** C. M. Daniels, "American Swimmers: Why They Have Been So Far Behind Those of Other Nations," *New-York Tribune,* March 4, 1906, 52.

3 **six hundred competitive swimmers:** At the turn of the century, America's Amateur Athletic Union's records of registered U.S. amateur swimmers list approximately six hundred.

3 **discarded as laughingstocks:** That American swimmers were considered laughing-stocks appears repeatedly in newspaper articles during this decade. One such article was written by the swimming expert and coach of Daniels, Louis de B. Handley, "C. M. Daniels, American Winner in Great Olympics, Is World's Greatest Swimmer," *Wilkes-Barre* (Pa.) *Times Leader,* July 22, 1908, 4.

3 **could not muster a decent stroke:** Daniels and Louis de B. Handley both recounted how he could not swim a decent stroke before December 1903. Ibid.; "C. M. Daniels, the Human Merman," *Victoria* (B.C.) *Daily Times,* May 15, 1911, 14.

3 **Invented the modern-day freestyle stroke:** Numerous articles from 1906 onward discuss Daniels's creation and evolution of what became the modern freestyle crawl, which are detailed more extensively later in the book. A few articles are "Handley Defends American Crawl," *Brooklyn Daily Eagle,* May 26, 1908, 23, and "Champion Daniels' New Kick Makes It Easy to Swim—Anybody Can Learn Trick," *Louisville* (Ky.) *Courier-Journal,* Aug. 9, 1908, 27.

4 **refusing to validate his achievements:** There are numerous newspaper and magazine articles from England, the United States, and even a few in Australia, as well as reports in the *New York Athletic Club Journal,* relating how England refused to acknowledge and/or believe any of Daniels's alleged times in America that beat their own records. One such account of that is by Handley, "C. M. Daniels, American Winner in Great Olympics," 4.

4 **crippling anxiety:** Louis de B. Handley wrote a few articles divulging Daniels's struggle with severe anxiety that he referred to as nervousness (a term of the era). One such article is ibid.

4 **body forged from steel:** The physical descriptions of Daniels and the European champion Zoltán Halmay were derived from photographs and various articles. See, for example, "Britain's Swimming Triumphs," *Athletic News* (London), July 27, 1908, 6.

4 **major conflict of interest:** Accusations of British referees' hometown bias or blatant cheating appeared in numerous articles and accounts by 1908 U.S. Olympians and their team's vocal leader, James E. Sullivan. One such article is "Toombs Says English Athletic Officials in Olympic Games Disgraced Their Nation," *Decatur* (Ill.) *Herald & Review,* Aug. 7, 1908, 13. This also addresses complaints about the British officials meeting in secret to "randomly" designate lanes and heats, with the resulting assignments often favoring the British athletes and disadvantaging the Americans.

4 **Its hundred-meter length:** The descriptions of the great stadium at Stamford Bridge and its hundred-meter Olympic pool are derived from numerous articles, Olympic records, and illustrations of the venue. See, for example, "Big London Stadium," *Montour American* (Danville, Pa.), May 21, 1908, 3.

5 **see the American fish defeated:** "Anything but an American," *Boston Globe,* Aug. 7, 1908, 5.

5 **next word from Mr. Hudson:** "Olympic Team Athletes Back with Complaints," *Evening World* (New York), Aug. 6, 1908, 6.

1: THE DROWNING BOY

9   **Charles never forgot the first time:** Mary Ellen McCormick interview.

11 **"My will to live":** Alfred Hajos, official Olympic archive, olympics.com.

12 **New York City claimed 352 millionaires:** Smithsonian, americanhistory.si.edu.

12 **"Mark Twain lives here":** This has been repeated in various accounts and newspaper articles about Twain's time in Buffalo. It has also been reported that the plaque read, "Mark Twain lives here and my father-in-law pays the rent."

12 **"a wild, sweet, enthralling zestfulness":** Luhan, *Intimate Memories,* 2.

13 **"Life flowed on":** Ibid., 3.

13 **"goody-goody"**: "Central School," *Buffalo Morning Express,* June 28, 1882, 4.

16 **Who's Who of guests:** "Wedding Bells," *Dayton Herald,* June 20, 1884, 3.

18 **"Whatever may have been the cares"**: Hill, *Hill's Manual of Social and Business Forms.*

18 **"Mr. T. P. Daniels greeted"**: "Personals," *Dayton Herald,* March 24, 1885, 3.

19 **"the very symbol"**: This quotation is attributed to Twain during a speech he made at Delmonico's in 1889 honoring the returning Albert Spalding and his epic world tour of baseball.

20 **friend arrived with a telegram:** Frank Fowler sent the telegram about Fred's accident to Mr. E. P. Matthews, a Dayton attorney and mutual friend. It read, "Meldrum was drowned this afternoon in James river at Balcony Falls. Body not yet recovered. Notify T. P. Daniels at once. Wire me what to do. Frank Fowler." "Death by Drowning," *Dayton Herald,* June 21, 1886, 3. Although this article supposes that Fred "was not an expert swimmer," other articles from Buffalo say otherwise. See "Fred Meldrum's Fate," *Buffalo Commercial,* June 21, 1886, 3. A further sad tragedy about this matter was that Fred's parents and younger siblings had departed for a European tour the day before and would not hear about Fred's death until they arrived in Europe a week later. Alice's older brother Arthur cabled his uncle in London to break the news and instruct them not to return home for the funeral because Fred's remains were beyond recognition. "Young Meldrum's Body," *Buffalo Commercial,* June 23, 1886, 3.

21 **"Great Retirement Sale"**: "Daniels & Meldrum Last Days," *Dayton Herald,* April 9, 1890, 1.

22 **finest houses of worship:** "A Church Consecrated," *New York Times,* Dec. 16, 1891, 9.

22 **$50,000 inheritance:** "Dead Men Who Left No Wills," *Buffalo Courier,* Nov. 13, 1891, 6. See also "Alexander Meldrum's Estate," *Buffalo Evening News,* Feb. 29, 1892, 7. After the widowed Mrs. Anna Meldrum received a third of the estate under law, the five surviving children received one-fifth each of the remaining two-thirds, which equaled approximately $48,840 apiece, before the proceeds from the sale of the family mansion at 309 North Street were factored in. See "For Sale," *Buffalo Courier,* April 2, 1892, 3.

22 **More than 100,000 horses:** Known historically as the Great Horse Manure Crisis of 1894, some estimated Manhattan's total horse population as high as 200,000. Each horse generated fifteen to thirty pounds of manure per day. To remove the daily manure accumulation, it would take a daily caravan of roughly 250 modern-day garbage trucks. See "The New York Horse Manure Crisis," *Power Trip: The Story of Energy,* WETA, weta.org.

23 **constant ball of nerves:** Louis de B. Handley wrote a few articles divulging Daniels's struggle with severe anxiety that he referred to as nervousness (a term of the era). See, for example, L. de B. Handley, "C. M. Daniels, American Winner in Great Olympics, Is World's Greatest Swimmer," *Wilkes-Barre* (Pa.) *Times Leader,* July 22, 1908, 4.

23 **"rest cure"**: Lutz, *American Nervousness, 1903.*

24 **Gebhard's Natatorium:** "Maids and Matrons in the Swimming Bath," *Buffalo Times,* April 24, 1898, 14.

25 **"swallowed enough water"**: "C. M. Daniels Is the Swimming Hero," *Buffalo Commercial,* Feb. 28, 1906, 6. This account of Daniels's first experience with swimming appeared numerous times over his career, with variations. One article incorrectly claimed that his father threw him into the NYAC tank. Some articles reported the quotation as if they interviewed Tom Daniels directly. Most likely Daniels recounted the story.

27 **"prominent New York businessmen"**: "The Klondike-Alaska Gold Co.," *Buffalo Evening News,* Aug. 5, 1897, 8.

27 **"no chances of failure"**: "H. F. Roesser: Well Known Hotel Man Talks of Klondyke," *Buffalo Times,* Aug. 3, 1897, 1.

27 **"Thomas P. Daniels of Porter & Daniels":** "Klondike-Alaska Gold Company," *Allentown* (Pa.) *Morning Call,* Aug. 19, 1897, 3.

27 **took five lessons:** "Learn How to Swim," *Gazette* (Montreal), Sept. 15, 1904, 2.

27 **"An even dozen":** "C. M. Daniels, the Human Merman," *Ogden* (Utah) *Standard,* May 13, 1911, 11.

27 **Newspapers across the country:** "Death of Hon. Charles Daniels," *Buffalo Evening News,* Dec. 21, 1897, 1; "Charles Daniels Is Dead," *New York Times,* Dec. 21, 1897, 7; "Ex-justice Daniels Dies," *Philadelphia Times,* Dec. 22, 1897, 12; "Death of Charles Daniels," *Chicago Tribune,* Dec. 21, 1897, 4; "Death of Charles Daniels," *St. Louis Globe-Democrat,* Dec. 21, 1897, 4; *San Francisco Call,* Dec. 21, 1897, 4; "An Ex-Supreme Court Justice Ill," *Sacramento* (Calif.) *Record-Union,* Dec. 21, 1897, 1; "Death of a Former Chief Justice of New York," *Spokesman-Review* (Spokane), Dec. 21, 1897, 2.

28 **Judge Daniels's handwritten will:** "Drawn by Himself," *Buffalo Courier,* Jan. 4, 1898, 5.

29 **"former champion swimmer":** "Queens Borough Resorts," *Brooklyn Daily Eagle,* July 3, 1898, 28.

29 **Alice began to suspect:** *Daniels v. Daniels,* divorce file, Court of Kings County, Brooklyn, 1904.

29 **When Alice confronted Tom:** Ibid.

2: CASTAWAYS

30 **Alice heard from Tom's siblings:** *Daniels v. Daniels,* divorce file, Court of Kings County, Brooklyn, 1904.

31 **fifty cases filed:** "The Sexy Secrets from NYC's Long-Sealed Divorce Records," *New York Post,* Aug. 16, 2016.

31 **1900 U.S. census:** Twelfth U.S. Census: New York, Borough of Manhattan, June 1–2, 1900.

32 **became even more interested:** Mary Ellen McCormick interview.

33 **"one thousand years without a bath":** Michelet, *La sorcière* (The witch; 1862).

35 **"toothache in my stomach":** Carleton Putnam, *Theodore Roosevelt,* vol. 1, *The Formative Years, 1858–1886* (New York: Charles Scribner's Sons, 1958), 26.

36 **Adirondack guidebook:** William H. H. Murray, *Adventures in the Wilderness; or, Camp-Life in the Adirondacks* (Boston: Fields, Osgood, 1870).

36 **summer population grew:** Terence Young, "The Minister Who Invented Camping in America," *Smithsonian Magazine,* Oct. 17, 2017, smithsonianmag.com.

36 **boarded a train:** "Incredible Golf Endurance Record Set at Sabattis 55 Years Ago Still Stands," 1971, IS, stated Charley's association with the Adirondacks began in 1900 when he began spending his summer vacations at the Hiawatha Lodge. We also know Alice's sister Flossie left Buffalo to vacation at the Hiawatha Lodge in early July 1900. *Buffalo Morning Express,* July 9, 1900, 5. Most certainly Flossie went to stay at the Hiawatha with Charley and Alice. Although the records of the Hiawatha's guests were long destroyed in a fire, these two citations seem conclusive as to the year.

36 **The settlement included:** *Brooklyn Daily Eagle,* June 17, 1900.

38 **befriended some of the local guides:** Louis de B. Handley, "C. M. Daniels, American Winner The Great Olympics, Is World's Greatest Swimmer," *Wilkes-Barre* (Pa.) *Times Leader,* July 22, 1908, 4. While Handley stated that Daniels was an experienced and practiced woodsman at age fourteen and that guides for miles around soon began to know him, it appears Handley's age for Daniels was a year or two off. There is no indication that Daniels visited the Adirondacks or did any scouting or outdoor activity until age fifteen.

38 **practiced his father's breaststroke:** Mary Ellen McCormick interview.

39 **"outclassed and did not finish"**: "American Swimmer Did Not Finish," *New York Times*, Aug. 12, 1900, 8.

40 **"Doc"**: *Popular Mechanics*, Dec. 1924, 81; *Chula Vista* (Calif.) *Star*, Feb. 23, 1950, 10.

40 **National Sportsmen's Show**: "Show for Sportsmen," *Lawrence* (Kans.) *Daily Journal*, Feb. 13, 1901, 3.

41 **a dozen to forty boys**: *Sun* (New York), July 17, 1901, 15, listed the names of seven boys at the initial opening up of camp with Seixas, which was most likely followed with more boys arriving. See also "Youthful Sportsmen," *Lincoln* (Neb.) *Evening News*, March 16, 1901, 3, which posts a picture showing closer to twenty boys attending the previous year's camp. Subsequent years stated upwards of forty junior scouts. Despite extensive research, history does not tell us for certain if sixteen-year-old Charley was among those boys at Camp Rainbow that summer. Reports cite Charley as an active member of Camp Rainbow during the National Sportsmen's Show that forthcoming spring, and he certainly attended the camp in subsequent summers. Handley's earlier claim that Charley had expert scouting skills as a young teen, coupled with his documented riflery prowess in March 1902, makes it highly likely that he was at Camp Rainbow during the summer of 1901. Given the circumstantial evidence, I felt it would be erroneous not to include Charley at Camp Rainbow.

42 **"ADDITIONAL CAPITAL SUPPLIED"**: *New York Times*, April 20, 1902, 23.

42 **she saw him**: *Daniels v. Daniels*, 1904.

43 **"Daniels Wins Rifle Trophy"**: "At Sportsmen's Show," *New York Times*, March 18, 1902, 6.

44 **"star"**: "Brooklyn's Fast Swimmers," *Boston Globe*, Jan. 12, 1902, 25.

44 **"wonderful," "marvelous"**: "Le Moyne Makes Another Record," *Boston Post*, Feb. 26, 1902, 3.

44 **"the coming champion"**: "Brooklyn's Fast Swimmers."

44 **hyped up a match race**: "Le Moyne of Brookline to Contest Swimming Championship with Schaeffer," *Boston Post*, Jan. 29, 1902, 3; "Le Moyne Would Swim Scheaffer [*sic*]," *Evening World*, (New York), Jan. 23, 1902, 8.

44 **showing every promise**: "This Youth Is Sure to Prove a Great Swimmer," *Buffalo Enquirer*, April 9, 1902, 4.

44 **"American record holders"**: Ibid.

3: THE UNBEATABLE BRITISH EMPIRE

45 **naval fleet larger**: Parliament's 1889 Naval Defence Act formally adopted the "two-power standard," stipulating that the Royal Navy should maintain a number of battleships at least equal to the combined strength of the next two largest navies.

47 **first-class bath cost sixpence**: Love, *Social History of Swimming in England*, 66.

48 **Sydney alone supported**: Charles Daniels, "American Swimmers: Why They Have Been So Far Behind Those of Other Nations," *New-York Tribune*, March 4, 1906, 52.

48 **drew a reported 100,000**: "Swimming," *Evening Mail*, July 12, 1905, 7.

48 **England registered about**: Daniels, "American Swimmers."

49 **so-called skyscrapers**: In 1900, the tallest building in Manhattan was the thirty-one-story Park Row Building in the Financial District, completed in 1899, then the world's tallest office building. Skyscrapers were defined as any building over ten stories. Prior to the Park Row, the tallest building in New York was the eighteen-story Manhattan Life Insurance Building, built in 1894.

50 **English newspapers reported**: "The Texas Hurricane," *Morning Post* (London), Sept. 21, 1900, 3.

50 **Modeled on the London Athletic Club**: New York Athletic Club, *Constitution, By-Laws, Rules, and Alphabetical Lists of Members* (1905).

51 **"The athletes of the clubs"**: Duncan Edwards, "Life at the Athletic Clubs," *Scribner's Magazine,* July 1895, 4–24.

51 **The NYAC's twenty watermen**: "Swimming. American Champion in London," *Sportsman,* Nov. 19, 1904, 5.

51 **an unwanted stepchild**: "Says Swimmers Must Have National Body," *New York Times,* March 18, 1917, 33.

51 **small gathering of curiosity seekers**: "Schaeffer Lowered Two Swimming Records," *Buffalo Courier,* July 9, 1901, 12.

52 **"nothing short of marvelous"**: "Swimming Records Were Shattered by Otto Wahle," *Buffalo Courier,* July 10, 1901, 12.

52 **three minutes slower**: *Leicester Chronicle and Leicester Mercury,* Aug. 11, 1900, 2.

52 **Wahle was shocked**: "Says Swimmers Must Have National Body," 33.

4: THE KNICKERBOCKER PREDICAMENT

54 **Greenwich Village apartment**: We know Alice and Charley lived at 53 Washington Square by March 1904. "Mrs. Daniels Gets a Decree," *Brooklyn Daily Eagle,* March 14, 1904, 22. History does not tell us exactly when they moved.

56 **"the most stunning girl"**: *Buffalo Times,* Aug. 3, 1902, 39.

56 **110 secondary school boys**: *Annual Reports of the Department of the Interior for the Fiscal Year Ended June 30, 1901: Report of the Commissioner of Education* (Washington, D.C.: Government Printing Office, 1902), 2:2199.

56 **Dwight School**: "Dwight School," *Brooklyn Daily Eagle,* Sept. 15, 1901, 6–7.

57 **NYAC's written application**: New York Athletic Club, *Constitution, By-Laws, Rules, and Alphabetical Lists of Members* (1905).

57 **"The only way"**: "Record Breaking Brookline Swimmer Is Expected to Beat Schaeffer," *Boston Post,* March 9, 1902, 7.

58 **more than fifteen hundred members**: *Club Book of the Knickerbocker Athletic Club* (1899).

58 **"the finest athletic clubhouse"**: "Amateur Men of Brawn," *New York Times,* April 27, 1890, 7.

58 **club's admissions committee**: *Club Book of the Knickerbocker Athletic Club* (1899).

59 **"recognized standing"**: Ibid., 45.

61 **first swimming records**: *Richmond* (Ind.) *Item,* May 30, 1903, 3; *Boston Globe,* Aug. 24, 1891, 3.

62 **Meffert disliked swimmers**: "Alex Meffert's Advice," *Austin* (Tex.) *American-Statesman,* July 22, 1905, 5.

62 **speed of 60.2 seconds**: "Swimming Baths," *Leigh Chronicle and Weekly District Advertiser,* Oct. 3, 1902, 6.

63 **described his stroke**: "Daniels Has Stroke Resembling Uppercut," *Pittsburgh Daily Post,* April 29, 1907, 6.

63 **Meffert's absolute cutoff**: Ibid.

63 **"A powerful effective kick"**: "Alex Meffert's Advice," 5.

63 **forcing a V**: Ibid.

63 **"Remember"**: Ibid.

64 **forming an X**: "Champion Daniels' New Kick Makes It Easy to Swim—Anybody Can Learn Trick," *Louisville* (Ky.) *Courier-Journal,* Aug. 9, 1908, 27.

64 **measured off a hundred-yard course**: Mary Ellen McCormick interview. See also Dave Epperson, "Self-Taught Olympic Swimming Champ," *Monterey Peninsula Herald,* Sept. 1950, IS.

64 **forty of his fellow scouts**: "Saranac Lake Has Good Roads," *New York Times,* July 20, 1902, 26.

64 **"by far the best contested race"**: "Resort News," *Brooklyn Daily Eagle,* Aug. 15, 1902, 7.

65 **Arthur Meldrum a "bankrupt":** *Buffalo Commercial,* June 18, 1902, 4.

65 **Charley recalled swimming:** Epperson, "Self-Taught Olympic Swimming Champ."

5: CHASING THE GOD OF SPEED

67 **trial of the century:** Facts regarding the Molineux trial are derived from several sources including the online Law Library: American Law and Legal Information located at law.jrank.org, newspaper articles, and Harold Schechter's *Devil's Gentleman: Privilege, Poison, and the Trial That Ushered In the Twentieth Century* (New York: Ballantine Books, 2007).

68 **$400,000 clubhouse mortgage:** "Knickerbocker Athletic Club Reorganization," *New York Times,* Aug. 22, 1902, 14.

68 **prominent notice:** "A Public Athletic Club," *New York Times,* Sept. 7, 1902, 15.

68 **stick with his training:** "Worked Hard for Success," *Pittsburgh Press,* April 21, 1907, 21; "Remarkable Bits of Sport," *St. Louis Post-Dispatch,* Feb. 24, 1908, 8.

68 **Knickerbocker Aquatic Club:** "To Form New Swimming Club," *New York Times,* Sept. 8, 1902, 3.

68 **L. de B.:** Ibid.

68 **Budd:** Ibid.

68 **Spike:** "N.Y.A.C. Water Polo Team Has Made a Fine Record," *Brooklyn Daily Eagle,* Oct. 22, 1905, 57.

68 **Dave:** *New York Athletic Club Journal,* Jan. 1905, 31.

68 **"Any healthy, normal child":** "Sports and Athletics," ISHOF archive, Joe Ruddy file, IS.

69 **to vacate:** "Fast Races by Swimmers," *New York Times,* Nov. 16, 1902, 10.

69 **"soundly beaten":** "Valley Man Swim Champ When Suits Were Knee Length," *Monterey Peninsula Herald,* Oct. 21, 1971, C. M. Daniels scrapbook, IS.

70 **Dave Bratton:** *American Carpet and Upholstery Journal,* Dec. 10, 1904, 68; *New York Athletic Club Journal,* July 1905, 21; *New York Athletic Club Journal,* Jan. 1905, 31.

70 **"Keep an eye on Daniels":** *Sail and Sweep* 3 (1904): 176. Original quotation by Meffert recounted himself telling Bratton to "keep his eyes on Daniels."

71 **The news was shocking:** "Cavill Swims 100 Yards in 58 3-5s," *New York Athletic Club Journal,* Nov. 1902, 22; "Swimming Record," *Sydney Morning Herald,* Sept. 26, 1902, 5.

72 **"kept his head entirely underwater":** "New Swimming Record," *Buffalo Commercial,* Oct. 8, 1902, 6.

72 **"crawl":** "Australians Still Making Onslaughts on Swimming Records," *Sun* (New York), Oct. 12, 1902, 10.

72 **Schaeffer was the first American:** L. de B. Handley, "Speed Swimming: The Three Recognized Methods," *Outing,* April 1906–Sept. 1906, 577.

73 **cheap swimsuit:** "C. M. Daniels, a Coming Swimming Champion," *Idaho Daily Statesman,* July 11, 1904, 3.

74 **"You can't make a peach":** *Pasadena Post,* Nov. 25, 1926, 4.

74 **propose Charley's name:** *New York Athletic Club Journal,* March 1903, 25; *New York Athletic Club Journal,* April 1903, 27; New York Athletic Club, *Constitution, By-Laws, Rules, and Alphabetical Lists of Members* (1905), 15–16.

76 **a prohibitive "mechanics" clause:** Matthew P. Llewellyn and John Gleaves, "A Universal Dilemma: The British Sporting Life and the Complex, Contested, and Contradictory State of Amateurism," *Journal of Sports History* 41, no. 1 (Spring 2014): 95–116.

77 **slight limp:** Joe Ruddy's and Edgar Adams's leg disabilities are described in "Three Swimmers Who Figured Prominently in Olympic Meet," *St. Louis Republic,* Sept. 11, 1904, 29.

78 **"Your wind is bad?":** "New York's Father Neptune: The Life and Times of Joe Ruddy and Other Famous Swimmers," MS, ISHOF archive, Joe Ruddy file, IS.

78 **annual salary of three thousand dollars:** *Baltimore Sun,* May 16, 1903, 9.

79 **ten yards short:** "Valley Man Swim Champ When Suits Were Knee Length."

79 **visit his fellow scouts:** "Schoolboys Compete at Camp Rainbow," *Sun* (New York), July 10, 1903, 10.

6: SKELETONS OUT OF THE CLOSET

80 **A little before noon:** "Raid Wall Street Firm," *New York Times,* Aug. 6, 1903, 12; "Raid Underwriting Outfit," *Sun* (New York), Aug. 6, 1903, 9.

81 **"no application will be considered":** "Raid Underwriting Outfit."

81 **more than $70,000:** "Bitten by Wall Street Brokers," *Rochester* (N.Y.) *Democrat and Chronicle,* Aug. 6, 1903, 12.

81 **"one of the greatest":** Ibid.

81 **"Late Justice Daniels' Son Under Arrest":** *Buffalo Courier,* Aug. 6, 1903, 6.

81 **"Thomas P. Daniels Held for Larceny":** *Buffalo Evening News,* Aug. 12, 1903, 11.

81 **a fraud and a swindler:** "Daniels in Court Swindling Case," *Evening World,* (New York), Aug. 15, 1903, 2.

81 **defrauded people:** "Martin Says It's False," *Daily News-Democrat* (Huntington, Ind.), Aug. 26, 1903, 1.

81 **A West Virginia man:** "Daniels, 'Banker,' Held in Court," *New York Herald,* Aug. 12, 1903, 7.

82 **Tom's former boss:** "Police Stopped 'Banking' Concern," *Stark County Democrat* (Canton, Ohio), Aug. 11, 1903, 4.

82 **Tom was married:** "Man Under Arrest Is Thought to Be Judge Daniels' Son," *Buffalo Evening News,* Aug. 6, 1903, 18.

82 **"Mrs. Minnie Brown Daniels":** "Daniels Gets Bail," *Buffalo Evening News,* Aug. 14, 1903, 8.

82 **list of local residents:** "Buffalo Folk Whom Daniels Had on Lists," *Buffalo Times,* Aug. 25, 1903, 1.

7: A GAME FOR BARBARIANS

87 **Baron Pierre de Coubertin:** Much of the information on Pierre de Coubertin stems from his two memoirs, *Les batailles de l'éducation physique* and *Olympic Memoirs.* Other main sources include Yvan de Navacelle de Coubertin, "The Coubertin Family—a Short History of a Noble French Family," International Society of Olympic Historians (2015), isoh.org, and George Hirthler, "Celebrating Pierre de Coubertin: The French Genius of Sport Who Founded the Modern Olympic Games," International Olympic Committee, Sept. 2, 2019, olympics.com. Further information on Pierre de Coubertin and James E. Sullivan originates from John Apostal Lucas, "Early Olympic Antagonists: Pierre de Coubertin Versus James E. Sullivan," in *John Apostal Lucas,* 41–55. A good description and background of Sullivan came from the article "This Man Planned Olympic Games for World's Fair in 48 Hours: Study of James E. Sullivan," *St. Louis Post-Dispatch,* April 24, 1904, 56. Numerous newspaper articles have also been used to confirm facts and bring to light new information, some of which are cited below.

88 **"an immense workshop of putrefaction":** Victor Considerant, *Destinée Sociale,* Paris, 1848, 290.

90 **"The Battle of Waterloo":** This quotation is popularly attributed to Arthur Wellesley, Duke of Wellington, commander at Waterloo and graduate of Eton.

91 **Olympian Festival:** "Olympian Festival at Wenlock," *Shrewsbury Chronicle,* Oct. 24, 1890.

92 **"Let us export our fencers":** Pierre de Coubertin, Nov. 25, 1892, Sorbonne.

92 **"viable nor useful":** Coubertin, *Les batailles de l'éducation physique,* 92–93.

92 **"Nowhere did the idea"**: Coubertin, *Olympic Memoirs,* 19.
94 **elbow room at the start**: Ibid., 24.
95 **inefficient, mismanaged, and incapable**: *Outing,* April–Sept. 1900, 98–99, 318–19.
95 **U.K. expressed doubt**: "The New Olympian Games," *Sheffield Daily Telegraph,* April 4, 1896, 4.
95 **"a thief, trying to strip"**: MacAloon, *This Great Symbol;* see also Hirthler, "Celebrating Pierre de Coubertin."
96 **superfluous, made-up word**: Coubertin, *Olympic Memoirs,* 67.
96 **"impractical, uninteresting"**: Pierre de Coubertin, "Les femmes aux Jeux olympiques," *Revue Olympique,* July 1912, 109–11.
96 **"not cut out"**: Attributed to Pierre de Coubertin, 1896.
97 **"Nothing could be more difficult"**: Coubertin, *Olympic Memoirs,* 61.
97 **"The Paris games"**: *Outing,* April–Sept. 1900, 566.
97 **"The whole series of sports"**: "The Paris International Meeting," *Field: The Country Gentleman's Newspaper,* July 28, 1900, 155.
97 **"To treat these events"**: John E. Findling and Kimberly D. Pelle, eds., *Historical Dictionary of the Modern Olympic Movement* (Westport, Conn.: Greenwood Press, 1996), 16–17.
98 **"There was nothing Olympic"**: Coubertin, *Olympic Memoirs,* 68.
100 **"The ball made by A. G. Spalding"**: *Spalding's Official Basket Ball Guide* (New York: American Sports Publishing Company, 1896–1897), 34.
100 **"Everything is possible"**: Geoffrey C. Ward, *Baseball: An Illustrated History* (New York, Knopf, 1994), 29.
101 **new union's goal**: "Uniform Athletic Rules," *Scranton* (Pa.) *Republican,* Oct. 16, 1900, 10.
101 **"luster" and "incomparable prestige"**: Coubertin, *Olympic Memoirs,* 76.
102 **"Surely the annals of athletics"**: *Referee,* (London), July 8, 1900, 7.
102 **"The Olympic Games held at"**: "Grand Olympian Games," *Buffalo Morning Express,* Oct. 14, 1900, 11.
103 **"We do not want it"**: "Olympic Games at Buffalo," *Rochester* (N.Y.) *Democrat and Chronicle,* Oct. 17, 1900, 13.
103 **Several other papers**: *Kansas City Times,* Oct. 21, 1900, 19; *Akron* (Ohio) *Beacon Journal,* Oct. 19, 1900, 7.
103 **"civilization's and humanity's eternal game"**: Walt Whitman, "Our Eminent Visitors: Past, Present, and Future," in *November Boughs* (Philadelphia: David McKay, 1888), 39.

8: UNDERWATER

107 **"conduct injurious to the good order"**: New York Athletic Club, *Constitution, By-Laws, Rules, and Alphabetical Lists of Members* (1905), 18.
107 **Dave had a story**: "Swimmers Lost in a Fog," *Sun* (New York), Dec. 18, 1904, 17.
109 **membership would expire**: New York Athletic Club, *Constitution,* 15.
109 **observed that no two of them**: "Champion Daniels' New Kick Makes It Easy to Swim—Anybody Can Learn Trick," *Louisville* (Ky.) *Courier-Journal,* Aug. 9, 1908, 27.
109 **Charley concluded that a swimmer**: Daniels, *Speed Swimming.*
109 **technique he called the "swordfish"**: "Says Swimmers Must Have National Body," *New York Times,* March 18, 1917, 33.
109 **"Why, that's the Australian crawl"**: Ibid.
111 **record from 220 to 500 yards**: "Review of Season on Track and Field," *Brooklyn Daily Eagle,* Dec. 20, 1903, 25.
111 **uninspiring seventy-two seconds**: "Columbia Swimmer Won," *New York Times,* Nov. 15, 1903, 15.

III   **"in the American style"**: Arthur Daley, "Sports of the Times, a Rather Damp Topic,"
ISHOF archive, Joe Ruddy, file IS.

II2   **"If a fellow sticks"**: Robert Edgren, "For Rough Games Football and Boxing Are
Not in It with the Gentle Sport Called Water Polo," *Buffalo Times,* Nov. 28,
1920, 47.

II2   **Unless the arm:** "Bill Corum Says . . . ," *San Bernardino Sun,* July 24, 1937, 15.

II2   **"If a fellow feels"**: "A Real Swimmer," ISHOF archive, Joe Ruddy file, IS.

II2   **"Once when I played"**: ISHOF archive, Joe Ruddy file, IS.

II2   **"Hey, Lou"**: Daley, "Sports of the Times, a Rather Damp Topic."

II3   **"We found them"**: ISHOF archive, Joe Ruddy file, IS.

II5   **Ladies' Day:** *New York Athletic Club Journal,* Jan. 1904, 11–12.

II6   **68 seconds:** Ibid.

II6   **67.6 seconds:** "Columbia Swimmers Won," *New York Times,* Dec. 13, 1903, 18.

9: STRUCK BY LIGHTNING

II7   **exerting himself in the pool:** *Sail and Sweep* 3 (1904): 176.

II7   **loved classical music:** ISHOF archive, Otto Wahle file, note from family.

II7   **"Upper arm starts the recovery"**: Daniels, *Speed Swimming,* 33.

II8   **"It was not possible"**: Arthur Schnitzler, *My Youth in Vienna,* trans. Catherine Hut-
ter (New York: Holt, Rinehart and Winston, 1970), 6.

II9   **An inch of snow:** *New-York Tribune,* Dec. 28, 1903, 12.

I20   **dispatched a cable:** "Next Olympian Games for the United States," *San Francisco
Chronicle,* Nov. 11, 1900, 8; "Talk of Olympian Games," *Chicago Tribune,* Nov. 12,
1900, 3.

I20   **an angry open letter:** "Olympian Games," *Rochester (N.Y.) Democrat and Chronicle,*
Nov. 14, 1900, 5.

I21   **Whitney used his magazine:** "The Sportsman's View-Point," *Outing,* Oct. 1900–
March 1901, 473–75.

I21   **"I am always willing"**: Coubertin, *Olympic Memoirs,* 74.

I21   **"The fight was on!"**: Ibid.

I22   **Coubertin believed few European athletes:** Ibid., 74–87.

I22   **"the greatest event"**: "Olympic Games at St. Louis," *Downs* (Kans.) *Times,* March 5,
1903, 1.

I22   **assigned the organizational responsibilities:** The St. Louis World's Fair Committee
was ultimately in charge of assigning a person to oversee the Olympic Games.
However, when the Games were awarded to St. Louis, the *Chicago Tribune* reported that Coubertin wrote to the Amateur Athletic Union to inform its officers
that they were to act as the representatives of the IOC at the St. Louis Games and
directed them to draw up the Olympic program for the Games. "A.A.U. at Olympian Games," *Chicago Tribune,* March 27, 1903, 7.

I22   **Tom Daniels was enjoying a drink:** *Daniels v. Daniels,* divorce file, Court of Kings
County, Brooklyn, 1904.

I23   **prosecution had decided not to move forward:** Magistrate's Court docket book—
Manhattan 1st District, Aug. 5, 1903.

I24   **qualify for the finals:** *Sail and Sweep* 3 (1904): 70.

I25   **same tank last February:** Ibid., 176.

I26   **Charley's slowest figure:** Ibid., 70.

I26   **"Daniels's effort cannot"**: "Swimming," *Sun* (New York), Jan. 17, 1904, 11.

10: IN SEARCH OF AN AMERICAN CHAMPION

I29   **find the fastest gait:** Daniels, *Speed Swimming,* 63.

I29   **was folly:** Ibid., 65.

129 **judge of tempo:** Ibid., 57.
129 **parents' divorce proceedings:** *Daniels v. Daniels*, divorce file, Court of Kings County, Brooklyn, 1904.
132 **entire lap behind:** "Daniel's Natatorial Miracle," *New York Athletic Club Journal*, March 1904, 9–10.
132 **Danny:** *Topeka State Journal*, July 16, 1904, 11.
132 **"a miracle":** "Daniel's Natatorial Miracle," 9–10.
132 **"New Swimming Records":** *Sun* (New York), Feb. 14, 1904, 9.
132 **"Record Swim at N.Y.A.C.":** *New York Times*, Feb. 14, 1904, 14.
132 **"Tank Records Fall":** *New-York Tribune*, Feb. 14, 1904, 7.
132 **"Boy Breaks Records":** *Boston Globe*, Feb. 14, 1904, 2.
133 **"What in all probability":** "Swimming Meet in Brookline," *Boston Post*, Feb. 28, 1904, 12.
135 **greatest natural-born athletes:** "Harry LeMoyne a Wonder," *Boston Post*, Nov. 8, 1903, 13.
135 **shot put record:** "Indoor Record Broken at Cambridge Meet," *Boston Post*, Feb. 9, 1904, 3.
135 **one-fifth to four-fifths of a second:** Daniels, *Speed Swimming*, 59.
136 **deep dives kill speed:** Ibid.
138 **new American record:** "Swimming Meet in Brookline," 12.
139 **ten feet behind:** Ibid.
139 **Ten days later:** "New Swimming Records," *New York Times*, March 10, 1904, 10.
139 **"LeMoyne, LeMoyne, LeMoyne!":** Finkbeiner, *From Harvard to Hagerman*, 82.
139 **Alice Daniels appeared:** *Daniels v. Daniels*, 1904.
140 **"MRS. DANIELS GETS A DECREE":** *Brooklyn Daily Eagle*, March 14, 1904, 22.
141 **broke four more American records:** "District Swimming Championships," *New York Times*, March 20, 1904, 14.
141 **twenty-seven seconds faster:** "A.A.A.U. Swimming Championships," *New York Athletic Club Journal*, April 1904, 23.
141 **more than half a minute:** Ibid.
141 **twenty seconds slower:** "Swimming Carnival at Newcastle," *Sydney Morning Herald*, March 15, 1904, 6.
141 **"The truth of the matter":** Frederick R. Toombs, "C. M. Daniels a Coming Swimming Champion," *Topeka State Journal*, July 16, 1904, 11.
141 **Dick Cavill:** "Australasians at Olympic Games," *New York Times*, March 26, 1904, 6.
141 **letter from Columbia:** Columbia University to C. M. Daniels, May 17, 1904, C. M. Daniels scrapbook.
142 **two-hundred-yard race:** *New York Athletic Club Journal*, May 1904, 11–12.
142 **fast 63.6 seconds:** Ibid.
143 **110-yard American record:** "Swimming Record," *Buffalo Commercial*, May 12, 1904, 6.
143 **"an act of boyish":** "LeMoyne Barred from Philadelphia Games," *Boston Post*, March 23, 1904, 10.
143 **letters to friends in Boston:** "Le Moyne as 'Dropped Student' Cannot Play for Harvard This Fall," *Boston Globe*, Sept. 20, 1904, 8.
143 **LeMoyne intended to return:** "Getting into Form," *Boston Globe*, Aug. 8, 1904, 9.
143 **Harry had skipped town:** ISHOF archive, Harry LeMoyne file.
144 **"spectacle of horror":** "1,000 Dead in Steamer Fire," *Chicago Tribune*, June 16, 1904, 1.
144 **"Mothers hugging their children":** Ibid.
145 **"That should be the resolve":** "Every Woman Should Swim," *New-York Daily Tribune*, June 25, 1904, 5.
145 **Tom Daniels reappeared:** *Daniels v. Daniels*, 1904.

146 **twenty-five-student graduation:** *Report of the Commissioner of Education for the Year Ending June 30, 1904* (Washington, D.C.: Government Printing Office, 1906), 2:2031.

147 **fifty-page briefs:** "Death of Hon. Charles Daniels," *Buffalo Evening News*, Dec. 21, 1897, 1.

11: AMERICA'S FIRST OLYMPICS

151 **"brilliant ceremony":** "St. Louis," *Daily News* (London), May 2, 1904, 7.

151 **more than 200,000 people:** "An Auspicious Opening of World's Fair: The Attendance Estimated at 237,000," *St. Louis Post-Dispatch*, April 30, 1904, 1.

152 **"indescribably grand":** Martha Clevenger, *"Indescribably Grand": Diaries and Letters from the 1904 World's Fair* (St. Louis: Missouri Historical Society Press, 1996), 3.

153 **"anthropological athletic meet":** "Coming Events," *St. Louis Globe-Democrat*, Aug. 7, 1904, 37.

153 **"The real legacy of the fair":** Robert Moss, "The 1904 World's Fair: A Turning Point for American Food," Serious Eats, Feb. 25, 2020, seriouseats.com.

154 **"Modern Olympic Games to Outrival Originals":** *Louisville* (Ky.) *Courier-Journal*, Dec. 27, 1903, 17.

154 **"World's Fair Meet Will Be the Best":** *Brooklyn Times Union*, Aug. 19, 1903, 5.

154 **"the fastest track in America":** "Stadium Is All Ready for Olympic Games," *Indianapolis News*, May 13, 1904, 14.

154 **Sullivan proclaimed thirty-five thousand:** "Great Olympic Games at the World's Fair," *Salt Lake Tribune*, March 6, 1904, 6.

155 **"In a word":** Lucas, *Olympic Games 1904*, 15.

155 **"Olympiad 1904":** "St. Louis 1904: The Medals," olympics.com.

156 **"I see that fellow":** *New York Times*, July 24, 1904, 17.

156 **weekly mid-distance practice:** "Daniels, Winner of Championships, Is Great Swimmer for His Age," *St. Louis Republic*, Sept. 11, 1904, 29.

156 **62.8 seconds:** "Remarkable Swim by C. M. Daniels," *Philadelphia Inquirer*, Aug. 21, 1904, 14.

156 **77 seconds:** "Swimming Records Go," *New York Times*, Aug. 28, 1904, 7.

157 **Newspapers reassured the public:** "Foreign Experts Will Meet Home Talent in Swimming Contests," *St. Louis Republic*, Aug. 28, 1904, 18.

157 **broke Charley's 220-yard:** *The World Almanac and Encyclopedia* (1905), 268.

157 **60.2 seconds:** "Mighty Effort of Australian," *San Francisco Call*, June 24, 1904, 10.

158 **"I hope I shall never":** Orville Schell, *Virtual Tibet: Searching for Shangri-La from the Himalayas to Hollywood* (New York: Metropolitan Books, 2000), 195.

158 **might send one swimmer:** "Notes on Swimming," *Nottingham Evening Post*, July 30, 1904, 6.

159 **"The results have confirmed":** *Guardian* (London), Aug. 20, 1900, 9.

159 **"The French people":** Lucas, *Olympic Games 1904*, 15.

159 **"There would have been six":** Coubertin, *Olympic Memoirs*, 76.

160 **"to add luster":** Ibid.

160 **Coubertin estimated at most:** Coubertin, *Les batailles de l'éducation physique*.

160 **"Now that [the Olympics] had":** Coubertin, *Olympic Memoirs*, 79.

163 **"The contest also showed":** "Praises City for Athletic Support," *St. Louis Post-Dispatch*, Nov. 6, 1904, 10.

165 **attendance at eight thousand:** "Swimming," *Sportsman* (London), Nov. 19, 1904, 5.

167 **fastest American open-water time:** "Gaul Lowers American Swimming Record for 50 Yard Straightaway," *Philadelphia Inquirer*, Aug. 16, 1903, 11.

169 **As the men's legs pushed off:** "Swimming Record Broken by German," *St. Louis Republic*, Sept. 6, 1904, 9; descriptions of Leary's stroke appear in numerous arti-

cles, such as "Stroke Turns Swim History," *Muncie* (Ind.) *Star Press*, June 13, 1942, 11, as does Halmay's crawl stroke.

169 **the Hungarian did a "trick":** "Daniels, Winner of Championships, Is Great Swimmer for His Age." *The St. Louis Republic*, Sept. 11, 1904, 29.

170 **"Foreign Swimmers Take Main Events":** *St. Louis Post-Dispatch*, Sept. 6, 1904, 14.

12: A GAME CHANGER

170 **the crawl:** As I researched the origins of the crawl through numerous old newspaper articles and scholarly studies, different variations and accounts emerged, as well as contradictions and debates. The version I present is based on articles quoting the Cavills' and Wickham's recollection as to its origin, as well as scholarly studies. I compared it with historical time lines, such as Sydney Cavill's journey to the United States, and when and what version of the crawl first surfaced at San Francisco's Olympic Club, as well as newspaper accounts of the crawl in Australia during this time (1890s to 1904) and Dick Cavill's first use in London in 1902. See L. de B. Handley and W. J. Howcroft, *Crawl-Stroke Swimming* (London: E. J. Larby, 1929); Gary Osmond and Murray G. Phillips, "The Bloke with a Stroke: Alick Wickham, the 'Crawl,' and Social Memory," *Journal of Pacific History* 39, no. 3 (Dec. 2004): 309–24; see also Forbes Carlile, "A History of Crawl Stroke Techniques to the 1960s: An Australian Perspective: Section II," in *Forbes Carlile on Swimming* (London: Pelham Books, 1963), 126–88; see also Dudley Hellmrich, *How to Swim Correctly* (Sydney: Caxton Printing Works, 1929), 11–15, and Trent Dalton, "The Truth Hasn't Been Told," *Weekend Australian Magazine*, Dec. 15, 2017. Outside these accounts, Zoltán Halmay used his leg-dragging version of the crawl in Paris in 1900, and it is unclear where he developed this. There are a few accounts that speculate Halmay picked it up from the Australian Freddie Lane or Dick Cavill.

171 **"not kicking her legs at all":** *Referee* (Sydney), July 1914.

172 **"Look at that kid":** *Sydney Morning Herald*, March 1, 1958, 10.

172 **arms and legs moved synchronously:** *Sydney Morning Herald*, Sept. 26, 1902, 5.

173 **58.6 seconds:** Ibid.

173 **"They lash the water":** "The Ojibbeway Indians," *Essex Herald*, April 30, 1844, 4.

173 **large crowd:** "Olympic Swimming Races," *Baltimore Sun*, Sept. 7, 1904, 9.

173 **record in the fifty-yard sprint:** "Swimming Event at St. Louis," *Chicago Tribune*, Sept. 7, 1904, 6; the judges wrongly declared this race a dead heat between Halmay and Leary and made the two enter a swim off, where Halmay beat Leary again. "World's Record by N.Y.A.C. Swimmer," *New York Times*, Sept. 7, 1904, 3.

173 **swept the hundred-yard backstroke:** "Swimming Records Broken," *Los Angeles Times*, Sept. 7, 1904, 15.

174 **almost two seconds:** "New Swimming Record," *Washington Evening Star*, Sept. 7, 1904, 9.

175 **"World's Record by N.Y.A.C. Swimmer":** *New York Times*, Sept. 7, 1904, 3.

175 **"Daniels of New York":** *St. Louis Globe-Democrat*, Sept. 7, 1904, 6.

175 **"Daniels' Great Race":** *San Francisco Call*, Sept. 7, 1904, 6.

175 **"Daniels a wonderful swimmer":** *Daily Gazette*, Sept. 7, 1904, 1.

175 **"Olympic" record:** "Swimming Records," *Sporting Life* (London), Sept. 7, 1904, 2.

175 **"a big German beerhorse":** Jamison Handy, "The Greatest Thrill of My Swimming Career," MS, ISHOF archive, Jamison "Jam" Handy file, 4.

176 **by sixteen seconds:** "Swimming Races at St. Louis," *New York Times*, Sept. 8, 1904, 5.

176 **"Amateur Athletic Union":** Mary Ellen McCormick collection of Daniels's medals.

177 **"For years this country":** Fred A. Wenck, "Daniels Home from Triumphs Abroad," 1906, C. M. Daniels scrapbook, IS.

177   **"the international competition"**: Otto Wahle, "Olympic Swimming," in Sullivan, *Olympic Games, Stockholm, 1912,* 149.

13: INTO THE LAIR OF GIANTS

180   **six-week European rest:** *Buffalo Sunday Morning News,* Sept. 4, 1904, 5.
180   **"Nothing worthwhile is accomplished":** Handley, *Swimming for Women,* 10.
181   **"Seldom was there an expression":** Finkbeiner, *From Harvard to Hagerman,* 3.
181   **"loss will be severely felt":** "New Athletes at College," *Sun* (New York), Oct. 9, 1904, 20.
182   **"Black care rarely sits":** Theodore Roosevelt, *Ranch Life and the Hunting-Trail* (New York: Century, 1896), 59.
182   **"Anna Daniels":** *Minnehaha* ship manifest of first-class passengers from New York to Southampton, Nov. 14, 1904, upon entry into U.K. Strangely, Charley is listed after "Anna Daniels" as what looks like "Clara Daniels," and Flossie is listed after "Alice Meldrum" as "Frances Meldrum" instead of "Florence Meldrum."
184   **"Daniels will at once":** "Champion Swimmer to Compete Abroad," *New York Times,* Nov. 5, 1904, 11.
184   **Dave Bratton, had died:** *New York Athletic Club Journal,* Jan. 1905, 31.
185   **According to *Modern Sanitation:*** *Modern Sanitation,* Dec. 1909, 208–12.
185   **"According to Daniels":** "American Champion in London," *Sportsman* (London), Nov. 19, 1904, 5.
187   **"The crawl is not pretty":** "In Doing the Crawl," *Wichita Daily Eagle,* April 30, 1905, 24.
187   **12.4 seconds:** "Local Swimmers Active," *New York Times,* Dec. 25, 1904, 9.
187   **fifty-yard record:** *New York Athletic Club Journal,* Feb. 1905, 22.
187   **American indoor century champion:** Ibid., 23.
187   **"If Budd should ever learn":** L. de B. Handley, "American Swimmers to Beat the World," *Recreation & Outdoor World,* July 1914, 30.
187   **began boasting:** "Schwarz a Coming Champion, Says M.A.C. Swimming Expert," *St. Louis Globe-Democrat,* Jan. 15, 1905, 43.
188   **"anyone not using the crawl":** "In Doing the Crawl."
190   **top men were absent:** "Oxford University v. Otter," *Sportsman* (London), June 19, 1905, 3.
191   **England's newspapers impugned:** "Swimming and Water Polo," *Athletic News,* June 19, 1905.
191   **"certainly Welched us":** C. M. Daniels scrapbook, IS.

14: THE AUSTRALIAN INVASION

193   **"Nothing succeeds like excess":** Oscar Wilde, *A Woman of No Importance* (1893).
193   **group also included:** "Arrival of B. B. Kieran," *Sportsman* (London), June 19, 1905, 3.
194   **every world record:** "Swimming," *Observer* (London), June 18, 1905, 3.
195   **"I can only say":** "Swimming," *Sportsman* (London), June 19, 1905, 3.
195   **"It is hopeful that":** "C. M. Daniels," *Athletic News,* June 12, 1905, 8.
196   **England's six-hundred-yard record:** "Swimming," *Sporting Life* (London), June 27, 1905, 6.
196   **"He is a fish":** "Swimming & Water Polo," *Sportsman* (London), June 27, 1905, 3.
197   **seven feet high:** "Swimming," *Sportsman* (London), June 21, 1905, 7.
197   **by almost four minutes:** *Oakland Tribune,* Aug. 24, 1908, 14.
198   **"high society was not":** Kellermann, *How to Swim,* 20.
198   **"I can't swim":** This quotation has long been attributed to Kellermann; however, its factual origin remains elusive, and this could be a paraphrase that evolved over time.

200 **fifty thousand spectators:** "Swimming at Blackpool," *Guardian* (London), July 11, 1905, 7.

202 **seventy yards ahead:** "Swimming," *Manchester Courier and Lancashire General Advertiser,* July 11, 1905, 9.

202 **"It will certainly be surprising":** "Swimming," *Sportsman* (London), July 19, 1905, 2.

15: THE AMERICAN CRAWL

206 **"I was weak, listless":** C. M. Daniels, "How I Won the Swimming Championship," *Topeka* (Kans.) *State Journal,* Nov. 25, 1905, 6.

206 **three hundred to a thousand:** "Geo. J. Munroe Arrested by Post Office Inspectors," *Joliet* (Ill.) *Evening Herald,* Nov. 21, 1906, 1.

207 **"I cannot promise":** Daniels, "How I Won the Swimming Championship."

207 **"Coming at the time it did":** Ibid.

209 **80 Washington Square:** *Thirteenth Census of the United States: 1910 Population,* April 23, 1910.

210 **"Do not become discouraged":** Handley, *Swimming for Women,* 26.

211 **Those "little tidbits":** Hill, *Hill's Manual of Social and Business Forms.*

211 **"Try smiling":** "Work, Relaxation Spelled Success for Gloria Callen," *Gallup* (N.M.) *Independent,* March 4, 1942, 3.

211 **"What was good for one":** "Daniels Praises the Crawl," *Sun* (New York), Jan. 28, 1906, 12.

212 **"The fish have to do":** "C. M. Daniels, the Human Merman," *Ogden* (Utah) *Standard,* May 13, 1911, 11.

212 **"They play havoc with condition":** Handley, *Swimming for Women,* 68.

212 **"Few things impair":** Ibid.

212 **the dizzying back-and-forth:** "Daniels Tells of the Crawl," *Sun* (New York), Aug. 11, 1907, 15.

213 **"Not in years have swimmers":** "Handy to Swim in the East," *Chicago Tribune,* Aug. 26, 1905, 8.

214 **"in order that athletics":** "Life at Athletic Clubs," *Scribner's Magazine,* July 1895, 5.

215 **developed his own side-breathing technique:** Jamison Handy, "The Greatest Thrill of My Swimming Career," MS, ISHOF archive, Jamison "Jam" Handy file, 6–8.

215 **crawl his way to victory:** "Handy Is Mile Champion," *Chicago Tribune,* July 21, 1905, 4.

215 **new American record:** "World's Record Broken in Swimming Race," *Brooklyn Daily Eagle,* Aug. 27, 1905, 43.

215 **Handy accused Charley:** Handy, "Greatest Thrill of My Swimming Career," 6–8.

215 **another American record:** "American Swimming Record," *Brooklyn Daily Eagle,* Sept. 5, 1905, 10.

215 **near-record time:** "Daniels Swims Fast," *New-York Tribune,* Sept. 3, 1905, 8.

215 **"Daniels is beaten!":** "New Swimming Records," *New-York Tribune,* Sept. 5, 1905, 10.

215 **63.2 seconds:** Ibid.

216 **The Boston Globe wrote:** "Daniels Makes New World's Record in Swimming," *Boston Globe,* Sept. 5, 1905, 8.

216 **forty-eight seconds faster:** "Kieran Successful," *Sydney Morning Herald,* Aug. 7, 1905, 7.

216 **almost two minutes faster:** "A World Swimming Championship," *Guardian* (London), Aug. 9, 1905, 10.

216 **impressive fifty-nine seconds:** "Swimming," *Western Daily Press* (Bristol, U.K.), Aug. 15, 1905, 7.

217 **a surprise Olympiad:** *Buffalo Morning Express,* Sept. 21, 1905, 8.

217 **this "session" in Athens:** Coubertin, *Olympic Memoirs,* 97.

217 **wise to leave well enough alone:** "Daniels Praises the Crawl."

218 **"There is not a man":** "Crawl Superior to the Trudgen," *Inter Ocean* (Chicago), Feb. 4, 1906, 14.

218 **330-yard record:** "Handy Wins Match Race," *Chicago Tribune,* Oct. 27, 1905, 10.

218 **five American records:** "New Swimming Records," *Boston Globe,* Nov. 22, 1905, 8.

218 **mid-distance American records:** "Two American Records," *Boston Globe,* Dec. 15, 1905, 6.

218 **1905's top national swimmer:** "National Champions of 1905," *Buffalo Evening News,* Jan. 1, 1906, 6.

219 **"Mrs. Thomas Daniels of New York":** *Buffalo Commercial,* Jan. 4, 1906, 14; *Buffalo Times,* Jan. 4, 1906, 11.

219 **"Australian Champion Swimmer":** *Buffalo Morning Express,* Dec. 23, 1905, 12.

219 **recalled Wahle being so insistent:** "Daniels Praises the Crawl."

220 **"In the Australian crawl":** "Says Swimmers Must Have National Body," *New York Times,* March 18, 1917, 1.

221 **new American record:** "Daniels Praises the Crawl."

221 **"So long as the flat side":** Ibid.

221 **felt as if a baby grand piano:** Rowdy Gaines interview, Sept. 24, 2021.

222 **"I think that it":** "Great Swimmers Not over Twenty," *Philadelphia Inquirer,* Jan. 29, 1906, 11.

223 **"wonderful work":** "Chief Sullivan to Receive Medal," *St. Louis Republic,* Nov. 3, 1904, 10.

223 **need to raise at least:** "Fund for Athletes for Olympic Games," *New York Times,* Jan. 11, 1906, 10.

224 **"Daniels seemed to positively crawl":** L. de B. Handley, "Daniels, the Boy Record Breaker," Daniels scrapbook, IS.

225 **fifty-eight-second world record:** "Swimming Records Broken by Daniels," *Pittsburgh Daily Post,* Jan. 14, 1906, 11.

225 **refused to acknowledge it:** *New York Athletic Club Journal,* March 1906, 12.

16: IN ROUGH WATERS

226 **"I am firmly convinced":** "Daniels Praises the Crawl," *Sun* (New York), Jan. 28, 1906, 12.

226 **"To see is to believe":** Ibid.

226 **"My advice to those":** Ibid.

226 **a thousand dollars toward the Olympic fund:** *New York Athletic Club Journal,* March 1906, 16.

227 **"Now for Daniels":** "Handy Returns to Form," *Inter Ocean* (Chicago), Feb. 4, 1906, 15.

227 **"This is absurd":** "Olympic Team Sails To-Day," *Kansas City Star,* April 3, 1906, 3.

227 **"He claims 420 yards":** Ibid.

227 **"We do hope your great crack":** Ibid.

228 **"Every one of these contests":** "Champion Swimmers in Their Greatest Carnival," *Philadelphia Inquirer,* Feb. 11, 1906, 34.

228 **"I think Schwarz":** "Missouri to Show N.Y.A.C. Swimming," 1906, C. M. Daniels scrapbook, IS.

228 **seventy of the country's best:** "Swimming Records Go in A.A.U. Championships," *New York Times,* Feb. 22, 1906, 8.

229 **"There is such a thing":** "Handy Will Not Swim in the East," *Inter Ocean* (Chicago), Feb. 14, 1906, 4.

229 **thirteen American records:** *New York Athletic Club Journal,* March 1906, 11.

229 **had raised only $14,864:** Sullivan, *Olympic Games at Athens, 1906,* 127.

229 **"Unthinking persons often smile"**: "American Swimmers," *New-York Tribune*, March 4, 1906, 52.
230 **"We may have been their laughingstock"**: C. M. Daniels, "How American Swimming Was Revolutionized," 1906, Daniels scrapbook, IS.
231 **"Dear Sir: I beg to advise you"**: American Committee of the Olympian Games at Athens, Greece, 1906, to Daniels, March 8, 1906, Daniels scrapbook.
231 **"will be watched"**: *New York Athletic Club Journal*, April 1906, 14–16.
231 **"We have been a good deal"**: L. de B. Handley, "Yankee Swimmers Should Win," 1906, Daniels scrapbook, IS.
231 **"A year or two ago"**: "Swimmers Who Will Race for America at Athens," *Philadelphia Inquirer*, March 11, 1906, 13.
232 **"We all look to Daniels"**: "Sullivan Starts for Athens," *Boston Evening Transcript*, March 16, 1906, 3.
233 **"without any provocation whatsoever"**: *Thomas P. Daniels v. Lydia S. Daniels*, Superior Court of Cook County, Illinois, divorce file, 1906.
233 **"sporting houses"**: Ibid.
233 **110-yard world record**: "Daniels Sets New World's Record in 110 Yard Swim," *Inter Ocean* (Chicago), March 23, 1906, 4.
234 **fifty-six seconds**: "Daniels Swims Fast," *Sun* (New York), March 24, 1906, 9.
234 **"Year's Most Important Event"**: *Evening World*, (New York), March 26, 1906, 6.
235 **"Old Glory"**: Sullivan, *Olympic Games at Athens, 1906*, 135.
235 **thirty-four athletes**: "Athletes Sail for Athens," *Chicago Tribune*, April 4, 1906, 12.
236 **fifteen-foot rogue wave**: Sullivan, *Olympic Games at Athens, 1906*, 133–39.
237 **By Easter Monday**: Ibid., 55.
238 **partitions about seven feet high**: Ibid., 139.
238 **"frighten the horses"**: Often attributed to King Edward VII, this quotation most likely evolved over time, originating from actual city ordinances of the day.
239 **"no longer a fit place"**: Attributed to Astor around 1890.

17: AWAKENING ZEUS'S THUNDERBOLTS

241 **far from his usual form**: *New York Athletic Club Journal*, June 1906, 16.
242 **Sunday morning, April 22**: Sullivan, *Olympic Games at Athens, 1906*, 5–7.
244 **"The people seemed enthused"**: Ibid., 21–23.
244 **biggest thrills of his life**: "Carmel Valley Olympics Trio Holds 9 Medals," *Monterey Peninsula Herald*, Oct. 8, 1964, 1.
244 **"Where in the world"**: Sullivan, *Olympic Games at Athens, 1906*, 11.
245 **disappointing tenth**: C. M. Daniels, "Daniels Tells of Athens Race," 1906, C. M. Daniels scrapbook, IS.
245 **"Daniels Picked to Win Finals"**: *Chicago Tribune*, April 25, 1906, 10.
245 **"One American Shows Class"**: *Spokane Chronicle*, April 24, 1906, 5.
245 **"Olympic Contests Begin"**: *New York Times*, April 24, 1906, 12.
245 **"dangerous competitors"**: "Swimmers Who Will Race for America at Athens," *Philadelphia Inquirer*, March 11, 1906, 13.
245 **"We have ever been a joke"**: Fred A. Wenck, "Daniels Home from Triumphs Abroad," 1906, Daniels scrapbook, IS.
246 **"Healy is one of those phenomenal"**: L. de B. Handley, "Yankee Swimmers Should Win," 1906, Daniels scrapbook, IS.
247 **Charley surveyed the ocean**: Daniels, "Daniels Tells of Athens Race."
247 **106-meter straightaway**: *Monterey Peninsula Herald*, Sept. 19, 1960, Daniels scrapbook.
248 **swimming painful**: Daniels, "Daniels Tells of Athens Race."
248 **"a new era"**: "Daniel's Victory," *Buffalo Commercial*, April 28, 1906, 6.

249 **"anything but satisfied"**: "Meeting of Champions," *Manchester Courier and Lancashire General Advertiser,* May 28, 1906, 3.

249 **"He Didn't Start"**: *Evening World,* April 27, 1906, 2.

250 **"[Bornamann's] opponents set"**: Daniels, "Daniels Tells of Athens Race."

250 **"Universal regret was expressed"**: Ibid.

250 **twenty-seven American records**: *Bisbee* (Ariz.) *Daily Review,* June 2, 1906, 3; "Sporting Twinkles," *Evening Star and Daily Herald* (London), June 11, 1906, 2.

250 **"while England"**: *New York Athletic Club Journal,* May 1906, 11.

251 **"Americans Win at Athens"**: *Buffalo Courier,* April 26, 1906, 10. See also Daniels scrapbook, 1906.

252 **"Hearty congratulations to you"**: Sullivan, *Olympic Games at Athens, 1906,* 45.

18: TAKING ON THE EMPIRE

253 **seven annual championship races**: Sinclair and Henry, *Swimming,* 349–66, 387–95, 402–18.

254 **"It must be confessed"**: "Meeting of Champions," *Manchester Courier and Lancashire General Advertiser,* May 28, 1906, 3.

254 **"Daniels claims"**: "America's Champion Swimmer," *Evening Telegraph* (London), Nov. 19, 1904, 5.

254 **"It is said"**: Natator, "Swimming," *Star,* (Christchurch, Australia), Sept. 27, 1906.

255 **"If this be true"**: "C. M. Daniels," *Athletic News,* June 12, 1905, 8.

255 **"The presence of the late"**: "Swimming," *Ottawa Journal,* June 9, 1906, 2.

255 **"As it is unlikely"**: "The English Championships," *Manchester Evening News,* May 1, 1906, 7.

256 **His method was to first**: "Tricks of the Racing Swimmer," *Courier* (Waterloo, IA), Aug. 28, 1911, 8.

257 **swim the race in his mind**: Rowdy Gaines interview, Sept. 24, 2021.

257 **"You should not care"**: C. M. Daniels, "How American Swimming Was Revolutionized," 1906, Daniels scrapbook, IS.

257 **"the only thing wanting"**: "England Losing Ground," *Manchester Courier and Lancashire General Advertiser,* June 18, 1906, 3.

258 **57.4 seconds**: "Swimming," *Daily Telegraph and Courier* (London), June 23, 1906, 8.

258 **"taking further advantage"**: "Sporting Twinkles," *Evening Star and Daily Herald* (London), June 11, 1906, 2.

259 **"This was more a social"**: "Valley Man Swim Champ When Suits Were Knee Length," *Monterey Peninsula Herald,* Oct. 21, 1971, Daniels scrapbook, IS.

260 **60.2 seconds**: Otto Wahle, "How Daniels Won Title," 1906, Daniels scrapbook, IS.

261 **"THE RACE"**: Racing bill from Nottingham's Victoria Baths, 1906, Daniels scrapbook.

261 **nerves were most intense**: Rowdy Gaines interview, Sept. 24, 2021.

262 **"appeared very nervous"**: Natator, "Swimming," Nov. 1906, Daniels scrapbook, IS.

262 **"nearing the end of each lap"**: "Australia's Crop of Sour Grapes," 1906, Daniels scrapbook, IS.

262 **Newspapers later reported that Halmay**: "Gala in Nottingham," 1906, Daniels scrapbook, IS.

262 **"dead heat"**: "Championship Swimming in Nottingham," *Nottingham Journal,* July 13, 1906, 6.

262 **"Another stroke"**: "Australia's Crop of Sour Grapes," quoting *Referee* (Sydney), 1906.

263 **Charley's was 58.6**: "A.S.A. Championship," *Daily Express* (Dublin), July 13, 1906, 8.

263 **"It was the opinion"**: "Australia's Crop of Sour Grapes," quoting *Referee* (Sydney), 1906.

263 **called such claims startling**: *Athletic News,* July 16, 1906, 8.

263 **"As soon as we have evidence"**: "Swimming Notes," *Australian Star* (Sydney), Sept. 27, 1906, 4.

264 **"very narrow victory"**: Natator, "Swimming," 1906, Daniels scrapbook, IS.

264 **"Healy had proved"**: *Referee* (Sydney), Jan. 19, 1907, as reported in "Swimmer Daniels' Victory," *Washington Evening Star*, Jan. 20, 1907, 60.

264 **"the young American"**: "Australia's Crop of Sour Grapes."

264 **"Swimming Officials Refuse"**: Daniels scrapbook, 1906, IS.

19: MUDSLINGING

265 **July 26, 1906**: SS *Baltic* Passenger List at Port of Arrival.

267 **"Quietly the curtain fell"**: Coubertin, *Olympic Memoirs*, 97.

267 **greatest ever held**: "World Athletes Ready for Games," *Chicago Tribune*, July 13, 1908, 11.

268 **"I propose to be frank"**: Posey, *III Olympiad*.

268 **"Well, I think that settles"**: Ibid.

269 **"Although Daniels is far"**: Fred Wenck, "Daniels Still the World's Best," 1906, C.M. Daniels scrapbook, IS.

270 **"Not one in one thousand"**: "The Sportsman's Niche," *St. Louis Post-Dispatch*, Sept. 13, 1906, 14.

271 **Top swimmers**: "Champion Swims Begin Thursday," *St. Louis Post-Dispatch*, Sept. 13, 1906, 14.

272 *Post-Dispatch* **published**: "Want to Bet Handy Will Defeat Daniels," *St. Louis Post-Dispatch*, Sept. 12, 1906, 6.

272 **"I would rather win"**: "M.A.C. Stands First in Swims," *St. Louis Post-Dispatch*, Sept. 15, 1906, 6.

273 **"I have been training"**: "Swimming Champion," *Buffalo Commercial*, Sept. 20, 1906, 5.

273 **"It must be that Daniels"**: "The Sportsman's Niche," *St. Louis Post-Dispatch*, Sept. 14, 1906, 7.

273 **"Never mind, Danny"**: "Swimming Notes," *St. Louis Post-Dispatch*, Sept. 15, 1906, 6.

273 **"Who's the current"**: "The Sportsman's Niche," *St. Louis Post-Dispatch*, Sept. 15, 1906, 6.

273 **"in the dim and distant"**: Ibid.

273 **"There is much dissatisfaction"**: "New Water Mark for Daniels," *Chicago Tribune*, Sept. 15, 1906, 10.

273 **"I do submit that"**: "The Sportsman's Niche," Sept. 15, 1906.

274 **"Now the West will brag"**: "Swimming Champion."

274 **"Is it not"**: L. de B. Handley, "Champion Daniels Agrees to Swim Handy for Title," 1906, Daniels scrapbook, IS.

275 **the *former* mile**: "Eastern Teams Want M.A.C. Basket Ball and Aquatic Dates," *St. Louis Globe-Democrat*, Oct. 21, 1906, 51.

275 *Buffalo Courier* **noted**: *Buffalo Courier*, Oct. 2, 1906, 5.

275 *Buffalo Evening News* **published**: "C. M. Daniels," *Buffalo Evening News*, Oct. 8, 1906, 20.

275 *Buffalo Commercial* **ran**: "Daniels and Handy in Swimming Match," *Buffalo Commercial*, Sept. 29, 1906, 10.

275 *Buffalo Sunday Morning News* **ran**: "World-Famous Athlete Here," *Buffalo Sunday Morning News*, Oct. 7, 1906, 6.

276 **"It was quite"**: Matt Mann, unpublished autobiography, ISHOF archive, Matt Mann file.

277 **$1.5 million**: "Great Swindle Uncovered in Milwaukee," *Akron* (Ohio) *Beacon Journal*, Nov. 21, 1907, 3.

277 **newspapers noted**: "Giant Frauds Alleged," *Washington Post*, Nov. 21, 1906, 11.

277 **twenty thousand smaller publications:** *The American Newspaper Directory* (New York: George P. Rowell, 1900).

278 **intercollegiate swimming league:** "Big Boom for College Swimming," *Washington Evening Star,* Dec. 16, 1906, 63.

278 **YMCA branches:** Wenck, "Daniels Still the World's Best."

278 **"We don't say":** "Handy Backs Out of Match," *Buffalo Enquirer,* Jan. 23, 1907, 8.

279 **Charley lined up:** "Daniels's Record Swim," *New York Times,* Feb. 3, 1907, 10.

279 **"Diamond Queen":** "Weds, Blocks Law, and Gets Money," *Inter Ocean* (Chicago), Dec. 15, 1906, 3.

280 **"taking advantage":** "Daniels and Handy Will Race Tonight," *Washington Times,* Feb. 23, 1907, 8.

280 **defeated the trio:** Ibid.

281 **forty-three seconds:** "New Records for Swimmer Daniels," *New York Times,* Feb. 24, 1907, 58.

281 **sixteen new American records:** "C.A.A. Swimmers Beaten," *Chicago Tribune,* Feb. 24, 1907, 13.

281 **special one-mile match race:** Fred A. Wenck, "Daniels Out for the Mile Mark, Too," 1907, Daniels scrapbook, IS.

281 **twenty-four seconds short:** *New York Athletic Club Journal,* April 1907, 31.

20: THE ENGLISH CHAMPION RETURNS

285 **a story arose:** "Naval Trick Frees Celtic from Fog," *New York Times,* May 1, 1907, 2.

286 **"There is no more reason":** Kellermann, *How to Swim,* 47.

286 **"My early physical misfortune":** Ibid., 34.

287 **"I just want to show":** *New York Athletic Club Journal,* April 1907, 23.

287 **fifty-seven seconds:** "Sporting News Items," *Daily Mirror* (London), April 15, 1907, 15.

287 ***Brooklyn Daily Eagle* asked:** "Swimmer C. M. Daniels Starts English Tour," *Brooklyn Daily Eagle,* Aug. 16, 1907, 15.

287 **"Human Fish Beaten":** "Human Fish Beaten," *Trenton Evening Times,* Aug. 20, 1907, 8.

287 **"America's Best Swimmer":** "Daniels Finished Third," *Buffalo Commercial,* Aug. 20, 1907, 8.

287 **"Zoltan Halmay Won":** "Zoltan Halmay Won World's Swimming Match," *Province* (Vancouver), Aug. 20, 1907, 11.

288 **"Daniels Was Third":** "Daniels Was Third," *New York Times,* Aug. 20, 1907, 8.

288 **"It is hard":** *New York Athletic Club Journal,* Sept. 1907, 18.

288 **two-fifths of a second:** "Daniels' Record Broken," *Brooklyn Daily Eagle,* Aug. 24, 1907, 10.

288 **missed the pole:** "Daniels Was Not Beaten in England," 1907, C. M. Daniels scrapbook, IS.

290 **60.8 seconds:** "Nottingham Swimming Club," *Nottingham Journal,* Sept. 7, 1907, 6.

290 **an even 57:** "Notes of the Week," 1907, Daniels scrapbook, IS.

290 **less than stellar:** "Notes on Swimming," *Nottingham Evening Post,* Sept. 7, 1907, 8.

291 **fourth lane:** "Swimming," *Sportsman* (London), Sept. 7, 1907, 3.

292 **six-beat crawl:** Historical records do not tell us the precise moment Daniels used a six-beat kick. However, given this was the fastest time he ever swam the hundred-yard race, it makes sense that he used it at this time.

292 **swimming downhill:** Rowdy Gaines interview, Sept. 24, 2021.

292 **Charley hit 55.4:** "English Swimming Records," *Spalding Athletic Almanac* (1908), 145.

292 **"Good golly!":** "History in Swimming," *Guardian* (London), Sept. 9, 1907, 4.

21: TO SWIM OR NOT TO SWIM

293 **"It was appropriate":** "Swimming," *Sportsman* (London), Sept. 9, 1907, 3.

293 **"Whirling in the water":** "Whirling in the Water World," *Athletic News*, Sept. 9, 1907, 7.

293 **"Sensational Swimming":** "Swimming and Water Polo," *Yorkshire Post*, Sept. 9, 1907, 12.

293 **"The race proved one thing":** "Swimming and Water Polo," *Daily News* (London), Sept. 13, 1907, 12.

293 **"If there are any admirers":** *New York Athletic Club Journal*, Oct. 1907, 28.

294 **"Well done":** C. M. Daniels scrapbook, 1907.

294 **London *Evening News*:** "Swimming Champion Explains the 'Crawl' Stroke," *Evening News* (London), 1907, Daniels scrapbook, IS.

294 **full-page exposé:** Ibid.

294 **"it will be surprising":** "Swimmers and the 'Crawl' Stroke," *Echo* (London), Sept. 14, 1908.

294 **beat it by two seconds:** "Swimming and Water Polo," *Sporting Life*, Sept. 11, 1907, 6.

294 **"I don't know how":** "C. M. Daniels, the Human Merman," *Ogden* (Utah) *Standard*, May 13, 1911, 11.

294 **"The colleges are very active":** "Swimmer Daniels Is Home Again," *Buffalo Morning Express*, Sept. 29, 1907, 23.

295 **"unknown in England":** "Englishmen Hold On To Their Trophies," *Hartford Courant*, Feb. 28, 1908, 12.

296 **hundred tickets:** "To Entertain Swimemr [*sic*] Daniels," 1907, Daniels scrapbook, IS.

297 **"The purpose of our gathering":** *New York Athletic Club Journal*, Nov. 1907, 14–17.

297 **"Daniels went to England":** Lyrics of "Didn't He Swamble," in ibid.

299 **"Never quit athletics":** "New York's Father Neptune: The Life and Times of Joe Ruddy and Other Famous Swimmers," MS, ISHOF archive, Joe Ruddy file, IS.

299 **"Some of these ex-athletes":** Ibid.

299 **advised against it:** "Daniels Invited to Australia," *New York Athletic Club Journal*, Dec. 1907, 15.

302 ***Los Angeles Times* even printed:** "Daniels Holds All Swimming Records" and "Swimming Pool for U.S.C.," *Los Angeles Times*, Jan. 5, 1908, 79.

302 **"knack and confidence":** *New York Athletic Club Journal*, Oct. 1907, 41.

302 **56.2 seconds:** "Daniels Outswims Handy at Sportsman's Show," *Brooklyn Daily Eagle*, March 6, 1908, 10.

303 **"as certain to eclipse":** "Preparing for the Revival of the Ancient Olympic Games in London—Will Eclipse All Others," *Washington Evening Star*, Dec. 15, 1907, 59.

303 **"the largest structure":** "Immense Stadium Is Nearly Finished," *Muncie* (Ind.) *Star Press*, April 17, 1908, 7.

304 **"will be the center":** "Big London Stadium," *Montour American* (Danville, Pa.), May 21, 1908, 3.

304 **"His own sheer force":** Attributed to Theodore A. Cook; see also Cook, *The Sunlit Hours: A Record of Sport and Life* (New York: George H. Doran, 1925).

304 **"Left in the care":** Coubertin, *Olympic Memoirs*, 98.

305 **"As this country has been the cradle":** *Official Olympic Report of 1908* (London: British Olympic Association, 1909), 24.

306 **"absolutely vital":** Coubertin, *Olympic Memoirs*, 101.

307 **intention to raise fifty thousand dollars:** "Comment on Sports: Olympic Games Fund," *New-York Tribune*, Feb. 10, 1908, 8.

307 **it was reported:** "Swimming Notes," 1908, Daniels scrapbook, IS.

307 **"That our swimmers":** "How America Will Be Represented in the Swimming Races in London," *San Francisco Chronicle*, June 28, 1908, 37.

308 **The Australians argued:** Daniels scrapbook, 1908, IS.

308 **67.2 seconds:** "Great Australian Swimmer," *Sun* (New York), May 17, 1908, 29.

309 **four greatest amateur athletes:** "Amateur Sports," *Los Angeles Times*, March 22, 1908, 88.

311 **"An athlete in any line":** "Swimmer Daniels Will Keep Trying," *Buffalo Commercial*, March 15, 1907, 6.

311 **"has made no trials":** "Swimmers Begin to Get in Shape," *Buffalo Commercial*, May 20, 1908, 6.

311 **69.2-second time:** "Try-Out for Swimmers," *Washington Evening Star*, June 5, 1908, 17.

311 **"It was disappointing":** "Olympic Games Affected Swimming Games at Home," *Pittsburgh Press*, Nov. 22, 1908, 18.

22: DANIELS IN THE LION'S DEN

313 **A political cartoon:** "Sports: Just a Moment, Please!," *Brooklyn Daily Eagle*, July 15, 1908, 18–19.

313 **"the most remarkable":** "America's Best to Take Part in Olympic Games," *Los Angeles Evening Express*, May 22, 1908, 14.

313 **"with great disfavor":** "France Now an Athletic Factor," *New York Times*, Feb. 9, 1908, 30.

314 **"America's Greatest Swimmer":** "Daniels Starts Off in Advance," *Buffalo Commercial*, June 17, 1908, 6.

314 **four days twenty hours and eight minutes:** "Lusitania Breaks Record," *Brooklyn Daily Eagle*, June 12, 1908, 1.

314 **"American Swimmers Face":** "American Swimmers Face Hard Task to Defeat Foreign Stars in Meet," *Anaconda* (Mont.) *Standard*, June 21, 1908, 27.

314 **"Daniels stands for":** "The Swimming World," *Manchester Courier*, July 13, 1908, 3.

315 **"If the American Line":** "On Board Ship with Athletes," *Buffalo Express*, July 16, 1908, 12.

316 **2.6 seconds short:** "The Belgians' Visit to Hyde," *Manchester Courier and Lancashire General Advertiser*, July 8, 1908, 9.

316 **three-fifths of a second:** "International Swimming," *Manchester Courier*, July 9, 1908, 8.

316 **What these splits revealed:** "Supremacy of the Nations," *Manchester Courier and Lancashire General Advertiser*, July 13, 1908, 3.

316 **0.8 second short:** "C. M. Daniels Fails at His Record," *Manchester Courier and Lancashire General Advertiser*, July 13, 1908, 3.

317 **"a little too fine":** "Olympic Team Athletes Back with Complaints," *Evening World* (New York), Aug. 6, 1908, 6.

318 **"The American team":** Joe Williams, "Our 1908 Olympic Squad—They Were Rowdy Heroes—Wouldn't Salute the King," ISHOF archive, Joe Ruddy file, IS.

319 **"And do you know":** Ibid.

320 **"the Olympic games of London open":** Cook, *Fourth Olympiad London 1908 Official Report*, 48.

320 **"rise above mediocrity":** "Olympic Games Affected Swimming Games at Home," *Pittsburgh Press*, Nov. 22, 1908, 18.

321 **"A more disgraceful":** "Life and Letters," *Academy* (London), July 25, 1908, 75.

321 **"English officials":** "400 Meter Race Controversy," *Evening World* (New York), July 23, 1908, 1.

321 **"The pulling of the Italian":** "Olympic Victors Home from London," *New-York Tribune*, Aug. 7, 1908, 5.

321 **"It was simply a case":** "British 'Fair Play' a Farce at Recent Olympic Contest," *Brooklyn Daily Eagle*, Aug. 16, 2008, 43.

321 **"Sports passions became raised"**: Coubertin, *Olympic Memoirs,* 98–99.

321 **"There seemed to be"**: Ibid., 99.

322 **"Both teams showed"**: Ibid., 103.

323 **65.8 seconds**: "Walking Record at the Olympia," *Courier* (London), July 18, 1908, 7.

324 **70.2 seconds**: "Americans Win 100-Meter Swim," *Elmira* (N.Y.) *Star-Gazette,* July 20, 1908, 1.

324 **"anyone but a Yankee"**: "Anything but an American," *Boston Globe,* Aug. 7, 1908, 5.

324 **"One of the big points"**: "Goessling—Twice an Olympic Swimmer," *St. Louis Star and Times,* Jan. 13, 1933, 19.

326 **"It's over"**: Dave Epperson, "Self-Taught Olympic Swimming Champ," *Monterey Peninsula Herald,* Sept. 1950, C. M. Daniels scrapbook, IS.

328 **65.6 seconds**: "Swimming," *Sporting Life* (London), July 28, 1908, 3.

328 **"American Wins"**: "American Wins Swimming Victory," *Buffalo Enquirer,* July 20, 1908, 1.

328 **"Daniels Equals"**: "Daniels Equals World's Record," *Dayton Herald,* July 20, 1908, 1.

329 **"Daniels made a grand win"**: "Americans Raise Flag of Victory," *Chicago Tribune,* July 21, 1908, 7.

329 **"now undisputed"**: "Daniels Won World's Swimming Title Through Hard Work and Yankee Pluck," *Brooklyn Citizen,* July 22, 1908, 3.

329 **"Daniels, World's Best"**: *Buffalo Express,* Sept. 6, 1908, 19.

329 **"An athlete of such marked"**: Louis de B. Handley, "C. M. Daniels, American Winner in Great Olympics, Is World's Greatest Swimmer," *Evansville* (In.) *Press,* July 22, 1908, 3.

331 **"the finest sprinter"**: "America Again to the Fore," *Sporting Life,* July 22, 1908, 6.

331 **"Athlete of the Year"**: "Charles M. Daniels, Won Olympic Swimming Medals," *New York Times,* Aug. 12, 1973, 59.

23: THE LAST CENTURY

332 **six days eighteen hours and fifty-eight minutes**: "Old Liner Close Second to New," *New-York Tribune,* Aug. 7, 1908, 4.

332 **East Coast press**: "Makes Swimming Easier," 1908, C. M. Daniels scrapbook, IS.

333 **"outrageous abandonment"**: "Chas. M. Daniels Weds," *Sun* (New York), June 8, 1909, 7.

333 ***Buffalo Times* reported**: "Wagner-Daniels," *Buffalo Times,* June 8, 1909, 6.

334 **"[Tom] says"**: "Swimming Notes," *Pittsburgh Press,* March 24, 1909, 17, Daniels scrapbook.

334 **broke Kieran's elusive 220-yard record**: "'Human Fish' Daniels Makes World's Record," *Pittsburgh Daily Post,* March 27, 1909, 9.

334 **father of Charles**: "Ex–Dayton Merchant Sought by Officials," *Dayton Herald,* May 3, 1910, 1.

335 **thirty thousand dollars in hand**: "Daniels Eludes Federal Court," *Leavenworth* (Kans.) *Post,* May 5, 1910, 3.

335 **J. A. Dent**: *Oregon Daily Journal,* April 18, 1915, 5.

336 **1911 220-yard AAU Championship**: "Daniels Equals His Own World's Record," *Pittsburgh Daily Post,* March 29, 1911, 9.

336 **500-yard race**: "Wanted: A Way to Get Daniels and Handy in Race for Swimming Title," *St. Louis Post-Dispatch,* April 1, 1911, 9.

336 **afraid of losing**: "C. M. Daniels, the Human Merman," *Ogden* (Utah) *Standard,* May 13, 1911, 11.

336 **56.8 seconds**: "Daniels Shades Other Swimmers," *New York Times,* March 25, 1911, 13.

336 **"The improvement shown"**: "Swimming," *Sydney Morning Herald,* May 17, 1911, 15.

337 **"I have decided"**: "About Swimming," *Buffalo Commercial,* Jan. 4, 1912, 9.

337 **"Olympic Team":** "Olympic Team to Lose a Big Star," *Washington Evening Star,* April 17, 1912, 21.

337 **"Team Crippled":** "Team Crippled in Swimming," *Grand Forks* (N.D.) *Herald,* April 24, 1912, 3.

337 **"Daniels absence likely":** "Daniels Out, America Has Little Show in Swimming," *Boston Globe,* April 17, 1912, 8.

EPILOGUE

341 **single black stripe:** *Asbury Park Press,* Aug. 16, 1978, 41, ISHOF archive, Jamison Handy file.

342 **"Baron Pierre de Coubertin":** Sullivan, *Olympic Games, Stockholm, 1912.*

344 **"If I can't swim to safety":** Mary Ellen McCormick interview.

BIBLIOGRAPHY

ARCHIVES AND DOCUMENT COLLECTIONS

Mayor's Committee of New York City. *Report on Public Baths and Public Comfort Stations*. Albany, N.Y.: Wynkeep, Hallenbeck, Crawford, 1897.

Willis, Joseph, and Richard Wettan. "Social Stratification in New York City Athletic Clubs, 1865–1915." Paper presented at the North American Society for Sport History Convention, Boston, 1975.

BOOKS AND PERIODICALS

Baily's Magazine of Sports and Pastimes. London: Vinton, 1908.

Barnes, Harper. *Standing on a Volcano: The Life and Times of David Rowland Francis*. St. Louis: Missouri Historical Society Press, 2001.

Bier, Lisa. *Fighting the Current: The Rise of American Women's Swimming, 1870–1926*. Jefferson, N.C.: McFarland, 2011.

Brownell, Susan. *The 1904 Anthropology Days and Olympic Games: Sport, Race, and American Imperialism*. Lincoln: University of Nebraska Press, 2008.

Cambridge Review: A Journal of University Life and Thought. Vol. 26. Printed by Faith and Tyler, 1904–1905.

Carson, Thomas E. *Unsung: The Ray Ewry Story*. A 4/20 Publications, 2017.

Chaline, Eric. *Strokes of Genius: A History of Swimming*. London: Reaktion Books, 2017.

Club Book of the Knickerbocker Athletic Club. New York: Knickerbocker Athletic Club, 1899.

Condron, Frank. *The I Olympiad, Athens 1896*. Vol. 2 of *The Olympic Century: The Complete History of the Modern Olympic Movement*. Toronto: Warwick Press, 2015.

Cook, Theodore Andrea. *The Fourth Olympiad London 1908 Official Report*. London: British Olympic Association, 1908.

Coubertin, Pierre de. *Les batailles de l'éducation physique: Une campagne de vingt-et-un ans*. Paris: Librairie de l'Éducation Physique, 1909.

———. *Olympic Memoirs*. Lausanne: Bureau International de Pedagogie Sportive, 1931.

Crain, Esther. *The Gilded Age in New York, 1870–1910*. New York: Black Dog & Leventhal, 2016.

Daniels, Charles M. *Speed Swimming*. With Louis de B. Handley and Otto Wahle. New York: American Sports Publishing Company, 1907.

Digby, Everard. *De Arte Natandi (The Art of Swimming)*. London, 1587.

Draper, Andrew Sloan, ed. *Sports, Pastimes, and Physical Culture.* Vol. 6 of *Draper's Self Culture.* St. Louis: Twentieth Century Self Culture Association, 1913.

Dunn, Edward T. *Buffalo's Delaware Avenue: Mansions and Families.* Buffalo: Buffalo Heritage Press, 2017. First published by Canisius College Press, 2003.

Finkbeiner, Myron. *From Harvard to Hagerman: An Incredible Journey of an Unknown Athlete: Harry LeMoyne.* Self-published, 2012.

Goodman, Ruth. *How to Be a Victorian: A Dawn-to-Dusk Guide to Victorian Life.* New York: Penguin Books, 2014.

Gordon, Ian, and Simon Inglis. *Great Lengths: The Historic Indoor Swimming Pools of Britain.* Swindon: English Heritage, 2009.

Handley, Louis de B. *How to Play Water Polo.* New York: American Sports Publishing Company, 1907.

———. *Swimming and Watermanship.* New York: Macmillan, 1922.

———. *Swimming for Women: Preliminary and Advanced Instruction in Competitive Swimming, Fancy Diving, and Lifesaving, Questions and Answers on Swimming Technique.* New York: American Sports Publishing Company, 1924.

Heffer, Simon. *The Age of Decadence: Britain, 1880 to 1914.* New York: Random House, 2017.

Hill, Thomas E. *Hill's Manual of Social and Business Forms: Guide to Correct Writing.* Chicago: Hill Standard Book Company, 1888.

Jackson, Robert. *Meet Me in St. Louis: A Trip to the 1904 World's Fair.* New York: HarperCollins e-books, 2004.

Jenkins, Rebecca. *The First London Olympics 1908.* London: Little, Brown, 2008.

Joyner-Kersee, Jackie. *A Kind of Grace: The Autobiography of the World's Greatest Female Athlete.* With Sonja Steptoe. New York: Warner Books, 1997.

Kellermann, Annette. *How to Swim.* London: William Heinemann, 1918.

Love, Christopher. *A Social History of Swimming in England, 1800–1910: Splashing in the Serpentine.* London: Routledge, 2008.

Lucas, Charles J. P. *The Olympic Games 1904.* St. Louis: Woodward & Tiernan, 1905.

Lucas, John. *The Modern Olympic Games.* South Brunswick, N.J.: A. S. Barnes, 1980.

Lucas, John Apostal. *John Apostal Lucas: Teacher, Sport Historian, and One Who Lived His Life Earnestly: A Collection of Articles and Essays with an Autobiographical Sketch.* Lemont, Pa.: Eifrig, 2009.

Luhan, Mabel Dodge. *Intimate Memories: The Autobiography of Mable Dodge Luhan.* New York: Harcourt, 1933.

Lutz, Tom. *American Nervousness, 1903.* Ithaca, N.Y.: Cornell University Press, 1991.

MacAloon, John J. *This Great Symbol: Pierre de Coubertin and the Origins of the Modern Olympic Games.* London: Routledge, 2008.

Mallon, Bill. *The 1900 Olympic Games: Results for All Competitors in All Events, with Commentary.* Jefferson, N.C.: McFarland, 1997.

———. *The 1904 Olympic Games: Results for All Competitors in All Events, with Commentary.* Jefferson, N.C.: McFarland, 1999.

———. *The 1906 Olympic Games: Results for All Competitors in All Events, with Commentary.* Jefferson, N.C.: McFarland, 1998.

Matthews, George R. *America's First Olympics: The St. Louis Games of 1904.* Columbia: University of Missouri Press, 2005.

McCash, June Hall. *The Jekyll Island Cottage Colony.* Athens: University of Georgia Press, 1998.

New York Athletic Club Journal. Jan. 1900–1912.

Nicholls, Rochelle. *Hell and High Water: Cecil Healy, Olympic Champion Whose Life Was Cut Short by War.* Newport, N.S.W.: Big Sky, 2018.

Oneill, Therese. *Ungovernable: The Victorian Parent's Guide to Raising Flawless Children.* New York: Little, Brown, 2019.

————. *Unmentionable: The Victorian Lady's Guide to Sex, Marriage, and Manners.* New York: Little, Brown, 2016.

Orton, George Washington, ed. *A History of Athletics at Pennsylvania, 1873–1896.* University of Pennsylvania Athletic Association, 1896.

Phelps, Michael. *Beneath the Surface: My Story.* With Brian Cazeneuve. New York: Sports Publishing, 2004, 2008, 2012, 2016.

Posey, Carl A. *The III Olympiad, St. Louis 1904, Athens 1906.* Vol. 4 of *The Olympic Century: The Complete History of the Modern Olympic Movement.* Los Angeles: World Sport Research and Publications, 2000.

Rose, Kenneth D. *Unspeakable Awfulness: America Through the Eyes of European Travelers, 1865–1900.* New York: Routledge, 2014.

Rozenblit, Marsha L. *The Jews of Vienna, 1867–1914: Assimilation and Identity.* Albany: State University of New York Press, 1983.

Sinclair, Archibald. *Swimming.* London: George Routledge & Sons, 1909.

Sinclair, Archibald, and William Henry. *Swimming.* London: Longmans, Green, 1893.

Social Register, Buffalo. Vol. 24. New York: Social Register Association, Nov. 1909.

Spalding, Albert G. *Feb. 28, 1901, Report of the Director of Sports.* Vol. 1 of *Report of the Commissioner-General for the United States to the International Universal Exposition, Paris, 1900.* Washington, D.C.: Government Printing Office, 1901.

Sprawson, Charles. *Haunts of the Black Masseur: The Swimmer as Hero.* New York: Pantheon Books, 1992.

Steele, Robert W., and Mary Davies Steele. *Early Dayton: With Important Facts and Incidents from the Founding of the City of Dayton, Ohio, to the Hundredth Anniversary, 1796–1896.* Dayton: W. J. Shuey, 1896.

Stoddard, S. R. *The Adirondacks Illustrated.* Self-published, 1893.

Sullivan, James E. *The Olympic Games at Athens, 1906.* New York: American Sports Publishing Company, 1906.

————. *Spalding's Official Athletic Almanac for 1903.* New York: American Sports Publishing Company, 1903.

————. *Spalding's Official Athletic Almanac for 1905: Olympic Games Number.* New York: American Sports Publishing Company, 1905.

————. *Spalding's Official Athletic Almanac for 1909.* New York: American Sports Publishing Company, 1909.

————. *Spalding's Official Athletic Almanac for 1910.* New York: American Sports Publishing Company, 1910.

————, ed. *The Olympic Games, Stockholm, 1912.* New York: American Sports Publishing Company, 1912.

Szabo, Lajos. "Hungary," *Journal of Olympic History,* Dec. 2006.

Universal Exposition, Saint Louis, 1904: Preliminary Programme of Physical Culture, Olympic Games, and World's Championship Contests. St. Louis, 1904.

Wigo, Bruce. *The Golden Age of Swimming: A Pictorial History of the Sport & Pools That Changed America.* Self-published, 2009.

Young, David C. *The Modern Olympics: A Struggle for Revival.* Baltimore: Johns Hopkins University Press, 1996.

PHOTO CREDITS

———

201   "Swimming and Life Saving" by Archibald Sinclair, 1906,
       London, 32.

203   New York Athletic Club

208   International Swimming Hall of Fame

213   New York Athletic Club

224   Courtesy of the Daniels family archives

234   Courtesy of the Daniels family archives

239   1906 Athens Olympic film footage

239   Library of Congress and the American Sports
       Publishing Company

245   American Sports Publishing Company

271   International Swimming Hall of Fame

283   Library of Congress

289   Courtesy of the Daniels family archives

290   Courtesy of the Daniels family archives

312   *The Fourth Olympiad London 1908 Official Report* and
       the British Olympic Association

323   Courtesy of the Daniels family archives (originally
       published in the *Buffalo Courier* on June 20, 1909)

326   Courtesy of the Daniels family archives

329   Courtesy of the Daniels family archives

330   International Swimming Hall of Fame

INDEX

Page numbers in *italics* indicate illustrations.

MICHAEL LOYND is chairman of the St. Louis Olympic Legacy Committee, a representative on the International Olympic Committee's World Union of Olympic Cities, a member of the International Society of Olympic Historians, and a sports attorney and lecturer. He is the author of *All Things Irish: A Novel*.

michaelloynd.com

facebook.com/michael.loynd

Twitter: @MichaelRLoynd

Instagram: @michaelrloynd

ABOUT THE TYPE

This book was set in Caslon, a typeface first designed in 1722 by William Caslon (1692–1766). Its widespread use by most English printers in the early eighteenth century soon supplanted the Dutch typefaces that had formerly prevailed. The roman is considered a "workhorse" typeface due to its pleasant, open appearance, while the italic is exceedingly decorative.